WOMEN, "RACE," AND WRITING IN THE EARLY MODERN PERIOD

Women, "Race," and Writing in the Early Modern Period is an inter-disciplinary examination of one of the most neglected areas in current scholarship. The contributors use literary, historical, anthropological, and medical material to explore an important intersection within the major era of European imperial expansion.

The volume explores:

- new perspectives on canonical European texts from the period;
- the conditions of women's writing and the problems of female authorship;
- the tensions between recent feminist criticism and questions of "race," empire, and colonialism;
- the relationship between the early modern period and postcolonial theory and recent African writing.

Women, "Race," and Writing in the Early Modern Period contains ground-breaking work by some of the most exciting scholars in contemporary criticism and theory. It will be vital reading for anyone working or studying in this field.

The contributors are Lynda E. Boose, Laura Brown, Dympna Callaghan, Natalie Zemon Davis, Carla Freccero, Kim F. Hall, Jean E. Howard, Margaret W. Ferguson, Stephanie Jed, Ania Loomba, Felicity Nussbaum, Patricia Parker, Juliana Schiesari, Irene Silverblatt, Jyotsna Singh, and Verena Stolcke.

Margo Hendricks is Assistant Professor of Literature at the University of California, Santa Cruz.

Patricia Parker is Professor of English and Comparative Literature at Stanford University.

WOMEN, "RACE," AND WRITING IN THE EARLY MODERN PERIOD

Edited by
Margo Hendricks and Patricia Parker

London and New York

First published 1994
by Routledge
11 New Fetter Lane, London EC4P 4EE

Simultaneously published in the USA and Canada
by Routledge
29 West 35th Street, New York, NY 10001

Typeset in Baskerville by Florencetype Ltd, Kewstoke, Avon
Printed and bound in Great Britain by
T.J. Press (Padstow) Ltd, Padstow, Cornwall

Printed on acid free paper

British Cataloguing in Publication Data
A catalogue record for this book is available from the British Library

Library of Congress Cataloging in Publication Data
Women, "Race," and Writing in the Early Modern Period / edited by
Margo Hendricks and Patricia Parker.
p.   cm.
Includes bibliographical references and index.
1. Literature, Modern—Women authors—History and criticism.
2. Women in literature.   3. Imperialism in literature.   4. Colonies
in literature.   5. Race in literature.   6. Feminism and literature.
I. Hendricks, Margo.   II. Parker, Patricia A.
PN471.W556   1994
809'.89287—dc20   93-17049

ISBN 0-415-07777-X (hbk)
ISBN 0-415-07778-8 (pbk)

CONTENTS

INTRODUCTION

Margo Hendricks and Patricia Parker

> Difference must be not merely tolerated, but seen as a fund of necessary
> polarities between which our creativity can spark like a dialectic. Only then
> does the necessity for interdependency become unthreatening. . . .
>
> (Audre Lorde, *Sister Outsider* [1984])

Two of the essays in this volume begin by alluding to Valerie Wayne's
recent introduction to *The Matter of Difference* (1991) and its frank
acknowledgment that, while that collection is focused on "difference," it
is regretfully "unable to address questions of race to any adequate
degree."[1] The scholarship that has emerged in the years since the
publication of *Rewriting the Renaissance: The Discourses of Sexual Difference
in Early Modern Europe* (1986)[2] has helped to redefine the contexts of
scholarly and theoretical engagement with questions of gender and the
position of European women in this period as part of what it terms "a
better appreciation of differences." Yet, until recently (with a few notable exceptions), "race" has largely been absent from or only peripheral
to such discussions. In fact, in the much contested arena of the marginalized position of women (or the position of women writers), very little has
been made of the racial (as well as class) positions constructed for and
assumed by early modern European women.

By contrast, the foregrounding of "race" – in the complex, multiform
and even contradictory senses of this term in the period between 1492
and 1800 – is central to the present interdisciplinary collection, one of
the ways it focuses explicitly on such differences. For if "race," in any
discussion, has to be placed within what in this sense are appropriately
named "scare-quotes," as influential anthologies such as *"Race," Writing
and Difference* (1985) and other recent work remind us,[3] then this caution
is even more critical in relation to the centuries and divergent cultures
that are the principal (though not exclusive) focus of this book.

As the essays here repeatedly stress, "race" as that term developed
across several European languages was a highly unstable term in the
early modern period, a period that saw the proliferation of rival

1

European voyages of "discovery" as contacts with what from a Eurocentric perspective were "new" and different worlds, the drive toward imperial conquest and the subjugation of indigenous peoples, and the development (and increasingly "racial" defense) of slavery. At the beginnings of this era, *raza* in Spanish, *raça* in Portuguese or "race" in French or English variously designated notions of lineage or genealogy, as in the sense of a noble (or biblical) "race and stock," even before its application in Spain to Moors and Jews or its eventual extension to paradigms of physical and phenotypical difference that would become the basis of later discourses of racism and racial difference. Similarly, in the sixteenth century, and from a more Anglocentric perspective, a sense of otherness led to the linking of the "wild Irish" with the Moors, the Scots as well as Scythians as members of a "barbarous nation," and the description of Spain itself as being of "all nations under heaven . . . the most mingled, most uncertayne and most bastardly."[4] It is both this varied meaning and its eventual development into later forms of racism and racial distinction that form the explicit focus of many of the essays here.

The second major concern of the present collection involves the foregrounding (rather than the effacing) of differences between women, as well as of tensions within contemporary feminism and feminist scholarship. In this respect (from its opening essay by Ania Loomba), its direct confrontation with and divergences from earlier feminist work (on the situation of female authors and of women's writing, on critiques of traditional scholarship of canonical texts) and its engagement with questions raised by feminists of color link this volume with descriptions by feminist scholars of color of the "appropriation of their experiences and struggles by hegemonic white women's movements," and critiques such as that of Chandra Talpade Mohanty, in "Under Western Eyes," of the tendency within Western feminist discourses to produce something homogeneously constructed as the "third world woman" as a "singular monolithic subject."[5] Such tensions within feminism – and between white or Western feminist writing and the critique articulated by feminists of color – has been the explicit focus of contemporary work as varied as Cherríe Moraga and Gloria Anzaldúa's *This Bridge Called My Back: Writings by Radical Women of Color*, Norma Alarcón's *Third Woman* journal, Amy Ling's *Between Worlds*, or Trinh T. Minh-ha's *Women, Native, Other: Writing, Postcoloniality, and Feminism*, as well as influential writing by Audre Lorde, Toni Morrison, Alice Walker, Maxine Hong Kingston, Paula Gunn Allen and others.[6] Such work, as Chela Sandoval has noted recently, involves a renewal rather than simply the first appearance of such tensions, just as bell hooks self-consciously echoes the question posed by Sojourner Truth to a convention of white suffragettes ("Ar'n't I a woman?") in her 1981 book *Ain't I a*

Woman: Black Women and Feminism.[7] Differently put, it involves, as hooks
herself notes in *Feminist Theory from Margin to Center* (1984), the challenging of the restriction of feminist theory to the "hegemonic dominance"
of "white academic women," or a response to Gayatri Spivak's description of the ways in which hegemonic feminist criticism, focusing on "the
literature of the female subject in Europe and Anglo America," has so
often reproduced "the axioms of imperialism."[8]

Recent anthologies such as *Conflicts in Feminism* (1990) have sought to
address these issues, including the ways in which (to paraphrase Valerie
Smith, one of its contributors) "the lives and cultural productions of
black [we would add, "and other"] women [of color] have been over-
looked or misrepresented within Eurocentric and androcentric discourses."[9] Work on the history of colonialism (such as Peter Hulme's
Colonial Encounters: Europe and the Native Caribbean 1492–1797) and
critiques of the assumptions of texts such as Tzvetan Todorov's *Conquest
of America: The Question of the Other* (1984), by both historians and
feminists, have already inspired almost a decade of work on earlier
encounters between Europe and the so-called "New World" that engages
with more contemporary writing on colonialism and postcoloniality.[10]
Studies of indigenous women such as Pocahontas or "La Malinche," the
interpreter and mistress-victim of Cortés (considered in Verena Stolcke's
essay here), or of Yucatec Maya women by historians such as Inga
Clendinnen, along with work on the feminization of new lands and
indigenous peoples in European discourses of "discovery," have already
begun to bring questions of gender and sexual difference into prominent relation with questions of cross-cultural encounters, of exploitation,
and of European dominance.[11]

Recent work on travel narratives and imperialism, such as Mary
Louise Pratt's *Imperial Eyes: Travel Writing and Transculturation*, has also
challenged academic tendencies to periodization and specialization by
spanning the historical distance between the second half of the eighteenth century and instances as recent as the 1980s.[12] The focus in the
present volume on the period from the early sixteenth to the late
eighteenth centuries similarly allows interconnections frequently obscured by a periodization that limits itself to a particular century. It
presents instead a series of interdisciplinary studies ranging across
several different languages and cultures in this period of almost three
hundred years. And it concludes with an essay (by Jyotsna Singh) that
starts from the complexities of "race" and "gender" in Shakespeare's
Othello (1604), reflects upon the conflation of the two categories (or
subordination of one to the other) that marks recent feminist treatments, and then moves to a consideration of non-Western texts from the
other end of the era of imperial and colonial expansion, and the complexities of the postcolonial construction of identities.

The volume as a whole, then, addresses the tensions noted by Mohanty, Sandoval, and others as much in the divergences between its various contributors and the dialogue and debate within its covers as in the departures its essays differently make from earlier or more traditional scholarship. Within what is increasingly designated as the "early modern period" – a term that includes not only a broader chronological range but a rejection of the kind of (Eurocentric and androcentric) valuation involved in terms such as "the Renaissance" or "the Enlightenment" – it thus joins work for the most part only recently beginning in the scholarship on these earlier periods, on the ways in which European women, including women writers and proto-feminist movements, contributed by their own agendas and Eurocentric constructions of the culturally other to the development of imperialist and domestic ideologies based on distinctions of "race" and social position.[13]

The volume, finally, seeks both to ask new questions about canonical and lesser-known texts, by both male and female authors, and to build bridges with contemporary work on "race," postcoloniality, and difference, in the hope that scholars separated by disciplinary, chronological, cultural, and linguistic boundaries can begin to see the historical interconnectedness of their labors and the potentially productive tensions of their differences. In this spirit, it also challenges the barriers that so often separate scholars working in different fields or languages as well as different disciplines – history, literary criticism, anthropology, cultural and postcolonial studies. In its focus on the differing roles and situations of women in particular – as agents and writers, as subjects and objects (of desire, curiosity, exchange), as commodified "woman" and as subverters, translators, transformers, and resisters – this book seeks not to hide but rather to highlight differences of perspective and approach as well as its own omissions or less central emphases – the importance, for example, of what Judith Butler calls "gender trouble" or the instability of gender boundaries themselves as markers of difference in this period; the problems of female rule that included not just Elizabeth the English Virgin Queen or Anne of Denmark but Isabella of Spain, in relation to the situation of Spanish Jews and Moors; further exploration of continental women and women writers, including those of Italy, and especially of Venice, city of famous courtesans as well as of female Moors; transvestite women travelers to non-European worlds; the recovering of voices of indigenous women; or the exoticism as well as anxieties of female rule that traverse, among canonical authors, for example, a writer as influential as John Milton, creator of the Eve and colonizing Satan of *Paradise Lost* and of the culturally alien Dalila of *Samson Agonistes*.[14] To name these is to name only a few of the topics that might well be treated as part of such a larger project, but which, because of the time and space constraints of a single volume, are necessarily if unfortunately omitted here. As a collection, finally, that includes work by the small but increasing number of women of color engaged in the study of early modern culture and history, the book that follows is also self-conscious in its hope that in this respect as well it will be ultimately left behind, a volume that in retrospect will be only a harbinger of the much more to come.

Although the collection is divided informally into sections that suggest some of the ways of organizing its concerns, what is equally important are the crossings between, as well as within, these informal groupings. Part I – "Defining Differences" – begins with Ania Loomba's "The Color of Patriarchy: Critical difference, cultural difference, and Renaissance drama," a study that issues explicitly from the varied points of intersection between Renaissance and postcolonial studies. Anticipating one of the volume's major themes, Loomba notes the critical omission of "race" from much of white feminist criticism, just as forms of New Historicism have been faulted for their eliding of problems of women, class, and gender. Questioning the status of "experience" in feminist work that forgets that women are a heterogeneous group, Loomba focuses on the problems involved (for feminists in India, for example) when the experiences and issues of Western feminism are offered as "natural" and insists that the primacy of gender can only be asserted by devaluing other social differences and thereby the "experiences" of "other" women. She then turns to the problematic status of agency within English Renaissance drama, examining the relation between the rebellious Vittoria and her black female servant in Webster's *The White Devil*, the interrelation of "race" and "gender" in Shakespeare's *Love's Labour's Lost* and *Much Ado About Nothing*, and, more extensively, the various textual and contextual linkages between patriarchal control, state power, parochialism, colonialism, and racial prejudice.

Lynda E. Boose's "'The Getting of a Lawful Race': Racial discourse in early modern England and the unrepresentable black woman" – which takes the quotation in its title from Shakespeare's *Antony and Cleopatra* – begins from the importance of not superimposing a peculiarly American history of race relations back onto their pre-slavery English origins. It then moves to the malleability of the term "race" in early modern England, in contexts that include not only Africans and Native Americans but the Irish (in Edmund Spenser's *View of Ireland* and other texts) and the figures of Venetian, Moroccan, and Jew in *The Merchant of Venice*. Touching briefly on Lady Mary Wroth's *Urania* and "miscegenated romances featuring a black man and white woman," Boose proceeds to concentrate on the less common narrative of white man and black woman, a narrative she argues is crucial to the development of the link between "race" and differences of color. Arguing that it is this pairing of white man/black woman that challenges what Janet Adelman highlights as the deepest patriarchal fantasy of male parthenogenesis, Boose ranges in this discussion from medieval romances to Peele's *Battle of Alcazar*, from Shakespeare's so-called "Dark Lady" sonnets recast as "Black Woman" sonnets to Ben Jonson's *Masque of Blackness* and *Masque of Beauty*. She then concludes this history with an anticipation of its future in "the resisted narrative of the black woman" as it re-emerges in postcolonial, post-slavery America.

The final essay in this part, Juliana Schiesari's "The Face of Domestication: Physiognomy, gender politics, and humanism's others," takes as its focus not England but the continent, and specifically the development in Italy of the discourse of physiognomy. Beginning from Joan Kelly's celebrated question "Did women have a Renaissance?" and its reminder that the new learning and its elites did not involve improvement in the condition of women, Schiesari concentrates on the demarcation of domestic space theorized by humanists such as Francesco Barbero and Leon-Battista Alberti, and the articulation of the new "science" of physiognomy in Giovan Battista Della Porta's *Della fisionomia* (1610). Her study of "the full panoply of humanism's exclusions" includes the complication of humanist praise of "the dignity of man" (in Pico della Mirandola's famous phrase) by "the various constructed others of European manhood: the feminine, the savage, the bestial" and the brutal reality of the era's exclusions, including of the Jews from Spain, women from public life, and the inhabitants of the Americas and Africa from their homelands and freedom. Expanding her discussion outward from Italy to Spain and France, she includes in the context of her argument the debates between Bartolomé de Las Casas and Juan Ginés de Sepúlveda, the defender of the New World conquest, and the exceptional position of educated women such as Madame de Sévigné and Madame de la Sablière.

Part II – "Male Writing, Exoticism, Empire" – begins with Carla Freccero's yoking of two chronologically opposed *termini* of the "early modern" – the combination of cannibalism, homophobia, and homophilia in the recent case of Jeffrey Dahmer and the mirror-image of the Eucharist in the virulent anti-semitism of the late European Middle Ages – in an essay entitled "Cannibalism, Homophobia, Women: Montaigne's 'Des cannibales' and 'De l'amitié'." Treating first of the designation of the cultural other as "cannibal" – whether Jew or the indigenous inhabitant of the Caribbean resisting colonial invasion – she then turns to two central essays by Montaigne ("Des cannibales" and "De l'amitié"), focusing both on the missing "voice" of the New World woman and the complicating of "normative heterosexual arrangements" in the former and, in the latter, on the tradition of male friendship from which women are excluded. Drawing diversely on the work of Eve Kosofsky Sedgwick and Luce Irigaray as well as de Certeau and Derrida, Freccero brings these two Montaigne essays into provocative juxtaposition, charting the complex relations between cannibalism, homophobia, male friendship as a communion between men, and homosociality as a "sociocultural endogamy" that disguises itself as exogamy while simultaneously excluding the participation of women.

Patricia Parker's "Fantasies of 'Race' and 'Gender': Africa, *Othello* and bringing to light," moves between the continental context of Freccero's essay and the English and British imperial focus of the rest of this section. It begins with the insertion of a story from Leo Africanus (of the women of "Barbarie") into the discussion of sexual relations between women as a thing "monstrous and difficult to believe" in Ambroise Paré's influential *Des Monstres et prodiges* and its English parallel in Helkiah Crooke's *Microcosmographia*, where a discussion of "Tribades" similarly refers the reader to this African narrator and his tale of "Barbarie." Arguing that Crooke's reference to the "deeply hidden" female sexual part that "Columbus imagineth he first discovered" is emblematic of the links between "the anatomist's opening and exposing to the eye the secrets or 'privities' of women" and the so-called "discovery" or bringing to "light" of what were from a Eurocentric perspective previously hidden worlds, Parker moves from the period's fascination with "monster" literature and its appetite for travel narratives, to the language of the ocular that connects narratives of "discovery," including Pory's English translation of Africanus, with both anatomy and the development of a domestic English network of informers and spies. She concludes with an analysis of *Othello* that relates both its uncovering of the "chamber" of a woman and its hunger for the exotic history of another converted Moor to these ocular obsessions and the apparently chiastic but "crucially *asymmetrical*" crossings of "gender" and "race" at work both in Shakespeare's *Othello* and in the surrounding culture's obsession with the "monstrous," the secret and the hid.

Jean E. Howard's "An English Lass Amid the Moors: Gender, race, sexuality, and national identity in Heywood's *The Fair Maid of the West*," focuses on Heywood's play as a way into the relation between the forging of "a sense of English identity" in "what we have Eurocentrically come to call 'the Age of Discovery'" and the emergence of a "language of racial difference in which skin color and physiognomy became over-determined markers of a whole range of religious and sexual and cultural differences by which the English were distinguished from various non-European 'others'." Focusing on the figure of the exceptional woman – eroticized but virginal (and hence complexly related to England's Queen Elizabeth) – as "a device for defining English values and for uniting men of different classes into a homosocial community of brothers," it explores the means through which Heywood's play (which includes a voyage to "Barbary" on a ship called the "*Negro*," and the construction of Islam and the "infidel" through a discourse of sexual libertinism) not only disrupts the English–Spanish binarism of post-Armada European politics through its insertion of a "Moor" but shifts "the focus of cultural anxiety from the body of the woman onto the body of the racial other."

Laura Brown's "Amazons and Africans: Gender, race, and empire in Daniel Defoe," continues into the eighteenth century the focus on Africa in Parker's and Howard's studies. Arguing that the figure of the Amazon is most usefully understood in the period as "an important form of mediation in the representation of imperialist ideology," Brown begins from "the trope of the Amazon" in eighteenth-century literary culture – including Dryden's translation of Juvenal's misogynist Sixth Satire and the echoes of Virgil's imperial epic in Pope's *Rape of the Lock* – and the relationship between trade, mercantile capitalism, and commodity fetishism in eighteenth-century discussions of female dress and adornment. She then moves to an extended treatment of Defoe, "one of the most prolific and eloquent apologists for mercantile expansion" in the first age of English maritime imperialism, the period sustained by "the slave trade, the colonization of the West Indies and North America, the wars against Native Americans and the early colonial ventures in Africa and India." Starting with Defoe's *Roxana*, Brown traces the combination of violence and empire with "a proto-feminist female autonomy" that raises problems of "the status of a feminism derived from a passionate advocacy of mercantile capitalism." Her discussion includes the links between empire and misogyny central to *Gulliver's Travels* and the poetry of Swift, and ends with Defoe's *Captain Singleton* (which includes a journey across the African continent) as "a final test case for the connection of the representation of difference with the ideology of empire." In conclusion, she raises the question of whether, "in placing gender analytically before race, we are forced to adopt the hierarchies of empire" and of the complications arising from "the argument for bourgeois liberty upon which much modern feminism depends."

Felicity Nussbaum's "The Other Woman: Polygamy, *Pamela*, and the prerogative of empire" begins from the eighteenth century's "appetite for consuming Africa, including its representations, its raw goods, and its human commodity, slaves" (an appetite that by the end of the century made a best-seller of Mungo Park's *Travels in the Interior of Africa*). Taking as its primary focus the relation between Englishwomen and African women mediated through contemporary preoccupations with polygamy, it ranges over British travel narratives, fantasies of cross-racial polygamy in texts such as Henry Neville's *The Isle of Pines* (1668), the polygamy tracts of the eighteenth century and Samuel Richardson's *Pamela*. Charting the justification of European sexual oppression of African (and slave) women, Nussbaum describes how the portrayal of

African women as "unabashedly seductive" was employed to justify the widespread fathering of illegitimate children of mixed race and the "unacknowledged polygamy" that involved using the wombs of female slaves as a means of increasing the slave population. She then concludes by focusing on three Englishwomen's views of the other woman – Anna Falconbridge's account of her voyages to Sierra Leone with her Abolitionist husband, Lady Mary Wortley Montagu's *Letters during her TRAVELS in Europe, Asia and Africa*, and Mary Wollstonecraft's discussion of polygamy in *A Vindication of the Rights of Woman* – in ways that raise troubling questions about the relation of European feminism to the status of this constructed other.

Part III – "Female Authorship and Negotiating Differences" – takes female authorship as its explicit subject, along with the tensions involved in forms of difference (class, "race," gender) that shape the work of particular women writers and the ways their subjects, and importance, are conceived. Dympna Callaghan's "Re-reading Elizabeth Cary's *The Tragedie of Mariam, Faire Queene of Jewry*," focusing on the drama of Elizabeth Cary that represented the first original play in English by a woman, starts from Valerie Wayne's introduction to *The Matter of Difference* (1991) and its assertion, "by omission," of the "importance of addressing more fully the issue of race in Renaissance literature." She addresses first what she sees as the tendency of past feminist criticism – and of a feminist archeology concerned with the subject position of the woman writer – to "take gender as the diacritical difference of culture and in so doing erase other systems of difference" such as race and class. She then treats of this tendency in past criticism of Cary's *Mariam*, stressing that it is set in Palestine ("displaced center of Christianity and the home of the infidel"), among the Jews (highly racialized as well as demonized in early modern England), and involves a plot where "a conspicuously white female protagonist and a tawny female villain constitute the focus of the tragic action." Callaghan argues, finally, that the suppression of "race" in much of the criticism of this play impairs not only our understanding of the role of gender distinctions within it but a truly critical understanding of the position of Cary herself as an English woman writer.

Kim F. Hall's "'I rather would wish to be a black-moor': Beauty, race and rank in Lady Mary Wroth's *Urania*" begins by joining "race" to the emphases on gender and political control in recent studies of early modern rhetoric and then focuses both on the "fair/dark" distinction that makes its appearance in the language of aesthetics "at the moment of intensified English interest in travel and African trade" and on the ways in which "tropes of blackness in descriptions of beauty function as markers of race which work to differentiate between women." Beginning from Shakespeare's so-called "Dark Lady" sonnets and the rejection of the darker Hermia in *A Midsummer Night's Dream* as "Ethiope" and "Tartar," Hall moves to a more extended reading of Lady Mary Wroth's *The Countess of Montgomerie's Urania* (1621), suggesting that Wroth and other women writers "demonstrate a heightened sensitivity . . . to the cultural implications of their own investment in the language of racial difference" and use "the arbitrariness of this aesthetic to strengthen their own rhetorical and social positions at the expense of more marginalized groups." Focusing primarily on Wroth, a member of Queen Anne's circle who helped stage Jonson's *Masque of Blackness* ("a defining moment of the British empire which used blackness to privilege white beauty") and who may have been present when Pocahontas was brought to court, Hall also notes that writers such as Emilia Lanier, Mary Sidney, and Elizabeth Cary stress more than their male contemporaries the color of Cleopatra as a threatening other woman. And she concludes that "in attempting to expose and escape destabilizing constructions of gender, these women position themselves at the site of other differences," thus complicating "the creation of 'the' female subject" in ways that have powerful implications not only for the study of "Shakespeare's sisters" in early modern England but for contemporary feminists, including feminists of color.

Stephanie Jed's "The Tenth Muse: Gender, rationality, and the marketing of knowledge," starts from the marketing category of "Tenth Muse" that links the seventeenth-century publication of two "New World" women poets, working in different languages, who have otherwise no contact or interaction with each other – Anne Bradstreet (whose poetry was published in 1650 under the title *The Tenth Muse, Lately Sprung Up in America*) and Sor Juana Inés de la Cruz (the first edition of whose works described her as "the Tenth Muse"). Arguing that the fiction of the "Tenth Muse" was "the effect of social relations among men of letters and commerce for whom the idea of a woman writer made no sense" – a form of commodification within a system of assumptions about authorship that made these female anomalies more "vendible" – Jed then relates this marketing taxonomy to the larger European construction of the "New World" as a museum. Tracing the European interrelation between commerce and culture to an earlier emblematic instance – the relation between the "natural history" assembled by Gonzalo Fernandez de Oviedo (1478–1557), and the Venetian administrator and knowledge-broker Gian Battista Ramusio (the European publisher of Africanus's *History*) – Jed then suggests what might enable the construction of a "Women's Archive," and the study of mutually isolated figures such as Bradstreet and Sor Juana through an exploration of "the conditions under which this relation of disconnection was produced," rather than focusing simply on "the images of disconnected women." She concludes with provocative remarks on the marketing of a more contemporary instance – *The Norton Anthology of Literature by Women*.

Margaret W. Ferguson's "Juggling the Categories of Race, Class, and Gender: Aphra Behn's *Oroonoko*" begins from the conviction that Joan Kelly's question "Did women have a Renaissance?" needs to be complicated by versions of that question for "groups *other* [than] white European women." Focusing on Aphra Behn's novella, she considers the ways in which the categories of race, gender, and class, "understood as historically contingent and relational rather than foundational concepts," might be applied both to that text and to the multiple ambiguities of Behn's own position, both as a woman writer "who explicitly if intermittently defined herself as oppressed by and financially dependent on wealthy men" and as "a member of an English 'family' of slave owners." In contrast to Todorov's *The Conquest of America* and much of early modern travel literature, Behn's novella, Ferguson argues, constructs the relation between Old World and New not as a simple binary opposition between self and other but as a series of complexly triangular "relations of sameness and difference among a black African slave, a white English woman, and a group of Native Americans." Her chapter concludes with an analysis of the effacement of Imoinda, the black wife, from the modern Norton paperback edition of this text and the complex interrelations of white woman (in this case, woman author) and the figure of the black woman.

Margo Hendricks's "Civility, Barbarism, and Aphra Behn's *The Widow Ranter*," finally, starts with another citation from *The Matter of Difference* and from her own position as "one of the small but growing number of scholars of color engaged in the study of Renaissance English racialism and racism." Her study of the "complex and often contradictory assumptions about race, class, and gender" at work in Aphra Behn's play *The Widow Ranter* treats of Behn's fictional revision of a historical event – Nathaniel Bacon's organizing of a "volunteer army of indentured English servants, African slaves, dissatisfied soldiers, and the laboring poor to wage war on the American Indians who resisted English hegemony." Arguing that in its representation of the Native Americans, the play "maps a central paradox of the concept of civility" and of the rhetoric of "civil" and "civilized" that permeates discussions of English domination in the New World, Hendricks focuses on Behn's displacement of Bacon's relationship with his English wife onto "a fictional 'star-crossed' miscegenous romance" between Bacon and an American Indian queen, indicating the ways in which Behn's own implication in the ethnographic stereotype of the sexually aggressive native woman serves "to deflect the very real anxiety in the racial ideology of English female sexuality." Invoking Mary Dearborn's use of the figure of Pocahontas and taking issue with Karen Ordahl Kupperman's *Settling with the Indians: The Meeting of English and Indian Cultures in America, 1580–1640,* Hendricks argues for the importance of the figure of the American Indian (and not just the African) woman as a register for the discourse of "race" in the period and for miscegenation as the undoing of the fiction of assimilation that lies at the heart of "civility."

Part IV – "Gender, Race, and Class: Colonial and postcolonial" – features four interdisciplinary essays devoted to specific aspects of the relation between Europe and other worlds: New France, New Spain, and the postcolonial recasting of Shakespeare's *Othello* by two twentieth-century African writers. Historian Natalie Zemon Davis's "Iroquois Women, European Women" focuses on the regions of what is now Canada, penetrated by the French. Beginning with the appearance, to the eyes of Montagnais and Micmac women, of European ships at the entrance to what would become New France and – across the Atlantic – Marie Guyart de l'Incarnation's dream of Amerindian lands and her subsequent arrival at Quebec, Davis's essay takes as its subject the similarities and differences in the situation and views of these women in the sixteenth and first half of the seventeenth centuries. Her goal is to decolonize the categories of historical writing by insisting upon the simultaneity of European and American Indian cultures, rather than seeing the latter as an "earlier" or "prior" form of European society, and upon the historicity of both cultures, rather than seeing the North American woodlands as static until the Europeans arrived. The focus is on comparison more than on encounter and on "experience," creative action, and consciousness more than on representation. Davis points to major differences in the two worlds in regard to property, structures of authority, and sexual boundaries, but also certain similarities in regard to women's access to public voice and to women's priestly roles. Using materials from archeology, ethnography, and collective memory, Davis describes changes in warfare, political organization and diplomacy in the Canadian woodlands in the late fifteenth century and sixteenth century that parallel those in Europe, with roughly similar implications for female sense of self and women's access to public voice. In both societies the male role as purveyor of political eloquence expanded. In both societies, Davis speculates, women expanded their voice in religious action – for the European women in both Catholic and Protestant reformations, for the Amerindian women in sooth-saying and dream interpretation, in anti-Christian denunciation, and in Christian preaching.

Anthropologist Irene Silverblatt's "Andean Witches and Virgins: Seventeenth-century nativism and subversive gender ideologies" begins from the proposition that "gender ideologies – the broadly construed meanings implicated in the making of women and men" – were intrinsic not only to Spanish structures of colonial order but to forms of Andean resistance to them. She therefore explores how Andean women, some called "witches" and others called "virgins," struggled to "carve out a space of challenge to Spanish attempts to destroy Andean culture." Starting from the ways in which Spanish colonial practices and institutions "pressured Andean gender relations" and handicapped or exploited women in particular, she charts the transformation, in seventeenth-century Andean communities, of the European icons of "witch" and Madonna-like "virgin" into instruments of native resistance, in the cases of "witches" such as Juana Icha and Francisca Cargua Chuqui and celibate indigenous women such as Asto Mallao and Francisca Guacaquillay, key figures in an Andean cultural revival that challenged the Spanish orthodoxy.

Social anthropologist Verena Stolcke also focuses on New Spain in her "Invaded Women: Gender, race, and class in the formation of colonial society" but across a broader historical period. She begins from the Spanish doctrine of "limpieza de sangre" or purity of blood ("Never stained," as Lope de Vega put it, "by Jewish or Moorish woman") as the basis for a study of the relationship between the influence of ideological categories that structured Spanish society (and were originally intended only for domestic consumption) and "the cultural and ideological burden transported by the conquerors to the so-called 'New World'." Noting that studies of the conquest of America often present it as "an affair between men," in accounts that "have systematically omitted the manner in which indigenous women and, shortly after, black women lived through the assault it involved on their personal and cultural integrity," Stolcke cites exceptions such as Inga Clendinnen's study of Yucatec Maya women (1982), Patricia Seed's *To Love, Honor and Obey in Colonial Mexico* (1988) and Irene Silverblatt's *Moon, Sun, and Witches: Gender Ideologies and Class in Inca and Colonial Peru* (1987). She then explores the contours of the experience – and representation – of indigenous women, including the controversial figure of Doña Marina or La Malinche. Noting that the conquest of America "coincided with the end of the so-called Spanish Reconquista and the politically and ideologically motivated expulsion or compulsory conversion of the Jews in 1492," Stolcke proceeds to chart the complex history of the interrelation between the development of "limpieza de sangre" doctrines in Spain and their transportation to the different context, and *mestizo* population, of the Spanish "New World."

The final essay in this part and the volume is Jyotsna Singh's "Othello's identity, postcolonial theory and contemporary African rewritings of *Othello*." She breaks with the early modern time frame of the other essays by examining the bridge between Shakespeare's *Othello*, the remarks of

Coleridge and Lamb on the "monstrous" and "revolting" union of Desdemona and the Moor (remarks she juxtaposes with a quotation from Aimé Césaire on "the Negro . . . separated from himself"), and two African rewritings of the relation of (black) male and (white) female in the play: Murray Carlin's *Not now, sweet Desdemona* (Uganda, 1968), where "the actor playing Othello is a black from Trinidad and the woman known as 'Desdemona' a white, South African heiress," and Sudanese author Tayib Salih's novel *Season of Migration to the North* (1969). Beginning from Western criticism of *Othello* that has "difficulty in reconciling Othello's role as a tragic hero with his blackness" (thus reinscribing a division of "civilized" and "barbarian" extrapolated from the play itself) and moving to a critique of recent treatments of "femininity" and "blackness" in the play that elide "the condition of black masculinity with that of white femininity," Singh treats the latter as symptomatic of "a tendency in contemporary Western feminist engagements with race which . . . implicitly *collapse* the categories of difference by assuming a common history of marginalization." Noting that non-European or Third World readers do not share this investment in "discursively eliding the different forms of victimization," and invoking the work of Franz Fanon and of Homi Bhabha on "mimicry," she then proceeds to a reading of Carlin's rewriting of *Othello* and Salih's novel – both products of the 1960s and the wake of African independence movements – including the ways in which they yield "a more complicated and often contradictory relation between the discourse of race and gender than the standard feminist position allows in its frequent insistence upon the shared experiences of women and marginalized ethnic groups."

Jyotsna Singh's essay and the volume, then, end with this simultaneous bridging and disjoining of the space between the "new world(s)" of the "Renaissance" or early modern period and the "Third World" of the postcolonial era. Echoing in a different context some of the polemical perspectives with which the volume began – in the essay of Ania Loomba – and providing a critical perspective on the interests and engagements of white, North American or European feminism, Singh offers a challenge not unlike that of bell hooks with which Kim F. Hall concludes her study of the links between contemporary feminism and the situation of woman writers such as Lady Mary Wroth – that

> only when we confront the realities of sex, race, and class, the ways they divide us, make us different, stand us in opposition, and work to reconcile and resolve these issues will we be able to participate in the making of a feminist revolution, in the transformation of the world.

Part I

DEFINING DIFFERENCES

1

THE COLOR OF PATRIARCHY
Critical difference, cultural difference, and Renaissance drama

Ania Loomba

Like Middleton's Beatrice-Joanna, but in conditions quite unlike hers, I "feel a giddy turning in me."[1] Mine is occasioned by an oscillation from Renaissance to postcolonial studies: the first being the right kind of thing an Indian student of English literature was supposed to do, and the other, a concern she ought to make a priority today. The oscillation defines me as a changeling in both areas – traditional Shakespeareans in India are upset at my suggestion that the bard be removed from the fulcrum of literary studies, other colleagues because I continue to teach Shakespeare even when I have the choice not to.[2] Out of the Indian context, I am resentful at the possibility of being ghettoized into talking solely about the intersection of race and gender, and upset when enough attention is not paid to that subject. On all counts, it is difficult to escape what Martha Minow has nicely described as "the dilemma of difference" whereby "both focussing on and ignoring difference risk recreating it."[3]

Thanks to the pedagogic and cultural hangovers of colonialism, these seemingly disparate areas occasionally intersect and make the giddy turnings worth while. The encounters are variegated: *Hamlet*, for example, is, for many male postgraduate students in Delhi, the ultimate representation of "the human condition"; it is also the name of a prize-winning variety of mango developed recently in Trivandrum in south India. In the small north-eastern border state of Mizoram, it approximates a folk cult show, while a road sign on a Himalayan highway cautions speeding drivers by asking them whether they want "to be or not to be." Together, these encounters reveal some of the strands of the postcolonial fabric.[4]

But Renaissance and postcolonial studies also meet each other via their common interest in marginalized peoples of different sorts, and in their disparate attempts to theorize and recover subaltern resistance (or agency) and locate it in relation to power. The difficulty of doing that with respect to the female subject has been an especially pressing concern within both areas and has almost become an index of critical

17

politics. It has been alleged, for example, that those histories and theories of the colonial encounter which find it practically and theoretically impossible to recover the female subaltern voice rehearse and contribute to the continuing marginalization of colonized people, especially women.[5] It appears that there are analogous problems in recent Renaissance studies. Some years ago, Walter Cohen's review of political criticism of Shakespeare astutely juxtaposed (but without especially interrelating) the "strangely quietist feel of these radical critiques" (referring particularly to new historicist work) with his contention that in these readings "women have disappeared."[6] More recently, some feminist critics have polemically amplified aspects of this critique, contending that the effect of new historicists' and cultural materialists' inadequate focus on female presence and agency in Renaissance drama "has been to oppress women, repress sexuality, and subordinate gender issues."[7]

Such critiques might appear to be manifestations of the by now widespread reservations about the politically quietist implications of "poststructuralism" and "new history" – reservations which are framed within the larger problem of squaring critical inquiry with politics which has so bedevilled poststructuralist theory in general. Women and "third world" critics have been especially uncomfortable with some poststructuralist assumptions and methods: it has been variously alleged that the agency of the marginalized subject is obscured when that subject is theorized as discontinuous, or as merely "the site" for the intersection of various discourses; that a Foucauldian emphasis on the relational aspects of power and resistance implies the ultimate containment of the latter; that if power is theorized as dispersed and fragmented then it emerges as either too benign or too pervasive; and that poststructuralist skepticism about knowledge and metanarratives only results in intellectual angst and political paralysis.[8] These problems point to very real difficulties involved in theorizing social difference – race, gender, class, caste, and other social differentials cannot be easily accommodated without risking an endless fragmentation of subjectivity.[9]

"The Renaissance" has been both an especially fruitful site for poststructuralist critical work and an embattled one.[10] The potential alliance between various strands of political criticism is becoming increasingly fissured, although there is widespread regret about these critical/political ruptures as well as continuing attempts to heal them. In the course of what Ann Thompson rather mildly characterizes as "an uneasy relationship" between feminism and various forms of historical and cultural materialist criticism, the sprawling debates that took place between Marxism and feminism in the 1960s and 1970s are revisited, but only implicitly, and often in a way that is not conducive to posing a viable alternative to these poststructuralist shortcomings in the theorizing of gender issues, and especially female agency, within Renaissance drama.[11]

Since this essay will run the risk of exemplifying what Lynda Boose rightly criticizes as "the contestatory model of scholarship" which "turns the literary profession into a shoot 'em out at the You're-Not-O.K. Corral," I want to underline the compulsion that a self-conscious criticism necessarily faces in having to confront the basis of its differences with others.[12] As Jean Howard puts it,

> essays which explain how and why one does and should read in a particular way are both more generous and more risky since they do not try to seal themselves off from what is polemical by aspiring to a timeless commonsense, but expose what is difficult and what is at stake in "making knowledge" at *this* historical moment.[13]

Boose criticizes the contestatory model by contrasting it with a sisterhood and a familial supportiveness that is supposed to mark the relations among American feminist Shakespeareans. My own differences with her and others are articulated in the hope that the exclusions which both "sisterhood" and "the family" have sometimes historically been party to need not be reinscribed in the present context.

Both Lynda Boose, in "The Family in Shakespearean Studies," and Carol Neely, in "Constructing the Subject," seek to redress the alleged neglect of women by cultural materialists and new historicists (who are conflated in different ways by both critics) by invoking their own experiences as critics (as I have done), and by situating these within the history and political agenda of American liberal feminism. Therefore, let me briefly discuss the question of critical self-reflexivity. Cultural materialists have been addressing this for some time, but today it has become almost fashionable: now there is a wider recognition and discussion of the ways in which Shakespearean criticism might "negotiate power relations in our own social context."[14] But there is a potential paradox here: even though it is increasingly acknowledged that intellectual differences about "what happened in history" or "textual meaning" are shaped by our own political differences, such a recognition does not end critical claims to a "truer" historicism or a "better" literary criticism. In other words, the desire to situate the writer-critic ostensibly stems from the need to contest universalist notions of knowledge or value but sometimes ends up replicating such notions. An analogous circularity is evident in those inquiries into cultural difference which are undertaken from, or which return to, a position of self-privileging. Orientalist discourses are of course notorious in this respect. But Gayatri Spivak argues that some influential French feminists also privilege Western culture precisely via their "occasional interest in touching *the other* of the West."[15] While at some level all inquiry stems from the question "who am I?," the distinction between situating oneself critically and critical self-obsession is still worth taking trouble over.

The issue of self-reflexivity is also involved with the historical and epistemological status of "experience," an issue which motivated feminist research to attach great importance to locating oneself in one's discourse. While "experience" is important in recalling the reality of both oppression and agency and thus a way of countering the debilitating effects of some recent poststructuralist perspectives, it is hardly a transparent concept. First, the gaps between what is "out there" and "what is internalized" cannot be swept under the carpet; second, experience itself is so profoundly colored by various social contexts and differentials that it only underlines the fact that women are a heterogeneous group.[16] The experience of one group must be placed alongside those of others: the relations between them also determine and circumscribe the validity of each. To make these connections is also one way in which we can negotiate the paradoxes of difference, and determine overlaps even as we pay attention to specific and varying contexts.

As Susie Tharu and K. Lalita point out (while setting their new anthology of women's writing in India in the context of the Western feminist academy), "when the new validity women's experience acquired as a resource that could be drawn on for critical discussion was conflated with the empiricist idea that experience was the source of true knowledge, experience lost the critical edge it had acquired as a political tool," feminism was annexed to a bourgeois humanist scheme of things, and finally, the experiences and issues of Western feminism were offered as "natural."[17] Such a trajectory is evident in both Boose's and Neely's essays. Their own experience is not understood as specific and relative; rather, it swells to define what both of them are at some pains to establish, that is, what Neely calls a female "subjectivity, interiority, identity which is continuous over time and is not the product of ideology" and "some area of 'femaleness'" which is understood as standing free of both history and context (7). Both of them begin by rightly pointing out the dangers of dissolving gender into analogies. Gerda Lerner's pioneering guideline for gender critique emphasized exactly this: "all analogies – class, group, caste – approximate the position of women but fail to define it adequately. Women are a category unto themselves; an adequate analysis of their position in society requires new conceptual tools."[18] I have expressed my discomfort with the way in which the analogies between gender and power relations in the Renaissance have been used to explicitly undermine the specificity of the former.[19] But where Lerner cautioned against letting the uniqueness of women's position deteriorate into asserting a simplistic hierarchy of oppression, Neely ends up reiterating that gender is "a primary category" (15). It has been pointed out in so many earlier feminist debates that the primacy of gender as an analytical category can only be asserted by devaluing other social differences and thereby the "experiences" of "other" women.[20] That this warning needs to be repeated in the context of Renaissance studies, especially at a time when such studies are beginning to consider issues of cultural difference, is perhaps a measure of the way in which the centrality of "The Renaissance" to Western culture constantly exerts a pressure to discuss it entirely within the values and parameters that are a legacy of that socio-cultural tradition.

"Sisterhood" has never precluded fundamental political differences among women. But in Boose's essay, and Neely's, it is invoked very easily precisely at the expense of all variegation between women even within the United States, let alone the rest of the world. It is not surprising, then, to find that while these critics reiterate Walter Cohen's point about the neglect of gender in political criticism of Shakespeare, they do not acknowledge his observation that "Third World and other ethnic studies are regrettably relegated to the same subordinate role (as women) despite their obviously political thrust" (19). A focus on woman and one on race and cultural difference are both collateral and divergent tasks. But Boose unfortunately chooses to pit them against each other: "when gender is not being ignored in materialist critiques, it repeatedly ends up getting displaced into some other issue – usually race or class" (729). Studies of race in early modern Europe (as a theoretical parameter, as a historically constituted category, and as a factor in analyzing textual strategies as well as responses to them) are pitifully few and I cannot think of even one instance where race is critically *prioritized* over gender.

Such a demarcation of gender from other categories of difference predictably maps onto a whole series of other divisions – notably the ones between text and context, gender and history, family and politics. In Boose's essay, all of the former are the terrain of feminism, and the latter the interests of Marxism. The twain can never meet, it is implied, not by pointing out the very real tensions between them but simply because "American feminists are committed to liberal rather than radical Marxist politics" and "what has never been clear to American liberal feminism is how one can serve feminism and Marxism too" (724). First, the long history of Marxist debates on the intersection between the social and the individual is reduced to a hackneyed caricature of a crudely deterministic materialist criticism which is the hallmark of right-wing attacks on cultural materialists,

21

which Boose would like to distance herself from (731, n. 22). Second, the interconnections between private and public are muted, and the binary oppositions which have historically rendered women invisible are resurrected. To argue, as Neely does (12), that "a focus on power, politics, and history, and especially, the monarch, turns attention away from marriage, sexuality, women and the masterless," is to abandon the former set of historically demarcated and contested spaces as those in which women cannot be inserted. Instead of positing the family as a privileged place for locating women, as both Boose and Neely do, feminists can demonstrate, as indeed they have done in other contexts, how these spaces are themselves gendered. I'll return to this later; here I only want to argue that surely the multiple alternative histories of the family which black and "Third World" feminists have been making visible, and the linkages between the development of the family and those of imperialism, colonialism, and capitalism, should problematize a simple invocation of that institution, and of the place of women within it.[21]

Michèle Barrett, among others, has discussed the ideological and historical contours of the ways in which the literary text, the psyche, and "woman" are linked by virtue of their compartmentalization from the social, the historical, and material.[22] Boose defends her rehearsal of this process by arguing that,

> given feminism's very different *historical* relationship to "history," it seems thoroughly consistent with the feminist goal of liberating women *from* their history that the mainstream feminist interpretations of Shakespeare did indeed marginalize the historical and concentrate instead on the literary text.
>
> (735)

One wonders where this leaves feminist historians, for whom "liberating" women entails rewriting history itself. Surely, it is possible to *question* dominant historiography without having to *retreat* from history. The "literary text," moreover, is at least as problematic a category for feminists as is "history," and a legitimate form of feminist critique has been to question canonical texts as well as their dominant cultural and institutional deployment, which notoriously also marginalized the historical in the name of the literary. This should hardly need to be restated today, except that skepticism on the part of other feminists about the special status of the Shakespearean text becomes the target of Boose's wrath. She is of course perfectly right in pointing out that canon-bashing (particularly in the case of the Bard) may cut the academic branches we perch on, because so many jobs depend on our continuing to teach Shakespeare. It is also true that women readers may take pleasure in Shakespeare, as in other canonical texts.

But possible pleasure and professional exigencies are strang
mutated into an insistence that we must not feel too alienated frc
Shakespeare's plays, or find them effecting patriarchal closures. Those
who do, like Kate McLuskie, are reduced to another tired caricature –
that of the "tough," "uncompromising," puritanical feminist, who, we
are told, can "only warn us away from Shakespeare in terms that warn
us away from pleasure" (725). Via this stereotype, our choices as feminists are narrowed and we are not allowed to question, beyond a certain acceptable point, the value of the Shakespearean text.

In the recent and lengthy controversy over Shakespeare in *The
London Review of Books*, an analogous pleasure-in-the-text formula
emerges. Boris Ford attacks cultural materialists thus:

> I found myself speculating when they last read one of
> Shakespeare's major plays as they might perhaps listen to one of
> Bach's unaccompanied cello sonatas or Mozart's string quartets:
> because they find them profoundly moving, or spiritually restor-
> ing, or simply strangely enjoyable.[23]

In both cases, pleasure-in-the-text quickly leads to pleasure-in-culture.
It is disturbing to find how close Boose comes to Ford in reading
Shakespeare as emblematic of Western culture and that culture as
self-evidently worth "enjoying" or valuing: "And logically,
Shakespeare must be only the beginning: if one is to renounce
Shakespeare for his patriarchalism, then surely one must also
renounce the enjoyment of most of Western drama . . . and for that
matter, most of Western literature" (725). Now the message of colonial education was precisely that if Indians did not find
Shakespeare's plays "pleasurable," they did not possess intelligence or
culture. "Pleasure" in that context was clearly synonomous with
approbation, and in continuing to conflate the two, Boose and Ford
deny the pleasures of negative critique, which (I am glad to report)
are considerable in the Indian academy where Shakespeare's hallowed
status is still institutionally secure. At a recent conference in New
Delhi (which ironically was devoted to interrogating the history and
ideologies of English in India), a well-known novelist similarly accused
political criticism of devaluing "emotion": "you have become too cold
and analytical" he informed me. I could only recount to him the passions that were unleashed in my classrooms once students had the
freedom to criticize the Bard, as opposed to the dull apathy that the
demand for reverence usually produced. "Pleasure" for many Indian
students of Shakespeare would critically hinge on whether or not they
were given the choice to agree or disagree, be moved or angry, re-
stored or bored – and not only by Shakespeare and the Western
canon, but by any text.[24] To say this is simply to recall the necessary

investment of marginalized readers in insisting on the freedom to re-spond to complex texts in multiple ways and the important role of feminist theory in stressing (even celebrating) exactly this possibility and the diversity of positions from which readers respond.

I do not intend to suggest that a negative critique is the only kind of pleasure that canonical texts make available to traditionally margi-nalized students/readers. To respond from the fullness of one's specific situations is also to discover *new and different sources of textual pleasure* or issues to identify with: I certainly find that I enjoy *Antony and Cleopatra* and *Othello* a great deal more today than I did as a student when I wasn't allowed to comment on the racial difference of their central figures. (In both cases, incidentally, I ended up thinking that Shakespeare wrote a better play than I did at first.) Stephen Greenblatt also notes a "tendency . . . in those explicitly concerned with historical or ideological functions of art to ignore the analysis of pleasure or, for that matter, play" but goes on to caution that "tran-shistorical stability or continuity of literary pleasure is an illusion . . . the task then would be to historicize pleasure, to explore its shifts and changes, to understand its interests."[25] This is an enormously difficult order and sensitivity to the diversity, shifts, and changes among con-temporary readers might be one way of equipping ourselves for reconstructing the identities and responses of past recipients of these texts.

The question of literary reception also allows us to interrogate the ongoing controversy about female agency in these plays. Those who find Shakespeare patriarchal are severely criticized by both Boose and Neely for somehow contributing to the neglect of women's power and agency. Carol Neely argues that feminist criticism needs to "over-read, to read to excess, the possibility of human (especially female) gen-dered subjectivity, identity and agency, the possibility of women's re-sistance or even subversion" (15). I think that is right, and in fact have argued, in the context of colonial history, why the recovery of subal-tern agency must presuppose its existence in order to unearth it from indifferent archives and hostile historiography.[26] I also disagree with many of those critics who read Renaissance theater as unmitigatedly patriarchal. But neither position needs to deny that women in the plays are tortured, mutilated, and punished for their attempted inde-pendence and agency.

To begin with, we may sift textual meaning from the fate of the characters within the plays: it can be argued that precisely these punishments expose the workings of a hostile patriarchal order and its strategies in suppressing women so that a feminist reading of *Othello*, for example, is not dependent upon a radically resistant Desdemona.[27] Agency is often made visible precisely by the violence of the dominant response against its expression, as I shall indicate via Webster's *The White Devil* later in this essay. This play, like so many others of the period, also demonstrates the ways in which agency can often manifest itself through compliance with the structures of power, through a utilization of dominant strategies, stereotypes, and ideologies.

Moreover, and this surely is the crucial question, whose agency is finally at stake for feminist criticism? That of Shakespeare's or Middleton's or Webster's female figures? That of the female critic? Or that of the women students, readers, spectators of the drama? Not only Lynda Boose and Carol Neely, but surprisingly Ann Thompson, writing from the opposite perspective of trying to reconcile materialist and feminist criticism, imply a straightforward connection between the agency of female literary characters and that of real women reading the plays. If, as Brecht remarked in relation to his Mother Courage, the purpose of playing is to make the *spectator* see, then the readers' agency does not exist in direct relation to that of the literary figures in the plays, and in fact the relation might actually be an inverse one. Such demarcation makes possible the positive politics of the negative critique. A feminist pedagogy should not have to gloss over the victimization of women – precisely the lack of agency in the represented lives of women can become a pedagogical and critical means for mobilizing consciousness and agency in the lives of the readers. The radicalism or otherwise of Renaissance and Jacobean theatre is a contentious and difficult issue within recent political criticism; the position that a critic takes on it can hardly be a reliable or straightforward index of her own politics.[28] It is indeed a strange (and dangerous) literary-critical maneuver which will suggest that I am complicit with colonial ideologies if I trace the powerful workings of colonial discourse in *The Tempest*. The ideological positions contained within a text – even if we could agree on what these are – are not binding on its readers/spectators/critics. Therefore, *The Taming of the Shrew*, with its less recuperable representation of women, could as effectively function as the basis of a radical critique of literary education in India or bardolatry in general (to take just two examples) as, say, *Antony and Cleopatra*.

The confusion about women's agency in this debate also has much to do with the privileging of text over history, which I earlier remarked upon. Benita Parry suggests that the agency of the colonized is either misunderstood or neglected by recent colonial discourse theorists partly because they do not pay sufficient attention to the various contexts of that voice, privileging discourses and texts over, say, institutions and political movements.[29] The distinction between the two sets is not unproblematic, but here I'm concerned that the very opposite suggestion is being made – that the *text* (as explicitly

25

contrasted to history) is offered as a sufficient ground for recovering the agency of the marginalized. That this should happen within non-traditional Shakespearean studies only indicates that the legacy of English literary studies of the last century is difficult to challenge on one of its central sites – the Shakespearean play.

In this essay, I have sporadically referred to the colonialist history of Shakespeare's plays and the current teaching situation in India not simply to insert my own critical stake into debates about Shakespeare and feminism, but also to point out that even discussions of race, imperialism, colonialism, cultural difference, and otherness can be insular. Boose's suggestion that "if race, ethnicity and religion have mapped a differential investment for blacks onto *Othello* and Jews onto *The Merchant of Venice*, gender construction has always already dictated a disproportionate feminist investment in a number of issues which span the canon" (721) reduces critical investment to only one of its many starting points. "Blacks" may also be invested in more than a rereading of *Othello*. The notion of "race" must transcend the black presence in the plays and inform understandings of gender, the state, political life, and private existences, otherwise the "others" within Shakespeare as well as in the Shakespearean academy or classroom will be granted only a token legitimacy which will disguise, among other things, the dynamic and intricate intersections of these categories in the creation of Renaissance culture as well as our own contemporary cultures. These connections would include the following: the relationship between the Western family and emergent colonial discourses; the overlap and tensions between various types of patriarchal ideologies in the early modern period; the construction of newer forms of patriarchal discourses via the deployment of canonical texts (such as Shakespeare) in a variety of contexts (for example, Indian and South African classrooms); the ways in which relations of gender and race inform and shape teaching situations in various parts of the world and the relationships between them. As I hope the rest of this essay will indicate, these difficult, even occasionally fuzzy, connections are conducive rather than detrimental to a critical focus on gender and the recovery of female agency.

The division between inner and outer was instrumental in defining both the patriarchal family and the parochial state in early modern England; at the same time, the state was patriarchal and the family parochial. Some of these overlaps are quickly traceable in Webster's play *The White Devil*. In this play, it is clearly the agency of the punished rebellious woman, Vittoria, which is at stake for feminist criticism and pedagogy. The process of its recovery would, I think, involve precisely those critical maneuvers which Boose and Neely say are antithetical to a "true" focus on women – tracing the ways in which the discourse of "blackness" is mobilized in order to circumscribe female transgression, connecting such repression with the question of class and state power, and acknowledging the possibly enabling interconnections between women's deviant agency and their compliance.

Zanche, Vittoria's Moorish servant, the "black fury" of the play (IV.vi.224), allows us to trace some of the divergences and convergences between different social hierarchies.[30] Although two-thirds of European slaves were female, the female slave is not proportionately visible in the drama of the period. Patriarchy as a *motor* of colonialism, rather than just an additional factor within it, has begun to be studied only recently and is often missing from the accounts of many historians of race, even those (such as Cedric Robinson) who are sensitive to other crucial connections such as the fact that medieval colonial slavery served as a model for Atlantic colonial slavery; that class differentials are often expressed in terms of race, or that racism is not just an effect of European geographical expansion but connected to its internal dynamics such as the growth of mercantilism. Robinson astutely points out that "the tendency of European civilisation through capitalism was . . . not to homogenize but to differentiate – to exaggerate regional sub-cultural dialectical differences into 'racial' ones."[31]

In *The White Devil*, "blackness" is a signifier for various forms of socially unacceptable behaviour. Flamineo says,

As in this world there are degrees of evils,
So in this world there are degrees of devils.
(IV.ii.57–8)

The term "black" is obsessively used to describe all of them. Monticelso calls Lodovico a "foul black cloud" (IV.ii.99); Flamineo, at the end of the play, sums up his own life as "a black charnel" (V.vi.267); there is "black slander" (II.i.60), "black lust" (II.i.7), "a black concatenation of mischief" (III.ii.29–30), "black deed" (V.iii.247), and Monticelso's "black book" in which "lurk the names of many devils" (IV.i.33, 36). Moreover, the variety of evils that the play identifies all feed into the construction of the deviant woman, as is evident from the range of analogies that Monticelso draws upon in defining Vittoria as a "whore" during her trial – poisoned perfumes, sweetmeats, alchemy, cold Russian winters, counterfeited coins, the fires of Hell, treasuries emptied by riot, dead bodies . . . (III.ii.79–101). This astonishing variety inscribes the transgressive woman by displacing onto her a whole spectrum of anxieties that beset Renaissance authorities, so that she is erased even as she is over-defined. However, it is also true that her stage presence and her

27

defiant answering back qualify and critique the success of discursive attempts to contain her.

Now the trial of Vittoria is also staged for the benefit of the six foreign ambassadors. Here, the staging of female deviancy, marked, defined, and controled, is shown to be crucial for the exercise of state power. *The White Devil* and other plays of the period establish the linkage between private and public authority by showing their common fear of uncontrollable female activity. Overlaps between the construction of women and cultural outsiders, which have by now been widely identified in other contexts, are similarly evident in the process of "naming" Vittoria. "Black lust" and a "black concatenation of mischief" are attributes of this "debauch'd and diversivolent woman" (III.ii.28–30). The "jade" Vittoria is obliquely referred to as a "resty Barbary horse" (IV.ii.93), and when Brachiano suspects Vittoria's fidelity, he describes her not only through the patriarchal stereotypes of "changeable stuff" and "whore," but as a "devil in crystal," whose beauty is fatal as a "heathen sacrifice" (IV.ii.43, 46, 85, 86).

The two female devils – black and white – coexist with a whole range of other evils such as the "wild Irish" and "the uncivil Tartar." Zanche and Vittoria come together most spectacularly in the scene where they attempt to kill Flamineo. White sister and black lover together occasion his outburst against "cunning devils." There is a momentary obliteration of class differences between men as servant invokes master in his diatribe against women: "Brachiano be my president: we lay our souls to pawn to the devil for a little pleasure, and a woman makes a bill of sale" (V.vi.145–6). But such bonding, male and female, is never free of the tensions of class and race – in the same scene, Vittoria has reminded Flamineo of her position as Zanche's mistress, and Zanche's own class and blackness continually mold the contours of her vulnerability as "the infernal" who provides "sport" for several men in the play (V.ii.214). Zanche longs for a situation where she will not be any man's "shame," as Monticelso defines her in relation to Flamineo (V.i.90). Her sexual identity can be celebrated and expressed only to a black man:

> I ne'er lov'd my complexion till now
> Cause I may boldly say without a blush
> I love you.   (V.i.209–11)

But Zanche simultaneously recognizes that racial bonding is precariously constructed across class and gender differences. Hence she woos the "Moor" with *money*, which will mask her color and confirm her desirability as a woman. Thus it is to her "black" lover that Zanche confesses her hope that her dowry will "make that sunburnt proverb false, /And wash the Ethiope white" (V.ii.248–9). Here we see both an internalization of the discourse of "whiteness" on Zanche's part – there is still the desire to be washed of her color – and some understanding of its contradictions – race is negotiable via money. Her desire to be white is also the fuel for whatever agency she displays. Hence "true" and "false" consciousness are inextricably entwined.

Indeed, the play shows both Zanche and Vittoria insistently *acting*, though without a full understanding or articulation of their desires, and always *provoking* their punishment. To focus on the punishment, then, is not simply to recount a sorry tale of victimization, but to identify agency and resistance, if only in the moments before they are snuffed out. It is also worth noting that Vittoria protests against her arraignment by grasping, inverting, and thereby challenging the division between the sexual and the political: in an incisively appropriative gesture, she calls her trial a rape and claims that the State and the Church have "ravish'd justice" (III.ii.271, 273). She, like Caliban, has learnt to curse in the language of the oppressor. All such gestures of appropriation necessarily indicate the gray areas that agency inhabits – areas that are inhabited by a whole range of oppressed and deviant women in the period. For example, the "witch" uses her confessions to find a position from which to speak out, or female pamphleteers use the arguments of male rationalists and humanists in order to dismantle their prescriptions for female behavior.

I have been suggesting the necessity of weaving between and even within different categories of difference: not just the category of "women" but also the category of "race" needs to be acknowledged as heterogeneous. The outsider in the literature of the period is not always literally of a different color, after all, the slave population of Europe consisted of Tartar, Greek, Armenian, Russian, Bulgarian, Turkish, Circassian, Slavonic, Cretan, Arab, African (Mori), and occasionally Chinese (Cathay) slaves. Peter Stallybrass rightly questions the assumption that the interests of different marginalized groups automatically, or simply, converge, and shows that in the case of Renaissance representations of "the world turned upside down" the unity of oppressed groups "emerged as a precarious alliance, often honoured as much in the breach as in the observance."[32] These tensions between various "others" serve as a crucial check against confusing intersections with parallels; against simply mapping various forms of oppression upon each other, cataloging endless "overlaps" to the point where the specificity of each is blurred. As Brittain and Maynard point out, "because there are cultural explanations for both racism and sexism does not mean that they deal with the same phenomenon . . . the oppression of black women undercuts the usefulness of the 'parallels' exercise." They also astutely note that

29

"the distinction we make between sex and gender seems to have no counterpart in the discourse on race."[33] Dominant discourses of course strategically collapse as well as emphasize distinctions in those they seek to control. British colonial strategy in India, for example, worked toward stratifying the local population into several races. The repeated distinctions drawn between Aryan and Dravidian rested upon an equation of the latter with Africans and worked toward persuading the Indian elite that they were not racially discriminated against. (As it happens, the precarious pan-Aryanism thereby suggested played some role in smoothing the course of Western literature in the Indian classroom, by offering connections between the "great" authors of both cultures.) At the same time, colonialist discourses constantly had to draw linkages between its various others; both strategies can be detected in the following pronouncements of Sir Harry Johnson, the first commissioner of British Central Africa, in 1894:

> On the whole, I think the admixture of yellow that the negro requires should come from India, and that Eastern Africa and British central Africa should become the America of the Hindu. The mixture of the two races would give the Indian the physical development which he lacks, and he in turn would transmit to his half-negro offspring the industry, ambition, and aspiration towards civilized life which the negro so markedly lacks.[34]

An analogous reminder of the ways differences are simultaneously marshaled and flattened by dominant discourses and institutions is offered by several studies that point out how the Irish provided a model for slavery and colonialist discourses in both Africa and India.[35] My point is that to recognize both differences between various categories of "difference" as well as the importance of alliances is necessarily to undertake a somewhat tortuous and dizzy critical path, one which is sensitive not just to "the text" but also to its placement. For example, the endless critical debates about Othello's precise skin color, one may recall, often strain to deny its political importance, so that, paradoxically, to insist on the crucial significance of blackness may involve moving away from the question of Othello's exact shade.[36] That play also demonstrates both the divergences and alliances between different sorts of patriarchy: black and white, familial and public, virulent and more "human," and the same variegation can be observed in other plays, both where there is a black presence and where there isn't.

The diversity of those who were regarded as "outsiders" and the overlaps between race, region, class, and gender do not minimize the importance of color consciousness, which already had a history which newer interactions drew upon and remolded. As Norman Daniel puts it:

. . . xenophobia and hysteria were compounded at the inception of the Crusades and it is a mistake to view them as isolatable phenomena. . . . Fighting and robbing, killing, trading, making profits, taking rents or tributes, all these were closely linked to philosophical and theological analysis, to the composition of history and propaganda, and even to love of one's neighbour. The Crusades renewed the idea that we need not do as we would be done by. They were also an expression of a much older history of suspicion. . . . The expectation of difference goes back to the cultural intolerance of "barbarians" which is one of the less useful legacies of Greece.[37]

To insert gender into this history is to note how similar dichotomies between woman and man, inner and outer, private and public, shape the development of family, nation, home, race, and culture. In *The White Devil* or *The Duchess of Malfi* domestic and State power are represented as occupying literally the same sites, and, as discussed above, the language of control uses (and fluctuates between) both gender and color. The way in which they are meshed together is evident from some of the material made available by Jean-Louis Flandrin, whose studies of the early modern family do not address either gender or race explicitly but who points out the ways in which the terms "kinsfolk," "*lignage*", "race," "home," and family appear in seventeenth- and eighteenth-century French dictionaries as more or less synonymous.[38] The concept of the house, writes Flandrin, is intermediate between those of *race* and of "household"; it "linked the continuity of the family with the perenniality of settlement in a particular place." This fluctuation between "race" and "house" is also evident in Montaigne's essay, "Of Names":

It is a wretched custom, and with most injurious consequences in our land of France, to call each person by the name of the estate, and it is the usage that most leads to confusion between different races. The younger son of a good house, having had as his appanage a piece of land under the name of which he has been known and honoured, cannot honourably abandon it; ten years after his death the land passes into the hands of a stranger who follows the same usage; you may well guess how confused we become when we try to ascertain the origin of these men.[39]

Flandrin points out that such ambiguity meant that descent could be traced through women whenever it suited the preservation of the household.

The dwindling of this concept of the household by the sixteenth century can be related to changes in class, gender, and race relations, each of which called for a stricter definition of the family in order to preserve property and cultural identity. While the lower classes (especially people like traveling salesmen) were perceived as black, actual contact with non-white peoples intensified parochialism into racism. The fear of female mobility and the fear of "outsiders" fuel each other – in early modern Europe, as in countless other patriarchal cultures. For example, we learn, from Flandrin again, that the exogamous policy of the Church was contrary to the everyday practice of the French peasantry:

> In many villages, if not in all, the "big boys" grouped together as an institution, made efforts to establish their monopoly over the marriageable girls of the parish. Every girl married to an outsider represented, in fact, for the less fortunate among them, an increased probability of remaining a bachelor and a servant in the house of another. Thus it was that with cudgel blows, if one is to believe Retif and some other observers, they dissuaded outsiders from associating with the village girls. Furthermore, they proclaimed the dishonour of such girls as became interested in others than themselves.[40]

In various cultures and historical contexts, female sexuality has been seen as "responsible" for a necessary tightening of the family structure and for the need for hierarchy, differentiation, and privacy. Renaissance and Jacobean plays, as well as other writings of the time, are literally littered with instances which demonstrate the linkage between deviant femininity and outsiders, even in the most casual or "insignificant" moments.[41] In *The Two Gentlemen of Verona*, for example, Proteus remarks that

> . . . the old saying is:
> Black men are pearls in beauteous ladies' eyes.

Julia's disavowal

> 'Tis true, such pearls as put out ladies' eyes;
> For I had rather wink than look upon them
> (V.i.11–14)

confirms her "lack" of sexuality and therefore her status as a desirable and moral woman. Black women are rare in the plays, but even when they are briefly invoked, their "place" is clear:

> DESDEMONA How if she be black and witty?
> IAGO If she be black and thereto have a wit,
> She'll find a white that shall her blackness hit.
> (II.i.131–3)

The unruly female body is both a symptom and the result of a threatened national culture: in Middleton and Dekker's *The Roaring Girl*, Moll's unfeminine attire consists of "the great Dutch slop," or breeches which her tailor promises her will be "open enough" to accommodate her desire for free movement; Sir Alexander Wengrave fears he has "brought up my son to marry a Dutch slop and a French doublet; a codpiece daughter" (II.i.88, 95, 97–8).[42] In the 1620 pamphlet, *Hic Mulier*, which virulently attacks female crossdressing, women who display the desire to fashion themselves and "mould their bodies" are described much in the same way as Vittoria is: they are "all Odious, all Devil," "Mer-Monsters" and if their activities "be not barbarous, make the rude Scythian, the untamed Moor, the naked Indian, or the wild Irish, Lords and Rulers of well-governed cities."[43]

This essay has only been able to gesture toward the various textual and contextual linkages between patriarchal control, state power, parochialism, colonialism, and racial prejudice that need to be made. Of course it is possible to use such connections to read gender relations, sexual anxiety, or threats from and to women as merely signs for something else – cultural anxieties, a crisis of governance, and so on. I have tried to argue that such reductionism cannot be corrected by matching it; instead we can use a fuller, if more heterogeneous and problematic, understanding of women to relocate them as central to all cultural and historical processes. Colonialism is manifestly the history of the intersection of various and color-coded patriarchies. The common operations of these patriarchies might lead us to posit a globally oppressed, transcultural womanhood, but even as we point to a widespread history of gender oppression, we must be alert to the difference that the color of patriarchy (and the color of feminism?) makes to an analysis of female subordination and agency. In so far as the Renaissance has provided a crucial "originary" moment for the supporting structures of Western culture such as the state and the family, the study of these structures can often become a culturally inward-looking exercise which takes these structures as universal, or worse, as normative. Even as students of the Renaissance today focus upon those constituencies and groups (women, blacks) who function as the enabling "others" of Renaissance culture, it becomes clear that no study that assumes as normative the structures of the state or the family (then or now) can develop a vocabulary sensitive enough to recover adequately the histories of oppression, let alone to reconstruct acts of disobedience. Further, our attempts to recover the agency of "woman" will constantly have to reckon with critical and pedagogic investments in the idea of "family"; the need is to dispense with the family romance, both in relation to the community of Shakespeareans today, and in the analysis of the Renaissance family. The widespread and sometimes strange existence of Shakespeare in postcolonial worlds is only one useful reminder of this diversity (of the black sheep, perhaps!) in the Shakespearean "family."

2

"THE GETTING OF A LAWFUL RACE"

Racial discourse in early modern England and the unrepresentable black woman

Lynda E. Boose

If ever a topic needed to be waylaid, queried, and "debrided" of acquired meanings before discussion of its origins might fairly begin, surely it is the discourse of race.[1] For while the twentieth century has generally presumed that skin color is its determining factor, what actually complicates any analysis of racial discourse is, to begin with, the pervasive ambiguity – in the late sixteenth or late twentieth century – surrounding the use of the term "race" itself. As Frank Reeves puts it:

> I may recognize others' discourse to be about race, when it employs a category which I am able to identify as having a referent corresponding to that designated by my own understanding of the term "race." It is not to be recognized solely by the occurrence of one particular linguistic symbol.[2]

In attempting to identify the parameters of the racial discourse of early modern England, we might well start by asking how it is possible to distinguish a set of signifiers indicating some specifiable notion of race, within a discourse as xenophobic as that of the Elizabethans and Jacobeans. In Shakespeare's plays, for example, certain canards about African characters like Othello, Aaron the Moor, and Portia's suitor, the Prince of Morocco, sound blatantly "racist" to our twentieth-century ears because they reflect the taxonomy of color through which we have come to rationalize our own racial fantasies. Portia's snide remarks about Morocco's "sooty bosom" would thus be much more likely to strike us as "racist" than would her disparagement of the German suitor, whom she dislikes because, as a German, he is, *ipso facto*, also a drunkard. But is it an accurate reading of sixteenth-century English prejudices – or twentieth-century and especially American ones – to see the former instance as being categorically the more virulent and systemic? Was skin color the most defining feature for constructing Otherness in sixteenth-century England? Precisely how do the attitudes toward black African

35

characters dramatized in Shakespeare's plays or those of his contemporaries differ from the general contempt attached almost indiscriminately to the various aliens/foreigners/Others/outsiders of Elizabethan England?

Because of its geographical isolation, sixteenth-century England was of all European countries the most unfamiliar with Africans; by contrast, the Spanish and Portuguese had enjoyed over 800 years of such contact.[3] Nonetheless, only a century later, "Britain had become the primary source of information and speculation about the assumed proclivities and capabilities of Africans . . . [and] vied with Holland for the monopoly in the buying and selling of black slaves."[4] The Britons had earlier participated in the European slave-trade and had, in fact, persisted in such commerce for several centuries after "Western and Central Europeans had generally banned the enslaving of fellow Christians."[5] But slavery as an English institution was not yet racial. The slaves that were sold out of and within the British Isles even as late as the fifteenth century were Britons, mostly Celts; and when England began to compete in the trade to supply slaves to the Spanish New World colonies, the driving economic impetus behind the venture had not yet been fully vested with an ideology of racist meaning. Although thirty London merchants, the Company of Adventurers, were granted the slaving concession as early as 1618,[6] it was late in the century – well after Shakespeare wrote *Othello* – that black Africans were conceptually reduced in the popular imagination to commodified objects of trade.[7] That they had darker skins was clearly recognized: but exactly what significance was attached to that fact? Where should the lines be drawn that separate the observation of difference from various degrees of prejudice and, finally, from what can legitimately be defined as a systemic form of prejudice such as we assume when we invoke the charge of "racism"?

If "race" originates as a category that hierarchically privileges a ruling status and makes the Other(s) inferior, then for the English the group that was first to be shunted into this discursive derogation and thereafter invoked as almost a paradigm of inferiority was not the black "race" – but the *Irish* "race." In tracts such as Spenser's *A View of the Present State of Ireland*, the derogation of the Irish as "a race apart" situates racial difference within cultural and religious categories rather than biologically empirical ones. But when that discourse then places the Irish into analogy with what twentieth-century Americans would call "peoples of color," within what category do these claims of difference belong – the biological, the cultural, or the theological? In early modern English treatises on New World "Indians" the Irish frequently appear as analogous because similarly primitive/barbaric. In *The White Devil*, John Webster repeatedly associates the black Zanche with the Irish.[8] It was not just the writers of Elizabethan and Jacobean England, however, who believed the Irish were a race apart. Even after the fantasy of skin color had been fixed in concrete by the French anatomist Cuvier's 1805 pronouncement of three major races in the world – white, black, and yellow – the Englishman's need to distance himself from the Irish by invoking the most powerful discourse of difference available was so strong that the terminology of primate behavior developed to describe the Africans as inferior was applied to the Irish as well. Thus an 1860 English traveler to Ireland writes:

> I am haunted by the human chimpanzees I saw along that hundred miles of horrible country. I don't believe they are our fault. I believe there are not only many more of them than of old, but that they are happier, better, more comfortably fed and lodged under our rule than they ever were. But to see white chimpanzees is dreadful; if they were black, one would not feel it so much, but their skins, except where tanned by exposure, are as white as ours.[9]

The writer of the passage is Charles Kingsley, writing his wife about his first trip to Ireland.

The delusion of race as contemporary Anglo-American culture understands it was an order that was quite probably just on the horizon by the end of the sixteenth century, just beginning to displace the notion of divine necessity as antecedent rationale for principles of difference. But it was also a moment when several systems of meaning were clearly still in competition. The discourse of race that the Tudor and Stuart eras produce is written into that gap.

The Englishman's overtly stated attitude toward almost all forms of cultural difference was unabashedly contemptuous. Thus sixteenth-century chronicler Robert Fabian, describing three New World natives who had been presented in court to Henry VII, writes that they were "clothed in beasts skins, & did eate raw flesh, and spake such speech that no man could understand them and in their demeanour like to bruite beastes." Coming across them again two years later, however, Fabian speaks of seeing "two [of them] apparelled after the maner of Englishmen in Westminster pallace, which that time I could not discerne from Englishmen, til I was learned what they were."[10] For Fabian, the Native Americans who were "bruite beastes" when their language, eating habits, and clothing differed from his suddenly become indistinguishable from the well-dressed Englishman. Clothes, or rather cultural signifiers, make the man and cultural and theological alignments – unlike biological ones – can always be changed. Fabian's story is a conversion narrative that would not have been possible had he seen these "bruite beastes" through the eyes of his later heirs, who almost certainly would have noted and invested meaning in specifically "Indian" physical fea-

LYNDA E. BOOSE

tures that would have pre-empted the inclusions that Fabian seems willing to grant.

Yet by the time Shakespeare wrote *Othello, the Moor of Venice* in 1603, Fabian's perspective was a way of thinking that was apparently under siege – as even the title of the play ambiguously suggests by the way it defines Othello as a dually constituted subject, a walking contradiction akin to something like "the Eskimo of Texas." Othello has converted to Christianity, has adopted the Venetian language, and, like the Venetians, imagines himself in opposition to the infidel/Turk. Desdemona, apparently once frightened by his darkness, has found his humanness in the stories of his suffering; Brabantio has invited him into his home; the Duke has entrusted him with nothing less than leadership in the defense of Venice from outside invasion. In terms of the theological and cultural categories, Othello is a Venetian. And yet, once his Ensign has raised the flag inscribing Othello within the difference of skin color, all the presumably meaningful differences Othello has constructed between himself and the infidel collapse. Thus alienated, he becomes the alien. Lying in death with Desdemona, the ineradicable visual difference embodied by Othello's presence is perhaps the ambiguous referent that makes the bed become, in Lodovico's ambivalent words, a "tragic loading," an "object [that] poisons sight," and something that suddenly impels the need to police the boundaries with "Let it be hid" (V.ii.373–5).

To chart early modern England's discourse of racial difference, we clearly need a more detailed cartography of what the English assumed within notions of the same. Did the English (or the French, Germans, Dutch, or Spaniards) participate in anything like the modern sense of some definitively *racial*, shared "Europeanness"? Or was the difference between a "Moor" and someone we would call a "European" conceptually organized around the religio-political geography of Christian vs. Muslim more than around a geography of skin color? How does the Jew fit into such schematics, especially if he is himself European ("Ashkenazi")? How are we to read the odd racial geography within which Jessica denominates her father by referring to Shylock's "countrymen" as "Tubal and . . . Chus" – the latter being the name which Elizabethans widely recognized as the original black African? Racial identities can be constituted by linguistic myths as well as by myths of origin. As a result of the mythic "history" that connected England to Rome and to Troy, did Englishmen feel "racially" connected to Italians? Or did they have any national sense of Germanic ties?

Since various early modern travel writers and playwrights insist on the distinction between "black Moors" and "white Moors," perhaps this figure identifies a particular social space where a notion of hierarchical difference in skin color was getting written over oppositions that had

38

been posited by the religio-political landscape of Muslim vs. Christian. The black Moor/white Moor was a prominent English fiction; but precisely what did this distinction mean to the English? Since Venice was Europe's predominant site of contact with the world of racial and religious Others and since *The Merchant of Venice* provides a multicultural mélange that includes two complete settings and plots filled with outsiders/aliens attempting to establish bonds with the dominant and privileged group, how might we schematize the play's various aliens in terms of the implied hierarchies of their (relative) acceptability to an English audience? What is the organizing principle behind Portia's various suitors? In the structure of the casket game, how does Morocco's position compare with Arragon's? Is Arragon to be understood as merely another member of the multitude of failed European suitors, or does his structural placement between the black Morocco and the white Bassanio, a Spaniard between a Moroccan and a Venetian, geographically imply that he occupies the space of the "white Moor"? In the grouping of the three suitors who are shown choosing the caskets, if Morocco and Arragon are set up along some implied moral continuum leading up to Bassanio, is the structuring principle tacitly presupposed along the lines of skin color? nationality? religion? Within a play that clearly values the act of "hazarding" and "risking all," this continuum defines the positive model of choice that is posed against the raft of European would-be's. Yet what should we infer from the fact that those same wanna-be's return home without forfeit while the two who do risk and lose – the two who also seem to be geographically and ethnically the most definably Other of the suitors – leave Belmont under penalty of perpetual celibacy, condemned never to reproduce themselves, no more successful in obtaining validation from the dominant group in Belmont than is Shylock in Venice? As I have been implying from the outset, it is the questions rather than the answers that are important. For by trying to situate *The Merchant of Venice*'s many constructions of Otherness in relation to some posited space of the English audience/self, questions such as these reveal just how many competing, potentially even contradictory, discourses lie tangled beneath the surface of the evolving notions of "race" in early modern England.

Shylock in particular raises special problems. According to the prevailing connection between skin color and race, "Jewishness" is not a race; nonetheless, it was and still is treated as if it were – as if Jews and Christians were fundamentally separated by something more incontrovertible than religious differences alone. Through the disclosure of prejudice built into the culture at every level, the kind of bias that collects around Shylock, modern readers glimpse a world that is most coherently identifiable to us as a version of contemporary racism. Yet if we assume a rudimentary racial theory based on skin color, how and where does Shylock's category of "Jewishness" fit? Does "non-Christian" sufficiently account for the way that "the Turk and the Jew" so often get phrased together as oppositional examples of some kind of similar Otherness? Or might the implied alienation of this pair be likewise empirically grounded in bodily difference – not the difference of "nature" signified by skin color but the difference that religion and culture had carved upon the (male) *body*? Did circumcision possibly set up a covert sense of body difference that made Muslim and Jew synonymously alien and, for a culture unused to the idea of such mutilation enacted upon male genitals, made that alienness as disturbing, deeply threatening, and by consequence as negatively value-laden to Christian Europe in the late sixteenth century as later centuries have imagined skin color and/or physiognomy? In Othello's concluding lines, speaking through the strangely bifurcated discourse in which he simultaneously occupies the positions of subject and object, conqueror and transgressor, Christian and Turk, what he invokes as the final, inclusive sign of his radical Otherness is not an allusion to his skin color. When the hero kills the transgressor, his actions are condensed inside a suicide cryptically encoded by, "I took by th' throat the circumcised dog, / And smote him, thus" (V.ii.264–5). Christian castration anxieties similar to those associated with Othello's threat of Otherness and his imputed theft of the high-born Venetian daughter likewise pervade Shylock's threat to cut off the pound of flesh from Antonio's body. In both Venetian plays, cultural anxieties are staged within a father–daughter–alien suitor triad in which seizure of the daughter is figured as castration.[11] And while such a threat of castration may be partially recuperated in the comic structure of *The Merchant of Venice* by a narrative that authorizes Christian appropriation of the Jew's daughter, both plots nonetheless participate in a fantasy that is suggestively produced by its location in Europe's paradigmatic space of market exchange and masculine competition, in the place of European rehearsal for engagement with the universe of foreign Others.

By the mid-seventeenth century, England would be competing with the Dutch for the dubious distinction of being the world's largest slave-trader. On the eve of that century, however, the nation had not yet come to embody the phenomenon of White Racism. As far as what initially triggered the formation of that response to Africans, some of the key factors obviously center on the discovery of the New World and the growth of a capitalist economic system that with relative ease converted human beings into property. But through a series of speculations inferred from the patterns of largely literary representation, I would like to propose that another source for that response lies in the patriarchally defined constitution of gender.

In the Shakespeare plays that include prominent outsiders, the disqualifying features that define men like Othello, Aaron, Shylock, and Caliban as aliens are not likewise invoked to disinclude the women marked as belonging to the outside. The Otherness of Jessica in *The Merchant of Venice* or of Tamora in *Titus Andronicus* is presumed to be convertible, as it would have to be if such women were to be incorporated into the group of insiders and go on to bear Lorenzo's or Saturninus's sons within that enclosure. In order for marriage to work in terms of the Lévi-Strauss model of social exchange, women who belong to an otherwise alien group must be perceived as assets whose assimilation will result in beneficial male social alliance on not only the *intra*- but also the *inter*-group level, including the bride's ability to reproduce the male whose children she will bear. Stories based on the "foreign bride" structure populate Western narratives. There is, however, one particular juncture in representation at which the model seems to break down and disappear completely, and that gap may point to a crucial juncture in the historical development of the racial fiction and its deep association with the (negative) primacy of skin color.

According to Winthrop Jordan, "in the long run . . . Englishmen found blackness in human beings a peculiar and important point of difference. The Negro's colour set him radically apart from Englishmen."[12] Exactly where this radical set-aside can be posited, however, seems to me a more gender-marked issue than is usually allowed. As the popular Anglo-American construction of culture explains it, White Racism has been, from its origin, a story about male competition. Thus the black male, imputed competitor for possession of the white male's prerogatives of power, wealth, and the assumed ownership of white females, poses the threat that marks the space where projected racial anathema begins. The explanation, however, not only seems as invested in projection as the fantasy it explains but effectively transposes the logic of historical cause and effect. The explanation that White Racism was instigated by a (projected) anticipation of black male violence smacks of a determinacy that acquired force within the slaveowners' very real fears of slave revolt; to assume it as the originary narrative is to superimpose the consequences of a peculiarly American history of race relations back onto their pre-slavery, English origins. And what this works to do is to defamiliarize and repress another story that would locate White Racism inside the norms of the culture's patriarchal system of transmission.

Elizabethan literary representation does, certainly, include deprecations of the black man. But curiously enough, the black male–white female union is, throughout this period and earlier, most frequently depicted as the ultimate romantic-transgressive model of erotic love. Othello is the romantic hero of his play who wins the love of Desdemona; the Prince of Morocco is placed into the position of one of three suitors who dare to venture the romantic quest for Portia; in Lady Mary Wroth's 1621 sequel pastoral, *Urania* (or *Urania II*), her heroine Pamphilia marries the noble black ruler, the King of Tartaria;[13] and the French Charlemagne Romances, translated into English as *Otuel*, feature a Moorish warrior hero, Otuel, who marries Belisant, the daughter of Charlemagne. Since "in the Romances, Moors were definitely black,"[14] there seems warrant enough to include *Otuel* in this list of miscegenated romances featuring a black man and white woman – romances which seem to *stop* sometime during the seventeenth century and go under-ground, eventually emerging in the post-slavery world transformed into degraded, pornographic narratives. But while the pre-slavery, black man–white woman narrative was still flourishing in drama, in epic, and in pastoral as the epitome of the romantically transgressive story, what seems conspicuously absent is any comparable tradition for a black woman–white man narration. The absence is especially noteworthy because this is the script that would seem, especially in light of the "captured alien bride" motif from which both Jessica and Tamora derive, to be the more expected pattern of the two. In light of Western Christianity's mystical models of the "black and comely" Shulamite woman of the Song of Songs and the frequently allegorized story of Soloman and Sheba, it would further seem that such a narrative, with its potential for catalyzing alliance, would have been authorized by the very existence of such precedents. It is, however, a narrative that essentially does not appear. And it may be here, at the site of this gap, that the division of people into categorically separate groups according to skin color may find its deepest, most unstated logic.

Clues to this logic float to the surface whenever English travelers to Africa try to puzzle through how black people (assumed as the deviant color) got that way. In *Purchas His Pilgrimage* (1613), Samuel Purchas presents with an open skepticism the various theories of skin color that had been received from classical learning:

> Now if any would looke that wee should here in our discourse of the Negro's assigne some cause of that their black colour: I ans-were, that I cannot well answere this question, as being in it selfe difficult, and made more by the variety of answeres, that others giue hereunto. Some alledge the heat of this Torrid Region, pro-ceeding from the direct beames of the Sunne; And why then shoulde all the West Indies which stretch from the one Tropike to the other, haue no other people? . . . why should Africa yeeld white people in Melinde? Some . . . attribute it to the drynesse of the earth: . . . as though Niger were here dryed vp. . . . Why then are the Portugalls Children and Generations white, or *Mulatos* at most, that is tawnie, in *St. Thomez* and other places amongst them? Some

ascribe it (as Herodotus) to the blacknesse of the Parents sperme or seede; And how made they the search to know the colour thereof, which if it hath (a thing by others denyed), by what reason should it imprint this colour on the skinne?[15]

As Purchas's insistent skepticism makes evident, sufficient contact with Africans had destabilized the climatological thesis of color that nonetheless remained the favored English explanation. But when Purchas begins to consider "Generation" and alludes to the rather whimsical theory that it is the literal "blacknesse of the Parents sperme or seede [that] imprint[s] this colour on the skinne," his discourse moves dangerously close to genetic considerations that the climatological explanation had worked to deflect. And at that point he suddenly brings the whole inquiry to a halt by asserting that "*Secret thinges*, both in Heauen and Earth, *they belong to the Lord our God*," and concludes with an apocalyptical vision in which "wee may all *be one*":

> the tawney Moore, black Negro, duskie Libyan, Ash-coloured Indian, oliue-coloured American, should with the whiter Europaean become *one sheepe-fold*, vnder *one great shepheard*, . . . (all this varietie swallowed vp into an ineffable vnitie) only the *Language of Canaan* be heard, only *the Fathers name written in their foreheads, the Lambs song in their mouths*, . . . *and their long robes being made white in the blood of the Lambe*.[16]

Happily for Purchas's readers, the bodily clothing to which "wee all" will ascend is still going to be white.

In 1578, an earlier English voyager, George Best, had sailed even closer to a recognition of genetic realities. In his *Discourse* of 1578 (reprinted in Hakluyt, 1600), Best took it upon himself "to proove all partes of the worlde habitable." Important to his argument was a refutation of any connection between skin color and proximity to the sun:

> Others . . . imagine the middle Zone to be extreme hot, because the people of Africa, especially the Ethiopians, are so cole blacke, and their haire like wooll curled short, which blacknesse and curled haire they suppose to come onely by the parching heat of the Sunne, which how it should be possible I cannot see: for even under the Equinoctiall in America, and in the East Indies, and in the Ilands Moluccae the people are not blacke, but tauney and white, with long haire uncurled as wee have, so that if the Ethiopians blacknesse came by the heat of the Sunne, why should not those Americans and Indians also be as blacke as they, seeing the Sunne is equally distant from them both, they abiding in one Parallel?[17]

As further illustration, Best quite literally brings the point home:

> Therefore to returne againe to the blacke Moores. I my selfe have
> seene an Ethiopian as blacke as a cole brought into England, who
> taking a faire English woman to wife, begat a sonne in all respects
> as blacke as the father was, although England were his native
> countrey, and an English woman his mother: whereby it seemeth
> this blacknes proceedeth rather of some natural infection of that
> man, which was so strong, that neither the nature of the Clime,
> neither the good complexion of the mother concurring, coulde any
> thing alter, and therefore wee cannot impute it to the nature of the
> Clime. . . . And the most probable cause to my judgement is, that
> this blackenesse proceedeth of some naturall infection of the first
> inhabitants of that Countrey, and so all the whole progenie of them
> descended, are still polluted with the same blot of infection. . . . by
> a lineall discent they have hitherto continued thus blacke.
>
> (262–3)

From here, Best goes on to invoke the story of Cham, Noah's disobedient son, whose lustful copulation with his wife was punished by the
blackness of the son that he fathered, Chus, who supposedly settled in
Africa and became originary father of the black Moors.

In his mini-narrative, what George Best has unwittingly recorded is, of
course, a rudimentary recognition about the way that genetic structure
resolves difference. When he reaches the disturbing acknowledgment
that not even the "good complexion of the mother . . . coulde any thing
alter," what he has really recognized is the dominance of dark pigmentation and its subordination/suppression of white – an arrangement that
wholly inverts the self-confirming presumptions that Best, Purchas, and
their white-skinned, English brethren have hitherto taken as articles of
faith. But it is crucial to note that Best's initial description of the
Ethiopian having taken a "faire English woman to wife" was itself free of
the animus usually attached to racism. The site of the problem that
prompts Best to digress from proving "all partes of the worlde habitable" is his confrontation with black dominance and suspicion of its
connection to "lineall discent." Upon reaching that perception, Best's
discourse begins reconstituting blackness into the sign of "infection so
strong it cannot be countered"; from there, it turns for theological
rationale to the story of Cham. But the tale of Cham and his son Chus
uncovers exactly the narrative that is, throughout the literature, always
under avoidance: the story of a black son fathered by a white father.
And while European travelers had no doubt fathered children in Africa
over the years, so long as such incidents occurred in Africa, white fathers
could attribute the darkness of the children to the climate. The black
child was not on hand to betray the secret.

In terms of patriarchal production, the implication of what Purchas hints at, Best sees, and Shakespeare stages in *Titus Andronicus* is disturbing. But by restricting themselves to narratives about offspring born to black fathers and "faire mothers," Shakespeare and Best protect themselves and their readers from the ideological disruption implicit in the story they do not tell. For even when the climatological explanation of blackness has lost force, the orthodox discourse about gender still works to contain the problem of color dominance within the black man–white woman paradigm: that a white woman married to a black man should bear a son who replicates the father actually fulfills the deepest patriarchal fantasy of male parthenogenesis (which the Aristotelian model of conception helped support), in which women were imagined primarily as receptacles for male seed. As is evident in much of the literature as well as in the behavior of historical figures like Henry VIII, the paternal fantasy of perfect self-replication was rudely disturbed by the production of daughters, whose arrival suggested the mother's outrageous substitution of herself. But even sons could be construed as products of the mother rather than the father. Commenting specifically on the way that *King Lear* "in effect distinguishes between Edmund as his mother's child and Edgar as his father's,"[18] Janet Adelman demonstrates how the authorizing distinction of legitimacy was defined less in terms of marriage to the mother than by erasure of her: while illegitimate Edmund is the product of the mother's womb, legitimate Edgar is the product of patriarchal law, the prerequisite for which is his apparently motherless status:

> Patriarchal society depends on the principle of inheritance in which the father's identity – his property, his name, his authority – is transmitted from father to son; . . . the father of a true son need "envie no father for the chiefe comfort of mortalitie, to leave an other ones-selfe after me." But this transmission from father to son can take place only insofar as both father and son pass through the body of a woman; and this passage radically alters them both. This is the weak spot in patriarchal inheritance: maternal origin and illegitimacy are synonymous in the Gloucester plot – and throughout *Lear* . . . whether or not the son is biologically his father's, the mother's dark place inevitably contaminates him, compromising his father's presence in him. For the son who has traversed the maternal body cannot be wholly "an other ones-selfe" for his father; the mother's part in him threatens the fantasy of perfect self-replication that would preserve the father in the son.[19]

In terms of the ideological assumptions of a culture such as that of early modern England, the black male–white female union is not the narrative that requires suppression. What challenges the ideology substantially enough to require erasure is that of the black female–white male, for it is in the person of the black woman that the culture's pre-existing fears both about the female sex and about gender dominance are realized. Through her, all free-floating anxieties about "the mother's dark place" contaminating the father's designs for perfect self-replication become vividly literal. It is even worth speculating that so long as marriage to outside/alien women was with women whose off-spring did not present so marked a visual contradiction of the patriar-chal image – marriages such as the oft-narrated union of the (white) Christian male and the Jew's daughter or even those between Englishmen and peoples like the Native American such as Pocahontas (peoples whom Best descriptively aligns with an English selfhood as being "not blacke, but tauney and white, with long haire uncurled as wee have") – perhaps racially based insults would remain somewhat local and "race" would not become an ideological, institutionally systemic concept. But in the untold story about the son produced by a "faire English man" and an "Ethiopian woman as blacke as a cole" lurks the impetus for a patriarchal culture's profound anxieties about gender to spill over into a virulent system of racial anathema. While such anathema would eventu-ally apply to everyone thus stigmatized, the locus of the transfer would be not the black male but the black female, whose signifying capacity as a mother threatens nothing less than the wholesale negation of white patriarchal authority. Within the symbolic order of that system, it is precisely that capacity that makes her unrepresentable. The logic of White Racism and even its need for special taboos to mark out a category of "miscegenation" (a United States' coinage that the OED first records in 1864, almost synonymous with Emancipation) are actually predictable from, if not inherent in, the unlocatable moment of patriarchy's con-frontation with genetic dominance. Essentially, this posits a new narra-tive for the formation of racism and endows that narrative with a "primal moment" located in a white male culture's discovery that not only was black more powerful than white and capable of absorbing and coloring it, but that in this all-important arena of reproductive authority, black women controlled the power to resignify all offspring as the property of the mother.

What helps bear out such a hypothesis is the treatment of black women in the few medieval/early modern representations of them that do exist. On the continent, where a medieval tradition of "le bon éthiope" apparently at least existed,[20] some space seems to have been opened up within literature and religious art for representation of figures like the Black Madonna (especially prevalent in France). But though the tradition existed, depictions of the figure – whose origin is shrouded in mystery and legend – apparently split into two distinctly racial representations, the less frequent, definably Negro one apparently suppressed (perhaps intentionally supplanted) by the other, dominant practice of imaging a madonna who was black-skinned but nonetheless Caucasian.[21] Even more telling is the absence noted by St Clair Drake: within the powerful Provençal tradition that spread across Europe of representing women as idealized love objects, "French troubadours did not sing about white knights enamoured of dark ladies. Except in Spain and Portugal, poets and troubadours did not make black women objects of romantic love, nor did artists depict them as such."[22]

In England, the few depictions of black women and what is avoided in them adds weight to such speculations. In Tudor and Stuart drama, black women most frequently appear in minor roles as lascivious servants whose depiction literalizes the patriarchal fear of the darkness of female sexuality. Zanche – whose presence in *The White Devil* forms a degraded mirror of the culture's collective views of her white mistress – is representative. Even on occasions where the black woman–white male yoking occurs in the main plot, the racial narrative nonetheless remains repressed, retarded from full articulation by its dissipation into figures like Shakespeare's Cleopatra or Marlowe's Dido, both of whom are only by the remotest suggestion represented as being Negro. According to Shakespeare's source in Plutarch, Cleopatra produced several sons to Antony (as well as to Julius Caesar). Antony's children are neatly left off stage in this play, removed from direct contact with the audience. Nonetheless, the implicit problem they may be thought to crystallize suggestively intrudes itself in the midst of one of Antony's most patriarchal diatribes. Having abandoned Octavia shortly after marrying her, Antony, returned to Egypt and now enraged at Cleopatra, here blames her as the cause why he has

> my pillow left unpress'd in Rome,
> Forborne *the getting of a lawful race*.
>   (III.xiii.107–8; my italics)

The black man is representable. But within Europe's symbolic order of dominance and desire, the black woman destroys the system, essentially swallowing it up within the signification of her body. By contrast to the way that repeated allusions to both skin color and physiognomy foreground the racial identity of the black male figure in *The Merchant of Venice*, *Titus Andronicus*, and *Othello*, the unrepresentability of Cleopatra's racial status is what gets foregrounded by *Antony and Cleopatra*'s use of only two such allusions, both of which help obfuscate rather than situate the issue. In the play's opening description of Cleopatra as the "tawny front" upon which Antony now bends his gaze (I.i.6), she is located within the term most often used to describe olive-skinned peoples – a term that Shakespeare invokes for ambiguously ethnic description in both "knight / from tawny Spain" (*LLL* I.i.173) and "tawny tartar" (*MND*

47

III.ii.273), and one that George Best had explicitly used to distinguish the skin color of the "tauney" peoples of America and the East Indies from that of black Ethiopians. Even when Cleopatra playfully describes herself as being "with Phoebus' amorous pinches black" (I.v.29), her reference sets skin color back into the old climatological description that avoids the challenge to white patriarchy. Lest one imagine, however, that Shakespeare or other writers of the era were yet unaware of the genetic connections that George Best had illustrated, not only Shakespeare's treatment of race in *Titus Andronicus* but George Peele's in *The Battle of Alcazar* suggests otherwise. In Peele, a white Moor, having married a black woman, has a black Moor for a son – and this son, as might be expected, is traitorous to his father and as black in perfidy as in complexion. And while the racial threat implicit within Peele's drama is defused by its geographical and religious dislocation, this play does at last present the otherwise avoided narrative of the son produced from a white male's union with a black woman.

Other than Peele's late sixteenth-century play, apparently the only other attempt to represent this story occurs in the legend of Morien, the Black Knight, an Arthurian tale (*c.* thirteenth–sixteenth centuries) of probable French origin that seems to have arisen after Central Europeans had made contact with the Moors in Spain and Portugal,[23] and that survives solely in German and Dutch translations. The tale plays out the return of the repressed: the arrival in Europe of the black, African-born son, his search for his father (who variously occurs as Sir Percival, his brother Agloval, or his father Gahmuret), and his demand for legitimation. If the legend in all its variants is read as the inscription of medieval Europe's initial speculations about the offspring of a white male's union with a black woman, then early modern England's repeated evocation of the climatological explanation suggests a rather marked repression of information that had seemed obvious enough to *Morien*'s thirteenth-century narrators. In the surviving Dutch version, the physical impression that Gahmuret's son makes upon Europe's foremost knights, Gawain and Lancelot, is striking:

> He was all black, even as I tell ye: his head, his body, and his hands were all black, saving only his teeth. . . . Then was the black knight blithe and drew near to Sir Lancelot, and bared his head which was black as pitch; that was the fashion of the land – Moors are black as burnt brands. But in all that men would praise in a knight was he fair, after his kind. Though he were black, what was he the worse. He was taller by half a foot than any knight that stood beside him.[24]

Equally striking, however, is the implicit refusal in Wolfram von Eschenbach's early thirteenth-century version to concede the realities of genetic dominance. In von Eschenbach's *Parzifal*, the black knight named "Feirefiz" is imagined as having skin that is mottled black *and* white and a name (cf. *vaire-fils*) that literally means "speckled son" or "multicolored son."[25]

The threat the black woman poses to the dominant system of representation is situated along a historical continuum of mis- and disrepresentation. In terms of modern assumptions about Shakespeare's texts, what would happen, for example, as Jonathan Crewe has asked, if "instead of always genteelly speaking of Shakespeare's Dark Lady sonnets, we could bring ourselves to call them the Black Woman sonnets"?[26] Why is the sonnet woman's "black" always referred to its other connotative possibilities and never to its racial one? And why do we insistently call her a "lady" when the sonnets themselves never do? Rather than the more conventional topic of sexual frustration and Neoplatonic transcendence, Shakespeare's sonnets directly address the issue of reproduction inside a framework in which the desired model of "fairness" and "likeness," produced as a political/cultural value, necessitates reading the addressee of the sonnets, the fair young man, as an explicit signifier for the white male. As Crewe comments in an unpublished paper, the black woman who begins to surface as object of desire/abhorrence from no. 127 onwards "dislocates the entire system of 'white' likeness, introducing more difference than the system can manage." In effect, the disruptive she whose introduction into the sequence abruptly terminates the sonnetteer's meditation on the fair young man's reproduction introjects herself not just as *a* difference, but as the very ground *of* difference, that which – as the evocation of "the old days" recalling the Song of Solomon in no. 126 implies – is even asserted as ontologically prior to the culturally presumed claim of white male subjectivity.

The problem of the black woman's unrepresentability received its most famous staging at the English court during Ben Jonson's debut as official masque-maker at the 1605 Twelfth Night performance of *The Masque of Blackness*. In *Blackness*, amidst Inigo Jones's elaborate staging effects, Queen Anne and eleven of her ladies, all costumed alike and painted as black African sea nymphs, arrived "*seated one above another; so that they were all seen, but in an extravagant order,*" inside a seashell that moved "*curiously,*" with "*six huge sea-monsters*"[27] swimming alongside. According to the fiction, these "*daughters of Niger*" come in search of a land whose name ends with "*-tania*" (165), where their blackness can be transformed by the power of its ruler, a temperate "sun" with beams bright enough "To blanch an Ethiop" (225). Having found the land whose "snowy cliff is Albion the fair" (180), the lucky ladies alight and dance before being sent off again with the promise that they may return to "Brit-tania" after a year has passed and their whitewash is complete.

Three years elapsed before the promised sequel, *The Masque of Beauty*, was finally enacted on Twelfth Night, 1608, in Whitehall. The Queen

49

with now fifteen ladies, no longer in blackface, entered on *"an island floating on a calm water"* sitting sedately on a *"Throne of Beauty, erected . . . by Ionic pilasters"* (144, 145, 146), ensconced, costumed, and defined no longer by exoticism and extravagant order but by the organizing resonances of the classical aesthetic. In this second, revisionary masque, hierarchical distinction – visually asserted by the jeweled crown that Queen Anne as "Harmonia" now wears – is rhetorically adumbrated into the Neoplatonic explanation that the *Masque* offers for the women's offstage transformation:

> When Love at first did move
> From out of chaos, brightened
> So was the world, and lightened. . . .
> Yield, night, then, to the light,
> As blackness hath to beauty,
> Which is but the same duty.
> It was for beauty that the world was made
> And where she reigns Love's lights admit no shade.
> (236–43)

In these two court productions (explicitly the latter), Jonson appropriates the masque as a political vehicle to argue his position in the aesthetic debates of early seventeenth-century poetry; within that context, race functions as a representational strategy. But by aligning blackness, night, and chaos against light, day, and generativity, and by invoking the Neoplatonic model of "Love's lights admit no shade," Jonson – whether wittingly or not – pushes the discourse of color difference outside any framework conducive to tolerance, let alone affirmation. In the production of the incipiently racist binary that makes "Beauty" the antithesis of "Blackness," what gets dismantled is the "black and comely" feminine ideal of the Song of Songs; what gets produced is a model of racial opposition constituted specifically along the axis of gender. Within the Jonsonian narrative, what is constructed as a threat to Albion's white face is the troop of women, who arrive in blackness and are sent away to wash themselves clean before they can return or be invited to stay on in "fruitful Kent and Essex fair" (255). As Kim Hall has shrewdly noted, "The cultural imperative of both masques is turning females white: none of the male 'Blackamoors' seems to feel any such need."[28]

Besides the aesthetic context, the race and gender issues woven into the two Jonson masques need to be read through the scenes of their performances and the decidedly different reactions the two inspired. For while *The Masque of Blackness* may not have been the first masque of blackamoor women to have been put on at the English court,[29] it was nonetheless the first time the court had been treated not only to the spectacle of Britain's Queen in black paint but, moreover, to a very pregnant black Queen who was known to be making her final public appearance before retiring to Greenwich pending delivery and who appeared in the masque with a fan inscribed, "a golden tree laden with fruit."[30] As Suzanne Gossett has ably illustrated, the decorum of the masque genre depended on the audience's recognition of a fully coherent symbolic identity between the court figures and the roles they played.[31] Since Queen Anne herself had conceptualized her appearance in the masque and had been instrumental in the whole production,[32] one can only guess at the extent to which the subversiveness of this performance was intentional. In *Blackness*, everything from Inigo Jones's elaborate artistic design to the signifying embodiment of the black-skinned and pregnant English Queen seems to have made it a magnet for the culture's anxieties about gender to coalesce around what Hall describes as "the unsettling vision" of the upper echelon of England's aristocratic ladies "posing as African nymphs,"[33] their blackened faces, hair, hands, and bosoms ornamentally highlighted with the priciest of pearls. It is unclear what James thought of the evening's or his wife's performance; but from Sir Dudley Carleton's correspondence to Sir Ralph Winwood, Carleton's view is amply clear:

> Their Apparell was rich, but too light and Curtizan-like for such great ones. Instead of Vizzards, their Faces, and Arms up to the Elbows, were painted black, which was Disguise sufficient, for they were hard to be known; but it became them nothing so well as their red and white, and you cannot imagine a more ugly Sight, than a Troop of lean-cheek'd Moors. . . . [The Spanish Ambassador danced with] the Queen, and forgot not to kiss her Hand, though there was Danger it would have left a Mark on his Lips. The Night's Work was concluded with a Banquet in the great Chamber, which was so furiously assaulted, that down went Table and Tresses before one bit was touched.[34]

Beyond its obsessive quality, there are two particularly revealing things about Carleton's description: one is his fantasized sense of a "Danger" that female blackness will leave marks on the white male who touches her, and the other is the way that this anxiety is immediately followed by a curiously punitive narration that depicts the "Night's Work" culminating in "furious assaults" that tore down "Tresses" within the great chamber. In a January 7 letter to Chamberlain, Carleton again obsessively elaborates the scene:

> The maske at night requires much labor to be well described; but there is a pamflet in press which will saue me that paynes. . . . The presentation of the maske . . . was very fayre, and theyr apparel rich, but too light and curtizan-like; Theyr black faces, and hands

51

which were painted and bare vp to the elbowes, was a very loth-some sight, and I am sory that strangers should see owr court so strangely disguised. The Spanish and Venetian Ambassadors were both there, and most of the French abowt the towne. The con-fusion in getting in was so great, that some Ladies lie by it and complaine of the fury of the white stafes. In the passages through the galleries they were shutt vp in seueral heapes betwixt dores, and there stayed till all was ended.[35]

Carleton first moves from a kind of unconscious introjection that meta-phorically constructs him as the pregnant party carrying a burden imagined as painful to deliver, to conjuring up the black ladies of the masque as sexually available objects. The "curtizan" image provokes an immediate denial that appears as violent antipathy toward the women's black bodies, followed by a rationalizing of that rancor into patriotic virtue. Then suddenly – by way of describing Whitehall's lack of space for the masque audience – Carleton narrates a scene of competition framed as sadistic desire for entrance, from which psychic location he is once again led toward a satisfyingly punitive vision of "fury" against "Ladies [who] lie by it and complaine" that is administered by staffs of phallic authority here used to prevent women's access. The authoritative signs are even remembered as "white."

Against the eroticized hostilities of Carleton's reaction to the vision of female disorder he associates with the production of *Blackness*, compare the glowing applause that both the King and the Venetian Ambassador shower on Anne after *The Masque of Beauty*. Having deferentially noted that this was a "spectacle . . . worthy of her Majesty's greatness," Ambassador Giustiniani insists that

what beggared all else . . . was the wealth of pearls and jewels that adorned the Queen and her ladies, so abundant and splendid that in everyone's opinion no other court could have displayed such pomp and riches. . . . it is evident the mind of her Majesty, the authoress of the whole, is gifted no less highly than her person. She reaped universal applause, and the King constantly showed his approval. At the close of the ceremony he said to me that he intended this function to consecrate the birth of the Great Hall which his predecessors had left him built merely in wood, but which he had converted into stone.[36]

Distinct from the pearls worn by the ladies in *Blackness*, those worn by the white-skinned women in *Beauty* articulate a vision of the pomp and splendor of the English court that is summed up by the masque's own definition of the women's function: "So all that see your beauty's sphere / May know th' Elysian fields are here" (343–4). Indeed, from the

Venetian Ambassador the masque provoked a paean of admiration. Implicitly, the Queen and her ladies were now seen as playing out their proper roles, their rewhitened bodies gracefully deployed as sites of status and desire for enunciating the purity of "Albion" and its aristocratic lineages. As Jonson's text records, James was apparently so pleased that he even interrupted the show midway to insist that the ladies dance several encores. Yet what nonetheless returns to haunt the King's response is the indigestible excess represented in the original masque by the pregnant blackamoor Queen – and it is this excess that finds its way back into James's conversation with Giustiniani in which he reveals his determination to convert the occasion into a masculine "birth" that he (rather than Anne) delivers to the nation, an edifice in stone appropriately named Whitehall.[37]

Jonson's two masques could together constitute a metanarrative of race and gender representation in English literature: the female blackamoors that made a symbolic foray on England's literary shores and attempted to enter early seventeenth-century representation were sent packing and welcomed back only when they had washed off their color. In a resolution that allowed Britain to contain difference within the much narrower sphere of intra-white hatreds, White Racism – conceived on English shores – was shipped off to the colonies along with racial difference, thus leaving the land called "Albion" virtually untainted – for centuries, at least – by racist imputations. To the Irish was left the job of playing out the English Other.

It would be some time before the resisted narrative of the black woman would be allowed to surface within English literature. When it did, it emerged on the American side of the Atlantic into a postcolonial, post-slavery, deeply anglicized United States of America that could neither send its blackamoors back[38] nor pretend, like its mother country, that it was a racially homogeneous culture in which difference was not an issue. It was a society that still valorized the biological connection between father and son upon which patriarchal organization is premised. But it was also one in which the ideology of slave-holding had rendered white men so dissociated from the cross-racial desire they commonly enacted in slave-cabins and so unidentified with the children they fathered that they were able to see even the sons from such unions as wholly outside of the otherwise definitive patrilineal model.[39] When this kind of festering desire was pushed into the open by Emancipation and surfaced in mid-nineteenth-century, white-authored American literature, it channeled itself into two deflective stories, one of which suppresses and the other of which reconstructs the black woman as the unrepresentable underlying object of desire. In the more familiar deflective pattern, white desire is projected onto the image of a black rapist whose imputed lust for white women must be severely punished by avengers disguising their identities in white bedsheets (thereby wearing, ironically enough, exactly the sign that the Elizabethans would have recognized as marking out the agent of the crime, not the avenger of it).[40] In the other narrative, the focus is on the mixed-race child that such forbidden desire has produced, who – by being a daughter instead of a son – facilitates a site for the disguised re-entry of the suppressed black woman, whose representation is collapsed into and hidden behind the figure of her daughter. This story of "the tragic mulatta"[41] that began emerging shortly before the Civil War is not, however, a story about just any mixed-race daughter. It is very specifically about the daughter who can pass for white, the liminal figure who signifies neither and both races, whose color obscures the black woman she smuggles into the text, and whose potentially undetected presence threatens white society with a newly dangerous return of the repressed in which the sins of the fathers will be revisited, played out this time in their own houses on suggestively incestuous ground. In the white-constructed tragic mulatta archetype, tragedy is inherently defined by the heroine's discovery that she has "black blood."[42] Within the melodrama of decision that such discovery precipitates, the purest act of love that the heroine can offer and what morally redeems her from the contamination she carries is to insure, by eliminating herself from the potential status of mother, that her poisoned blood will not destroy the white male's family line by marking it with that sign of blackness that Dudley Carleton had so many years earlier feared might rub off.

3

THE FACE OF DOMESTICATION
Physiognomy, gender politics,
and humanism's others

Juliana Schiesari

In Ariosto's Fifth Satire, the character bearing the poet's name advises his interlocutor on the proper way to manage a wife. Arguing for a motivational or rather manipulative approach, since "enticements work better than the chain," "Ariosto" repeats a common Renaissance *topos* that a wife should be domesticated in a way similar to the treatment of certain animals, especially dogs.[1] Obviously humanism's praise for the "dignity of man," as in Pico della Mirandola's famous work of that name, did not exclude a more demeaning view of women.[2] As Joan Kelly first argued in her celebrated essay "Did Women Have a Renaissance?," the lofty idealism of the new learning and the rise of the new commercial elites that we associate with the fifteenth and sixteenth centuries did not signal an improvement in the condition of women.[3] While traditional historians like Jacob Burckhardt have argued that the women of the Renaissance freely partook in the unshackling of medieval strictures, most women in fact found their limited privileges revoked and their few realms of power eroded.[4] The rising capitalist organization of society, Kelly argues, went hand in hand with the increasing restriction of women to the domestic space of the home. This exclusion of women from the public sphere, however, was not just a socioeconomic process. It was championed and legitimated by humanist thought itself, whose many commentaries on domestic life and family structure, as Kelly bluntly puts it, "sharply distinguish an inferior domestic realm of women from the superior public realm of men, achieving a veritable renaissance of the outlook and practices of classical Athens with its domestic imprisonment of its citizen wives."[5] Theorized by such humanists as Francesco Barbaro and Leon-Battista Alberti, the Renaissance demarcation of domestic space had incalculable effects in restricting women's possibilities of expression and freedom to move.[6] Recent scholarship into such Renaissance phenomena as the *Querelle des femmes* has also shown the parallel between misogyny and privatization, on the one hand, and early feminism and resistance to domesticity, on the other.[7]

More to the point, the ideology of the early modern *pater familias* seems to view women quite precisely as creatures to be domesticated. Perhaps no text so clearly rehearses the relation between paternity, husbandry, and domestication as Alberti's *I Libri di Famiglia*. For Alberti's characters of Giannozzo and Lionardo in that book, the distinction between public and private is the difference between the "manly things to do among men, fellow citizens and worthy and distinguished foreigners," (207) and the domestic enclosure of subservient beings including women, servants, children, effeminate males, dogs, and geese. The latter two are especially important in the household because they are "animals that are watchful and both suspicious and affectionate" (219), thus providing protection for the *pater familias'* belongings while he is away doing "manly things among men." The ideal wife is one who shares the same function as a good guard dog: "The woman, as she remains locked up at home, should watch over things by staying at her post, by diligent care and watchfulness" (207–8). In addition to the well known *Libri di Famiglia*, Alberti also wrote a training manual on horses, *Il Cavallo Vivo*, in which he discusses the proper raising of horses in terms of a good master's treatment of slaves and then produces the rule of thumb that "the diligence of the father of the family" (*padre di famiglia*) will always resolve problems in the proper manner.[8]

Coincidentally, the court culture of the northern Italian princes witnessed a revival in the keeping of companion animals, a custom lost since the end of Roman antiquity. Phobias about animals ran rampant in a Middle Ages obsessed with "Satanic" cats and races of dog-people (the so-called Cynocephali) worshipping the goddess Hecate. Dogs were kept only for the hunt, and only noblemen were allowed to hunt; yet beginning in fifteenth-century Italy, we begin to see lapdogs kept by women at court – the Maltese, the Bolognese, and the diminutive Italian greyhound.[9] If Ariosto is any indication, the development of these new breeds (*razza di cani*, or races of dogs), typically owned by women, contributed to the construction of the modern domestic sphere with its enforced privatization of women, children, and selected "companion" animals. From the point of view of early modern patriarchy, all three were in need of the same domestication.

Renaissance anxieties about gender relations are here expressed – transferentially, to borrow a term from psychoanalysis – through the language and figures of animal husbandry. In calling attention to the overlap between figures of women and figures of animals, my point is not just to reaffirm certain stereotypical correlations between femininity and bestiality in Renaissance and post-Renaissance culture. It is also to reassess the relations between culture and domination as they are evidenced in paradigms of representation that apply to all those entities – whether human beings of other genders and ethnicities or "non-human"

56

creatures – viewed as needing to be "domesticated."[10] What humanism constructed was a range of others to the entity "man," whose dignity was praised and who was given exclusive rights over the public realm. These "others" were either subject to the privatized enclosures of domestication (women in the home, children in nurseries, the mad in hospitals, dogs in their kennels, sheep in enclosed pastures) or banished to the edge of civilization (noble savages). A definition of humanity coterminous with the public sphere meant the deployment of massive exclusionary procedures to maintain that sphere as a masculine privilege. Advising Francesco da Carrarra, lord of Padua, on the city's governance in a letter of 1373, Petrarch already urges that the public streets and thoroughfares be cleansed of wailing women and roaming pigs.[11] And sumptuary, vagrancy, and enclosure laws became the questionable achievements of subsequent jurisprudence in the attempt to domesticate the others of humanism.

One of the most blatant and systematized forms that this domestication took was the "science" of physiognomy, as developed most notably by Giovan Battista Della Porta's *Della fisionomia dell'uomo* (On the Physiognomy of Man), published in 1610.[12] Presented as an interpretive grid to understanding human character as manifested in physiological and above all facial features, physiognomy quickly developed into a taxonomy of human physical characteristics correlating types of behavior with psychological attributes. Facial features occur as a kind of graphism or writing which in turn is in need of the systematic decoding that physiognomy claimed to provide. The perniciousness of physiognomy becomes evident, of course, when its conclusions are extended to entire groups of human beings based on their sharing certain common *physical* characteristics. Indeed, a working definition of racism can be found precisely in the attempts of the "science" of physiognomy to attribute common behavioral characteristics to shared physical features. While it is hard to argue that early modern physiognomy is *per se* racist in the sense that nineteenth-century phrenology or the writings of Gobineau incontestably are, there can be no question that physiognomy played a crucial role in the construction of race as well as gender. At its best, physiognomy was a psychological study of the psyche's imprint on the individual's anatomy (i.e. a kind of symptomatology); at its worst, however, it proceeded to a highly suspect classification of humanity based upon the assumed behaviors imputed to derive from bodily types. Anatomical difference thus became the pretext for prejudicial moral judgments, e.g. dark-skinned people are lazy, slant-eyed people are duplicitous, and so forth. The move from individual symptomatology to ethnic characterization is mediated, once again, through the figure of the beast. In fact, it is precisely the figure of the beast that allows for the explanation of individual quirks by inserting them into an identifiable group of beings (i.e. certain kinds of melancholic behavior are "found" to resemble that of wolves, a condition from which arose the term lycanthropy and the search to identify further "wolfish" characteristics in the physical appearance as well as the conduct of lycanthropes or "werewolves"). These correlations relied heavily on a highly suspect analogical process that superimposed the faces of animals onto humans, leading ultimately to a pernicious but effective essentializing of racial, gender, and bestial characteristics that justified the ideology behind those characteristics through an ambitious work of cross-referencing (e.g. men are courageous and honest like lions, while women, like the leopard with its spots, are cowardly and deceitful). Needless to say, *all* of the assumed behaviors of genders, races, and species were imaginary products of the society that produced this so-called "science." Nonetheless, what needs to be stressed is that the legitimation of this form of thought through the cross-referencing of the received stereotypes occurred in a way that bolstered their acceptance by making of them something "natural" as well as essential. By such a move, the "science" of physiognomy could claim to have disclosed the "true" nature of each being.[13]

Let us look more closely for a moment at Della Porta's text. Denouncing other divinatory sciences like chiromancy (or palm reading) and metoposcopy (or analysis of the forehead) as "vain, false and pernicious," (15) the author claims to base physiognomy upon "natural principles" (15) whose basis seems to be scattered observations of how changes in one's mental state lead to corresponding physical alterations. Bodily manifestations of psychic vicissitudes inevitably seem to trigger comparisons with animal behavior. For example, upon losing her empire, Hecuba is said to have started "barking like a bitch" (22). Lycanthropy then appears as a general example of how an internal state is revealed on and in the body through animalistic analogy (23–4). Chapter 3 makes a significant revision of this approach by ambitiously suggesting that "from the signs of the body one is able to know the inclinations of other animals" (24). In other words, bodily symptoms are not simply the translation of a mental or emotional disposition; they are the trans-species signs of those dispositions. Having deduced the supposed physical (i.e. bestial) traits of some psychological conditions, Della Porta now wishes to find a way to reveal those conditions through a systematized key of animal characteristics. Lycanthropy would thus be found in any creature that physically or behaviorally resembled the wolf. A complete inventory of the physical features of animals with their corresponding behavioral qualities should then provide the key to understanding human psychology; it is only a question of linking the right human physical features with the right animal. The bulk of Della Porta's book is composed of such comparative anatomies, richly illustrated with figures that juxtapose human with animal faces or bodies.

Della Porta's prime justification for this study occurs in chapter 3 with a discussion of dog breeding that is key to the book's subsequent development. Citing ancient sources, he describes the physical characteristics of a good hunting-dog, as if the aptitude to hunt were solely derived from these physical attributes: large body, flat nose, wrinkled brow, dark, shiny eyes, short and delicate ears, delicate hindquarters, slightness of head, long neck, short tail, robust chest (24–5). It is not easy to see how this list adds up to a description of any of the hunting breeds then or now; but Della Porta as a good humanist cites ancient learning rather than speaking from any particular experience of hunting-dogs. Nor does he cite any of the authoritative works on canines such as Gaston Phébus's *Traité de la vénerie* or Guillaume Tardif's *Livre des chiens pour la chasse* (1492). Rather, his motivation would seem to be to arrive at the maximum number of attributes in order later to compare such a representation of a hunting-dog with that of an aristocratic human hunter. In the drawing that accompanies this description, a single trait (a brow ridge over the nose) is said to characterize fierce, warlike men such as Hercules, Achilles, Alexander the Great, or Azzolino di Padua (the man pictured in the drawing). What seems to matter is that the hunting-dog is not to be confused with the housedog, which Della Porta describes in the following terms, although this time his recourse is not to ancient authorities but to personal prejudice:

> The housedog . . . has a flat, serene and distended forehead, similar to those who adulate; the voice is injurious and full of malediction; ruddy, inflamed eyes, the upper gums extended outwards at the canines, the mouth is very open; the tip of the nose is narrow; the eyes wide open. It is a custom or a habit that he likes to scream; malicious, always capable of biting; he is injurious, adulatory, gluttonous, cruel, crazy, irascible, pitiless and inconsiderate.
>
> (59)

It is noteworthy that the description of the housedog is not any more specific than that of the hunting-dog. What has taken place is that the physical features of the housedog are merely negations of those attributed beforehand to the hunting-dog (flat rather than wrinkled brow, eyes that are red and irritated rather than dark and shiny). It is also noteworthy that while the hunting-dog was described only in physical terms, its domestic counterpart is portrayed by a long string of derogatory and somewhat incompatible psychological attributes. The reasoning behind this inventory becomes evident only later on when we are again given a picture of a domestic dog next to a man who can only be understood as a servant or "domestic." Those whose smooth brow resembles that of the housedog (as opposed to the furrowed brow of hunting-dogs and noble-men) are said to be "obsequious, eager to please, but not innocent, because in front of you they adulate you, but behind your back they slash you" (137). What we can see clearly here is that Della Porta is not describing "real" animals, but collecting a vast array of animalistic traits to be used for the description of human beings in ways that sustain and accredit the dominant social order. In the case of the difference between hunting-dogs and housedogs, the discourse of physiognomy serves as an ideological apparatus to preserve class hierarchy.

The same "method" is applied to gender difference in chapter 26, "How from knowing the parts of man and woman, one is able by their customs to conjecture many customs." Again, the supposition is that conduct can be deduced from physical form, and that an inventory of these forms will allow one to deduce the behavior of men and women, understood as anatomically determined. After a paragraph-long list of male attributes (from big body, big face, thin arched eyebrows, square jaw, large and robust neck, etc. to habits that are generous, intrepid, just, simple, desirous of winning), Della Porta describes the form of the lion with a list of attributes that corresponds to man in such a way as to "demonstrate among all the animals the model of maleness" (95): medium-sized head, somewhat of a square face, not big-boned, a square forehead, slightly protruding eyes, big eyebrows, a firm, straight neck, etc., and customs that are "magnanimous, generous, desirous of win-ning, mild, just and a lover of those with whom he is in the habit of conversing on a familiar or domestic basis [*conversare domesticamente*]" (96).

Again, these characteristics do not combine in any obvious way into some representable male or lion; not do the attributes of man and lion exactly replicate each other. Rather, one again has the impression that an entire set of qualities is being generated to be used later for the disciminatory purpose of separating the "true" manliness from all of its others: femaleness, servility, savagery, etc. Why else should we be given such biologically and even ideologically unleonine features as "mildness" or "a lover of those with whom he is in the habit of conversing on a familiar or domestic basis" (96)? It would seem that this last bit of unverisimilar anthropomorphism is supposed to describe the lion's mythic sense of fidelity; but Della Porta's periphrasis, with its insistence on "conversation" and "domesticity," all but gives away the human milieu whose classification and regimentation make up the physiognomi-cal agenda. And this agenda cannot be hidden even by the attempt to represent man and lion in visually parallel ways that portray their bodies as a play of contours and rotundities.

The agenda becomes even more apparent when Della Porta brings his discourse to bear on the real topic of this chapter, namely femininity. In a point-by-point negation of the initial description of man, woman is described as having "a small head, a small and narrow face, relaxed eyebrows, small and resplendent eyes, a meaty face, a small and always smiling face, round, hairless jaw, delicate neck"; in habits she is of "little spirit, thieving and full of deceit, delicate, prone to anger, fraudulent, and at once timid and audacious" (97). Della Porta, however, is not content with this obvious reversal of male positivity into female negativity. He thus cites Plato (and adds Galen's and Aristotle's confirmation) that "in all the ways that you compare her to man, she is more stupid and imperfect" (97). He also adds that Plato says that "nature gave to man a beard, in order to show him as more worthy and venerable than all, and that he have a great ornament to bear" (97). Displaying a remarkable command of the misogynist tradition, Della Porta then cites Seneca to say that "there is nothing more unstable than woman, nor more inimical to duty; whose lack of faith has advanced infamy; a shop full of quarrels and fraudulence; it is impossible for peacefulness and woman to lodge under a single roof" (97). The weight of ancient authority is thus added to define and legitimate femaleness as the systematic negation of maleness. Conversely, certain male features, such as facial hair, are given meaning only through this operation of contrast. It is significant, however, that a male *physical* trait, beards, appears in contrast to female *psychological* qualities: stupidity, imperfection, instability, deceit, unruliness. The man's beard, a "great ornament," stands as a symbol of male perfection and superiority, the implication being that the beard's ornamental value can only be imperfectly mimed by women through the duplicity of make-up and baubles. Again, the physical differences that the physiognomist depicts are the pretext upon which he makes a judgment upon the supposedly corresponding psychological characteristics.

Della Porta pursues this use of physiological description in an ensuing discussion of the animal that most accurately typifies femininity as the lion did masculinity, namely the leopard: a small face, small whitish eyes, the body badly put together and badly proportioned, of changeable color, a long subtle neck. In its habits it is effeminate, delicate, irascible, insidious, fraudulent, at once audacious and timid. "To these habits, the form of the body corresponds very well," he says. The "ancient sages of Egypt" are cited as comparing the leopard to "the man who tries to conceal his malicious and wicked soul" because the leopard stalks other animals without letting them know his speed and force of attack (99). Interestingly, woman is described as a leopard described as an evil, deceitful *man*. What woman is, in other words, for the science of physiognomy is a devalued form of man, represented by a creature, the leopard, that is positioned as the antithesis of the courageous and magnanimous lion. Or rather, physical and behavioral stereotypes of

61

men and women are attributed to animals, whose condensed figurations of those qualities, in turn, legitimate the stereotypes as a self-evident principle of nature. Thus, other paradigms of gender difference are proposed in the difference between masculine eagle and feminine partridge, and between masculine serpent and feminine viper. It is interesting to note that gender difference is never understood as a difference of gender, i.e. as a difference within a species, but rather as a difference between species. In other words, gender difference is never understood as specifically *gender* difference. For Della Porta and his epigones, the argument is not that there are male and female lions, eagles, and leopards, but that men are like lions and eagles, and women are like leopards and partridges. And on the other hand, woman, leopard, and partridge are defined as lesser or "more imperfect" forms of man, lion, and eagle. The criterion of imperfection is borne out by the relation between serpents and vipers, since the viper, with whom women are associated, cannot be considered as anything except a subgroup of serpents (99). Vipers are a kind of serpent, presumably (keeping in mind the figure of woman as leopard as deceitful *man*) as women are a kind of man. Of course, this is the schema typical of humanism, which understands "man" in all his "dignity" as the generic human being, and woman as a particularized, derived, or "deviant" manifestation of that being. Physiognomy adds to this construction by correlating the connotations of misogyny with a certain bestial mythology in such a way as to *naturalize* humanist ideology. The viper is a particular kind of serpent, one whose negative characteristics, such as its venomous bite, become analogous to woman as a poisonous variant of "man."

Interestingly, while we have visual as well as textual representations of the other animal analogues (lion/leopard; eagle/partridge), the serpent/viper difference is *not* pictured. Most likely this is because this difference is not adequately representable in terms of the stark similarities and contrasts that Della Porta's book demands. Certainly, parallel drawings of a serpent and a viper could not suggest the contrast shown between lion and leopard or between eagle and partridge. More important, the question of pictorial representation points to the elision of gender difference by species difference, for a similar problem of contrast would emerge in trying to draw a male and a female eagle side by side. While a good naturalist could certainly draw such a pair, the image would fail to exposit the ideology of sexual difference that this chapter in Della Porta is at pains to demonstrate. In fact, what is at first surprising is that the obvious physical contrast between the male lion and his mane (like the man's beard) and the lioness is left unexploited for the even greater physical and ideological contrast offered by the leopard. Della Porta puts the book together as if there is a risk that gender difference *cannot* be represented, that it might be invisible or at least imperceptible. Because of this risk the need arises to underscore that difference *graphically* by the analogue of species difference, for physiognomy depends upon the most acute differences in bodily inscription to legitimate the essentialism that underwrites its ideology of psychological difference. This is exactly what the conclusion of this important chapter stresses when it sets out to enumerate the weaknesses of women: "But females are more mean spirited, impudent, greedy, shy, stupid and unjust" (99). All of these traits are supposedly written on the gendered face, according to the ensuing closing paragraph, which offers an example of Solomon's wisdom when a woman, the Queen of Sheba, tested him by disguising some young beardless men as women (100). Solomon was easily able to separate the boys from the girls after having made them all wash their faces, presumably to efface the duplicitous feminine *écriture* of make-up. Solomon's wisdom, then, is defined by his physiognomic ability to wipe out the risk of gender ambiguity by reading the gender of these biblical crossdressers as self-evident in their faces.

In the ensuing chapter (27), "Of the citizen and the savage, and how we can conjecture their customs," Della Porta expands his discussion to address cultural difference, although here again he constructs an imagined relation between human and animal types into an ideology of social hierarchy. Just as masculine and feminine behavior can be read out of male and female body forms, so is there posited a similar relation between behavior and form in the paired entities wild or savage (*selvaggio*) and domestic or urban (*domestico o cittadinesco*). The base opposition here is between wild and domesticated animals, which Della Porta claims differ not only in behaviors (independent versus trained) but also in physiques: among other qualities, wild animals are said to be thin-faced with slim, hard, knotted bodies, heavily furred, with big bones, sharp nails, yellowish eyes and ugly, yellow fur, while domesticated animals are meaty, soft, and delicate in body, thin-furred, with small bones and nails, and of a happy red color (*di color rosso allegro*). In behavior, wild animals are said to be "sharp tempered, inhuman, unfriendly, irascible, cruel, furious, solitary, coleric and melancholic, ferocious, implacable, insidious, fraudulent, mean spirited, impulsive, quick, and opposed to justice" (102), while domestic beasts are "pleasant, sweet tempered, goodnatured, slow to the task, soft, delicate, sociable, just and temperate" (102). As we have seen before, one would be hard pressed to make these qualities coalesce into a description of any single animal (it seems especially curious to describe animals as "inhuman" or "opposed to justice"). The point of these enumerative characterizations becomes clear, however, when the bestial metaphor is reapplied with the authority of nature to the human animal. When the above-listed signs are seen in human beings, says Della Porta, it becomes possible "to judge which ones are savage, uncultured, melancholic; and which ones are mild and human, sweet and sociable" (102). The veneer of the "natural" is suddenly effaced to reveal the full panoply of humanism's exclusions, especially if we remember Della Porta's initial assimilation of the urban and the domestic, which underscores the root sense of civilization as city life (from Latin *civis*: city) by opposition to what lies outside the city in the woods (*silva*), where the rustic is the equivalent of the savage (*selvaggio*). Suddenly, vast categories of humanity are denied their being human: the primitive as well as the rustic, the uneducated as well as the mad and melancholic; in fact, everyone except the cultivated and mannered city dweller, the urban elite purged of any irrational elements. Moreover, the reappearance in the list of savage attributes of many of the attributes the previous chapter assigned to women (irascibility, cruelty, fraudulence, mean-spiritedness, insidiousness, unjustness) suggests the already implicit exclusion of women from the glowing city of humanism. The swiftness of Della Porta's move here in this extremely short chapter also seems to preclude any visual representation of the argument. In fact, there are no further illustrations of humans or animals in the rest of this first of the five books that make up *Della fisionomia*. (The last four books dedicated to the more systematic study of detailed resemblances between human and animal anatomy resort again to the liberal use of visual representation to advance the arguments made there.)

Furthermore, the sudden revelation of humanism's multitudinous others implicitly raises the specter of a cultural pluralism and thus forces a careful redefinition of the physiognomical project in the last few chapters of Book 1. While admitting the vast diverseness of the human creature, Della Porta nonetheless reduces that multiplicity to a single rule of nature, namely that "everything falls or comes from temperament [*temperamento*]" because temperament is what "makes the customs and forms the parts of man" (103). This temperament is what makes "the Italians different from the Spanish, and the Spanish from the Germans and the Turks" or even "the Neapolitans different from the Calabrians, and the Calabrians from the people of Puglia, and these from the people of Abbruzzi" (103). The problem is to understand the source of this temperament. It is certainly not surprising that he proposes that similar body parts in humans and animals reveal similar customs in their behavior, suggesting a common physical source for temperament. He then tries to locate such a source in the climatological variants of Galen's humoral medicine, which superimposed the categories of hot and cold onto the fourfold system of humors. But Della Porta discontinues this direction after noting, following Galen, that the cold climate of Thrace produces men who are very pale and white and who (because heat is concentrated in the body to the point of "boiling") are bold and rash, whereas in Arabia and Ethiopia, the inhabitants' bodies are "hard, dry, burnt and black" and because they are thus so "deprived of their own heat, they become timid" (104). (Of course, this thermo-humoral theory posits an inverse relation between surface and internal temperature – pale skin means internal heat, dark skin inner cold – which is absolutely at odds with the physiognomic project of reading the body *from* its surface.[14] Still not satisfied, Della Porta then discusses astrological influences on temperament, cites the "rhetoricians" whose *topos* of the "ages of man" claims changes in humor to be a function of years lived, and finally repeats the argument that food alters behavior (i.e. we are what we eat).

Faced with this destabilizing plethora of grids in order to explain human diversity in ways contradictory to the premises of physiognomy, Della Porta retreats from pluralistic empiricism into logic and the appeal to a fixed, unified nature. In an abstruse chapter "On the way to judge which signs we should prefer," he attempts to determine which signs are "proper" and which are not. The best system, he pronounces, is physiognomy itself because it is based "not on a single sign, nor even on two" but rather on the observation of "all the signs" (106–7). In other words, the comparative approach of physiognomy is correctly able to triangulate the properness of a given sign by crossreferencing it with the same sign in other species and with adjacent bodily and behavioral signs in the same creature. Physiognomy, Della Porta then informs us, is etymologically derived from *physis* and *gnomon*, "as if it were to say the law or rule of Nature; that is, for certain the rule, norm and order of Nature one knows from a given form of the body a given passion of the soul" (108). A final chapter treats of the correct syllogistic reasoning which physiognomists use to "refind those proper signs" (*ritrovar questi proprii segni*) "through which one can come to know the inclinations of the soul; and finally the science of Physiognomy will be true" (109).

This long, abstruse attempt to justify physiognomy's ability to read the proper signs of temperament by which body and soul are linked also helps explain Della Porta's rejection of climatology, astrology, and both age and digestive theories, for all four of those approaches are more or less relativistic in bent, supposed to explicate human temperament as a function of external or environmental factors such as climate, date of birth, years lived, and nutrients ingested. Even climatology, whose development can be seen to have legitimated the stereotyping of non-European peoples from Jean Bodin to Montesquieu and Rousseau, presupposes that a change in environment will alter both body and spirit, and that human beings share a common humanity. Della Porta's physiognomy, on the other hand, strives to maintain an essentialism established through an understanding of anatomical and psychological features elaborated from a fixed set of supposed animal/human analogues. Physiognomy seeks to establish a kind of Platonic bestiary of humanity, a textual and visual catalogue of "ideal" (and significantly, "less than ideal") types as different from one another as are species of animals. This essentialism, combined with the exclusionary definition of humanity we saw earlier, assures that the relations amongst kinds of men remain unchangeable because it legitimates those views that wish to see higher and lower forms of humanity. Certainly, any view that ascribes an unchanging behavioral essence to human beings bearing a physiological characteristic merits the epithet "racist." Della Porta clearly marks one starting point for the historical trajectory of that way of thinking from late Renaissance physiognomy to Lavater to Gobineau. Nevertheless, there is a certain *ad hoc* quality to the physiognomic analysis that makes it much less systematized and categorical than modern racist ideology. In other words, its construction through compilation, typical of much Renaissance thought, favors the listing of particulars, no matter how contradictory, over the conceptual rigor of the logic of non-contradiction. This is not to say, however, that racist and sexist ideo-logemes do not often guide, whether consciously or unconsciously, the terms of specific discussions within the larger compilation. In Della Porta's work, those terms, as I have been arguing, are taken from the field of animal husbandry, whose broadest aim seems to be coterminous with the establishment of domestic space (the very foundation of civiliza-tion if we are to remember Della Porta's slippage between the two terms), with prescribing the rule of the home under the "husband," whose creatures (women, children, servants, workers, and beasts) are all assigned a determinable role in the hierarchy. But while it could be shown that the husband at home can easily transpose this set-up as the colonialist abroad, what about the more immediate risk of domestic upheaval?

Such a risk is indeed the secret fear of Della Porta's physiognomy. Far from positing temperament as essentially unchanging, the book is full of examples of strange metamorphoses both of body and of soul. In fact, the anxious project of physiognomy might very well be seen as the attempt at domesticating such metamorphoses, of explaining, control-ing, preventing, stabilizing, and curing them. An earlier chapter in Della Porta broaches the problem of changes that occur from the transposition of human souls into animal bodies. The first example is that of "the human soul com[ing] into the body of a dog." The claim is made that the dog's "intellect" still remains in the dog and that it will "not have customs other than those of the dog" (82). The same is then said to be true of the wolf, whose invasion by a human soul will not hinder it from acting like a wolf. What happens in cinanthropy or lycanthropy is that an alteration in human temperament takes place through the effects of burnt black bile (*malinconia brusciato*), which "makes it similar to a temperament of the dog, he howls and barks like a dog or a wolf, goes wandering about at

66

night in cemeteries, and finally performs all the actions of the dog or the wolf; moreover, he becomes similar in the face to a wolf or a dog" (83). Animality thus seems to draw the human soul into behavioral and even physical change, although the soul itself seems to remain unaffected even as it is locked within the foreign body and temperament of the beast.

The proof of this is made by an allusion to Plutarch's discussion of the Circe episode in the *Odyssey* where Ulysses "asks the men converted into various kinds of animals about the customs of those animals, because being animated in the bodies of those animals, they are informed about their customs" (83). Not only does this passage explicitly correlate the soul with humanity and the body with animality; the mediating agent of the human soul's (implicitly degraded) metamorphosis into the body of an animal is a figure of a powerful, seductive femininity. Like the deceitful leopard stealthily stalking its unsuspecting prey, Circe draws Ulysses' men into her secluded (savage) abode to transform them into beasts, albeit rational beasts still in command of their linguistic abilities and thus able to communicate their dilemma to their resourceful captain, who has proven himself well skilled at undoing the snares of various seductive women/monsters in the course of his travels. Of course, Ulysses demonstrates himself to be just as duplicitous and manipulative as any of the stereotypes of dangerously deceptive women. Nonetheless, the Circe reference defines the danger of animality, i.e. that of the soul's entrapment within the body, as the threat of a certain femininity. Otherwise put, women drive men to act like beasts. Physiognomy would then be the discourse that reads the traces of animality on the human body both to assuage the inscription of threatening femininity and to recuperate the soul of man hidden within the feral recesses of corporeality. The consequences include, on the one hand, the explicit depictions in a chapter from Book V of lascivious or libidinous women as being half beast. On the other hand, there remains the question of whether women or animals or "savages" have souls if what they represent for "man" is the danger of embodiment, or, by chiastic deduction, the embodiment of danger.

Although not explicitly raised by the physiognomists themselves, the question of who had or did not have souls was a recurrent topic of scholarly debate during the late Renaissance. While Della Porta's physiognomy reaffirmed social hierarchy according to naturalized ideologies of species difference, he nonetheless needed to attribute different temperamental and ethical capacities to animals in order to elevate analogous human characteristics to the height of the social order. In this idealization of higher forms of animal life, he differed sharply from a long-standing train of thought (inspired by Aristotle and culminating in Descartes) that distinguished animals sharply from humans and pos-

67

itioned women categorically, rather than through the subtler figure of Circe, below all men and close to all animals. Aristotle's work, which defined woman as a defective man, had already done much to cast woman as merely somewhat above animals. However, this hierarchical placement was quite tenuous since many commentaries, as Ian Maclean has shown, disputed whether women even possessed souls.[15] The debate reached a peak of sorts with the polemics surrounding the 1595 publication of Alcidalius's *Disputatio nova contra mulieres*, which argued that women were not even human. Not surprisingly, the same work also links women to demons and dogs.[16]

As James S. Serpell has eloquently argued, according to Christian tradition animals were on earth to serve man, and this role was to be firmly understood as the result of their not having souls. The earth, animals and plants were created specifically to serve the interests of humanity. By humanity, however, was meant specifically the male human being, having dominion over all other life. The less capable of reason, the more all such life should serve man. Such writing, stemming from Aristotle, fostered a master–slave ideology; Aristotle used the same argument to condone the Greek slave-trade. In *The Politics*, he argued that savages and barbarians were less rational than Greeks and therefore were created to serve them. Animals were deemed imperfect creatures since they were devoid of reason: they merely copulated, ate, and excreted. This prerational bodily function, which so disgusted Aristotle, was later incorporated into Christian doctrine mainly through the efforts of the Dominican, St Thomas Aquinas.[17] (Hence, later we might remark, the great debate in Vallodolid, Spain, in 1550–1 between the Dominican friar Bartolomé de Las Casas and the Aristotelian-inspired defender of the Conquest, Juan Ginés de Sepúlveda. Sepúlveda argued the absence of soul in the autochtonous inhabitants of the New World and thus their fitness to be treated only as beasts of burden; Las Casas argued that they had souls and that efforts should therefore be made to convert and save them from damnation.)[18]

Hence, also, but with a difference, the seventeenth-century debate over whether animals had souls, or were, as Descartes put it, mere machines or automatons, whose actions are explainable by "the arrangements of their organs" in the same way as the movement of a clock is explained by the disposition of "wheels and springs."[19] The criterion of difference, as in the case of Della Porta's cinanthropes and Ulysses's sailors seduced by Circe, is the ability to use language, which is taken as a sure sign of the existence of a soul. Language is, of course, explicitly defined by Descartes in such a way as to exclude any possible animal language. But it is also important to remember that Descartes is never able to prove "clearly and distinctly" except by faith in God's goodness either that other people are not "hats and coats which may cover automata" or even that he himself has a body, only that he is a "thinking substance."[20] In fact, in his late *Passions of the Soul*, he can only explain emotions and other psychological states as the effect of the body on the mind and thus as transmitted through "animal spirits" (*esprits animaux*), whose effect must be overcome by a stoical force of will.[21]

Descartes's analysis follows in the line of Aristotle and Aquinas, and opposes the Italian naturalist school of Giordano Bruno and Pierre Gassendi, who were more open to a reconciliation between matter and soul and hence less driven to distinguish categorically between the soulful and the soulless, between the rational and the irrational, between human and animal. And even though Cartesianism's emphasis on "innate" reasoning found many adherents among educated women institutionally excluded from erudite practices and the sanctioned scholasticism of Aristotelean inspiration, some of Descartes's most steadfast opponents on the issue of animal souls were found in the same educated women. Madame de Sévigné, for instance, praises the Bishop of Lyons for being an "ardent Cartesian" who also maintains that animals think ("there's my man," she writes of him). Elsewhere, she claims that "Descartes never pretended to make us believe" in the theory of animal machines.[22] Her Cartesianism would thus seem to be at best a markedly revisionist one.

Madame de La Sablière, on the other hand, ran a salon famous for bringing together aristocrats, scientists, and writers in a way that prefigures the progressive Enlightenment salons of Madame de Lambert and Madame de Tencin. A glance at those attending her salon would reveal a number of free-thinking and often anti-Cartesian followers of Gassendi: the mathematician Gilles Personne de Roberval, the writer Charles Perrault, the stridently anti-Cartesian doctor Antoine Menjot (who was also Madame de La Sablière's uncle), and most impressively, the philosopher François Bernier and the poet Jean de La Fontaine. Bernier wrote for Madame de La Sablière an *Abrégé de la philosophie de Gassendi* (1675), his *Doutes* (1682), and, by way of a gift, a work on the "diversity of human races" (written in 1684) as well as other works of philosophy and criticism. La Fontaine used Bernier's *Abrégé* as the philosophical basis for his famous "Discours à Madame de La Sablière," which explicitly attacks Descartes and argues for the existence of animal souls.[23] Perhaps her most celebrated protégé, La Fontaine was regarded by Madame de La Sablière, writes Chamfort, "almost as a pet." After her furniture was moved to a new home, she said: "In my old home, all I have left is myself, my cat, my dog and my La Fontaine." Pellison and D'Olivet claim a similar remark made by her after she had fired all her servants: "I have only kept my three pets, my dog, my cat and La Fontaine."[24] Having won a legal separation from an abusive husband, and thus having truly become the mistress of her own home, Madame de La Sablière was signally able to overturn the domestic politics of her era, to counter the Cartesian drift of her time with a Gassendist-inspired coterie that polemically argued for the souls of animals, the intelligence of women, and the plurality of cultures and "worlds" (Fontenelle's famous *Entretiens sur la pluralité des mondes* was dedicated to her daughter).[25] Far from being some man's domestic creature, Madame de La Sablière assembled around her a great company of literate men and kept her own pets, be they dogs, cats, or poets. Efforts like hers inscribe a history of resistance to the triumph of restrictive humanism and patriarchal social formations in early modern Europe.

Apart, however, from such exceptional women or signs of resistance, domestication of the private sphere and imperialism abroad are conjoined in the early modern period by ideological practices that sought to restrict and dominate the various constructed others of European manhood: the feminine, the savage, the bestial. Humanism's praise of the "dignity of man" appears predicated upon the abjection of what it considers the "non-human." And behind the face of domestication, exposited by the physiognomists in their attempt to decode an *écriture* of the body itself, lies the brutal reality of the era's numerous exclusions: of Jews from Spain, of women from public life, of the inhabitants of the Americas and Africa from their freedom and homelands, and, as we know since Foucault, of the "unreasonable" from everywhere but the confinement of prison-hospitals.

Part II

MALE WRITING, EXOTICISM, EMPIRE

4

CANNIBALISM, HOMOPHOBIA, WOMEN

Montaigne's "Des cannibales" and "De l'amitié"

Carla Freccero

Eating parts of his victims, the detective's report says, "was his way of keeping them with him even longer and making his victims part of himself."

("Clues to a Dark Nurturing Ground for
One Serial Killer," *New York Times*, August 7, 1991)

"He ate body parts, the purpose of which [was] so that these poor people he killed became alive again in him," attorney Gerald P. Boyle told the jury.

(*The Washington Post*, January 31, 1992)

[Homicide detective Dennis Murphy] also said Dahmer told police that he ate parts of three of his victims and that "he ate only the people he really liked and wanted to keep with him."

(*The Washington Post*, Saturday, February 1, 1991: A8)

Dahmer's "central fantasy," [Frederick Berlin, psychiatrist, director of the sexual disorders clinic at Johns Hopkins University] said, is "finding someone in a live state, beginning to relate with them, continuing in a transitional state between life and death and continuing after death."

(*The Washington Post*, February 4, 1992)

"We're dealing with some of the same dynamics that we can see in Gacy: the dysfunctional family, a guy who denies his homosexual feelings to erase whatever shame he might feel in committing these acts, who destroys the people who attracted him in the first place, . . . he's punishing himself and punishing them at the same time."

(Ted Cahill, in *The New York Times National*,
Sunday, August 4, 1991: 30 L)

"Client states he knows he prefers male partners but client feels guilty about it."

(Donna Chester, in *The New York Times National*,
Sunday, August 4, 1991)

73

"He talked openly about why he shouldn't be gay, that there was something wrong with it."

("Secrets of a Serial Killer: Jeffrey Dahmer," *Newsweek*,
February 3, 1992: 46)

Many serial killers tend to murder types of people they have a grudge against or people who have something in common with them.

(*Newsweek*, February 3, 1992: 46)

I

In her study of anti-semitism and the later Middle Ages, Louise Fradenburg analyzes the roles of ideology and fantasy in the Christian European abjection of Jews at the very moment "when Christians undertake economic expansion at home and territorial and religious expansion abroad":

> Medieval Jews did not use the blood of Christian children in their rituals, nor did they crucify them, nor even did they slit their throats and throw them into privies; these stories were, precisely, fantasies, however much, as fantasies, they may have been supported by the "truths" of Christianity.[1]

Fradenburg thus confirms Peter Hulme's assertion that "boundaries of community are often created by accusing those outside the boundary of the very practice on which the integrity of that community is founded."[2] Indeed the fantasies mentioned by Fradenburg resemble precisely those aspects of Roman Catholicism that were considered most distinctive to it as a theological belief and practice: the ritual use of the sacrificial blood of a scapegoat (also a child) and crucifixion (human sacrifice in general). Another practice of which the Jews were accused, the one that primarily concerns Hulme in his study of early relations between Europeans and the indigenous inhabitants of the Caribbean, is anthropophagy. Hulme notes that the Fourth Lateran Council in 1215 proclaimed the literality of the Eucharist, "the host becoming, upon the priest's words, the actual flesh of Christ" (85), and argues that the psychic processes of repression and projection and the ideological process of constructing an ensuing need for the self-defense of the community, both produce "a comprehensive ritual purging of the body of European Christendom" (85) and prepare the way for the designation of the cultural other (an external other this time) as cannibal.

The confidence with which Fradenburg, in the late twentieth century, can affirm the absurdity of the medieval Christian accusations against Jews only underscores the extent to which the myth of New World cannibalism constitutes European identity and undergirds its persistent (neo)colonial discourse. The statement that cannibals as such do not exist does not, for the Euro-American scholar, resonate with self-evident clarity, and yet the other attribute of the Caribs reported as hearsay by Columbus, that they "had one eye in the forehead," seems rather too ridiculous seriously to entertain.[3] Dictionaries, furthermore, confirm the rumor that the slippage Columbus (whomever we mean by this textual designation) initiated between "ethnic name and definitive social behaviour" (*Colonial Encounters*, 68), between the inhabitants of the Caribbean and the ferocious eating of human flesh, is so ideologically congealed as to seem unproblematically to designate an anthropological reality. Webster's tells us that cannibal comes "from 15th century Arawakan *caniba*, *carib* (forms *recorded by* [my emphasis] Columbus in Cuba and Haiti respectively), of Cariban origin; akin to Carib *calina*, *calinago*, *galibi* Caribs, literally, strong men, brave men" and lists as its first definition "a human being that eats human flesh." The *Petit Robert* goes further in its definition by spelling out the distinctive difference between anthropophagy, the eating of human flesh, and cannibalism, with its connotation of cruelty or ferocity in the eating.[4] We have, thus, in the history of this term, a Nietzschean genealogy: the strength and courage of a group of men who resisted colonial invasion is redefined by the empire as an unduly ferocious eating of people.

This initial digression into the peculiar construction of a European ideology-concept, cannibalism (defined by Hulme, without scare-quotes, as "a term meaning . . . 'the image of ferocious consumption of human flesh frequently used to mark the boundary between one community and its others,' a term that has gained its entire meaning from within the discourse of European colonialism" [86]), occurs as a prologue to a discussion about Montaigne's famous 1580 essay, "Des cannibales." It is impossible to speak about "his" or any other cannibals without first thus digressing, for to do so would be to participate in and collude with the very mechanisms of colonial discourse that construct cannibalism as an object of New World discussion, Montaigne's or "our" own. Although many insightful critical essays have been written about "Des cannibales" and about Montaigne's interrogation of contemporary ideology, few, if any, have questioned the premises of his very title, while his own acceptance of cannibalism as a practice seems a lapse in his more customary hermeneutics of suspicion.[5]

David Kastan, Peter Stallybrass, and Nancy Vickers remark that "Montaigne directly confronts what were the two most crucial points of colonial differentiation as they were constructed within the violent hierarchies of sixteenth-century travel narratives: polygamy and cannibalism."[6] These social practices, which most radically seem to differentiate the "cannibals" from "civilized" and Christianized Europe and which ultimately confirm their inferior alterity, become the occasion for Montaigne to discern supreme instances of culture.

CARLA FRECCERO

> And lest it be thought that all this is done through a simple and
> servile bondage to usage and through the pressure of the authority
> of their ancient customs, without reasoning or judgment, and
> because their minds are so stupid that they cannot take any other
> course, I must cite some examples of their capacity. . . . Now I am
> familiar enough with poetry to be a judge of this: not only is there
> nothing barbarous in this fancy [*imagination*], but it is altogether
> Anacreontic.[7]

If for many European contemporaries of the New World people, literacy as writing was the definitive mark of cultural superiority, for Montaigne that mark is "poetry" (*poësie*) or song (*chanson*).[8] The only direct citations of "cannibal" speech in the essay, which includes nevertheless "direct" observation by the visitors to Rouen (reported as indirect discourse), are two poems, a warrior song (*chanson guerrière*) and a love song ([*chanson*] *amoureuse*), each produced as artifact to substantiate the non-barbarity of cannibalistic and polygamous practices.

Where do these songs come from? In a useful essay, Bernard Weinberg collates Montaigne's extensive borrowings from some of the cosmographers who described the Tupinamba (*Toüoupinambaoults*) of America to sixteenth-century France: André Thevet, Nicolas Barré, and Jean de Léry.[9] These other accounts include "direct" speech and song around the question of eating the enemy and being eaten but they are not presented as evidence of poetry. David Quint observes that "[Montaigne] should be credited for the alimentary conceit . . . that the cannibals are eating not only the flesh of their fathers and grandfathers that has gone into nourishing the captive they eat in turn, but, as the captive says, their own flesh" (472).

> I have a song composed by a prisoner which contains this challenge, that they should all come boldly and gather to dine off him, for they will be eating at the same time their own fathers and grandfathers, who have served to feed and nourish his body. "These muscles," he says, "this flesh and these veins are your own, poor fools that you are. You do not recognize that the substance of your ancestors' limbs is still contained in them. Savor them well; you will find in them the taste of your own flesh."
>
> ("Of Cannibals," 158; 261)

Quint convincingly argues that Montaigne "made up" the prisoner-cannibal's song in order to underline the self-consuming nature of a cannibalistic society (473). He does not mention, however, why a love song, absent in the cosmographers' accounts, should also be produced in the essay.

Each of the two poems follows upon the practice in question, as though to "illustrate" that practice. Michel de Certeau notes that "Cannibalism . . . is approached from the angle of the victim (the heroism of the vanquished) and not the perpetrator," and polygamy "is seen from the point of view of service (the 'solicitude' of the women), not masculine domination" (*Heterologies*, 75). He thus suggests that Montaigne constructs what Jacques Derrida refers to as a "sacrificial structure": "The subject does not want just to master and possess nature actively. In our cultures, he accepts sacrifice and eats flesh."[10] Montaigne therefore creates subjects for sacrifice, men whose honor lies in eating and being eaten by the other, women whose honor lies in their "solicitude."[11]

But the love song does not correspond symmetrically to the sacrificial schema de Certeau discerns in the prose passages on cannibalism and polygamy. For although Montaigne's entire argument regarding polygamy depends upon the assertion that it is practiced with the consent of the co-wives, in the same way as cannibalism is accepted by the prisoner, nowhere does Montaigne display (or produce) the "voice" of the New World woman that would substantiate his claim. The song is sung, if we assume an "accurate" "transcription" (and normative heterosexual arrangements), not by a woman, but by a man:

> "Adder, stay; stay, adder, that from the pattern of your coloring my sister may draw the fashion and the workmanship of a rich girdle that I may give to my love [*m'amie*]; so may your beauty and your pattern be forever preferred to all other serpents."
>
> (158; 262)

It is worth pausing to examine the potential crux represented by this song. If the "transcription" is incorrect, then the symmetry of the poems as examples is preserved (a woman is speaking about a man); if the "transcription" is correct, and we presume symmetry, are we then hearing about the love between co-wives? Finally, if the "transcription" is correct and the speaking voice is a man, we can conclude that the examples are indeed asymmetrical and that perhaps this is no transcription at all, but Montaigne's own composition.[12] In any of these cases, there remains the ambivalent image of the adder. De Certeau asks whether it is the serpent of division, but another feature of the adder, one that is suppressed because the focus is on appearance rather than agency, is its poison (*Heterologies*, 76). In both instances, then, these poems about war and love constitute sites of disturbance: in the first there is the "addition" that eating the other is eating the self (being eaten); the second, by all appearances Montaigne's invention, both raises and elides the question of the woman's voice and troubles "love" with a hint of danger.

II

Stephen Orgel points out that "Cannibalism, Utopia, and free love [*sic*] reappear throughout the century as defining elements of New World societies."[13] Montaigne marks his entry into utopia by way of a "reply" to Plato:

> This is a nation, I should say to Plato, in which there is no sort of traffic, no knowledge of letters, no science of numbers, no name for a magistrate or for political superiority, no custom of servitude, no riches or poverty, no contracts, no successions, no partitions, no occupations but leisure ones, no care for any but common kinship, no clothes, no agriculture, no metal, no use of wine or wheat.
>
> (153; 255)

The use of negatives is the "privileged figure of utopian discourse," appearing in descriptions of the Golden Age in Hesiod, Virgil, Ovid, and in More's description of Utopia proper.[14] Likewise, hearsay (Montaigne's "go-between," to use Stephen Greenblatt's term) and exhibitionistic forgetting ("They mentioned three things, of which I have forgotten the third, and I am very sorry for it" [159; 263]) also mark the utopian boundaries of Montaigne's description. As I have argued elsewhere, utopia is a rhetorical figure for loss or failure, a loss or failure Montaigne refers to numerous times in the essay, first as the loss of Nature in "civilization" (152–3; 254–5), then as a loss of judgment (153; 255); military losses (157; 260–1); and finally, as the loss that will accrue to the Tupinamba themselves as a result of "contact" with Europe: "these men [are] ignorant of the price they will pay some day, in loss of repose and happiness, for gaining knowledge of the corruptions of this side of the ocean" (158; 262).[15] This loss (of a prelapsarian European innocence?) produces the cannibals as nostalgic ideal, cannibals who, as Gérard Defaux rightly points out, turn out to be Montaigne himself ("Un cannibale," 953, 957). In the book that is his body, Montaigne melancholically incorporates a lost ideal, which in turn is figured, symptomatically, as a cannibal.[16]

In another essay more explicitly about loss, nostalgia, and self, Montaigne's "De l'amitié," the thematics of cannibalism may be said to (re)appear around the question of friendship and the incorporation of the (love) object into the self that occurs, Freud tells us, with loss.[17] Montaigne's melancholic elegy to his dead friend, Etienne de La Boétie, thematizes an uncanny merging enacted, as absence, by the (missing) inclusion of de La Boétie's poetic corpus. The merging Montaigne describes between himself and his friend is accompanied by metaphors of nourishment, hunger, tasting, communion:

Friendship feeds on communication.

(136; 232)

Friendship, on the contrary, is enjoyed according as it is desired; it is bred, nourished, and increased only in enjoyment, since it is spiritual.

(137; 234)

In the friendship I speak of, our souls mingle and blend with each other so completely that they efface the seam that joined them, and cannot find it again.

(139; 236)

It is I know not what quintessence of all this mixture, which, having seized my whole will, led it to plunge and lose itself in his; (c) which, having seized his whole will, led it to plunge and lose itself in mine, with equal hunger, equal rivalry.

(139; 236)

The secret I have sworn to reveal to no other man, I can impart without perjury to the one who is not another man: he is myself.

(142; 239)

In short, these are actions inconceivable to anyone who has not tasted friendship.

(142; 240)

I was already so formed and accustomed to being a second self everywhere that only half of me seems to be alive now.

(143; 241)

In the sacrificial structure Derrida describes and Montaigne enacts, eating the other and being eaten by him form the basis of the most lofty intersubjective communion between men, or rather, of subjectivity itself: "The so called nonanthropophagic cultures practice symbolic anthropophagy and even construct their most elevated socius, indeed the sublimity of their morality, their politics, and their right, on this anthropophagy."[18]

This relation of spiritualized anthropophagy (or symbolic anthropophagy, as Derrida calls it) is a relation of love, of friendship; it is a relation in which women have no part. Montaigne writes that "the ordinary capacity of women is inadequate for that communion [*conference*] and fellowship [*communication*] which is the nurse [*nourrisse*] of this sacred bond; nor does their soul seem firm enough to endure the strain of so tight and durable a knot" (138; 234). He points out that ideally this spiritual anthropophagy would include the physical, that the resulting friendship would thereby be rendered more complete:

And indeed . . . if such a relationship, free and voluntary, could be built up, in which not only would the souls have this complete enjoyment, but the bodies would also share in the alliance, (c) so that the entire man would be engaged, (a) it is certain that the resulting friendship would be fuller and more complete.

(138; 238)

But the love that Montaigne commemorates in "De l'amitié" depends upon the repudiation of the physical. In a phrase immediately following this one, Montaigne declares, "(a) And that other, licentious Greek love is justly abhorred by our morality" (138; 234), thus precisely illustrating one of the meanings of homophobia, as an excessive fear of the same that founds itself on a disavowal of desire for the same.[19] The exclusion of the feminine from this bond would also, presumably, constitute a repudiation, inasmuch as the nurse (nourisse) who nourishes (nourrit) such a bond is Woman (or, perhaps more appropriately, a part-object, the breast that is, nevertheless, a *female* breast). In "The Politics of Friendship," Derrida argues that the "double exclusion of the feminine [friendship between women, friendship between a woman and a man] in the philosophical paradigm of friendship would thus confer on it the essential and essentially sublime figure of virile homosexuality."[20] However, in this masculine economy of the same (what Eve Sedgwick has called "homosociality"), homosexual relations among men are pro-scribed, "because they openly interpret the law according to which society operates," that is, a "sociocultural endogamy" that disguises itself as exogamy, while in fact excluding the participation of women.[21] "A sociocultural endogamy would thus forbid commerce *with* women. Men make commerce *of* them, but they do not enter into any exchanges *with* them," Luce Irigaray asserts, echoing Montaigne's economic comparison between marriage and friendship:

As for marriage, for one thing it is a bargain [marché] to which only the entrance is free – its continuance being constrained and forced, depending otherwise than on our will – and a bargain ordinarily made for other ends. . . . whereas in friendship there are no dealings or business [commerce] except with itself.

(137–8; 234)

With regard to the question of an economy or social order, Derrida analyzes a paradigmatic opposition in the discourse on friendship, in Montaigne and others, between singularity and universality:

On the one hand, friendship seems to be essentially foreign or unamenable to the *res publica* and thus could not found a politics. But, on the other hand, as one knows, from Plato to Montaigne, from Aristotle to Kant, from Cicero to Hegel, the great philosophical and canonical discourses on friendship (but my question goes precisely to the philosophical canon in this domain) will have linked friendship explicitly to virtue and to justice, to moral reason and political reason.

("The Politics of Friendship," 641–2)

Thus the canonical discourses on friendship both found *and* destabilize the oppositions between singular and universal, private and public, familial and political (643). And, Derrida argues, "the exclusions of the feminine would have some relation to the movement that has always 'politicized' the model of friendship at the very moment one tries to remove this model from an integral politicization" (642). His essay on friendship concludes on a note of (admittedly very) cautious optimism by suggesting that Montaigne's model introduces a rupture in the history of friendship ("Shall one say that it depoliticizes the Greek model or that it displaces the nature of the political?" [644]), a rupture that allows for the entry of the question of feminine exclusion. This would in turn permit a politicization such as the one Irigaray performs on the construction of the Western humanist subject in and for a hom(m)o-sexual (homosocial) or patriarchal order. The optimism derives from the "not yet" of Montaigne's phrase, "But this sex in no instance has yet succeeded in attaining it [friendship]" (138; 234). And indeed, it would seem that in both of Montaigne's essays on relations between men, or between self and other, in both "De l'amitié" and "Des cannibales," the question of Woman must be raised. But in "De l'amitié," she must be brought in to be repudiated, and in order for the essayist to repudiate the physical between men, for as Irigaray points out, "once the penis itself becomes merely a means to pleasure, pleasure among men, *the phallus loses its power*" (193). That power is what founds the subject as a man, as a same in relation to an other (same), sociocultural endogamy, where "man engenders himself, where man produces himself as man" for another (man) (185).

In a later interview, Derrida revises his previous formulation of friendship by describing the sacrificial structure of the discourses of the subject in/of Western humanism as

the idealizing interiorization of the phallus and the necessity of its passage through the mouth, whether it's a matter of words or of things, of sentences, of daily bread or wine, of the tongue, the lips, or the breast of the other.

("Eating Well," 113)

That idealizing interiorization of the phallus "through the mouth" is the melancholic incorporation of the other in Montaigne's essay; it is friendship, the spiritual or symbolic eating of and being eaten by the other,

81

that founds the sacrificial subject himself. How then to interpret the literalized (and presumably "horrific") interiorizing through the mouth of the "muscles," "flesh," "veins," and "limbs" of the other (man) in the cannibal's song? Does the literalization of spiritual anthropophagy introduce the phantasm of an erotic union that must, instead of love, be called war, with someone who, instead of friend, must be called an enemy?[22] Is cannibalism then the return of the repressed of/in friendship?[23] Is that return to be described as a return of the materiality of eating the other? Could the question of polygamy constitute then a literalization of the figurative or symbolic exchange and sacrifice of women (as Irigaray suggests it does in her discussion of Lévi-Strauss [170]) described in "De l'amitié" as marriage or the killing of a daughter (140; 237)? If Quint is right that Montaigne, in "Des cannibales," is criticizing the endogamous or self-cannibalizing social relations that consist in devouring an other that is really a self, whether they be found in Brazil or in France, how then to explain the valorized masculine merging of self and other that constructs the sacrificial subject of symbolic anthropophagy in the essay on friendship? How, indeed, to explain the repudiation of the feminine as the material condition of the possibility of eating the other (receiving nourishment) that constructs the humanist subject himself?

If, in fact, the cannibal's song can be said to figure both the violence and the eroticism of the subject's relation to the other, then perhaps some clue to the puzzle of the love song may emerge. Could the love song appear "belatedly" as the reinscription of the prohibition that the cannibal's song threatened to violate? Would it then constitute a reinstatement of a compulsory heterosexuality of sorts?[24]

If the image of the adder can be said to be ambivalent, then a chiasmatic relation is set up between the two poems: on the one hand a warrior song to an enemy conveys latent eroticism, and on the other an erotic song to a girlfriend conveys latent aggression. Cannibalism and polygamy as the (repressed) twin foundations of that other social order that is the Western humanist subject ("the political, the State, right, or morality, you will have the dominant schema of subjectivity itself. It's the same," says Derrida ["Eating Well," 114]). After all, Montaigne writes (of the cannibals), "they have a way in their language of speaking of men as halves of one another" (159; 263).

Derrida wants to call this schema carno-phallogocentrism, a "carnivorous virility" that founds "this," "our" Judeo-Christian humanist culture, extending to the symbolic what Carol Adams discusses in *The Sexual Politics of Meat*.[25] He formulates what seems to me one of the principal ethical challenges to European humanism when he remarks that "the 'Thou shalt not kill' – with all its consequences, which are limitless – has never been understood within the Judeo-Christian tradition . . . as a

'Thou shalt not put to death the living in general'" ("Eating Well," 113). Children; animals; women; men and women who were Caribs, Arawaks, Tupinamba . . . (not to mention gay boys of color). It would be tempting indeed to read the second poem as an accurate transcription of an erotic love song sung by a woman to a snake about its beauty, the skillful weaving of her sister, and the gift of the girdle she will give to her girlfriend:

> "Adder, stay; stay, adder, that from the pattern of your coloring my sister may draw the fashion and the workmanship of a rich girdle that I may give to my love [*m'amie*]; so may your beauty and your pattern be forever preferred to all other serpents."

But I would be misreading, forgetting history. Fradenburg writes that the "heroization of suffering *for*," what I am calling, after Derrida, sacrificial culture, what Juliana Schiesari calls melancholia,

> typically devalorizes actual suffering, and devalorizes those who attempt to avoid it as well as those prohibited from inflicting it. . . . The heroization of suffering *for* has in fact been one of the chief means of occluding the history of suffering and its relation to the history of violence.[26]

To return then, finally, to the question of the cannibals, we might also ask what became of the others, those who did not or were unable to "fiercely resist"? And what will become, we might ask, along with communities of color in Milwaukee, of those who are not now, even symbolically, the subjects of sacrificial culture, but are nonetheless subjected to it?

5

FANTASIES OF "RACE" AND "GENDER"

Africa, *Othello* and bringing to light

Patricia Parker

the lap or privity dilated or laide open. . . .

(Helkiah Crooke)

. . . descried and set forth the secretes and privities of women.

(Eucharius Roesslin)

In the 1573 edition of *Des monstres et prodiges* – in a passage so controversial that it was finally moved to his less accessible technical treatise on anatomy – the influential French surgeon Ambroise Paré included a section on the secret parts of women which "grow erect like the male rod," making it possible for them to "disport themselves with them, with other women," and hence necessary "with such women" that "one must tie them and cut what is superfluous because they can abuse them."[1] Paré's text pauses at this point to defend his mention of such practices, however incredible they may seem ("Now that these women, who by means of these caruncles or nimphes, abuse one another is a thing as true as it is *monstrous and difficult to believe*"). He does so, in a passage added to the 1575 edition, by appealing to the testimony of Leo Africanus, the converted Moor whose *Geographical Historie of Africa*, written in Arabic and Italian in 1526, had been widely translated and reprinted in Europe after its publication by Gian Battista Ramusio in Venice in 1550.[2] This confirming testimony is found in a story Africanus tells of some women of Fez in Mauretania who, claiming familiarity with demons, "rub one another for pleasure, and in truth . . . are afflicted of that wicked vice of using one another carnally." Sometimes, the interpolated story reports, women of the town who wished to join these female traffickers with "demons" in "carnal copulations" would use their husbands as unknowing accomplices in their own cuckoldry, as go-betweens to fetch or to prepare feasts for a "venerable band" of such women, leaving the wife free to go where, and with whom, she wished (though some husbands, it notes, would "get the spirit driven out of their wives' bodies with a good hard clubbing"). Paré's text then links this story out of Africa with another part of the *Geographical Historie*, on clitoral excision:

84

That is what Leo Africanus writes about it, assuring us in another
place that in Africa, there are people who go through the city like
our castrators . . . and make a trade of cutting off such caruncles,
as we have shown elsewhere under *Surgical operations*.

Paré's *On Monsters and Prodigies* was a popular and much-cited text,
part of the burgeoning "monster" literature of the European sixteenth
century and its vogue for quasi-pornographic display. In this sense it was
a phenomenon parallel to the growing European appetite for travel
narratives at the threshold of the early modern period – filled by texts
like the repeatedly translated one of this converted Moor.[3] Janis
Pallister, in her recent translation of Paré, notes the derivation of
"monsters" both from the root of warnings or "signs" (*monere* + *-strum*)
and from a sense of bringing forth to "show" (*monstrare*). But what is
being "warned" about here – and then "shown" more graphically
through illustration from Africanus's *Historie* – are not foreign "monsters" but civic or domestic ones, the dangerous practices of women close
to home made paradoxically more credible by reference to women of
"the principall citie of all Barbarie."[4] When in 1579 Paré suppressed the
story taken from Africanus's *Historie* – the only concession made to his
censors – he replaced it by mention of the case of two French women,
Françoise de l'Estage and Catherine de la Manière,[5] accused of being "so
abominable that they hotly pursue other women, as much or more than
a man does a woman" ("femmes tant abominables qu'elles suyvent de
chaleur autres femmes, tout ainsi, ou plus, que l'homme la femme") and
who narrowly escaped being put to death. In the textual history of this
African anecdote, the crossings multiply between civil and barbarous,
exotic and domestic: a forbidden (and threatening) female sexuality at
home is projected on – and verified by – a story of the women of
"Barbarie"; and the story then returns home, to local instances.

Paré's text of monsters – supplemented by the anecdote from
Africanus incorporated into the text of his *Anatomy* – offers a glimpse
into the secret sexual lives of European women, with validating reference to the women of "Barbarie." (This link, of course, would not
disappear from medical and scientific writing: Freud speaks of the "dark
continent" of female sexuality and Marie Bonaparte, at a signal moment
of psychoanalytic history, tells of his having given her Felix Bryk's *Neger
Eros* to read concerning clitorectomy or the "ritual sexual mutilations
imposed on African women since time immemorial," as confirmation of
the psychoanalytic dogma of orgasmic transfer from the "infantile"
clitoridal zone to the more "mature" vagina.)[6] The history of the anecdote in Paré is finally also a history of repression: by the time the French
surgeon's anatomical writings were translated into English by Thomas
Johnson in 1634, both the larger discussion of this hidden and secret

female part and the anecdote from Africanus had been relegated to a footnote on this "obscene part" that only the more curious, or determined, reader might pursue.[7]

This early modern linking of fascination with the secrets of female sexuality to a story out of "Barbarie" provided by the travel narrative of a converted Moor does not, however, appear only in the work of Ambroise Paré. It also figures in Helkiah Crooke's English anatomy – *Microcosmographia: A Description of the Body of Man* (London, 1615) – largely a translation of the medical authorities of the continent. Treating of "the Lap or Privities" of woman, Crooke writes of the "clitoris" or "the womans yard" that

> although for the most part it hath but a small production hidden under the *Nymphes* and hard to be felt but with curiosity, yet sometimes it groweth to such a length that it hangeth without the cleft like a mans member, especially when it is fretted with the touch of the cloaths, and so strutteth and groweth to a rigiditie as doth the yarde of a man. And this part it is which those wicked women doe abuse called *Tribades* (often mentioned by many authours, and in some states worthily punished) to their mutuall and unnaturall lustes.

In the margin appears in Latin "Tribades odiosae feminae." Beside it "Leo Africanus."[8]

Crooke goes on in this text to note that by the "motion and attrition" of this female member, though for this "businesse it was not necessary it should be large," the "imagination" of women

> is wrought to call that out that lyeth *deeply hidden in the body*, and hence it is called aestrum Veneris & dulcedo amoris; for in it with the ligaments inserted into it is, the especiall seate of delight in their veneral imbracements, *as Columbus imagineth he first discovered*.

The "Columbus" cited here along with his "discovery" is not Christopher but Renaldus, who in 1559 claimed to have brought this previously unknown territory to light.[9] Some clear link exists, then, in these European treatises of anatomy – Paré's in French, Crooke's in English, and the Latin treatise of another Columbus – between the anatomist's opening and exposing to the eye the secrets or "privities" of women and the "discovery" or bringing to light of what were from a Eurocentric perspective previously hidden worlds. Crooke's discussion of the female "Lap or Privities" draws on the early modern sense of "lap" as something "folded" which the anatomist's description, like his diagrams, then unfolds, displays, or opens to the eye. And indeed, it furnishes illustration of this "cleft" of the lap or privity *"dilated or laide open"* to the reader's view.[10]

* * *

. . . regions of the material globe . . . have been in our times laid widely
open and revealed.

(Francis Bacon, *The New Organon*)

Africa, which for a thousand yeeres before had lien buried . . . is now
plainely discovered and laide open to the view of all beholders.

(Jean Bodin, in praise of Leo Africanus)

What is striking in these early modern texts – of "monsters" shown to the
eye of the curious or the "privities" of women opened simultaneously to
scientific "discovery" and the pornographic gaze – is thus not only the
crossings they negotiate between domestic and exotic or, in the references to Africanus, between Europe and "Barbarie," but the shared
language of opening, uncovering or bringing to light something at the
same time characterized as "monstrous" or "obscene."[11] Such a language
of "opening" to the eye's inspection what had been secret, closed, or hid
characterizes European discovery narratives from the beginning. The
Epistle to Charles V reproduced in the English translation of Peter
Martyr's *Decades* in 1577 includes in its praise of the Emperor that

the divine providence, from the time that he fyrst created the
worlde, hath reserved unto this day the knowledge of the great and
large Ocean sea. In the whiche tyme he hath *opened the same*, chiefly
unto you (most mightie Prince)

– a passage which involves both opening and ownership. Its wider
context is the emphasis on "ocularly recognizing" that links accounts of
the uncovering of previously unknown worlds to the language of early
modern science and anatomy.[12]

Crooke's provision of a diagram of the hidden place of woman
"dilated or laide open" to the view is part of the ocular impulse of
anatomy more generally – its preoccupation with what William Harvey
called "ocular inspection," an impulse that has led several recent com-
mentators to align it with the specularity and scopophilia of theater.
Francis Bacon – principal theorist of the emergent epistemology –
routinely used Columbus, Magellan, and the "distant voyages and travels" through which "many things in nature have been *laid open and
discovered*" as emblems of the potential development of science itself as a
"masculine birth of time," opening and laying bare "the remoter and
more hidden parts" of a feminized "nature." European and English
curiosity about Africa or "Barbarie" is, then, in this respect part of a
characteristic early modern preoccupation with the ocular, an appetite
which, as with the appeal of prodigy and "monster" literature, involved
the hunger to "know" as a desire to "see."[13]

87

The presentation of Leo Africanus to an English audience is also marked throughout by this emphasis on the ocular, and its substitutes. The text of John Pory's translation, in 1600, of *A Geographical Historie of Africa Written in Arabicke and Italian by Iohn Leo a More* literally enacts the experience of unfolding and exposing to the eye, including as it does in its prefatory materials a map of Africa folded and closed upon itself, which, when opened up, brings before the reader's gaze the land of monsters, of Amazons, of prodigious sexuality and of peoples who expose those parts which should be hid.[14] Its frontal material evokes the desire to see and know "the secrets and particularities of this African part of the world" – which it promises to disclose "at large" – through Africanus's narrative "now *plainely discovered and laide open to the view of all beholders.*" To the text of this African *Historie* – the first to open the interior of Africa to European inspection – is affixed an "approbation of the historie ensuing" by none other than Richard Hakluyt, the veteran of New World "discovery" who persuaded Pory to undertake the translation of Africanus into English. It affirms this traveler's narrative to be "the verie best, the most particular, and methodocall, that ever was written, or at least hath *come to light* concerning the countries, peoples, and affaires of Africa." It is joined in this same preface by reference to the account of "John Baptista Ramusius, Secretarie to the State of Venice," treating of the manifold difficulties he had earlier undergone in order "to bring the important discourses therein *to light.*"[15]

The "secrets and particularities" of unknown parts of the world were visually displayed not just by the opening of pages or unfolding of maps but by the early modern textual innovation of an "index" – still in this period heavy with its etymological meaning of "informer" – an indicator or pointer that made the contents of these massive volumes even more accessible to ready survey by the eye. One text promises, for example, to bring before its reader

> the most famous and memorable laws, customes, and manners of all nations . . . collected, abridged, digested, and compacted together in this short and compendious Breviary; wherein you may easily finde whatever you have occasion to looke for . . . *lying open before thine eyes.*[16]

Travelers and "discoverers" were themselves informers to a European audience, bringing reports of matters otherwise hidden and unseen – an ocular emphasis that frequently makes the activity of reporting on the foreign or exotic one of "informing" in the sense of espial or spying out. Hakluyt calls upon this complex when he urges English voyagers to Virginia (simultaneously named after a Virgin Queen and suggestive of yet unopened virgin territory) to strive "with *Argus eies* to see" what this new territory might be made to "yield" – a visual language of espial reminiscent of the sexualized currency of other contemporary discourses.[17]

It is this shared language of "discovery" as informing or spying on something hid that gives to so many of these exotic histories their affinities with the ocular preoccupations of the growing network of *domestic* informers and spies charged with ferreting out secret or hidden crimes, those least accessible to "ocular proof."[18] Historians of early modern England speak of the "dilations" or "delations" ("secret accusations") that were a crucial part of this new domestic apparatus of "discovery" in this other sense of bringing something hid to light. (The "close dilations" of the informer Iágo in *Othello* depend, as we shall see, both on the meaning of "close" as "secret" and on this contemporary network of "informing," evoking not just a dilating or opening up – in ways simultaneously visual and sexual – but the whole domestic world of "delators" and spies.).[19] One text from the 1590s reports on the omnipresence of "secret spies" who "do insinuate themselves into our company and familiarity" with such pretence of "zeal, sincerity, and friendship" that they are able to "give intelligence" of the most "secret intents." Francis Walsingham, the Elizabethan secretary of state who extended this nascent network into the first national secret service, was described as "a most diligent searcher of *hidden secrets*."[20] Once again, the similarity in language charts a crossing of foreign and "domestic," exotic secrets and ones closer to home.

There was, moreover, an even more important link between this domestic preoccupation with informing and the testimony provided by travelers' histories. Pory reproduces from "Ramusius" an account which speaks of the delight of the European audience of Africanus's *Historie* to have unfolded through it a report "Concerning which part of the world, even till these our daies, we have had no knowledge in a manner out of any other author, or at leastwise never any *information so large* " (in the early modern sense of "dilated" or set out "at large") or "*of so undoubted truth.*"[21] Pory's promise to unfold "at large" and hence bring to light formerly unknown regions of Africa is a promise to bring what had been hid, or revealed only in part, before his readers' eyes. But the gaze is a vicarious gaze, a substitution of narrative or report for what a later such text would call the eye-witness or "occular . . . view."[22] The principal criterion for such substitutes for the directly ocular therefore became their reliability as testimony. Not only did they need to provide lifelike description, bringing the unseen as if before the eye through verbal *enargeia* or the rhetorical creation of convincing pictures (the root of seeing or "illustration" that links *enargeia* – or *evidentia* – to the "*Arg*us" of the many eyes); they also needed to be trustworthy messengers. Yet it is precisely the reliability of their testimony which was repeatedly questioned. Proliferating accounts of the monsters and prodigies of foreign lands circulated in the early modern period in an environment prey to the danger, and constant accusation, of counterfeit report, of substitutes for ocular proof that put the reader in "false gaze," as it is said at the beginning of *Othello* of the report of "Signior Angelo" that ominously anticipates the falsified informing of Iago, the figure whose name evokes not Venice but England's Iberian rivals in the African trade.[23] What the English translator of one travel text calls the "multitude of Mandivels" that "wander abroad in this pampletting age in the habite of sincere Historiographers," relating "meere probabilites for true," casts doubt on all reported "ceremonies & customes used in certaine countries, which seeme so *absurde*, *monstrous* and *prodigious*, as they appeare utterly voide of credit."[24]

Leo Africanus was one of these informing messengers, bearing tales from territories formerly off the stage of European history. Pory's presentation of his report thus raises more than once what appear to be needed "vouches" or warrants of his reliability, in a climate it too notes is populated by "mountebanks and Mandevilles." His prefatory "To the Reader" presents this African narrator as worthy "to be regarded" because, though "by birth a More, and by religion for many yeeres a Mahumetan," his "conversion to Christianie," along with "his busie and dangerous travels," render him a reliable informer on matters that before "were either *utterly concealed, or unperfectly and fabulously reported.*"[25] Africanus's own narrative, in Pory's translation, repeatedly invokes the language of the eye-witness, or where "ocular proof" was unavailable, the informer whose information bears the stamp of truth. Its "vouches" are filled with the sense of bringing vicariously but reliably before the gaze, as a credible substitute for the directly ocular:

> These are the things memorable and woorthie of knowledge seene and observed by me John Leo, throughout al Africa, which countrey I have in all places travelled quite over: wherein whatsoever I sawe woorthy the observation, I presently committed to writing: and *those things which I sawe not,* I procured to be at *large declared unto me by most credible and substantiall persons,* which were themselves *eie-witnesses* of the same.
>
> (358)

As Pory's presentation of Africanus to his English audience makes clear, that which is narratively declared "at large" becomes a substitute for what the eye has not seen, as well as testimony whose reliability must be vouched for.

* * *

This would not be believ'd in Venice,
Though I should swear I saw't.

(*Othello*)

Othello has long been linked both with Mandeville's "fabulous" reports
and with this converted Moor's African *Historie* through the "travellours
historie" (as the Folio text has it) provided by Othello, the Moor of
Venice, in answer to charges of "witchcraft" in the wooing of a white
Venetian bride.[26] It is this tale of "Cannibals that each other eat, / The
Anthropophagi, and men whose heads / Do grow beneath their
shoulders" (I.iii.143–5) that Othello provides first to Brabantio, a prominent Venetian citizen eager to hear his story, then in response to
Desdemona's prayer "That I would all my pilgrimage dilate, / Whereof
by parcels she had something heard" (153–4), and finally (in its staging
simultaneously) to a Venetian and English audience ignorant of events
in a double sense by them unseen – the monsters and adventures of
these exotic worlds and the offstage wedding (and in Iago's vivid *enargeia*, the imagined bedding) of a Venetian virgin by a "lascivious" Moor,
an "extravagant and wheeling stranger / Of here and every where"
(I.i.136–7). As a "travellours historie," its presentation evokes all the
familiar contemporary associations of such travelers' tales – the
European appetite or hunger for report (synecdochally by its reference
to the "greedy ear" of Desdemona that did "devour up" this stranger's
discourse, subtly and chiastically linking this form of domestic consumption with the figures of the "Cannibals" in these same lines); the converted Moor whose narrative is accepted as a reliable "vouch" (I.iii.106)
of events to which his European audience has no direct eye-witness or
"ocular" access; and, later, the questioning of its credibility as report,
when Iago (the figure who will soon become a "domestic" informer in
every sense) charges that this Moor's tales are mere "bragging and telling
. . . fantastical lies" (II.i.223).[27]

The links between Othello's exotic "travellours historie" – its verbal
pictures bringing offstage events vicariously before the eye – and Iago's
manipulation of *evidentia* (vicarious substitute for ocular "evidence")
when attention turns to the domestic secrets of a Venetian woman,
become part of this play's own extraordinary emphasis on bringing to
"light," on the hunger to "know" as the desire to "see," and its obsession
with offstage events, domestic and exotic, related both to the sexualized
"chamber" of a woman and to the origins of an outsider Moor. The two
combine in the vivid fantasies of miscegenation exploited in the opening
scene, in Iago and Roderigo's verbal evocations of "an old black ram /
. . . tupping your white ewe." They continue in Othello's "dilation" of his
"travellours historie," and finally in his hunger to see and know through
the medium of *his* native informant, to spy out the secrets of a woman

whose "honor" is an "essence that's *not seen*" (IV.i.16).

The play itself suggests – in one unmistakable and striking verbal echo – this central chiastic crossing of foreign and domestic, exotic and sexual. The "travellours historie" provided by the Moor of Venice in answer to Desdemona's entreaty that he might "all [his] pilgrimage dilate" (I.iii.153) has its clear echo in the sexualized object of the "close dilations" of the Temptation Scene (III.iii.123), where Iago, Venetian informer on these more domestic secrets, begins to "unfold" not hidden exotic worlds but the "close" or "secret" place of Desdemona's sexuality which his informing promises to bring to "light" (I.iii.404). It is these "close dilations" (with their pun on the "delations" or secret accusations of the informer and their beginning, like Othello's dilated narrative, from what is first glimpsed only in "parcels" or in part) that lead to the Moor's conviction that this informer "sees and knows more, much more, than he *unfolds*" (III.iii.242–3). The language of dilating, opening, or unfolding (enacted in Pory's presentation of Africanus's exotic *Historie*, with its enfolded map and promise to dilate "at large" what is hidden from the eye) begins, as *Othello* narrows to domestic secrets, to mark this new hunger to bring before the eye something unseen, offstage, hid – a movement that leads first to the "napkin" or handkerchief which both substitutes for "ocular proof" and increases the appetite for it, and finally to Desdemona's hidden "chamber," only in the final Act brought forth to "show."

To "dilate" in early modern usage came not only with a sense of opening or enlarging something "too much closed," but with this sense of opening up to "show" – "displaying some object . . . first of all through a lattice or inside a wrapping, and then unwrapping it and opening it out and displaying it *more fully to the gaze*." This is the double sense invoked in the scene of Othello's exotic "travellours historie." At the same time, however, it carried with it resonances of a specifically sexual opening, and, combined with the visual, of a voyeuristic, even prurient desire to "know," not just a way to open or "spread abroad" something closed or hid but a means through which "to open the bosom of nature and to *shew* her branches, to that end they may be *viewed and looked upon, discerned and knowen*."[28] It is this simultaneously eroticized and epistemological impulse to open up to show that thus enables the easy movement between rhetorical and sexual opening exploited in the link between *Othello*'s evocation of tales of African or New World discovery and the simultaneously visual and sexual "close dilations" of Iago's domestic informing, pruriently, even pornographically exposing a hidden "chamber" to the eye.

Within the almost unbearably protracted Temptation Scene, the "close dilations" which lead to this demand for "show" are echoed in a passage whose terms are strikingly both epistemological and sexual:

IAGO My lord, I would I might entreat your honor
      To *scan this thing no farther*; leave it to time.
      Although 'tis fit that Cassio have his place –
      For sure he fills it up with great ability. . . .
                                        (III.iii.244–7)

Hidden within the visual language of this informer's advice to "scan this thing no farther" is the "thing" which elsewhere is the "common thing" (III.iii.301–2) Emilia offers to her husband, the female privity or *res* that Iago vulgarly sexualizes when she intrudes to offer him what he terms a "trifle" (322). Advice that appears to speak only to an epistemological hunger to "see" and "know" introduces into the lines that follow the double meanings of a "place" Cassio "fills up" with "great ability," a "place" whose sexual inference is joined by the threat to Othello's "occupation" (III.iii.357) through the obscener sense of "occupy." What is secret or unseen here is the ambiguous sexual "place" of all the double-meaning references to the place Cassio might occupy as Othello's place-holder or "lieu-tenant." [29]

From the beginning, the protracted process of "unfolding" in *Othello* involves not only fascination with what is hidden from the eye, but, as Karen Newman and Michael Neill have differently remarked, a sense of bringing forth to "show" some "monster" too "hideous" to be "shown," a link made in the lines that lead into this informer's "close dilations" as a glimpse of something to be brought to light:

      By heaven, thou echo'st me,
    As if there were some *monster* in thy thought
    Too *hideous* to be *shown* . . .
      If thou dost love me,
    Show me thy thought.
                                        (III.iii.106–16)

The passage plays on the link between "monstrous" and "shown" already exploited in a "monster" literature that displays vicariously to the eye the otherwise "monstrous and difficult to believe" (as Paré had put it in citing Africanus's "Barbarie" as verification of "monstrous" domestic female sexual practices). And it links the dilating, unfolding, or opening to the eye made possible through Othello's "travellours historie" – with its monstrous "Anthropophagi" and "Cannibals" – to Iago's "close dilations" of a hidden female place which, as in Crooke, is both "dilated and laide open" to the gaze and "too obscoene to look upon." "Hideous," as Neill suggests, is in this complex pun "virtually an Anglo-Saxon equivalent for the Latinate 'obscene,'" that which according to a powerful if false etymology should be kept "offstage," linking the *scaenum* or stage to the obscene as what should be hidden, unseen, not "shown."[30]

93

Othello itself, however, provokes a constant, even lurid, fascination with the offstage or in this sense ob-scene, starting from the vividly racialized rhetoric of Iago and Roderigo at its opening, focused on an unseen sexual coupling, or imagined coupling, involving the "monstrous" opening of a Venetian virgin by a "lascivious Moor." The fact that these and other secrets of this imagined "chamber" are offstage and hence barred from vision prompts what mounts in the play both as hunger for more narrative or report – Othello's entreaty that *his* informer might "*all* [his narrative] *dilate*" – and as desire that what is "hid" be brought forth to "show." The desire to show or bring this "monstrous" place on stage also involves, however, a pornographic doubleness that simultaneouly panders to the eye and averts the gaze,[31] a movement that leads, after the final bringing of this hidden "chamber" to "light," to the opposing desire to "Put out the light" (V.ii.7), to reclose what has been unfolded and disclosed ("The object poisons sight, / Let it be *hid* ").

* * *

My mother had a maid call'd Barbary.
(*Othello*)

. . . this thing of darkness I / Acknowledge mine.
(*The Tempest*)

Othello's "dilated" traveler's tale, opening to Venetian (and English) eyes exotic worlds beyond the direct reach of vision, combined with the "close dilations" of a Venetian informer on the secrets of Desdemona's "chamber," chart the crossing in this play of domestic and exotic, "civil" and "barbarian," explicitly within the register of fascination and the vicariously visual. The evocation of a female *res* or "thing" available to be "dilated and laide open" to the eye in Iago's "scan this thing no farther," links it to the language applied to Othello the Moor ("the sooty bosom / Of such a *thing* as thou," I.ii.70–1), a language that returns in the description of Caliban – possible anagram of "Cannibal" – as the "thing of darkness" Prospero will later call his own. Both sexualized and racialized "thing" converge in *Othello* in the trifling "thing" Emilia offers to her husband – the handkerchief or "napkin" which becomes the sign at once of Desdemona's unseen "honor" (IV.i.16) and of Othello's exotic history, linked with Africa and with Egypt ("that handkerchief / Did an Egyptian to my mother give"; "there's magic in the web of it," III.iv.55–8; 69ff.). Embroidered "alla moresca" in the play's Italian source, "spotted with strawberries" (III.iii.435) in Shakespeare's addition, it evokes, as Lynda Boose has argued, a specific form of bringing forth to "show" the hidden sexual place of woman as a token of "opened" or lost virginity, the "bloody napkin" that figures not just in exotic or African narratives

94

but as a resonance within domestic European anxieties surrounding the secrets of female sexuality and its control.[32]

Paré's text, in its English version, cites the "bloody linnen cloth" described by "Leo the Affrican" in the midst of a discussion not just of virginity but of the "deceit of bauds and harlots" who, "having learned the most filthy and infamous arts of bawdry," seek to make men "to beleeve that they are pure virgins" – a passage which resonates against the language of another converted Moor ("I took you for that cunning whore of Venice / That married with Othello," IV.ii.88–9).[33] In *Othello*, the evidence of the spotted "napkin" presented as substitute for direct or "ocular proof" conjures in one powerfully economical image the token of opened virginity and hence of a chamber potentially kept by a "bawd," and the exoticized origins of the stranger Moor, split between that history and the perspective of a Venetian husband informed of secrets that in Venice are not only "monstrous" but withheld from "show" ("In Venice they do let God see the pranks / They dare not *show* their husbands," III.iii.202–3).

What links, then, what might be termed the "fantasies" of "race" and "gender" exploited within this play of dilating, uncovering, and bringing to light is something like the crossing of exotic and domestic already traced in several early modern contexts, but also the extraordinary series of exchanges and divisions in which Desdemona and Othello cross and occupy each side of that divide. The play produces a series of powerful chiastic splittings. Desdemona the white Venetian daughter becomes, as it proceeds, the sexually tainted woman traditionally condemned as "black," part of the representational schema that gives ironic resonance to the choice of the name "Bianca" ("white") for the character most explicitly linked to that taint and that releases the "demon" within her own name. "Desdemon" (as she is called by Othello in V.ii.25) sings toward the end the song of a "Maid call'd Barbary" (IV.iii.26) while Othello the Moor, the "Barbary horse" (I.i.111) and "erring barbarian" (I.iii.355) of the opening Act, comes to occupy the perspective of a wronged Venetian husband, executing judgment on a "blackened" or erring wife (III.iii.387–8: "now begrim'd and black/ As mine own face").[34]

It is not insignificant in relation to these crossings in both directions that the loci of this play are Venice and Cyprus. Venice, on Europe's margins, was the port of entry or opening to Africa (it is through "Ramusius, Secretarie to the State of Venice," that Africanus's *Historie* was first introduced). Homophone of "Venus," it was paradoxically both open and closed, impregnable "Virgin Citie" and a place notorious for its courtesans. Cyprus was both the classical refuge of Venus and the contemporary colonial outpost most vulnerable to invasion from the "barbarian" Turk. (The link between the sexual invasion of Desdemona by an "erring barbarian" and the vulnerability of Cyprus – threatened by Turkish invasion throughout the sixteenth century and in Turkish possession by the time of the play – is underlined by the defeated Brabantio's response to the Duke: "So let the Turk of Cyprus us beguile, / We lose it not, so long as we can smile," I.iii.210–11.) Venus was denounced by Stephen Gosson as "a notorious strumpet" who "made her self as common as a Barbars chayre" and "taught the women of Cyprus to set up a Stewes." Desdemona is associated with "Barbary" through suspicion of her "common" sexuality (IV.ii.72–3).[35] In the paranomastic play on "Moor" and "more" made easier by the variable orthography of early modern English, *Othello, the Moor of Venice* already contains within it the corresponding suggestion of the "More" of "Venus," chiastically linking the "Moor" so often spelled "More" with a potentially uncontrollable female excess.[36]

This crossing of exotic and domestic, "Moor" and female "more," within *Othello*, is rendered even more complexly layered by the resonances within this play of another eliding of an imperial encounter with a domestic one. Othello's "travellours historie," reminiscent of travel narratives both ancient and contemporary, possesses the power to "detaine" that Bodin ascribed to Leo Africanus's exotic and extended *Historie*.[37] But both in its opening and in this power to "detaine," the story "dilated" by the Moor and unfolded to Venetian Desdemona's "greedy ear" also recalls an earlier precedent for the encounter of Europe and Africa, female and male, itself a *locus classicus* for the dilation of all such visually evocative narratives. This is the tale of Aeneas to African Dido, a "Moore among the Moores," told by another "extravagant and wheeling stranger" to the ear of a woman of "Barbarie."[38] The tale of Othello the converted Moor is thus strangely put in the place of the traveller Aeneas – Trojan and ultimately Roman standard-bearer of a triumphant Western and European history – a figure who abandons a woman and "Barbarie" at once.

An echo of Aeneas and African Dido in a tale already overlaid with echoes of contemporary narratives of "discovery" should not come as a surprise in the work of the playwright whose *Antony and Cleopatra* and *The Tempest* similarly conflate different moments in the history of empire, or for that matter in a century of imperial rivalry that gave to one Spanish New World outpost the name of "Carthago." It might even be expected in a play that turns, as *Othello* does, between the poles of war and love, the competing calls of duty and the domestic. In relation to the play's repeated references to Desdemona as "our great captain's captain" (II.i.74) and commanding "general" ("Our general's wife is now the general," II.iii.315) – as well as its broader evocation of *pavor feminae* – it needs also, however, to be remembered that Aeneas's sojourn with Dido was in this period a powerful monitory emblem (both domestic *and* imperial) of domination by a woman. *Antony and Cleopatra* draws on the familiar Virgilian opposition of the virility of imperial Rome to the effeminating influence of this African queen, in that confluence of misogyny and orientalism that linked Cleopatra's Egypt with Dido's Carthage as exotic kingdoms ruled by women. Closer to home, the outlines of this imperial history hovered in complex ways around the rule of an *English* kingdom by a queen linked in name with Dido or "Elissa" as well as with Aeneas her putative Roman male ancestor, a queen associated with what John Knox denounced as the "monstrous regiment" of female rule. This other Dido/Elissa, both patron of English imperial ventures and the Virgin whose virginity figured the inviolability of England's borders, was a queen whose realm was not only highly vulnerable to invasion but sailed upon by self-styled Aeneases. To add to this complexity, however, she was also the monarch who ordered the expulsion of "Negroes and blackamoors" from that realm, on the grounds that the incursion of these particular outsiders had become excessive.

Othello's dilated narrative in Act I – with its effect on a woman whose "greedy ear" did "devour up his discourse" – casts the pair of outsider Moor and white Venetian daughter from the beginning, then, as an Aeneas and Dido, the pair echoed in *Antony and Cleopatra*'s more explicit version of this imperial history. In so doing, it crosses gender and racial identities, (mis)placing Othello in the position of Aeneas the "European" male and Desdemona in that of a dominating (and abandoned) female "Moor," a woman of "Barbarie" whose chastity in this tradition was suspect and open to question.[39] The crossing of female and black, Europe and "Barbarie," is thus adumbrated in the play even before Desdemona, "blackened," sings the song of an abandoned "Maid call'd Barbary" – the song which turns out to be the Willow Song already linked with Dido, the African Queen.[40] The associations of Moorish Dido – a woman of "Barbarie" who dominates a man, is tainted with an adulterous sexuality and is finally rendered passive and abandoned, in striking contrast to her earlier command – hover around the representations of Venetian Desdemona, the woman who is both "half the wooer" and forthright in her speech, but who becomes, as the play proceeds, the increasingly passive figure for whom hearing a stranger's tale also involves a disastrous consequence.

If, then, in this evocation of an ancient imperial history of male and female, Africa and Rome, Othello evokes Aeneas, male and "European," Desdemona the figure of Dido, female and Moor, the splitting of Desdemona into "white" and "black" in relation to her "fidelity" is mirrored by the splitting of Othello into faithful Venetian general and Turkish "infidel." The echo of African Dido and Roman Aeneas early in the play invokes the history of imperial conquest in the context of the tragedy that is Shakespeare's most intimately domestic, focusing as it does on bringing to light the "chamber" of a wife suspected of infidelity, as well as on the adulterating union of "white" and "black" at a time when the meaning of "adultery" included the taint of miscegenating mixtures. Othello's "dilated" traveler's tale recalls Africanus, Mandeville, Pliny, and the rest as well as the domestic English hunger for such narratives, in the context of a plot which turns on the reliability of an act of informing or report. But it does so by also summoning an echo of the "greedy ear" of a woman of "Barbary," and hence not just the history of imperial rivalries but the complex and crucially *asymmetrical* crossings of "gender" and "race" at work in the period – a period which could figure Desdemona as becoming "black" while retaining, in another register, her class and insider position or celebrate the imperial Roman heritage of English Elizabeth even as it linked her with the threatening female rule of a Moorish queen.

Othello as a whole is filled with such split chiastic exchanges and divisions: in the case of Othello himself, one crossing maps the apparent move from outsider to insider, from the perspective of "stranger" Moor to that of Venetian husband suspicious of the purity or "whiteness" of his wife. Othello, the converted Moor and enemy of the "Infidel," is explicitly split between insider and outsider in the scene of the night brawl on Cyprus, the island anxiously guarded from invasion by the Turkish fleet ("Are we *turn'd Turks*, and to ourselves do that / Which heaven hath forbid the Ottomites? / For *Christian* shame, put by this *barbarous* brawl," II.iii.170–2). By the play's end, in the speech that leads to the self-division of his suicide, these split identities are embodied in yet another travel narrative, one of which he now is simultaneously both object and subject ("And say besides, that in Aleppo once, / Where a malignant and a turban'd Turk / Beat a Venetian and traduc'd the state, / I took by th' throat the circumcised dog / And smote him – thus," V.ii.352–6). And in their notorious textual confusion, the final lines suggest a proliferating series of exoticized others – "base Indian" (Q1) or "Judean" (F1), "Arabian," and perhaps obscure allusion to the Jews and Edomites from the story of Mariam and Herod, another husband who in a fit of jealousy had his wife killed.[41]

* * *

    Friends all, but now, even now,
In quarter, and in terms like bride and groom
Devesting them for bed. . . .
                    (*Othello* II.iii.179–81)

The pervasive echoes in *Othello* of European Aeneas and a queen of "Barbarie" chart the complexly and asymmetrically interrelated issues of race and gender in this play, in a context that also summons the role of dilation as both engrossing narrative and bringing to "light." But even this account of the play's complex exchanges of "barbarous" and domestic is not complete without reference to one other of its crossings, and asymmetrical splits. Othello comes in one respect to "occupy" the place of a Venetian husband, in a play that insistently calls attention to the occupying or changing of "place." But in the process he also becomes the more passive receiver of another's informing, his ear "pierced" (I.iii.219), "abused" (395), or – in a different metaphorics – "colonized" by that informer, his "occupation" gone as he himself is "occupied," in a process described as bringing a "monstrous birth" to light (404). This other coupling complicates the heterosexual erotics of the play with all of its insistent homoerotic imagery, climaxing in the parody-marriage of Iago and Othello in Act III and adding to the already multiple senses of "informing" that of the "monstrous" shaping or giving form that comes of this displaced insemination and conception. It thereby adds to the play's fantasies of heterosexual miscegenation (the coupling of white Desdemona and "lascivious" Moor) the complications of a monstrous union of Iago and the Moor – a relation in which this Moor is by implication sexually "fallowed" ("as asses are," I.iii.402) rather than loyally "followed" by his Venetian subordinate (I.i.58), a reversal of their hierarchical relationship into a form of "service" frequently associated with such racialized others in the period of the play.[42]

We started with women "abusing themselves with women" – a phrase loaded with all the early modern freighting of *abusio* as a term for "unnatural" sexuality and linked in Paré's account with the practices of "Barbarie." We need to complete this picture – again, chiastically but asymmetrically – by bringing into this play's (and its culture's) projections, crossings, and splittings a sense of all that was involved in the designation of the "barbarous," including this other "abusive" and "monstrous" practice projected onto the other and outside, as the opposite to the "civil" or "civilized." In the example from Paré, the projection of "monstrous" female sexuality from cases close to hand onto an otherness called "Barbarie" appears to link certain European and African women as "monstrous" others in an exchange of alien and domestic reflected in the common currency of "bringing to light," while still retaining the ethnographic separation of the exotically different. In *Othello*, Iago "abuses" the ear of a Moor of "Barbary,"[43] a form of penetration that leads (with Desdemona excluded) to the "monstrous birth" that becomes the only progeny of the fantasies of miscegenation that haunt this play from its beginning, starting with Iago's vivid imagining of all that is to ensue from the adulterating of "kind" ("your daughter cover'd with a Barbary horse, you'll have your nephews neigh to you . . . coursers for cousins, and gennets for germans," I.i.111–13).

The "monstrous" in this play – as in its culture – includes the *abusio* of homoerotic practices as yet another barbarous form of "sin against kinde," the coupling that in the equally charged *enargeia* or vivid description of Cassio embracing Iago in bed (III.iii.413–26) produces Othello's "O monstrous! monstrous!" (427), glancing as it passes at the term for the "monstrous" abuses of an English theater in which the "secret" of Desdemona included the fact that she was acted by a boy. The domestic "open secret" of male sexual relationships (both private and prominent, as in the cases of Francis Bacon or James I, the monarch before whom *Othello* was performed) coexisted in complex and contradictory ways with denunciations of this other "monstrous" sexual practice, projected onto non-European or non-English others (including Iberians and inhabitants of "Barbary") as yet another familiar staple of "travellours histories."[44]

I put this pressure, finally, on more of what was included within the early modern designation of the "monstrous" because we have to do, both in this play and in its culture, with the violence of projection itself, propeled by the uneasy sense of "occupation" that comes from the blurring of boundaries between alien and civil, outside and an inside already occupied by "adulterating" mixtures.[45] *Othello* provides us not only with this violence, and its chiastic splittings, displayed and summoned forth to "show," but with the charged oxymoron of the "*civil* monster" (IV.i.64), a phrase which, detached from its immediate context, might be applied to the Venetian/Iberian figure of Iago, producer of the "monstrous" sight that "poisons sight," but which in more general, pervasive, and unsettling ways exposes the contradictions at the heart of the civilized or "civil." It is this only apparent oxymoron from *Othello* that perhaps best conveys the sense in the play, or more largely within early modern culture, of the projected other as both mirror and split chiastic counterpart of the "monstrous" at home, a home already "occupied" and hence unsettingly incapable of fortification against "invasion." Within the realm of the visual, it might also name that particular form of crossing and othering in which what is brought to "light" is at the same time that which cannot – or *must* not – be "seen."

6

AN ENGLISH LASS AMID THE MOORS

Gender, race, sexuality, and national identity in Heywood's *The Fair Maid of the West*

Jean E. Howard

In the introduction to *Nationalisms and Sexualities*, the editors argue that nationalism and questions of sexuality and gender have been inappropriately separated by philosophical and critical traditions which tacitly accept the categorization of the latter as matters of "private life," having little to do with the work of the public sphere, with nation-building.[1] My project is to look at several texts from the early modern period to suggest the particular ways sex and gender, as well as race, entered into discourses of the nation in early modern England.[2] I do not mean that England in the late sixteenth and early seventeenth centuries had a concept of the nation or a discourse of nationalism identical to those that became dominant in the nineteenth century. Tudor–Stuart England was an absolutist state, a historical formation more centralized than strictly feudal modes of social organization, but one in which social identity was in large measure constituted, not by an identification as citizen with a geographically bounded entity called the nation, but by one's place in vertical status hierarchies and by one's allegiance as subject to a monarch whose authority was genealogically and dynastically constituted.[3] As Benedict Anderson has specified, such states were in theory organized centrally, around the monarch, and had porous and indistinct borders able, for example, to be altered by marriages among royal families.[4]

I will argue, however, that even in Tudor–Stuart England something I simply wish to call a discourse of national identity was emerging which, despite many differences, shares with modern nationalism a supposed fraternity of subjects within an imagined community defined in part by a bounded geographical essence and in part by cultural and racial *differences* from other such imagined communities.[5] This discourse of national identity sometimes had a class valence. In the public theater, for example, it often emerged in texts bearing the stamp of the "middling sort," the proto-bourgeoisie, and could conflict with aristocratic discourses, such as those of chivalric romance, which saw men of the same rank forming a community that cut across national lines.[6] Gender, moreover, often *does* play a role in definitions of national identity. While woman, for example, could represent the nation in a symbolic sense, the enfranchized and dominant actors in the nationalist imaginary were overwhelmingly men. And perhaps most important, in what we have Eurocentrically come to call "The Age of Discovery," a sense of English national identity took shape in relation to an emerging language of racial difference in which skin color and physiognomy became overdetermined markers of a whole range of religious and sexual and cultural differences by which the English were distinguished from various non-European "others."[7]

In this chapter I cannot offer a genealogical account of the emergence of an early modern discourse of English nationalism. What I propose instead is a case study of a single text, Thomas Heywood's *The Fair Maid of the West, Part I*, which strikingly illuminates how gender, race, sexuality, and national identity were interarticulated in productions of the public playhouse in the twilight years of Elizabeth's reign or shortly thereafter. Probably written between 1600 and 1604, the play uses an exceptional woman, Bess Bridges, as a device for defining English values and for uniting men of different classes into a homosocial community of brothers, into a nation. Eroticized but virginal, Bess seemingly transcends the limitations of her gender – and must do so – to become the emblem of England. Yet her gender, and her sexuality, constitute threats to the fraternal nation, threats that in the final instance can only be handled by a stunning act of displacement: a shifting of the focus of cultural anxiety from the body of the woman onto the body of the racial other.

Not surprisingly in a post-Armada text, *Fair Maid* from its opening moments defines the English as the moral and religious antithesis of their great European rivals, the Spanish. But more interesting than the simple operation of the English–Spanish binarism is the way the play deploys a third term – the Moor – to construct a field of racial and sexual difference which at once situates the Moors as subordinate to their English trading partners and allays the anxieties about castration, female power, and female sexuality occasioned by Bess Bridges, the heroine who both is and is not a stand-in for the much grander Elizabeth who was Heywood's monarch until 1603. The play thus reveals how gender and sexuality could at once be mobilized in the service of emergent nationalism and could threaten to undo it; and how a discourse of race could be used to manage that threat and give "Englishness" a properly patriarchal inflection.

THE VIRGIN BODY AND THE WORK OF
NATION-BUILDING

The absences in texts are always important. In *Fair Maid*, certain absences in the list of dramatis personae are striking. The play has a large cast; in fact, about thirty individual characters are listed, as well as unspecified numbers of "Spanish and English Sailors," "Moors," "Captains," and "a Chorus." But of all these figures, only two are women. One is a nameless kitchen maid, the other Bess Bridges, the fair maid of the west from whom the play draws its title. In essence Bess exists in an all-male world, but she proves absolutely central to that world and to the text's construction of an English national identity.

The most astonishing aspect of Bess's dramatization is the enormous attention focused on her sexual status. She is a virgin, but an eroticized one, desired and desiring. This fact constitutes her power and enables her body to represent England as a virtuous and intact "maiden isle" (V.i.90); this fact also renders Bess problematic and dangerous, since the men of the play repeatedly assume she will give over her chastity and begin to employ her sexuality promiscuously, making them her common and interchangeable sexual objects. From the first scene, characters repeatedly discuss Bess's surprising virginity – surprising, that is, to those who assume that a woman who serves wine in a tavern must also, like a Mistress Quickly, serve sex. Both her class and her gender render Bess suspect. When the gentleman, Mr Carroll, arrives in Plymouth in the first scene, he is told by two captains of this "flower / Of Plymouth" (I.i.19–20) and of her beauty, sweetness, and modesty. Incredulously, he exclaims: "Honest, and live there? / What, in a public tavern, where's such confluence / Of lusty and brave gallants? Honest said you?" (I.i.24–6). As long as Bess inhabits the tavern world her chastity remains a subject of wonder and doubt. Even her beloved, the gentleman Mr Spencer from whom she is separated in Act I, can't quite seem to believe in her virtue even though, as he recounts to his friend, Goodlack,

> I have proved her
> Unto the utmost test, examin'd her
> Even to a modest force, but all in vain.
> She'll laugh, confer, keep company, discourse,
> And something more, kiss; but beyond that compass
> She no way can be drawn.

> (I.ii.57–62)

I wonder what is involved in examining Bess "even to a modest force." She has obviously withstood some fairly stiff pressure, and Spencer obviously feels he has the right to "test" her in this way.

When this same man later believes he is dying from a wound incurred

103

in the Spanish Azores, he intrusts Goodlack with a will leaving Bess a legacy of £500 a year. But the legacy hinges on a proviso which again reveals his doubts about her faithfulness and chastity.

If at thy arrival where my Bess remains,
Thou find'st her well reported, free from scandal,
My will stands firm; but if thou hear'st her branded
For loose behavior or immodest life,
What she should have I here bestow on thee,
It is thine own.

(II.ii.82–7)

A moment later he remembers that he has also left his picture with Bess, and even more vehemently he tells Goodlack that if Bess "be rank'd amongst the loose and lewd, / Take it away (I hold it much undecent / A whore should ha't in keeping), but if constant,/ Let her enjoy it" (II.ii.95–8). Obviously, even the man to whom she has pledged herself cannot quite reconcile the public nature of Bess's position in the tavern, her literal circulation among gallants, with the idea of her chastity. And there is a kind of horror of contamination in his urgent request that Goodlack rescue his picture – simulacrum of himself – from this woman should she prove "loose and lewd." In fact, there is a telling symbolism in the tokens Bess and Spencer exchanged at their parting in Act I. She gave to him a ring, emblemizing her virginity and implicitly pledging to him sole use of her vagina, and he gave to her his picture, emblemizing his masculine and familial honor (I.iii.35–92). What haunts his imagination, even at the point of death, is the fear that her "ring" has circulated out of his control, and that his honor is defaced by female sexual promiscuity.

Bess's sexual potential, then, remains a threat in the male mind, even though her chastity has often withstood men's "utmost tests." To be what she becomes in this text – a symbol of English values and a figure in whose service all Englishmen are united – Bess's chastity must be fetishized. As that oxymoronic thing, a virgin in a tavern, Bess emerges as an exception to her sex, a paragon of modesty and faithfulness. As such she functions as a unifying symbol of the nation and as a catalyst to transform and perfect the men around her. Masculine fear of female sexuality thus leads to idealization of the virginal woman, and through service to her a homosocial community of men is constituted, but one in which, ironically, women themselves will have almost no place.

Especially in Acts II and III, when Bess runs her tavern in Foy, her transformative powers as an exceptional woman are astonishing. Goodlack, for example, whose name none too subtly suggests moral deficiency, undergoes a reformation at her hands. When Spencer commissions Goodlack to deliver his will and inheritance to Bess, Goodlack hopes he will find Bess unchaste so that he can keep the money for himself. When he meets her, he verbally abuses her, telling her he knows she is a whore (III.iii.67) and that Spencer knew she was a whore and had asked Goodlack to wrest his picture from her (III.iv.17–22). In short, he speaks Spencer's worst fantasies as if they were the simple truth, but like a patient Griselda, Bess never wavers in her love for Spencer or in her courtesy to his abusive friend. Charmed by her goodness and her vow to die because of Spencer's unkind thoughts, Goodlack repents – "Had I a heart of flint or adamant, / It would relent at this" (III.iv.77–8). Thereafter he lacks no goodness, becoming Bess's faithful captain on her ensuing voyage to the Azores to rescue Spencer's body and avenge English honor on the Spanish.

Bess has an even more profound effect on Roughman, whose name also signifies his own particular failings. He is a bully and a coward, a man who pretends to be a fighter and a man of honor, but who in actuality only takes his aggressions out on women and servants. To deal with him, Bess dresses herself "like a page with a sword" (s.d. before II.iii), meets him alone in a field, and forces him to throw down his sword, tie her shoe, untruss her point, and lie down on the ground so she can walk over him (II.iii.67–73). Aware that she breaks with convention in dressing like a man and wielding a sword, Bess justifies herself by saying:

> Let none condemn me of immodesty
> Because I try the courage of a man
> Who on my soul's a coward; beats my servants,
> Cuffs them, and, as they pass by him, kicks my maids;
> Nay, domineers over me, making himself
> Lord o'er my house and household.
>
> (II.iii.27–32)

In short, in the tradition of Mary Ambree or Long Meg of Westminster to whom she explicitly compares herself (II.iii.13), Bess puts on male clothing to right social wrongs, specifically to make Roughman a proper man, less cowardly and more protective of women. In this regard, Bess performs one of the more conservative meanings of crossdressing.[8] As a crossdresser who knows how to wear and use a sword, Bess *could* be that threatening figure from the masculine imagination: the castrating woman who turns the world upside down. But Bess temporarily dresses as a man to teach a man to be more manly, and when her lesson is taught, she reassumes her female dress. Miraculously, Bess's treatment works. When Roughman learns he has been humiliated by a woman, he finds that she has "kindled that dead fire of courage" (III.i. 132) in him, and he rushes into the street to fight with whatever man he first meets. Thereafter he becomes an exemplary soldier who, along with Goodlack, becomes an officer on Bess's ship and a savage fighter against the Spanish.

What we see in Bess is the almost miraculous power of the virgin woman to make flawed gentlemen into exemplary servants of the Protestant State. In the process, divisions within the nation – between men and women, between classes, between male rivals – are elided and aggressions are channeled outward against a common enemy, Catholic Spain. Importantly, the opening Acts of the play depict an England shot through with interclass and intraclass rivalry and aggression. In the first Act two gentlemen, Carrol and Spencer, fight over whether Bess, a mere tapstress, can sit with them at their tavern table. In Act II, when he lands at Fayal, Spencer tries to separate two English captains who are fighting, and he himself is given a nearly deadly wound. In the tavern at Plymouth in Act I the drawers constantly make references to the unwillingness of gallants to pay what they owe to the tavern-keeper. As one drawer says: "It is the commonest thing that can be said for these captains to score and to score, but when the scores are to be paid, *non est inventus*" (I.iv.2–4). And his friend replies: "'Tis ordinary amongst gallants nowadays, who had rather swear forty oaths than only this one oath: 'God let me never be trusted'" (I.iv.5–7). The drawers have had to petition the Mayor of Plymouth to get the English general to pay their master what he is owed by the officers. Rather than a quarrel between gallants, the antagonism here is between spendthrift gentlemen and an industrious, thrifty tavern-keeper and his servants. Later, in Foy, Roughman, a "swaggering gentleman," shows a similar contempt for mere servants and for Bess in her new role as innkeeper. In III.i he bullies Bess, strikes Clem twice (III.i.50 and III.i.86) and kicks at the kitchenmaid (III.i.66). This is a commonwealth rife with social antagonisms.

The play's structure suggests, however, that once Bess's influence has spread and her power increased, the antagonisms internal to the nation will disappear. Gradually, the exceptional woman transforms the members of a factionalized, strife-ridden community into a harmonious band of brothers. The ship on which Bess sets sail for Fayal in Act IV is the stage on which this fantasy of national harmony is acted out. On board this vessel, which emblemizes the English nation in miniature, all men live as virtuous brothers. The reformed Goodlack is now captain of the ship, with Roughman as his lieutenant. Even Clem, the clownish tavern servant, has a place and vows to "prove an honor to all the drawers in Cornwall" (IV.ii.103–4). Crucially, even as class rivalries are suppressed or elided, the ship provides a space where the troubling potential of disruptive female sexuality is further muted. In essence, Bess now occupies the position of virgin widow. It is her betrothed's body she goes to retrieve, and while the men who travel with her are united through their service to her, none is her lover. As a virgin pledged to perpetual chastity because of her love for a dead man, Bess can seemingly inspire devotion devoid of sexual desire. Moreover, even her clothing now de-emphasizes Bess's specifically female qualities. When she goes to sea, it is with "rich apparel / For man or woman as occasion serves" (IV.ii.87–8), and she dresses "like a sea captain" (s.d. before IV.iv) until she lands in Barbary.

When Bess appears in men's apparel, the ironies surrounding her centrality to the national project are most striking. While she functions as a necessary unifying symbol of England, the actual nation forged around her is overwhelmingly male. When, furthermore, English national virtue is to be put to the test in a military encounter with the Spanish, the exemplary woman takes part only when she is transformed, sartorially, into a man. An enormous act of cultural suppression is enacted through this representational sequence. While an actual woman was or recently had been England's monarch, while women's wit and work were essential to England's commercial prosperity, and while women's reproductive powers were essential to the multiplication of England's citizens, almost none of this is overtly acknowledged by Heywood's text. In essence, the only woman in the play is an idealized exception to her sex, and at a crucial and defining moment she herself appears in the clothes of a man.

Obviously, this way of portraying the power of the exemplary woman owes much to representations of Elizabeth I: the Virgin Queen who occupied the masculine position of monarch and who gained much of her power in a patriarchal culture from her conscious decision to remain unmarried and so "above" the common fate of private women.[9] I want to stress, however, that Bess is *not* simply a screen for Elizabeth. Her depiction is much more complicated than such a simple identification of a female subject with her monarch would suggest. First, note the play's title. Bess is a fair maid "of the west." She is identified with a particular region of the country, not with the court. Her father came from Somersetshire (I.ii.18), and she was set to service in Plymouth. The title of the play thus seems to suggest that form of nationalism which defined itself in relationship to the land of England and its distinct regions, a nationalism which Richard Helgerson has posited as an alternative to the monarch-based ideologies of dynastic statehood.[10] Only secondarily, I think, does the title suggest that the "real" fair maid is Queen Elizabeth, the Protestant monarch from the island to the west of Europe.

The drama's play with its heroine's name is another signal of the contra-dictory forces shaping her depiction. For most of the play she is called Bess, a homely reminder that she is no queen, but a tanner's daughter, a fact stressed early in the play when Goodlack reproves Spencer: "One of your birth and breeding thus to dote / Upon a tanner's daughter!"

(I.ii.16–17). It is only in Act IV, when Bess is a wealthy tavern-owner and courted by the Mayor of Foy's son, that she begins to be nominated "fair Mistress Elizabeth" (IV.ii.9). And it is only in Act V that Mullisheg, the King of Fez, pointedly calls attention to the fact that Elizabeth is also the name of "The virgin queen, so famous through the world / The mighty empress of the maiden isle" (V.i.89–90), a nomination that calls explicit attention to the way the virgin body of the Queen – and so of Bess – can be made to emblemize the territorial integrity of England. Bess modestly disclaims any resemblance between herself and England's Queen, "the only phoenix of her age, / The pride and glory of the Western Isles" (V.i.99–100), but clearly the comparison is more than random.

To the extent that Bess *is* Elizabeth she embodies Englishness in the exemplary virgin body of the female monarch whose powers are at least in theory linearly derived and patriarchal in nature, whatever her own particular sex.[11] To the extent, however, that Bess is a tanner's daughter who through her virtue and hard work enjoys a spectacular rise in her fortunes, her powers have another derivation – simple entrepreneurship. In her representation several ideologies and several class positions are knotted together. For example, while it is crucial that Bess be a virgin throughout the text, it also is important that she have a beloved, Spencer, with whom she is finally united and whom she longs to marry. This differentiates her from that greater Elizabeth who dallied with marriage, but in the end remained wedded only to England and her own power, and it allies her with the values of the emergent middle classes who paid increasing attention to marriage as an affective, as well as an economic, institution.[12]

Bess's entrepreneurship also links her to the emergent middle class. Though she gets her first advance in life by being given Spencer's tavern in Foy to keep until his return, it is less aristocratic largesse than her own effort and thrift that are the foundations of Bess's ever-increasing wealth. Until she takes ship for the Azores, Bess is typically depicted working in the tavern, first as a simple barmaid in *The Castle* in Plymouth, later as the mistress of the *Windmill* in Foy. Self-discipline and hard work, along with modesty and chastity, are the hallmarks of her character. In this, she is an embodiment, not of aristocratic or monarchical virtues, but of the values of the artisans, shopkeepers, and merchants of the towns and cities of England. The subtitle of the play, of course, is *A Girl Worth Gold*. There are wonderful multiplicities of meaning in the phrase. Bess's chastity and virtue, of course, are part of her treasure. But increasingly her literal wealth is what makes Bess "worth gold," certainly to the Mayor of Foy who sees her as a prospective mate for his son.

Bess, moreover, uses her wealth for the good of her country, implying that among Eliza's best and most patriotic subjects are her entrepreneurial merchants and shopkeepers. Consider Bess's will.[13] Before she goes to sea, Bess writes a formal will giving away much of the money she has accrued through her labor. Some money she leaves to help maimed soldiers; some to set up young beginners in their trades; some to her servants, and so forth. She is, in short, a philanthropist concerned with the well-being of her town, and the well-being of the ex-soldiers and apprentices of her nation. Wealth generated by private labor and thrift is thus used to support the public good.[14] Moreover, Bess spends the rest of her money to purchase a ship in which to sail to the Azores to retrieve Spencer's body. Once there, partly because she believes the Spanish have desecrated that body, she in essence becomes a privateer against the Spanish. Aggressively seeking out Spanish ships, Bess vows to "face the fight / And where the bullets sing loud'st 'bout mine ears / There shall you find me cheering up my men" (IV.iv.91–3), a vow she keeps. In these battles, Bess is not only an emblem of the Virgin Queen, but a figure who can fuse the energies of the artisans, shopkeepers, and merchants of a commercializing nation with the chivalric gallantry of the traditional aristocracy.

A great deal is invested, obviously, in the figure of Bess in this play. In her service the divisions and antagonisms internal to the body politic of England seem magically overcome. At one and the same time she embodies the extraordinary power of Elizabeth, the Virgin Queen, and the erotics of provocation and denial associated with her, and also the commercial values of the emerging middle class and an erotics that posits marriage as its telos. Thus, through Bess, aristocratic symbols and ideologies are refashioned and fused with the values of another social class. But the exceptional woman who does all this work of social mediation never quite ceases to be a threatening figure in the homosocial nation of men she helps to call into being. In short, while Bess is a figure used to provide imaginary resolutions to actual social tensions, she is also a figure of crisis, whose centrality signals the very strains in the social fabric she is, magically, to resolve and who continually evokes men's fears of women's power and sexuality. The duplicitous whore, the castrating crossdresser, the disruptive woman on top – these negative representations of the "public woman" lurk just behind the positive aspects of her portrayal, betraying themselves, for example, in Spencer's worries that Bess has played the wanton in his absence, and in the self-conscious way Bess is made to articulate a defense of her crossdressed defeat of Roughman. Predictably the play's overheated insistence on Bess's chastity underscores what seems to be her most frightening quality: her sexuality. The play attempts in a number of ways to contain the threat posed by Bess's sexual desire and desirability, but the most important lies, unpredictably, in its handling of Bess's sojourn among the Moors.

THE SPANISH AND THE MOORS IN THE ENGLISH
MAPPING OF A NATIONAL IDENTITY

The striking fact I have so far elided from my account of Bess's voyage to the Azores is the name she gives her ship. Deliberately, she christens it the *Negro*. Her exchange with her men about this choice is important. To Goodlack she says:

> you said your ship was trim and gay;
> I'll have her pitch'd all o'er: no spot of white,
> No color to be seen, no sail but black,
> No flag but sable.
> GOODLACK 'Twill be ominous
> And bode disaster fortune.
> BESS   I'll ha't so.
> GOODLACK Why then she shall be pitch'd black as the devil.
> BESS She shall be call'd the *Negro*. When you know
>   My conceit, Captain, you will thank me for't.
>   (IV.ii.77–84)

The conceit seems to rest on the fact that, unbeknown to her crew, Bess is undertaking a journey of mourning to retrieve Spencer's body. The blackness of her ship signals her deep grief and the monstrousness, to her, of Spencer's death. But to indicate darkness and mourning, the ship could have been named many things besides the *Negro*. This specific choice links the ominous and devilish associations of the color black in the Western imagination directly to the peoples of Africa.[15] And, as Anthony Barthelemy argues, management and control of this black ship signal in a striking fashion the English desire for mastery and command over these dark peoples.[16] The name may even subliminally suggest a link between English and European shipping and the trade in Negro slaves, even though in this play the English merchants and privateers who visit Barbary are not slavers.[17] More broadly, the name given to the ship, the site where English national unity and national character are most fully displayed, suggests that the construction of Englishness depends on the simultaneous construction of what is non-English. In the elaboration of this grid of difference, the Spanish and the Moors play equally important, but quite different, roles, the former being constructed in the oppositional binarisms of mimetic rivalry, the latter in terms of racial inferiority and sexual danger.

Such is the power of modern forms of racism that to contemporary readers it may come as a surprise that the Spanish are more overtly demonized in *Fair Maid of the West* than are the Moors. This can partly be explained by the state of the commercial, religious, and political rivalries among the European powers at the end of the sixteenth century and partly by the particular history of English involvement with the western Maghreb during the same period. The Spanish, the great Catholic power of Europe, had attempted an invasion of England in 1588 and had firmly established themselves as the leading colonial force in the Americas. At least until the time James I composed a peace with the Spanish, they were popularly constructed as the religious and moral antithesis of their English counterparts. In *The Fair Maid of the West, Part I* the difference between Spanish and English is figured as a series of binary oppositions, and the relations between the two powers are straightforwardly antagonistic. The Spanish are Catholic, cruel, and rapacious; the English are Protestant, merciful, and generous. For example, while the Spanish have what they believe to be Spencer's body removed from the church where it was buried because they hold him to be a Protestant heretic (IV.iv.39–44), Bess and the English engage in no such acts of desecration. The Spanish captives from whom Bess learns this heinous news are granted their lives and sent away with money, no revenge taken (IV.iv.57–9).

As is true in much of the English writing about Spanish activity in the New World, moreover, the Spanish are consistently portrayed in this text as barbarously cruel.[18] When Spencer and the English merchant ship are captured by a Spanish ship, the captain tells Spencer that "strappados, bolts, / And engines to the mainmast fastened / Can make you gentle" (IV.i.22–4), while Bess, when she in turn captures the Spanish ship, seizes the boat and the goods aboard it, but releases the captain and his crew in their long boat (IV.iv.118–20). In a lovely example of the conquered being made to speak in praise of their conquerors, the Spanish captain declares that the "Famous Elizabeth" and "her subjects both are merciful" (IV.iv.122–3). Perhaps Clem, who always speaks the "low" matter of the play, characterizes the "difference" of the "Spanish" most scabrously when he connects them with excremental incontinence by calling them "you Don Diegos, you that made Paul's to stink" (IV.iv.110–11), a reference to a famous, though perhaps apocryphal, incident of excremental desecration of the famous cathedral by a Spaniard.

While the Spanish are obviously intended to be seen as the antithesis of the English in matters of religion and moral decency, they are, however, also constructed *in relation* to the English in a way that suggests a subterranean fraternal bond between the two nations, a bond defined precisely by rivalrous antipathy. Both nations, for example, are trying to exert control of the seas around the Azores; both are eager for booty and bullion; both claim to possess the true version of Christianity; and structurally, English actions in the play are often staged as a reactive and exemplary alternative to Spanish actions. These two European powers are national rivals and enemies, but necessary to one another's self-definitions. Their predictably appropriate mode of interaction is the hand-to-hand, ship-to-ship combat of masculine equals, though in their fictional sea battle the English, of course, must win.

The relationship of the English to the Moors is quite different. In one sense the Moors are supplemental to the highly orchestrated opposition of the two European powers. Most of the Moorish scenes occur in Act V, and though a feeling of danger courses through all the encounters between Mullisheg and the English adventurers, they are not presented as overt enemies. This may be due in part to the history of trade and diplomacy between the English and the Moroccan Moors in the sixteenth century and to the tantalizing, often-discussed possibility of an alliance between the two against the Spanish. As Jack D'Amico has detailed, England and Morocco were fairly consistent trading partners during the period, the English getting gold, sugar, dates, and saltpeter from the Moors and in turn supplying them with iron and military supplies, including munitions.[19] Despite the eventual establishment of a Barbary Company, much of this trade was unregulated, and English merchants sometimes found their ships impounded or detained in the ports along the Barbary Coast and had difficulty getting effective help from England in arranging their release. Some of this trade was also controversial, since European powers such as Portugal, who fought the Moors at the battle of Alcazar in 1578, did not want England supplying "the Infidel" with guns and ore. However, at times the English seemed to have hoped for an alliance with "the Infidel" in that they proposed Morocco join with England in an attempt to put the Portuguese Pretender, Don Antonio, on the Spanish throne; and in 1600 a sizeable Moorish embassy went to England to discuss matters of trade and diplomacy.

Some of this history of relations between the two powers is visible in the play. When Spencer has been miraculously cured of his wound while on Fayal, it is the ship of a London merchant that takes him to Mamorah, a town in Barbary where Bess later lands to get water for her crew. This town, near Rabat, is described by Leo Africanus as "built upon the mouth of the great river Subu," making it a convenient place for trading-ships to land and to take on fresh water.[20] Mullisheg is very aware of how he can benefit from the presence of European merchants in his land. In the first scene in which we see him, he has just established himself as King of a united Barbary. To put his kingdom to rights he speaks of establishing laws and enriching the depleted public treasury. In regard to the latter he says:

> Then give order
> That all such Christian merchants as have traffic
> And freedom in our country, that conceal

The least part of our custom due to us,
Shall forfeit ship and goods.
                    (IV.iii.15–19)

Apparently a number of merchants have run foul of Mullisheg's ordinances. Spencer says that the merchant who brought him to Mamorah "Hath by a cunning quiddit in the law/ Both ship and goods made forfeit to the king" (V.ii.3–4). And Bess, at the entreaty of Clem, gets Mullisheg to release Italian and French sea-captains whose boats have been detained in his ports. At one level the play simply acknowledges the vexed but well-established trade relations that existed between Morocco and a number of European nations, especially England.

This does not mean, however, that the representation of the Moors in *Fair Maid* is either ideologically benign or straightforward. These Moors who dare to interfere with English merchants and to court an English woman are made to embody a dangerous but effeminate otherness that finally renders them safely inferior to their European visitors. A much vaster gulf of difference yawns between them and the English than between those sworn enemies, the English and the Spanish. The ground of this difference is partly racial. Skin color functions in this play as a defining mark of difference and one basis for establishing relations of dominance and subordination between the English and Mullisheg and his court.

When speaking specifically of the inhabitants of North Africa, many writers of the period draw a distinction between tawny Moors and black Moors.[21] This play emphatically does not. Largely thanks to Clem's graphic comments, there is little doubt that Mullisheg, King of Fez, is to be understood as a black man. For example, when the King has granted Bess's request that a French merchant escape paying a fine, Clem exclaims, "May'st thou never want sweet water to wash thy black face in, most mighty monarch of Morocco" (V.ii.64–5), a backhanded expression of thanks in that it implies that the black face needs some cleansing water, probably a reference to the proverb about the futility of washing an Ethiop white.[22] When Bess a bit later kisses the King, Clem exclaims: "Must your black face be smooching my mistress's white lips with a Moorian? I would you had kiss'd her a ——" (V.ii.80–1). And Mullisheg himself comments, with happy anticipation, "she in a Negro / Hath sail'd thus far to bosom with a Moor" (V.i.8–9), seeming to equate his blackness with that of the ship Bess has chosen for her own.

Clem's disgruntlement at the kiss between his white mistress and the black King quite graphically voices a racist fear of miscegenation, of the contamination of the white woman by a polluting and inferior blackness.[23] Spencer had earlier imagined the contamination of his male honor, symbolized by his picture, by Bess's sexual promiscuity. Now

113

woman's body is the vehicle of sexual *and* of racial pollution. That Bess enters into conversation with the Moorish King, lifts her veil for him (V.i.33), and twice receives his kiss (V.i.66 and V.ii.79) seems to put her in the compromising position of encouraging his desire. She is both in danger and the source of danger. As Ania Loomba says in regard to the union of Desdemona and Othello:

> what is especially threatening for white patriarchy is the possibility of the *complicity* of white women; their desire for black lovers is feared, forbidden, but always imminent. . . . Even if she is passive, however, the white woman's contact with the alien male pollutes her.[24]

To Clem, the most outspoken member of the English entourage, there is no doubt that Mullisheg's color, and Bess's physical intimacy with him, threaten such pollution.

The particular construction of Islam in this text further heightens the sense that Mullisheg embodies a dangerous and polluting sexuality. The Moors in *Fair Maid* are not only black; they are also Muslims. In fact, in one brief scene Bess begs the life of a Christian preacher imprisoned for trying to convert the Moors to Christianity (V.ii.73–5). In many plays of the period Muslims, often designated simply as "Turks," are portrayed as devilish enemies of the West and of Christianity.[25] By contrast, *Fair Maid* does not construct the Moor primarily as a religious threat to England. Certainly Spanish Catholicism poses a greater threat in that regard. Historically, of course, the Ottoman empire never extended its reach fully across the Maghreb to encompass the conquest of Morocco.[26] It is conceivable that Heywood knew this fact and so did not conflate Moroccan Moors with the barbarous Turk, the traditional enemy of Western Christendom.[27] It is also possible that England's mercantile and political involvements with Morocco and her use of ports along the Barbary Coast to conduct raids against the Spanish were what allowed Heywood to present Moorish Muslims as something other than the enemy of English Protestantism.

These Moorish Muslims *are*, however, a *sexual* threat to the English, and Islam enters *Fair Maid* primarily as a discourse of sexual libertinism and danger.[28] In the only scene in which Mullisheg appears in Act IV, he speaks first of the laws he intends to promulgate and the wealth he intends to accrue to his newly united kingdom, and then he says:

> But what's the style of king
> Without his pleasure? Find us concubines,
> The fairest Christian damsels you can hire
> Or buy for gold, the loveliest of the Moors
> We can command, and Negroes everywhere.

Italians, French, and Dutch, choice Turkish girls
Must fill our Alkedavy, the great palace
Where Mullisheg now deigns to keep his court.
                                        (IV.iii.27–34)

A bit later he adds: "If kings on earth be termed demigods, / Why should we not make here terrestrial heaven? / We can, we will; our god shall be our pleasure, / For so our Meccan prophet warrants us" (IV.iii.37–40). In this speech the racist discourse of the lascivious black man and the Orientalist discourse of the libertine Muslim fuse to create Morocco as a place of sexual danger to the West. Of course, constructing the other as dangerous in this way has historically been the prelude for enslaving or "correcting" him/her.

Perhaps most striking is the threat of castration that hovers around Mullisheg's court. Clem, of course, is the figure upon whose body this threat is literally enacted, and the deed is presented in such a farcical manner that at first it is difficult to register the fact that the clumsy servant's "best jewels," as he calls them, have been cut off (V.ii.127).[29] Clem undergoes this "cutting honor" after Bess has asked Mullisheg to show her beloved Spencer some favor. Mullisheg, with what I hope is a delicious irony, offers to pay his romantic rival the honor of making him his chief eunuch. "He shall have grace and honor. – Joffer, go / And see him gelded to attend on us. / He shall be our chief eunuch" (V.ii.91–3). Bess is horrified, but her silly servant Clem offers to take the "honor" upon himself. Twenty-five lines later he comes running on the stage to exclaim: "No more of your honor, if you love me! Is this your Moorish preferment, to rob a man of his best jewels?" (V.ii.126–7). In trying to figure out why this grotesque episode occurs, it may be worth remembering that Clem has earlier come on stage "as a fantastic Moor" (s.d. at V.i.109). In the land of the Moors he, an Englishman, wears a version of Moroccan attire and for doing so seems to get a grotesquely hideous warning of the dangers of "going native." The idea seems to be that if the white European gives himself to the customs of Barbary, his manhood may be lost.

But the castration of Clem is also, I believe, connected to another set of anxieties about the gender and sexuality of Bess that resurfaces in Act V when the heroine, her military conquests over, once more puts on her female dress. In Act V Bess is again thoroughly sexualized. She arrives like a beauteous queen in Mullisheg's court, and at her first kiss the black King cries: "This kiss hath all my vitals ecstasied" (V.i.67). As I have begun to suggest, the erotic and racial politics of their encounter are extremely complex. As Clem's racist observations make clear, Bess is in part presented as endangered by black sexuality. At the same time, Mullisheg is put in the effeminating position of being so overwhelmingly attracted to this white goddess that he loses the power to refuse any of her requests. And she, by the initiative she takes in their encounters, invites being read as the sexual wanton Spencer and others earlier suspected her to be.

It is at this moment of greatest sexual tension that a miraculous resolution is effected by the "discovery" of Spencer. Alive and in Barbary with the English merchant who brought him from Fayal, Spencer comes forth in the final Act to take Bess as his bride and thus conveniently to displace his Moorish rival. This shadowy husband figure has a complicated status in the play. On the one hand, he needs to exist so that Bess can be seen to be committed to marriage; on the other, he needs to be absent for great stretches of the play so Bess can play the part of virgin warrior and emblem of England. Consequently, for much of Acts III and IV everyone in England assumes Spencer is dead; and when Bess actually sees him on the high seas in Act IV, she assumes he is a ghost come crying for revenge (IV.iv.135–52). Nearly fainting, she has to be led off to her cabin. But it is as a flesh-and-blood reality that Spencer returns in Act V, and it is imperative he do so to allay the intolerable anxiety surrounding Bess's sexuality and her status as an unmarried, and so unmastered, woman.

The wooing of Bess by Mullisheg, Spencer's return, and then the castration of Clem together embody complex acts of subordination and substitution by which the play attains a tenuous ideological resolution. Perhaps the most crucial event is Bess's imminent marriage to Spencer, an occurrence that promises the subordination of her will and sexuality to the control of a husband. No longer a warrior, queen, entrepreneur or sea-captain, Bess is about to be ushered from the public eye into the private home, the space allotted to woman in the emerging nation state. "Englishness" will then be identified with heterosexual marriage and with the masculine enclosure of female sexuality, not within the Moorish harem, but within the English home.

Simultaneously, the sexual threat formerly embodied by Bess is displaced onto the Moors. Mullisheg becomes the sexual libertine and the castrator, and he exists "in another country," one whose danger and contamination a prudent Englishman – unlike Clem – can elude by appropriate acts of caution and self-restraint. Thus, while it was Bess who stood accused throughout the play of sexual looseness and Bess whose prowess with a sword raised the specter of a woman so powerful and powerfully alluring that she could effeminate the men around her, it is the Moorish King who actually *displays* the rapacious sexual appetites so feared in Bess, and the Moorish King who literally submits a man to the razor of castration. Mullisheg finally substitutes for Bess as the play's chief figure of sexual danger, even as he himself is sexualized and effeminated by his excessive adoration of the English Elizabeth.[30] He is disempowered both by a discourse of racial inferiority and by his effemi-nating enthrallment to a woman. And Clem, the lower-class scapegoat, substitutes for all those Englishmen who felt endangered by the power of the castrating woman and then by her substitute, the castrating Moor. The implication is that only a servant is "really" endangered by either a Bess or by a Mullisheg, while further psychic distance on the threat of castration is achieved by its essentially comic representation.

What emerges from the final movement of this play is a vision of English national identity permeated by fear of female sexuality and by a racism constructed in part through a discourse of color, as well as cultural, difference. The drama's anxiety about women's power and sexuality can only be surmounted by its displacement onto the Moorish other, while woman herself is contained within the confines of marriage, out of the public arena. In this drama of emerging nationhood, the play's condescension to the Moors, seemingly more benign than the antipathy directed at the Spanish, is in actuality deeply consequential. While the English certainly fight with the Spanish, these two European nations are linked through a mimetic rivalry which constitutes them as equals and worthy antagonists. England's relation to the Moors is very different, for in an emerging colonial context, Moors are not so much potential fraternal rivals as potential slaves. They are represented as black, licentious and sexually dangerous – not only different, but infer-ior. When Spencer seizes Bess, the sexual prize, away from the effemi-nated Mullisheg, his act equates Englishness both with racial superiority and with a patriarchal masculinity insistent on the control of female sexuality. Ironically, the story of the girl worth gold and of "Mighty Mullisheg, / Pride of our age and glory of the Moors" (IV.iii.5–6), helps to construct an idea of English nationhood in which neither the black man nor the white woman will have places of privilege, and from which the black woman will all too often, as in this play, simply be erased.

7

AMAZONS AND AFRICANS
Gender, race, and empire in Daniel Defoe
Laura Brown

This essay[1] uses a reading of a powerful trope in the representation of women as a kind of workshop on the discursive relation between gender and empire in early eighteenth-century literary culture. Despite my title, I will focus mainly on Amazons – in eighteenth-century literature variously and in Defoe's *Roxana* (1724) at some length. Recently, the image of the Amazon has attracted the attention of feminist theorists and cultural historians, as well as classicists, anthropologists, and literary critics; and Amazons have been seen variously as emblems of female autonomy, figures of myth, examples of misogyny, or thematizations of romantic heroism.[2] In literature, outside the classical, the focus has been on the drama and epic of the Renaissance;[3] the Amazon has not seemed an active figure in the literary culture of the eighteenth century. I want to try to argue here that the Amazon is – though covertly or indirectly – a significant image in the discourse of the representation of difference in this period; that this figure is most readily perceived and most usefully understood specifically in terms of contemporary representations of exchange, accumulation, and commodification; and finally that the Amazon is for this period an important form of mediation in the representation of imperialist ideology. In focusing on Defoe, I have chosen to view this trope through the eyes of one of the most prolific and eloquent apologists for mercantile expansion in early eighteenth-century literary culture. That is to say, I stand in the place of the imperialist, and I view the "other" from the perspective of the dominant ideology. This perspective inevitably places gender before race, because gender represents a category of difference constituted primarily within the geographical purview of the dominant culture, while race in this period remains mainly extrinsic, geographically foreign, a category of difference defined as an external object. For that reason, the argument here will come to the African through the figure of the Amazon, and it will use Defoe's image of the African in *Captain Singleton* (1720) as a final test case for the connection of the representation of difference with the ideology of empire.

I will raise at the end of the essay the question of whether or to what extent, in taking the perspective of the imperialist and in placing gender analytically before race, we are forced to adopt the hierarchies of empire. Does such a perspective systematically exclude us from access to forces of subversion, resistance, or autonomy outside the range of imperialist thought? These questions grow out of a larger polemical purpose that I hope this essay will help to exemplify. In confronting critically the political consequences of this reading, I would like to raise the issue of political utility for recent new historical or Foucauldian or "political" criticism. This work has successfully placed the relationship between literature and society at the forefront of concern for contemporary students of literary culture. But the significance of asserting that relationship is still implicitly a subject for discussion. The old new historicists – those writing from the late 1970s to the mid- or late 1980s[4] – were criticized variously for emphasizing the coercive strategies of structures of power, for neglecting women, in history and in literature, and for omitting any self-conscious or systematic account of the assumptions or aims of their argument. The new new historicists – from the late 1980s to the early 1990s[5] – have taken up issues of gender and race, feminism and colonialism, working-class culture and male and female homosexual desire. Out of these developments has come a new self-consciousness about theoretical assumptions and a new self-criticism about political ends. As a contribution to this new discussion, I want to take up the issue of the assumptions and aims of "political" criticism in a concrete and local context, and to define the methods and ends of a specifically radical "political" critique.

I will propose here that "political" criticism stands its best chance of finding a progressive use if it attends to issues of inequity and exploitation as they arise in literary history in such a way as to further the struggle to bring an end to such conditions in our own period: that is, if it is oriented at least partly toward recovering or explicating liberationist positions, or if it provides us with a means of demystifying and then challenging a seemingly monolithic oppressive discourse. The purpose of this project is both to recover the expression of a socially critical position and to uncover the functioning of an oppressive ideology, by reading symptomatically a figure of subordination and difference. That is, this project claims to find in its explication of the image of the Amazon a potential political use – both a positive model and a negative lesson. I am proposing, in making such a claim, to define a specific sort of political purpose for contemporary "political" criticism, or – using this purpose as a model – to distinguish among recent "political" readings by their political ends.

119

I

One of the most disturbing images in Juvenal's Sixth Satire – a work that served as an influential model for the representation of women in eighteenth-century England – is not so much the famous figure of the lady in her dressing-room, though we shall return later to that trope, but rather the one that depicts female soldiers and gladiators, the description of the women at their military exercises. This is Dryden's translation:

> In every Exercise the Mannish Crew
> Fulfils the Parts, and oft Excels us too:
> Prepar'd not only in feign'd Fights t' engage,
> But rout the Gladiators on the Stage.
>
> .   .   .
>
> Behold the strutting *Amazonian* Whore,
> She stands in Guard with her right Foot before:
> Her Coats Tuck'd up; and all her Motions just,
> She stamps, and then Cries hah at every thrust,
> But laugh to see her tyr'd with many a bout,
> Call for the Pot, and like a Man Piss out.[6]

In part Juvenal's effect here is simply comic reversal: the woman playing the man's role. The laughter is rather brief, though, and the image conceals more anxiety than mere ridicule would warrant. The figure of the woman who "thrives on masculine violence" ("quae figut a sexu, vires amat")[7] – either by practicing it directly or by associating herself with men who do so – shows up in a variety of forms thoughout Juvenal's long and diffuse work. She is the one who joins the rough crew of sailors, braving the difficult and dangerous voyage to Alexandria, to elope with a gladiator. It is of her that Juvenal says "ferrum est quod amant":[8] the sword is what they love, or in Dryden's words: "But 'twas his Fencing did her Fancy move; / 'Tis Arms and Blood and Cruelty they love."[9] That same "ferrum" returns in the last lines of the poem, when women become the most horrific of "Fiends," a whole sex that will coolly commit murder for money – subtly, with poison, if that is most convenient, or brutally, with the sword: "These days, / Where e're you walk, the *Belides* you meet; [these are fifty sisters who killed their fifty husbands on their wedding night] / And *Clytemnestras* grow in every street."[10]

This movement from laughter to violence is characteristic of Juvenal's attack on women. As Dryden's translation puts it – with the typical neoclassical emphasis on generic distinctions – the satire slips into tragedy: "You think this feign'd; the Satyr in a Rage / Struts in the Buskins, of the Tragick stage. . . . / Wou'd it were all a Fable, that you Read . . ."[11] The image of the armed and warlike woman is the agent of this generic transformation. She is the point where comic transvestism turns to tragic violence, the apocalyptic telos and the serious message of Juvenal's misogyny.

These murderous women are described as springing directly from the money, luxury, and peace of the Roman empire.[12] The figure of the Amazon is in this respect an emblem of the *pax Romana*. Although politically women were marginal to the construction of the Roman or the British empires, culturally the constellation of discourses that served to represent the initiation, consolidation, celebration, defense, and even the critique of imperialism is intimately involved with the representation of women – in Rome and especially in eighteenth-century England – and the manlike, murderous woman plays a crucial role in this discourse.

The image of the warlike or murderous woman that we find in Juvenal supplies a prototype for the trope of the Amazon in eighteenth-century literary culture. This trope was evidently a resonant one in the period, and a variety of writers turned repeatedly to Juvenal's misogynist satire as a model and an inspiration. Dryden's translation had seven printings between 1692 and 1735. But the poem was also translated by Henry Fielding in 1725, by Edward Burnaby Greene in 1763, and by Edward Owen in 1785.[13] Fielding rendered Juvenal's verse in Hudibrastics and with contemporary references that bring the problem of the threatening Amazon up to date: "Have you not heard of fighting Females, / Whom you would rather think to be Males? / Of Madam *Sutton*, Mrs. *Stokes*, / Who give confounded Cuts and Strokes?"[14] Fielding refers to Mrs Sutton, a female prize fighter of the day, and to Elizabeth Stokes, another genuine female gladiator, who fought at both boxing and quarterstaff in public bouts at London amphitheaters.[15] Aside from their appearance in the unambiguously Juvenalian tradition, armed women also arise in the periodical and popular literature of the eighteenth century. Addison in the *Spectator* papers supplies a thumbnail sketch of a society of female warriors in which "No Woman was to be married till she had killed her Man,"[16] and Johnson translated a French text (by the Abbé de Guyon) as *Dissertation on the Amazons* and speculated in the *Idler* on the possibility of a nation of warlike women conquering men.[17]

Dianne Dugaw has recently argued that a widespread cultural fascination with fighting females characterizes the social life and popular literature of this period. She sees such female prize fighters as Sutton and Stokes – among others – along with the appearance of actual female soldiers in male dress, the interest in female physical vigor and autonomy, and the obsession with crossdressing in fashion, masquerade, and disguise, as an indication of a fundamental and ongoing questioning of gender roles.[18] For example, *The Female Soldier; Or, The Surprising Life and Adventures of Hannah Snell* (1750) recounts the career of a woman who in search of her husband took up male disguise and became a soldier, fought with apparent bravery in several battles, and was even seriously wounded without betraying her gender. Snell's enlistment in pursuit of her husband is a common convention in the ballad literature about the female soldier, as well as in the Juvenalian tradition that we have already canvassed, where the "Amazonian whore" goes to sea in pursuit of her gladiator lover. The opening passage of Hannah Snell's story suggests the ideological investments that might lie behind this popular woman warrior:

> [The author describes first] this dastardly Age of the World, when Effeminacy and Debauchery have taken Place of the Love of Glory, and that noble Ardor after warlike Exploits, which flowed in the Bosoms of our Ancestors, genuine Heroism, or rather an extraordinary Degree of Courage, are Prodigies among Men. . . . [and through this condemnation of the present age, he introduces the alternative of Hannah Snell's conduct in battle] tho' Courage and warlike Expeditions, are not the Provinces by the World allotted to Women since the Days of the *Amazons*, yet the female Sex is far from being destitute of Heroinism.[19]

Dugaw speculates that the female heroism that proved so fascinating in this period of almost continuous warfare might have called contemporary male heroism into question.[20] Here, Hannah Snell is quite explicitly defined as a heroic female alternative to a contemporary male depravity; her exploits evoke both the anti-heroism of the present-day male soldier and a kind of proxy heroism portrayed by the woman warrior. This role, as we shall see, connects the popular Amazon with the more canonical figures of fighting females in the period.

Perhaps the most canonical version of the trope occurs in the neoclassical format of Pope's *Rape of the Lock*, where it is joined directly, in the manner of Juvenal, with representations of the *pax Britannica* and the contemporary expansion of English commerce and prosperity – that is, with some of the period's strongest explicit images of empire. In this context, one might best describe *The Rape of the Lock* as a displacement of the *Aeneid* – the song of "arms and the man" and of the founding of the Roman empire – onto the figure of the "woman who thrives on masculine violence." Virgil's poem is a representation of continuous warfare, of unrelenting, unmitigated, and ultimately horrific "masculine violence" evoked ambivalently as a retrospective justification and apologia for imperial Rome. Pope's poem echoes Virgil's not only in the numerous details of rhetoric and event so familiar to the neoclassicist sensibility – the machinery of the gods, the journey to the underworld – but also in its structure of repetition, in the obsessive proliferation of scenes of battle, violence, and conquest. In this regard, the Amazon trope is the poem's central metaphor. Belinda "puts on all [her] Arms"[21] in Canto I, and engages in skirmishes and "Murders" (V.145) through the last lines of the poem, most notably in the card game at Hampton Court which is presented in the language of Aeneas's campaigns against the Latins.[22]

The familiar toilet scene, which echoes Juvenal's influential dressing-room passage, sets up another version of the conjunction of women and empire. Here, Belinda equips herself for battle, and the image of the "woman who thrives on masculine violence" is seen also as the self-consciously self-adorned female figure. The "Arms" (I.139) that she puts on are, of course, the commercial spoils of imperialist expansion. She is "deck'd with all that Land and Sea afford" (V.11), the "glitt'ring Spoil" and "unnumber'd Treasures . . . of the World" (I.129–36). Trade provides the means to this female adornment, and trade pervades the poem. Even the ubiquitous presence of coffee and tea is a signal of this engagement with mercantile prosperity: according to Defoe's *Review*, "*Coffee, Tea*, and *Chocolate* . . . it is well known are now become the Capital Branches of the Nations Commerce."[23] The Amazon here is a product and emblem of empire, in her person and in her Virgilian battles. Pope's poem, like Juvenal's, uses the murderous female figure – in which mercantile expansion and the activities of "masculine violence" are conjoined – as a kind of discursive center, from which the whole constellation of images and issues associated with empire emanates.

II

Roxana is a far cry from Hampton Court, or maybe not so far. Certainly Defoe's novel is socially and generically very distant from Pope's aristocratic and neoclassical poem; *Roxana* comes close to a popular tradition and views issues of class status from the opposite end of the hierarchy that *The Rape of the Lock* casually affirms. What does the very different cultural context of Defoe's *Roxana* add to this particular account of the representation of women in eighteenth-century literary culture? First and most obvious is the novel's pervasive engagement with the figures and problems connected with female adornment and dress. The center-piece of this engagement is Roxana's Turkish costume, which seems to have a mystical power of its own to attract men and women alike. In the process of her self-merchandising, Roxana repeatedly identifies with the material stuff in which she is dressed, resolving her problems through changes of clothes, and defining her success by what she is enabled to wear. She describes a gift of three gorgeous suits of clothes and a necklace of diamonds from the French Prince as a kind of proof of her unique ability to prosper and succeed;[24] with great delight she disguises herself as a Quaker – a form of moral legitimation by dress – to avoid her old acquaintance and begin a new life; and indeed she names herself (and her narrative) after her infamous Turkish dress. Thus the narrative too, and in particular the moral ambivalence of its treatment of Roxana's glamorous and lucrative career, is entangled with the issue of dressing. The Preface claims that if the history that follows is not as beautiful as Roxana is, as diverting as the reader wishes, and if it is not ultimately instructive, this must be the fault of the "Relator . . . dressing up the Story in worse Cloaths than the *Lady*, whose Words he speaks, prepar'd it for the World" (1). Everything in this narrative is dressed, including any claims to moral improvement, but it is Roxana's dressing that directs all others.

At the height of her career, Roxana's preferred form of adornment – the Turkish dress – both enables her to market herself in the most lucrative context, and itself evokes the spoils of an expansionist culture. It was, she says:

> the Habit of *a Turkish Princess*; the Habit I got at *Leghorn*, when my *Foreign prince* bought me a *Turkish* Slave, . . . the *Malthese* Man of War had, it seems, taken a *Turkish* Vessel going from *Constantinople* to *Alexandria*, in which were some ladies bound for *Grand Cairo* in *Egypt*; and as the Ladies were made Slaves, so their fine Cloaths were thus expos'd; and with this *Turkish* Slave, I bought the rich Cloaths too.
>
> (173–4)

The dress is the counterpart of the slave, and in this passage indistinguishable from her, and both are made available through the agency of imperialist aggression, here the unofficial imperialist rivalry of piracy. Indeed, the outfitting of the English female body in the complete and gorgeous dress of an exotic and exploited other is one dimension of the powerful motif of female dressing that characterizes eighteenth-century imperialist ideology. In *Oroonoko*, Aphra Behn's protagonist acquires a similar costume made from "Feathers, . . . whose Tinctures are unconceivable. I had a Set of these presented to me, and I gave 'em to the King's Theatre, and it was the Dress of the *Indian Queen*, infinitely admired by Persons of Quality; and was unimitable."[25] Belinda's toilet scene, where the Amazon arms herself with the spoils of empire, evokes local and specific products of mercantile capitalism. Behn's and Roxana's dresses call up the more generalized cultural obsession with the connection of female adornment and trade, exploitation, and empire. In one typical contemporary poem, James Ralph's *Clarinda*, women inspire the whole process of mercantile capitalist exploitation:

> For them the Gold is dug on Guinea's Coast,
> And sparkling Gems the farthest Indies boast,
> For them Arabia breathes its spicy Gale,

124

And fearless Seamen kill the Greenland Whale.

.   .   .

For them the *Merchant*, wide to ev'ry Sail,
Trusts all his Hopes and stretches ev'ry Gale,
For them, O'er all the World, he dares to roam,
And safe conveys its gather'd Riches home.[26]

The heroic merchant seems to be employed simply in dressing woman-kind, and by this means the acquisitiveness of the European male is replaced by the image of female adornment.[27]

Even when Roxana repudiates art, her claim to complete naturalness only serves to confirm her absolute implication in artfulness. The French Prince hesitates to touch her face, assuming she is painted, and receives a different sort of lesson in vanity:

> as he saw the Tears drop down my Cheek, he pulls out a fine Cambrick Handkerchief, and was going to wipe the Tears off, but check'd his Hand . . . I took the Hint immediately, and with a kind of pleasant Disdain, *How, my Lord!* said I, *Have you kiss'd me so often, and don't you know whether I am Painted, or not? Pray let your Highness satisfie yourself, that you have no Cheats put upon you; for once let me be vain enough to say, I have not deceiv'd you with false Colours:* With this, I put a Handkerchief into his Hand, and taking his Hand into mine, I made him wipe my Face so hard, that he was unwilling to do it, for fear of hurting me.
>
> (72)

She next dramatically washes her face before him with hot water: "This was, indeed, more than Satisfaction, that is to say, than Believing; for it was an undeniable Demonstration, and he kiss'd my Cheeks and Breasts a thousand times, with Expressions of the greatest Surprize imaginable" (72–3). The immediate consequence of this performance is the Prince's gift of "a fine Necklace of Diamonds," which he accounts for as a form of necessary completion: "I love, Child, *says he*, to see every thing suitable; a fine Gown and Petticoat; a fine lac'd Head; a fine Face and Neck, and no Necklace, would not have made the Object perfect" (73). Despite the purported preference for an unpainted face, this passage locates "per-fection" in the adornment, not the undressed original. Between the necklace and the face, between the dress and the female body that wears it, ornament and unadorned original are in effect indistinguishable. *The Rape of the Lock* produces the same symptomatic confusion in a much more familiar passage:

Now awful Beauty puts on all its Arms;
The Fair each moment rises in her charms,
Repairs her Smiles, awakens ev'ry Grace,

125

And calls forth all the Wonders of her Face.
Sees by Degrees a purer Blush arise,
And keener Light'nings quicken in her Eyes.
(I.138–44)

What Belinda sees in the mirror is paradoxically both her undressed self and the same image of fully adorned "perfection" preferred by Roxana's Prince. And the artfulness that confers that perfection seems to be both subsidiary and trivial – only heightening or embellishing qualities already present by nature in the female form, and at the same time constitutive of the beauty that emerges in the passage – in this sense there is no unadorned original. Like Roxana, Belinda need not be painted or even dressed at all to embody the necessary implication of adornment and dress with the representation of women. In both cases, even when it is unadorned or undressed the female body itself incarnates a central cultural engagement with accumulation and expansion.

This connection of women and the material objects with which they are adorned can be seen as a primary cultural emblem of commodity fetishism, where the physical products of human labor seem to take the place of human beings themselves. Relations between things replace relations between people, as exchange value usurps use value;[28] and here the association of the female figure with the material products of trade conceals the real structure of human relationships underlying those values dictated by exchange, the imperialist structure of male expansion and accumulation. As an object of commodification, then, Roxana is enlisted in the service of imperialist ideology, to mystify its most aggressive forces.

But Roxana's implication in mercantile capitalism has another, related, and higher stage. Through her investment of the profits from her alliances with the jeweler and the Prince, she becomes, in her own words, "from a Lady of Pleasure, a Woman of Business, and of great Business too . . . by managing my Business thus myself, and having large Sums to do with, I became as expert in it, as any She-Merchant of them all" (171, 131). She learns her business in Holland, which in this period was for English advocates of trade the national exemplar of successful management.[29] And indeed at this stage in her career she represents Defoe's ideal merchant. It is as a direct result of her engagement in trade that Roxana comes to call herself a *"Man-Woman,"* and that she is explicitly named as an "Amazon" (171) by Sir Robert Clayton (the only historical personage in the novel). In this context, Roxana rejects any form of subordination to men, in particular matrimony. She says:

I told him [Sir Robert Clayton], I knew no State of Matrimony, but what was, at best, a State of Inferiority, if not of Bondage; that I had no Notion of it; that I liv'd a Life of absolute Liberty now; was free as I was born, and having a plentiful Fortune, I did not

126

understand what coherence the Words *Honour* and *Obey* had with the Liberty of a *Free Woman*; that I knew no Reason Men had to engross the whole Liberty of the Race, and make the women, notwithstanding any disparity of Fortune, be subject to the Laws of Marriage, of their own making; that it was my Misfortune to be a woman, but I was resolv'd it shou'd not be made worse by the Sex; and seeing Liberty seem'd to be the Men's property, I wou'd be a *Man-Woman*; for as I was born free, I wou'd die so.

(170–1)

Roxana's elevation to the status of "She-Merchant" coincides with an extended attack on marriage, of which this brief discussion is only a final precis. She argues at length on the topic with the Dutch Merchant, who seeks to persuade her to marry him. The definition of female liberty that emerges from this discussion originates in a concern with financial control – she says: "tho' I cou'd give up my Virtue . . . yet I wou'd not give up my Money" (147) – and it ends in a radical assertion of sexual egalitarianism:

I return'd, that while a Woman was single, she was a Masculine in her politick Capacity; that she had then the full Command of what she had, and the full Direction of what she did; that she was a Man in her separated Capacity, to all Intents and Purposes that a Man cou'd be so to himself . . . it was my Opinion, a woman was as fit to govern and enjoy her own Estate, without a Man, as a Man was, without a woman; and that, if she had a mind to gratifie herself as to Sexes, she might entertain a Man, as a Man does a Mistress.

(148–9)

Not surprisingly, *Roxana* has been seen as a proto-feminist work, and for good reason.[30] At this, her most "feminist" moment, Roxana is also closest to Defoe's ideal of mercantile success; in claiming female liberty she maintains her right to control and increase her own profits. Indeed, Defoe connected liberty quite directly with a prosperous trade: he says in the *Review*, "among all the Advantages this Nation enjoys from Liberty, the Liberty of Trade is none the least, nor has it been any of the least Occasions of the growing Wealth of this Nation."[31] For Defoe, the right to free trade was essential to national prosperity; and trade itself was the ideal result of the cooperation of God, Providence, and Nature, dispensing mutual benefit over a variety of different customs and cultures, producing different species of things, and enabling nations of different climates and geographies to profit from each other's bounty. Money is the necessary medium of this utopic process, and the accumulation of money is the signal of its proper functioning.[32] But what is the status of a feminism derived from a passionate advocacy of mercantile capitalism, for Defoe or for us? And where does this Amazonian image lead?

To a supererogatory, Juvenalian violence. As an Amazon, Roxana figures a specific threat – violence – and that violence materializes at the end of the novel in the cold-blooded murder of her daughter by Amy, Roxana's surrogate and a successful "Woman of Business" in her own right (245). In a sense, the Amazon trope is simply following its scheduled trajectory. But the specific shape it receives from Defoe's narrative illuminates its function in eighteenth-century literary culture. Here, feminism issues in the most unwomanly form of violence – the murder of the woman's own child; that is, the logical conclusion of the extension of the ideal of mercantile capitalist profit to women is a brutal and uncontrollable violence, a violation of the supposedly natural and benevolent forces of trade. But trade itself has produced this Amazonian feminism. Through its evocation of the feminist Amazon, this text brings trade and violence into a symptomatically significant proximity. *Roxana*, like *The Rape of the Lock* and Juvenal's Sixth Satire, portrays an aggressively expansionist culture but omits any account of the "masculine violence" at its base. It is women who commit the violent acts in these works, never men. For Juvenal, the peace of the Roman empire was sustained by masculine violence, by a constant military presence at the periphery of the Roman world – in Britain, Africa, Arabia, and Egypt, and on the Danube, the Rhine, and the Euphrates. In the Sixth Satire, this continuous masculine violence is never mentioned, the "Victorious Arms" of Roman imperialism find a perverse proxy in the representation of the "women who thrive on masculine violence": "'Tis Arms and Blood and Cruelty they love." For Defoe, of course, the prosperity of the first age of English maritime imperialism was sustained by the slave-trade, the colonization of the West Indies and North America, the wars against the Native Americans, and the early colonial ventures in Africa and India. In *Roxana*, the explosion of aggressive energy and exploitation that characterized this early phase of mercantile capitalist adventurism emerges in the threatening figure of the "man-woman." In the image of the Amazon, then, we can catch sight of the violence that sustains empire, and we can see through the paired myths of peace and humanism that define and justify imperialist ideology.

The fully elaborated development of the Amazon motif in Defoe's novel produces a constellation of ideological contradictions, in which profit and murder, violence and empire, commodification and trade – with a proto-feminist female autonomy joined to all of these – are variously and reciprocally superimposed. One part of this process, as we have seen, produces a connection of empire and violence. The Amazon secretly comes to serve as a proxy for the imperialist: but in this process her private and local murder exposes his public and official violence. In the same way, commodification and trade are brought into an uncomfortable proximity. The figure of the commodified woman is a scapegoat for mercantile capitalist accumulation, serving to mask the male acquisit-iveness that fuels the energies of imperialism. But Roxana's metamor-phosis from a fetishized object into a merchant with her own profits makes that mask irrelevant: the she-merchant is no proxy, but an object of fetishization and an agent of exploitation at once, and this connection makes the alienating implications of accumulation and consumption the responsibility of the merchant and the product of mercantile capitalism. Through all these symptomatic contradictions, the category of female autonomy functions as the catalyst and in the process holds its own rendezvous with violence and receives its own repudiation. In this sense, then, the perceived threat of female equality betrays the historical alie-nation and brutality of the first age of English imperialism.

This conjunction of the Amazon with the representation of mercantile capitalist ideology suggests one way of understanding the function of misogynist writing in this period. The attack on women with which Defoe's narrative concludes can be referred, as we have seen, to a systematic unacknowledged connection of women and empire. The same connection can at least partly explain the misogyny implicit in *The Rape of the Lock* and, as I have argued elsewhere, the systematic attacks on women in Swift's poetry and in *Gulliver's Travels*.[33] Indeed, the attribution of commodification and violence to the female figure is the most common topic of misogynist literature in the eighteenth century. Significantly, the idealization of the woman as a repository of cultural value and meaning can also be linked to the same conjuncture, the implicit association of women with the acquisitive, progressivist, and civilizing enterprises of an expansionist culture. But in the early eigh-teenth century, at a time of comparative ideological consensus in England, when the benefits of empire were rarely disputed, it is in misogynist literature that the disturbing and disruptive effects of mer-cantile capitalism are felt. Perhaps this unacknowledged connection with the most significant and unresolvable problems of the age begins to explain the extraordinary, seemingly supererogatory violence of eighteenth-century satires on women. We might even argue – to take this point one step too far – that misogyny can find a perverse justifi-cation in its connection with imperialism, that the great misogynist statements of the eighteenth century stand in the place of an explicit critique of empire. Certainly in Defoe's case the unwitting critique with which the novel concludes seems to be generated by the misogynist turn of the narrative from female liberty to murder.

But the fighting female has yet another major role to play.

III

Prominent among the tropes that constructed the European understanding of racial difference in the long process of exploration, discovery, and exploitation that characterizes the extension of Western European culture over the globe from the Renaissance to the modern period is the recurrent description of a race of Amazons. The travel literature of this period is full of such accounts. Columbus in his journals recounts a discovery of warlike women with stores of gold or copper in the West Indies; narratives of Cortés's travels reproduce descriptions of wealthy Amazons in Mexico. Amazons with vast supplies of gold and silver were supposed to be found in the present-day Caribbean, Central America, Colombia, Peru, Chile, and in the Amazon basin.[34] Among the accounts retailed in one of the most widely circulated compendia of travel narratives in the period – *Purchas His Pilgrimes* – Amazons were described in Brazil and in the region of the Amazon river.[35] Walter Raleigh gives an account of Amazons he claims to document in Guyana:

> The nations of these women are on the South side of the river in the provinces of Topago, and their chiefest strengths and retracts are in the Islands situate on the South side of the entrance some 60 leagues within the mouth of the sayd river. The memories of the like women are very ancient as well in Africa as in Asia . . . in many histories they are verified to have bene, and in divers ages and provinces: but they which are not far from Guiana Doe accompany with men but once in a yere. . . . If they conceive, and be delivered of a sonne, they returne him to the father; if of a daughter they nourish it, and reteine it. . . . It was farther told me, that if in these warres they tooke any prisoners that they used to accompany with those also at what time soever, but in the end of certeine they put them to death: for they are sayd to be very cruell and bloodthirsty, especially to such as offer to invade their territories. These Amazones have likewise great store of these plates of gold.[36]

Various travelers place Amazons in parts of Africa, especially Ethiopia. Father Francisco Alvarez describes a race of warlike women in Ethiopia, a "kingdom of the Amazons":

> I was . . . assured, that on the Frontiers . . . as you travell toward the South there is a Kingdome governed by women, which may be called Amazones . . . they have no King but a Queene that hath no certaine Husband, but suffereth any man to lye with her, and to get her with child, and the eldest Daughter succeedeth in the Kingdome.

According to this account, "They gather great store of Gold in this

Kingdome" and their supplies serve as the source of the gold that is thence exported to other parts of Africa.[37] And elsewhere in *Purchas* we can find similar stories of African Amazons: in the report of Pigafetta's travels there is an empire in the Congo called Monomotapa, whose prize warriors are female legions: "These Women doe burne their left paps with fire, because they should be no hindrance unto them in their shooting, after the use and manner of the ancient Amazons." They too keep only their female children.[38] And also in *Purchas* Bermudez, another traveler to Ethiopia, has heard of Amazons there as well: "neere to Damute, [there is] a Province of women without men: which doe live after the manner of the ancient Amazones of Scythia."[39]

Throughout this period Amazons are purportedly sighted at the verges of European geographical penetration, and they are freqently possessed of the mythical precious metals that inspired those early dreams of exploitation. These Amazons are always warlike races, typically accomplished and bloodthirsty fighters who are often said to amputate or cauterize a breast in order better to use the bow. Their sexual arrangements are a common source of comment; they are sometimes said to have intercourse with male prisoners of war or at infrequent, prearranged times with neighboring tribes. By some reports, they return any male children to their fathers, and sometimes they are said to murder male offspring, a form of programmatic violence that is taken as another emblem of their unnatural and threatening brutality.

Raleigh and others allude to a venerable tradition that shapes these "discoveries" of warlike women: "the memories of [Amazons] *are* very ancient" [my italics] in Western European culture. In classical discourse Amazons serve as a figure for the uncivilized races beyond the boundaries of the known world – in Libya, Ethiopia, and Central Asia – and for the threat of barbarian invasion posed by those alien peoples. In the medieval period the story of an Amazon society entails an inversion of Western European social and cultural structures and thus defines the limits of social stability, and again this alien society is typically located in Ethiopia or in India. In representing their encounter with the worlds beyond Europe, their confrontation with the disorienting experience of geographical and racial otherness, the Renaissance chroniclers availed themselves of a version of the figure that had represented racial difference for over two millennia, locating and shaping that historically efficacious figure according to the new requirements of the expansionist ideology of Western European imperialism.

We have here a rather stark logical contradiction. The Amazon of one pervasive contemporary discourse is a figure for the native; but in another powerful canonical and popular construct, the Amazon is the *alter ego* of the male European imperialist. Finding this figure on both sides of the imperialist coin suggests that the Amazon functions as a strong common denominator in mercantile capitalist ideology: a common denominator for difference. I think our reading so far of the image of the female Amazon has given us the right to speculate a bit on the components of that common denominator. The woman and the native could be seen as equivalent categories in the construction of difference: both represent objects to be controled, manipulated, and exploited – economically as well as sexually, and thus they might fall together under the same figure. But also, both the female other and the native other evoke a complex social, political, and sexual threat, a threat compactly realized in and constituted by the Amazon image. Roxana, as we have seen, comes to control the profits accruing from the exploitation of her body, and so moves from an object of commodification to an agent of trade. And natives, too, might be seen as potential agents in their own context. To the extent that they are viewed as possessing their own land and property – in particular gold and precious metals, they might move from exploited object to threatening agent in their own right. As Raleigh says, "they are . . . very cruell and bloodthirsty, especially to such as offer to invade their territories." That is, the category of difference in this period embraces duplicitously both object and agent, exploitation and resistance. We can approach the structure of this ambiguity through a final reading of the representation of the African and of the relation between difference and trade in Defoe's *Captain Singleton*.

This diffuse novel falls into roughly two parts. The first, initiated by a mutiny, describes the travels of a small group of European sailors across the African continent from present-day Mozambique to Guinea (or West Africa), their encounters with the natives, and their discovery, mining, and accumulation of gold. By Singleton's account, the European adventurers are the first human beings in the African landscape. The narrative repeatedly asserts that "Never Man, nor a Body of Men" crossed the desert they encountered before they did; "no human Hands" fished in the great lake they find in their way.[40] These Eurocentric assertions of discovery directly contradict the narrative's simultaneous accounts of the populousness of the country. The Africans are ubiquitous and significant in the novel. In contrast to the countryside, which is represented as "very pleasant and fruitful, and a convenient Place enough to live in," the Africans are typically described as "a Parcel of Creatures scarce human, or capable of being made sociable on any Account whatsoever" (21). Because they are not seen as human, their difference – racial or otherwise – from the European adventurers is at first barely recognized; they form a part of the landscape like the trees, rivers, and hills (73). Though they are heard to speak, they seem to have no intelligible language (48); their speech is confused with animal noises (81, 107); and if they can be made to communicate, they use only signs in response to the Europeans' speech (82). The Africans whom the travelers manage to domesticate and who travel with them as guides and cargo-bearers, occupy two categories. Either they are Europeanized – like the Black Prince, an Oroonoko-like character endowed with a chivalric notion of honor and heroic accomplishments to match. Or they are the crucial figures in maximizing gold accumulation; they point it out to the travelers variously throughout their journey, and they perform the labor essential to its extraction.

The centrality of gold in the African section of *Captain Singleton* is a significant anachronism. At the time of the novel's writing – in 1720 – and also at the time of its setting – about twenty years earlier – gold was much less significant than slaves in the African trade. In this novel and in his numerous periodical essays on the Royal African Company (between 1709 and 1713), Défoe writes almost exclusively about the accumulation of gold.[41] Slavery is an occasional matter, subsidiary often to the discovery and extraction of the African gold. This anachronism need not suggest that slavery was a problematic issue for Defoe; but the focus on gold does seem to indicate that primitive accumulation and its logical extension into trade occupy a crucial position in the text. Significantly, it is mainly in relation to precious metals that the subjectivity of the natives arises. That is, the point at which the Africans briefly acquire human status – albeit of a negative sort – occurs in their relationship to these vast supplies of gold with which they are surrounded. They are fools for not knowing its worth; and fools are human. Even though the explorers acknowledge that gold is of no use without trade (127), and even though the acquisitiveness which it inspires is also occasionally associated with Satan through the kind of moralistic anachronism typical in Defoe's writings (131), each time the Africans innocently direct the travelers to deposits of gold which they show no interest in possessing themselves, or choose some more useful metal over golden ornaments (93, 107), they are made to seem strikingly defective in discernment. On these occasions, they are treated not as trees or beasts, but as human beings remarkable for their difference from the Europeans. The implicit assumption of the narrative at these points is that trade defines civilization; and that an understanding of exchange value is inherently superior to a dependence on use value. Civilization and racial superiority are thus associated with exchange value. Trade and money are the catalysts here, producing the text's only acknowledgment of racial difference in the context of an assertion of racial superiority. We might say that trade, or the potential for trade, transforms the natives from trees or beasts into human others – just as the association with trade transforms Roxana from an object of commodification to a figure of female autonomy.

The African section of *Captain Singleton* is succeeded by a long second half recounting Singleton's exploits as a pirate. The account of piracy

133

has the same telos as the African travels of the first section: the accumulation of riches. Both represent the aspiration to subject the world to capitalist exchange. Like the travelers of the first half, the pirates are single-mindedly devoted to the pursuit of profit; so much so that the narrative of their exploits and adventures is notably tame, focusing exclusively upon the goods and riches they accumulate. Appropriately, most of the wealth they carry off is the intercepted product of imperial trade with what we would now call the Third World. In short, *Captain Singleton*'s piracy – "the Plunder of so many innocent . . . Nations" (266) – is another redaction of European mercantile capitalism. This is a version of the common contemporary process, in this period of early capitalist development, by which an apparently erratic and private form of exploitation becomes a legitimate and official dimension of imperialist expansion.[42] Indeed, *Singleton*'s pirates are interchangeable with traders. The Quaker William serves as the linking figure between piracy and trade. He acts as the pirates' trading agent on more than one occasion (250), and he makes it clear that money is the real goal of their enterprise:

> Why, says *William* gravely, I only ask what is thy Business, and the Business of all the people thou hast with thee? Is it not to get Money? Yes, *William*, it is so, in our honest Way: And wouldst thou, says he, rather have Money without Fighting, or Fighting without Money? O *William, says I*, the first of the two, to be sure.
>
> (153–4)

From this perspective, he can argue against attacks on some unruly natives at Java, explaining "your Business is Money" (219) rather than vengeance. And he can, when profit calls, trade in slaves (164) despite his sympathy for the Negroes taken in a slave ship earlier in the narrative (157, 160). Thus William functions as an exemplar of capitalist ideology, programmatically subordinating morality to profit and ingeniously increasing the pirates' profit at every turn. He merges unobtrusively with the pirates, or emerges unobtrusively from them, first claiming he is made a pirate by force, then claiming he is a pacifist (144, 212), but swiftly making their work his own. The pirates, like Roxana, are protected morally by association with the Quaker, and this trick helps save the image of rapacious accumulation from criticism. William, then, functions as one of the means by which the ideology of capitalist expansion systematically obscures its necessary racism, violence, and exploitation through claims of egalitarianism and benevolence.

But just as it makes the pirates traders, this superimposition of piracy and trade makes all traders pirates. That is, it connects an illicit form of violence with the supposedly benevolent official processes of capitalist accumulation. Like *Roxana*, then, *Captain Singleton* systematically converts its protagonist's primary activity into trade, and in the process functions to reveal the necessary violence of imperialist ideology. Trade is the common denominator between *Singleton*'s two parts, integrating the acquisition of gold (in Africa) and goods (through piracy) as joint dimensions of the urgent enterprise of primary accumulation. And again as in *Roxana*, the association of trade and violence governs the unconscious structure of the novel. For both narratives, the figure of difference is constituted through this treatment of trade. The Africans become significantly other only through reference to their gold, just as Roxana becomes an Amazon through becoming a merchant, which is accordingly and paradoxically the source of her otherness. Ironically, the more a male, mercantile sensibility is attributed to Roxana, the more threatening and different she becomes. And the natives in *Captain Singleton* become more different the closer they come to a capitalist concept of trade and exchange. That is, the difference both of the native Amazon and of the female Amazon is a product of their relation to empire. In this sense, *Roxana* evokes the other within, the disruptive power of a category of difference internal to the dominant ideology. And *Singleton* reveals the other without the gates, measuring and taming difference with the European yardstick and bludgeon of accumulation.

IV

Under the sign of difference, the Amazon illuminates a whole constellation of ideological categories and functions. As a proxy or scapegoat, the representation of difference serves discursively to deflect the responsibilities and anxieties of empire. That process of deflection itself – by which the other takes on the powers of the merchant or the potential to engage in exchange – functions to demystify imperialist ideology. Dressed thus by deflection in the guise of power, the Amazon briefly serves to formulate a discourse of radical difference, a feminist reading of the bourgeois category of liberty. The repudiation of that radical critique is in turn a catalyst for the demystification of imperialist ideology. Finally, as a figure for the other, the image of the Amazon includes and thus conjoins both women and natives. This conjunction is founded on the discursive proximity of difference and trade, and that proximity in turn serves as the grounding prerequisite for the various odd configurations in the dramatization of imperialist ideology that this reading of the figure of the Amazon has enabled us to observe.

I raised two issues at the outset of this essay. The first was a specific question: does the fact that we have viewed the Amazon through the discourse of the dominant ideology make any account of resistance or subversion of that ideology inaccessible to us? If we generalize from this question, we can arrive first at the other issue to which I promised to return. That is, if we ask abstractly how this essay figures as a form of radical political criticism, we can begin to propose a political purpose for recent "political" readings.

One purpose of this particular reading resides in part in the recovery and representation of a critical position relevant to a progressive politics – the argument for female liberty. The advocacy of women's liberty as a product of the advocacy of exploitation might seem a violation of the supposedly egalitarian assumptions of a liberationist critique, even if the ultimate repudiation of female autonomy did not seem to make its original assertion irrelevant. In other words, how can we use a feminism that comes out of imperialism and that is so vehemently disowned by its author? We can use it to open up the argument for bourgeois liberty upon which much modern feminism depends; it shows us that the female liberty defined by Roxana is the logical extension of the bourgeois ideal of a universalist humanism that underlies the notion of free enterprise and economic individualism. And it casts light on the radical potential of that ideal just as it provides a cautionary indication of its limitations. It enables us to engage the important and politically useful question of the extent to which the argument for female liberty can be disentangled from capitalist ideology.

This reading can also be used symptomatically, as political demystification rather than recovery. We have seen through this account of the Amazon how ideology functions to incorporate or subsume categories of difference and turn them to its own ends; how an ideology that seems hegemonic and self-justifying unwittingly produces its own negation; how the universalist perspective of a dominant ideology might be fissured or flawed. In this way, a reading of the dramatization of an ostensibly monolithic ideology can provide various forms of leverage, various sightings of alternative categories, various points of contention that displace, disorient, or disrupt that discourse. Ends like these might justify the complex process of explication through which modern essays in "political" criticism – like this one – construct literary culture.

But I would like to conclude with a further, more speculative possibility, which I will raise in partial answer to the question of the limitation of our perspective to the view of the imperialist. Perhaps this argument indicates that even in the context of the dramatization of an oppressive ideology representations of difference cannot be suppressed. The use of the marginal as a proxy for power, while it seems a perfect act of appropriation, might trigger the potential for subversion, however ambiguously it is realized. Furthermore, the Amazon, in occupying the position both of the native other and of the female other and functioning in both places to expose the universalist humanism of imperialist

136

ideology, might mark an instance of joint disruption, a point of articulation where a common system of oppression encounters a common resistance. This point of articulation, if we can reach it, might take "political" critics beyond political readings to a liberationist politics.

8

THE OTHER WOMAN
Polygamy, *Pamela*, and the prerogative of empire

Felicity Nussbaum

It is manifest that there is a necessity of sacrificing one part of womanhood to preserve the other.

Bernard Mandeville,
A Modest Defence of the Public Stews (1724)

Nay, don't give us India. That puts me in mind of Montesquieu, who is really a fellow of genius too in many respects; whenever he wants to support a strange opinion, he quotes you the practice of Japan or of some other distant country, of which he knows nothing. To support polygamy, he tells you of the island of Formosa, where there are ten women born for one man. He had but to suppose another island, where there are ten men born for one woman, and so make a marriage between them.

Samuel Johnson in Boswell's
The Journal of a Tour to the Hebrides (1785)

"Africa is indeed coming into fashion," Horace Walpole wrote to Sir Horace Mann in July 1774 upon James Bruce's return from Abyssinia. In January 1799 Mungo Park's *Travels in the Interior Districts of Africa* was a best-seller.[1] Its 1,500 copies sold out within a few months, and three other editions were issued before the.end of the year. Translated into French and German and published in an American edition as well, the book testified to the appetite for consuming Africa, including its representations, its raw goods, and its human commodity, slaves. As Robin Hallett has written, "By 1750 no countryhouse library could be reckoned complete without one of those great multi-volumed *Collections of Travels*,"[2] and Africa, the unknown continent, nearly always figured prominently in these collections. European ignorance about West Africa persisted until increased trade prompted penetration beyond the coast, and Mungo Park's narrative especially sparked the imagination of layperson and merchant, scientist and missionary. Joseph Banks, himself a voyager and the treasurer of the African Association, wrote that Park had opened a road "for every nation to enter and extend its commerce and discovery from the west to the eastern side of that immense continent."[3] And the Preface to a book which was part of Joseph Banks' library, *A New Voyage to Guinea* (1744), acknowledges that it aims to satisfy the public's appetite for the foreign:

> The present Curiosity of the Publick for whatever may contribute to the rendring the Produce of distant Countries and the Manners of Foreign Nations, fully and certainly known, was what encourag'd the Publication of this Work. . . . There is no Part of the World with which we are less acquainted than the interior Part of *Africa*.[4]

Willem Bosman anticipated these ideas in his voyage to New Guinea written earlier in the century: "But 'twas an ancient Saying among the Romans, that *Africa* always produces something *New*; and to this day the Saying is very just."[5] Africa and its products, material and human, sold well in the expanding market, and it was regarded as a welcome producer of the new and the novel.

These travel accounts encouraged commerce deeper into the unmapped interior, and European manufactures were sent to West Africa in exchange for African slave labor in the Americas. As was characteristic of the larger print world in the eighteenth century, explorers' accounts were seldom dependent on patronage for publication and more exactly aimed at writing for an anonymous market.[6] As "Africa" was invented and consumed, the printed word about it gained a commodity status. Africa was increasingly included in the extraordinarily popular collections of travels in spite of the fact that the same accounts were often simply reprinted or slightly altered before Park's monumental voyages at the end of the century. Compelling information or fantasy, recycled as new, produced the desire for more such travel narratives and novels, even though very little new information emerged after the travels of Labat in 1725 and Moore in 1738, apparently because the urge to exploit Africa's wealth was not sufficient to overcome the obstacles to penetration.[7] Though the struggle for power over West Africa (colonized by the Portuguese, French, English, and Dutch) was intense in the eighteenth century, Africa's interior remained largely unmapped by Europeans. In short, the commercial market, especially in the mid- and late eighteenth century, gave evidence of a passion to consume the unknown and uncharted, the "new" blank space of Africa.

When the human object of obtaining something "new" from Africa speaks, however, as in the case of Ignatius Sancho, an African living in England, it is with incredulity, anger, and contempt for the misuse of his land and people. Sancho writes in his letters (1782),

> The grand object of English navigators – is money – money – money – for which I do not pretend to blame them – Commerce

attended with strict honesty – and with Religion for its companion – would be a blessing to every shore it touched at. – [but] In Africa, the poor wretched natives – blessed with the most fertile and luxuriant soil – are rendered so much the more miserable for what Providence meant as a blessing: – The Christians' abominable traffic for slaves – and the horrid cruelty and treachery of the petty Kings – encouraged by their Christian customers. . . . But enough – it is a subject that sours my blood.[8]

The European pleasure in consuming Africa exacted a high cost.

Power relations between the nations, between the colonizer and the colonized, may also be regarded as power relations between the sexes, "races," and classes. Here I want to consider one aspect of those power relations, the consumption of the Other with particular attention to the production and consumption of the Other woman. I mean to define this Other woman both geographically and sexually – that is, the African woman who is the "'other' of the 'other,'"[9] doubly colonized, *and* the Other woman of polygamy, women who make Others of each other in competition for the male prize. Focusing on women and polygamy as central terms in the expanding empire offers an alternative way of understanding history.

Polygamy is a multiplicity of practices that may set women against each other or, contradictorily, may bond them together in collective pleasure and mutual benefit. Polygamy in the eighteenth century was defined as a husband's taking more than one wife, marrying after the death of his first wife, and even his seducing a woman while married to another and therefore being responsible for her ruin. Johnson's *Dictionary* (1755) explains polygamy as "a plurality of wives," but polygamy may also mean simply having sexual commerce with more than one woman on an ongoing basis. As Caleb Fleming writes in *Oeconomy of the Sexes . . . the Plurality of Wives* (1751)

> I shall use the term, *polygamy*, for a man's having more than one wife at one and the same time; without any regard to the term bigamy or digamy [a second legal marriage after the death of the first spouse]: because monogamy be transgressed, for the same reason that a man has two wives, he might have twenty.[10]

England's national imperative to control women's sexuality in the later eighteenth century derives in part from the increasing demands of colonization. Further, polygamy brings together issues of gender, empire, and sovereignty to negotiate the erotic and the exotic. I want to explore some of the profound historical contradictions that emerge when polygamy, a crux of desire and domination, is invoked in British travel narratives of West Africa, the polygamy tracts of eighteenth-century England, and Samuel Richardson's *Pamela*.

In spite of the century's passion to create taxonomies of the species and maps of every colonial territory, the Other can never be fully "known" except in reference to the self. If imperialism uses the Other to consolidate the imperialist self, the Other also consolidates the European woman. "Colonial power produces the colonized as a fixed reality which is at once an 'other' and yet entirely knowable and visible," Homi Bhabha argues.[11] The European woman is doubly removed from these travel narratives because, in large part, she is represented rather than speaking. It is her civic duty to reproduce, and maternity, especially at midcentury, displaces her sexuality. The domestic monogamous Englishwoman, an emblem of maternal womanhood, frequently contrasts to the wanton polygamous Other.

The African woman is even less likely than the Englishwoman to represent herself. Africa is frequently, of course, represented visually as a woman, a scorched and naked mother under the heat of the sun, flanked by devil and lion, carrying gifts to Europe, a pharaoh's head and pyramids in the background, and tropical trees behind (figure 8.1).[12] It has become a current understanding that the eighteenth century is a time when "Africa" was invented for European consumption, but what has been less recognized is the way in which the African *woman* was invented as well as made coherent and consistent, especially in relation to the European domestic woman. Woman, like Africa, is something to be defined, charted, probed, exploited, and overcome. Metaphors of seduction, penetration, and conquest permeate the language of colonialism to define taming the wild exotic, and especially the imagined unbridled sexuality of the Other.

The notion of a separate history of women becomes particularly prominent during the eighteenth century, and women also figure so significantly that they are sometimes called the barometer of civilization.[13] Woman's status, whether she is a laborer or a leisured person, is often taken as the measure of a society's achievement. By some accounts, a past golden age of ideal womanhood existed, and education corrupted the noble savage woman after that lost moment of perfection. Alternative accounts claim the opposite: that civilization brought progress, and that woman's nature has been steadily improving from a base originary point. Contemporary eighteenth-century Englishwomen exemplified the superiority of a commercial and manufacturing society over a pastoral or primitive society that does not have the leisure to treat its hard-working women well. Montesquieu, Adam Ferguson, William Robertson, John Millar, and others argued for woman's improved status in "civilized" society. In these conflicting accounts of loss or progress, the indigenous woman, like the Englishwoman, was both the worst and the best of nature.

Figure 8.1 Frontispiece by G. Child to *A New General Collection of Voyages and Travels*, Volume II (London, 1745) 4 vols [compiled by John Green?] (London, 1745–7). Reproduced by permission of the British Library.

Discussions of polygamy in England were nearly as common as discussions of divorce, and notables such as William Cowper, Lord Chancellor of England, defended polygamy in order to vindicate his own *ménage à trois*. Bishop Burnet, Bernardino Ochino, Lord Bolingbroke, Patrick Delany, and the Deists also took up the pressing questions surrounding the timely issue.[14] In *Reflections Upon Polygamy* (1737) the pseudonymous P. Dubliniensis writes, "Polygamy is a doctrine daily defended in conversation, and often in print, by a great variety of *plausible* arguments."[15] Polygamy negotiates the distance between Englishwomen and their Others in the imagined present of the (European) eighteenth century and its reified notions of the primitive. Polygamy is treated in remarkably benign ways in the African travel accounts before missionary zeal began to preach monogamy as a tenet of colonization. John Millar's treatise draws distinctions between polygamy in "opulent and luxurious nations" and "barbarous countries." In the former women are reduced to slavery by polygamous practices. Further, children are so numerous that paternal affection is severely diminished, wives demonstrate great jealousy amongst each other, and they are strictly regulated by the father/husband. On the contrary "in barbarous countries, where it is introduced to a great measure from motives of conveniency, and where it is accompanied with little or no jealousy, it cannot have the same consequences."[16]

The popular African narratives nearly always mention polygamy or, in a few instances, its remarkable absence. Most notable is Olaudah Equiano, who reports of his native Ibo tribe that "The men . . . do not preserve the same constancy to their wives, which they expect from them; for they indulge in a plurality, though seldom in more than two."[17] Jerom Merolla da Sorrento comments about the Congo that

> Every one of these Negroes takes to wife as many women, be they slaves or free, it is no matter, as he can possibly get: these women, by his consent, make it their business to charm men to their embraces.

Moore and Stibbs remark that every man may take as many wives as he wishes, even up to a hundred, in the Gambia, and Barbot says that "as many wives as he can keep" enhances a Guinean man's reputation. Grazilhier comments that every man in Guinea "may have as many Wives as he pleases." William Smith reports that men may take as many wives as they want in Barbary, as many as they can maintain in Cape Monte, that there is much polygamy in Dahomey, and that wives are a measure of status from the ordinary man's 40–50 to the King's 4,000–5,000. He finds, following Alexander and Millar, that such practices are vestiges of an earlier time.[18] Sometimes distinctions between wives and concubines are reported, though not always. In some instances, polygamy is presented as commercially sound, and the wives are treated as inheritable property. The women work excessively hard in the field and in the bed, and all the wives, except the rich man's foremost two, may prostitute themselves to other men. In other cases, a wife's infidelity is grounds for selling her to the Europeans.

William Smith's *Voyage to Guinea* follows the popular assumption that African women are excessively sexual, the climate rendering the African coast and interior a torrid zone:

> As for all the rest, they may be accounted little better than his Slaves, nevertheless they live in Peace together without envying each other's Happiness, and he in their Turns, renders to them all, if able, due Benevolence: But if that be not sufficient for those hot constitution'd Ladies, they very well know how to supply such Defects elsewhere, without fearing any check from the Husband, who generally makes himself easy in those Cases, provided he duly receives such Profits.
>
> (146)

According to Paul Lovejoy's recent findings, women slaves for export apparently cost up to one-third more than men in spite of the greater supply of women. Lovejoy's explanation for this disparity is that women are in greater demand as sexual objects:

> The extraction of surplus labour is certainly a factor in explaining why the price of female slaves was greater than that for males. . . . Women worked hard at most tasks, and sometimes they could be made to work harder than males. But women's "work" also included sexual services.[19]

William Smith also comments that polygamy helped propagate bodies for slavery and allowed explorers to take sexual advantage of the indigenous population – "a man sometimes in one Day [may] . . . have Half a Dozen Children born to him" (202) because the polygamous men do not live with pregnant or menstruous wives. Frances Moore writes of the willingness of the Gambian women:

> The Girls would have People think they are very modest, especially when they are in Company; but take them by themselves, and they are very obliging . . . if any White Man has a Fancy to any of them, and is able to maintain them, they will make no Scruple of living with him in the Nature of a Wife, without the Ceremony of Matrimony.
>
> (121)

Smith adds, "Most of the Women are publick Whores to the *Europeans*, and private ones to the *Negroes*" (213). The women

144

miss no Opportunity [for sex, he writes], and are continually contriving stratagems how to gain a Lover. If they meet with a Man they immediately strip his lower Parts, and throw themselves upon him, protesting that if he will not gratify their Desires, they will accuse him to their Husbands.

(221)

Claiming this kind of seduction, Smith of course takes an African woman for his own. Polygamy, Smith suggests, varies not so greatly from European practices under the guise of courtship: "We often spend several Years therin [in courtship]; in which we at one Time, address this young Woman, write to that, and keep criminal Conversation with a Third" (260). Smith elides the differences among sexual practices, and his point is to show the superiority of Europeans while allowing for the strange excellence of "savage" ways. Smith concludes his account with a description of a paradisial liaison, "At Midnight we went to Bed, and in that Situation I soon forgot the Complexion of my Bedfellow, and obey'd the Dictates of all-powerful Nature. Greater Pleasure I never found" (254).

The sexual traffic between European men and African women is much remarked upon in the British travel voyages, as is the troubling question of color. For John Barbot too the women of Guinea are also proud and lascivious, seeking to attract Europeans even at a small profit: "such manner as might prove sufficiently tempting to many lewd *Europeans*; who not regarding complexions, say, *all cats are grey in the dark*" (239). (Barbot also notes that most Europeans keep three or four women "as if they were marry'd to them," 36). This trope of the European male congratulating himself for ignoring the color of his female bedmate in the dark is common in these accounts. Color is very much on the minds of the travelers with fantastic reports of spotted or mottled women, children who are half black and half white, twins in which one is black and the other white, and children born white who turn tawny or black in a matter of time, all presented as accurate history. In male sexual desire the color of the bedfellow is erased, and men's sexual oppression of women is justified by their assertion of the absence of racism. Portraying African women, especially the wives of other men, as unabashedly seductive and unclaimed for monogamy was necessary for European travelers who were impregnating African women and fathering illegitimate children of mixed race. Similarly the issue of polygamy becomes grimly relevant when we remember that white slaveowners participated in unacknowledged polygamy and used the slave woman's womb for increasing the slave population. Harriet Jacobs's *Incidents in the Life of a Slave Girl*, though written in the nineteenth century, gives voice to the slave woman's perspective: "Southern [white]

women often marry a [white] man knowing that he is the father of many
little slaves. They do not trouble themselves about it. They regard such
children as property, as marketable as the pigs on the plantation."[20] In
short, one threat of polygamy is that it makes legal, visible, and public
what has gone on all along – serial monogamy and especially adultery by
white men who claim African women as their sexual property and who
wish to bring to market their progeny in such unions. Polygamy is
further justified as a practical solution to slavery's disruption of family
life in *Some Historical Account of Guinea, its Situation, Produce, and the
General Disposition of its Inhabitants with an Inquiry into the Rise and Progress
of the Slave Trade* (1788) when male slaves are wrenched from their wives
and children and taken to another state.

In Henry Neville's popular erotic novella *The Isle of Pines*, the political
rule of the polygamous protagonist is also a sexual monopoly.[21] First
published in 1668, and reissued thirty times in six languages during the
eighteenth century, the novella recounts the prince's tale of shipwreck
and being left with four women. His polygamous relationship with all of
them repopulates the island. Polygamy here is figured as male magnani-
mity in spreading the sexual wealth to his sex-starved female com-
panions. He writes,

> Idleness and Fulness of every thing begot in me a desire of enjoy-
> ing the women, beginning now to grow more familiar, I had
> perswaded two Maids to let me lie with them, which I did at first in
> private, but after, custome taking away shame (there being none
> but us) we did it more openly, as our Lusts gave us liberty; after-
> wards my Masters Daughter was content also to do as we did; the
> truth is they were all handsome Women when they had Cloathes,
> and well shaped, feeding well. For we wanted no Food, and living
> idlely, and seeing us at Liberty to do our wills, without hope of ever
> returning home made us thus bold.
>
> (12)

Racial difference becomes something to reckon with, though class seems
less significant:

> One of the first of my Consorts with whom I first accompanied (the
> tallest and handsomest) proved presently with child, the second
> was my Masters Daughter, and the other also not long after fell into
> the same condition: none now remaining but my *Negro* who seeing
> what we did, longed also for her share; one Night, I being asleep,
> my *Negro*, (with the consent of the others) got close to me.

"I," he continues, "willing to try the difference, satisfied my self with
her" (12). The shipwrecked group enact the ultimate male fantasy as the
women become the breeders and he the stud: "So that in the year of our

being here, all my women were with child by me, and they all coming at different seasons, were a great help to one another" (12). The issue here is sexuality rather than maternity. Race and class, subordinate to fulfilling the fantasy of male sexual desire and voyeurism, are erased as the passionate women become interchangeable in the hero's mind. These and other discourses of polygamy locate the (sexual) passion to colonize the Other in the body of the woman.

Polygamy serves both as a male fantasy and as an economic rationale for deploying female sexuality. Eroticizing having more than one wife makes polygamy into a sexual practice and tends to obscure its economic uses. If one considers these matters within the context of nascent empire, rather than simply the English scene, Martin Madan's massive 1780 vindication of polygamy, ostensibly written to protect seduced women, becomes nuanced in surprising ways.[22] Those who argue in defense of polygamy, and those who argue against it, often claim to have the woman's interests at heart. William Cowper's cousin, Madan incited a controversy of over two dozen responses. Madan's ill-received book espouses the views published a decade before by his great-uncle, Lord Chancellor Cowper. In spite of his having been an enormously popular preacher, Madan was forced to resign as the chaplain of the Lock Hospital because of the resulting controversy.

Madan's *Thelyphthora* proposes polygamy as a serious solution to an epidemic of seduction or female ruin. Polygamy becomes a means to deal with excess females and to dispose of their living carcasses which become wastage after consumption. In the explorers' accounts and also in England there is a kind of litany concerning the loss of control over female sexuality, and it is particularly troublesome in its *public* manifestations. Prostitutes are visible everywhere: "our streets abound with prostitutes and our stews with harlots at present and the crimes of *adultery* and *seduction* are grown to an enormous height."[23] Richard Hill believed that Madan's proposal would actually *increase* the number of prostitutes. "Prostitutes swarm in the streets of this metropolis to such a degree," writes Saunders Welch,

> and bawdy-houses are kept in such an open and public manner, to the great scandal of our civil polity, that a stranger would think that such practices, instead of being prohibited had the sanction of the legislature, and that the whole town was one general stew.[24]

Polygamy resolves "the woman problem," and is a way to deal with the public embarrassment of unmarried and ruined women who show themselves in the street. Yet *Thelyphthora* was paradoxically crucial in fixing the monogamous family and in claiming private property. Madan proposes to control women's excess sexual passion in the purported cause of alleviating women's oppression, while those who oppose him

147

also cite emergent feminist sentiments in defense of women's investment in monogamy.

Another important justification for polygamy is to relieve the sexual deprivation of men, especially when eighteenth-century middle-class women are being urged to suckle their own children for long periods of time. As is well known, the practice of women's nursing their own children, rather than giving them over to a wetnurse, was firmly reinstituted during the eighteenth century. Sexual intercourse was discouraged during nursing as spoiling the milk, men's sexual deprivation became the object of concern, and sexuality was separated from maternity. (Not surprisingly, the question of women's sexual deprivation during this time seldom arose.) These matters became subject to comment when British voyagers represented foreign practices as exemplary or instructive to Englishwomen. John Matthews, for example, in his *A Voyage to the River Sierra-Leone* (1788) commends the domesticity and attentive maternity of the women:

> They never wean their children till they are able to walk . . . for, during the time a child is at the breast, the woman is not permitted to cohabit with her husband, as they suppose it would be prejudicial to her milk.[25]

David Hume's essay on the subject, while it finally argues against polygamy, treats it as potentially releasing men from their extreme passions for women by allowing them to indulge them to the fullest.[26] Hume openly acknowledges the political nature of sexual mores. Dividing and conquering the women who quarrel for his favors, the polygamist resembles a sovereign who politically manipulates one group against another in order to maintain his power. By analogy then, the best ruler is the monogamist who manages to keep his authority without pitting one wife or one faction against another. Similarly Mungo Park in his *Travels in the Interior Districts of Africa* sets up a paradigm of benevolent colonialism through the metaphor of polygamy. Park observes that husbands hold complete command, but the wives do not resent it, and in fact remain cheerful and compliant. The husband is not cruel, but the community supports his right to mete out punishment. Polygamy encourages women to quarrel, and the husband rules, judges, and punishes. "When the [African] wives quarrel among themselves, a circumstance which, from the nature of their situation, must frequently happen, the husband decides between them; and sometimes finds it necessary to administer a little corporal chastisement," he writes. In these public hearings, the wife's complaint is seldom taken seriously, and if she protests "the magic rod of *Mumbo Jumbo* soon puts an end to the business."[27]

The British travelers in Africa and elsewhere had considerable investment in reporting that polygamy was completely acceptable to the women involved. Polygamy may have encouraged female companionship and allowed an excess population of women to be protected through marriage, but it seems especially tied to patriarchal practices in most of its manifestations. Polygamy becomes a way for the enervated man to regain sovereignty through his sexual and political authority over his female property. England's toying with and ultimate rejection of polygamy near the end of the eighteenth century is part of the nation's defining itself both as distinct from and morally superior to the polygamous Other. Monogamy is instituted as part of England's national definition, and whatever practices its explorers might find to tempt them in other worlds, England asserts its public stance that marriage means one man, one wife, at least in law. As David Hume writes, "The exclusion of polygamy and divorces sufficiently recommends our present European practice with regard to marriage" (195).

II

I want to turn now to Richardson's *Pamela* II (1741) as a local instance of English monogamy and the tensions between women set in play to sustain monogamy's public face before turning finally to three Englishwomen's views of the Other woman. In Richardson's hastily composed sequel to the popular *Pamela*, *Pamela* II, a penchant for polygamy is one of Mr B's peculiarities. By "polygamy" Mr B seems to mean an adulterous affair – sexual relations with more than one woman – and the tantalizing possibility of keeping both available to him. *Pamela* II is a response to the commodification of the novel and the need to purchase another when the first has been consumed. According to Richardson's biographers Eaves and Kimpel, "By January 1741 the whole town had read *Pamela* I and by the summer Richardson had determined to write a sequel to counter a spurious continuation."[28] The first version, like the first wife, is somehow not sufficient to the desire – though of course Pamela proves her virtue and sufficiency at the cost of the sauciness that enlivened and complicated Part I. The Pamela of the sequel replays Otherness on the domestic rather than the African terrain. Pamela II is as unchanging in her maternity and virtue as the Pamela of the first part is volatile, maddening, and uncertain in her sexuality. Part II, as Terry Castle has shown, offers "a paradoxical kind of textual doubling" to its predecessor.[29] Part II revises and refutes Part I's empowering of Pamela and places her within a more familiar sexual traffic in which women are a form of exchange between men. Pamela II is also a polygamous second wife to Mr B in a realization of the driving fantasy of providing different women for different functions. In *Pamela* I this was already displayed in his liaison with Sally Godfrey and mani-

149

fested in the embodiment of Mr B's illegitimate daughter. In *Pamela* II Mr B meets Pamela's demand for breastfeeding with his own threat of "that vile word *polygamy*."[30] This debate centers on Pamela's belief that it is her natural duty, and thus a divine duty, to nurse her child, but "if the husband is set upon it, it is a wife's duty to obey" (III.48). Appealing to scriptural, legal, medical, natural, and parental authority, she musters considerable argument to insist on her duty to the child. To do otherwise, she believes, would be to indulge in "the sin of committing that task to others, which is so right to be performed by one's self" (III.50). But Mr B defines the question as one of hierarchy and priority – is the husband's will to be honored as superior to divine or natural law? How much authority over his wife does a husband have? Pamela wonders to her friend Miss Darnford, "Could you ever have thought, my dear, that husbands have a dispensing power over their wives, which kings are not allowed over the laws?" (III.5). Male sexual desire is coded as male sexual prerogative boldly intertwined with the political.

In the sequel Pamela (Mrs B) becomes the ideal wife who limits the demands of maternity in order to be sexually available to her husband. The wetnurse, a virtual double for Pamela, assumes those aspects of the maternal which threaten Mr B's sexual prerogative and keep the two functions of the breast distinct. Pamela is tormented everywhere she turns by other women who are under Mr B's control: he flirts with Pamela's nemesis, the Countess, with whom he travels, dallies, and converses in Italian. Pamela daily confronts a reminder of Mr B's sexual liaison with Sally Godfrey in the presence of their child Miss Goodwin; and Pamela herself is confined within Mr B's increasingly intense strictures to submit her will to him. No longer the Pamela of the first book who can withstand male prerogative, she withdraws into the tempering of her "self."

For Mr B the issue is both class privilege and male prerogative. He wishes to prevent Pamela's descending to her origins. He fears that she will become "an insipid, prattling nurse . . . a fool and a baby herself" (III.56), absorbed in the nursery instead of learning French and Latin. Calling on patriarchal authorities, Mr B teases Pamela with the threat of polygamy but then retreats:

> The laws of one's own country are a sufficient objection to me against polygamy: at least, I will not think of any more wives till you convince me, by your adherence to the example given you by the patriarch wives, that I ought to follow those of the patriarch husbands.
>
> (III.53)

When Pamela intones, "*Polygamy* and *prerogative*! Two very bad words! I

150

do not love them," Mr B demands that she ought to be angelic about this, rather than a *mere woman*.

Until Pamela becomes pregnant, there is little to say about the virtuous domestic married woman, no story to be told. Polygamy seems to be inextricably linked to pregnancy as an assertion of male prerogative when men find themselves faced with the female authority that women's pregnancy releases: "For ladies in your way," Mr B argues, "are often like encroaching subjects: They are apt to extend what they call their privileges, on the indulgence showed them; and the husband never again recovers the ascendant he had before" (III.63). It is an invasion of his "province." Mr B's patriarchal retort here and elsewhere is a physical reminder of his authority: a tap on her neck as he says, "Let me beat my beloved saucebox." Later Mr B commands, "Speak it at once, or I'll be angry with you; and tapped my cheek" (III.153). The community of readers, just as in the case of Mungo Park's Africa, supports the husband's right to mete out physical punishment and to regulate the women who quarrel over him.

For Pamela, the question concerns a woman's authority over her own body, her child, and her will, and she perseveres though Mr B finds her saucy and perverse:

> Upon my word, he sometimes, for argument's sake, makes a body think a wife should not have the least will of her own. He sets up a dispensing power, in short, although he knows that that doctrine once cost a prince his crown.
>
> (III.53)

Her parents do not hear her plea: "But do you take it *indeed*, that a husband has such a vast prerogative?" (III.56). Pamela succumbs, and the two are reconciled. But Mr B has been duplicitous in becoming involved with the Countess, the bold Italian nun at the masquerade, even though the reader is encouraged to believe that it was a harmless platonic flirtation. Mr B expresses the longing upon which monogamous marriage in the eighteenth century is based, the longing that *love* will mask the power relations that guarantee male prerogative.

Mr B's alleged affair with the Countess occurs near the time of Pamela's first lying-in. The rest of the novel is, after all, about polygamy, the production of female desire directed toward Mr B, and the regulation of that desire. Mr B is able to take plural "wives" in the sense of one sexual Pamela and one maternal Pamela, but also more literally a chambermaid and a countess, and apparently make them seem to be the same. The sympathetic Lady Davers reports to her,

> What vexes me is, that when the noble uncle of this vile lady [the Countess] . . . expostulated with her on the scandals she brought

upon her character and family, she pretended to argue, foolish creature! for polygamy; and said, She had rather be a certain gentleman's second wife, than the first to the greatest man in England.

(III.171)

Pamela, who had survived the wicked Mrs Jewkes, now finds herself cowering at the prospect of meeting the Countess. Again, as in the first volume, the reader remains uncertain if Pamela is overreacting.

Mr B literally plays them off against each other when he arranges for them to meet. The Countess wins at the harpsichord when each plays; and her equestrian skills are reported to be superior to those of the class-bound Pamela. Seldom is a comparison between women so blatant except in misogynous satire. Mr B reports the Countess's questioning concerning the superiority of face, hair, forehead, brows, complexion, eyes, cheek, nose, lips, smiles, teeth, chin, ears, but when he threatens to move lower, the lady calls a halt. No need, however, for the facial features may easily be read as codes for sexual parts.[31] In the second telling of this twice-told tale of the encounter between Pamela and the Countess, the beauty contest between the "incomparable" ladies is made very particular:

> For black eyes in my girl, and blue in your ladyship, they are both the loveliest I ever beheld. – And, Pamela, I was wicked enough to say, that it would be the sweetest travelling in the world, to have you both placed at fifty miles distance from each other, and to pass the prime of one's life from black to blue, and from blue to black; and it would be impossible to know which to prefer, but the present.

(III.229)

The Countess cuffs him in response, and he "kissed her in revenge." Pamela cries out in disgust: "Fine doings between two Platonics!" which leads Mr B again to exercise his physical authority and tap her neck. The former chambermaid and the Countess, reduced to parts of themselves as they compete for the polygamous male, are interchangeable women in spite of social class. Mr B, like the weak sovereign of David Hume's essay "Of Polygamy," "must play one faction against another, and become absolute by the mutual jealousy of the females. *To divide and govern*, is an universal maxim" (185). Hume says polygamy means male prerogative, male governance, and male authority. This enables us then to see the way masculine privilege is integrally connected to the territorial prerogative of empire. Pamela is Mr B's territorial domain to conquer as the power relations of *Pamela* I are reversed, and she fully submits her will to his. Pamela wins out over the nobility through the display of her

152

superior beauty and virtue, but we can imagine Mr B's continuing to produce polygamous rivals only to be once again chastened by the moral order of monogamy.

The progress of *Pamela* II reveals Mr B's apparent libertinism yet supposed fidelity. In the unsatisfying resolution of the plot, Pamela rather than Mr B is put on trial. The Countess, it turns out, was quoted out of context, and the entire epistolary affair may now be reread and reinterpreted to free Mr B from imputation. He unequivocally rejects polygamy as outside the bounds of his country. He claims that it was only advanced "in the levity of speech, and the wantonness of argument" (III.223). In sum, *Pamela* II re-establishes an order in the world made topsy-turvy in *Pamela* I. It replaces the first Pamela with Pamela II, who is in turn interchangeable with the sexual and maternal parts of the Countess or Sally Godfrey. One nursing breast is equal to another, one sexual organ substitutes for another. But polygamy is un-English. It is an exotic tease that occurs at masquerades and in the eyes of a jealous woman, an appearance rather than reality, and *Pamela* II becomes a triumphant assertion of monogamy. Richardson, like Hume, seems finally to argue that the best ruler, in the home as well as the state, is the monogamist who does not need to pit factions against each other in order to maintain authority. He rules by the willing submission of woman's will, which relies on her sexual competition with other women.

Polygamy operates on two fronts at once – the domestic and the colonial. At home its imagined possibility maintains a husband's sovereignty over his wife's body and its parts by threatening to replace it with another female body. Yet to legalize its practice, even for the benevolent purpose of providing husbands for ruined women and taking up a surplus of useless women (as Martin Madan's *Thelyphthora* proposed), proves too disturbing for England's sense of itself as moral and Christian. Instead the supposed free market, renewed in its energy at the end of the century, prevails. On the colonial front, polygamy represents men's control of women as property. To penetrate the seraglio is to take pleasure in penetrating another man's property, just as the colonizers penetrate and possess the African continent. In documenting this penetration, they succeed in displaying themselves as sovereign. The sovereign male, the counterpart to the woman who realizes her civic duty in mothering, freshly expresses his patriotism and his Englishness in polygamy abroad and public monogamy at home.

III

For the Englishwoman, the stance is even more intensely fraught with contradiction. In this context I want to turn briefly to three European women's views on polygamy, Anna Falconbridge, Lady Mary Wortley

Montagu, and Mary Wollstonecraft. In tension with the cult of domesticity represented in *Pamela* is the increasingly strong female voice, readership, and authorship – a tension between empowerment and domestication, an uncertainty that keeps the lines between the sexes unstable when politics and science would wish to demarcate them more rigidly. The profound historical contradiction revealed is that Africa (the Other) provided the justification for strange practices, but also a threat that the Other may have been too similar for comfort to the European if the practice is then justified and shared. The polygamous sensualized yet ugly African woman is produced in order to make possible the domestic Englishwoman. One effect is to depoliticize the bourgeois woman and insist that there are no public or global implications to the domestic sphere.

In this context we might well ask what use pitting women against each other serves at a time of emergent feminism, of newly rigidified differences between the sexes, and of the formation of empire. Both Falconbridge and Montagu focus on the female body of the Other in their accounts of polygamy, while Mary Wollstonecraft concerns herself instead with its social implications. In these three accounts there is a sense in which the Other is the self displaced in a veiled and even skewed recognition of its own colonization. These Englishwomen consume the Other woman through their gaze and their texts.

Anna Falconbridge, writing a narrative of her voyages to Sierra Leone where she traveled with her Abolitionist husband, comments on how unusual it is for an Englishwoman to visit Africa.[32] In conversation with another European woman, a Portuguese who envies Englishwomen, Falconbridge can acknowledge their sameness and their mutual oppression: "I thanked her in behalf of my country women, for her good opinion, but assured her they had their share of thorns and thistles, as well as those of other countries" (122). But her initial reaction to the women she finds there is to remark on her distance from them: "Seeing so many of my own sex, though of different complexions from myself, attired in their native garbs, was a scene equally new to me, and my delicacy, I confess, was not a little hurt at times" (21). She champions "My own sex" yet considers their "different complexions"; she positions herself as the delicate and squeamish one, for they are not yet mapped in terms of gender because of the difference in color.

Falconbridge, like other travelers, locates racial difference in the fetishized breasts of the Other, the exposed breasts of the polygamous king's many wives. These breasts place the women in a conjunction of the sexual and maternal which is difficult, if not impossible, to reconcile in the Englishwoman, and the way she reconciles them in the African woman is through judging them to be aesthetically repellent. Breasts, like pudenda, mark racial differences between European and African

154

women. Their breasts – large, long, stretched by nursing, "disgusting to Europeans," are reminiscent of the near-constant invocation of the legendary Hottentot breasts which women supposedly threw over their shoulders for the comfort of the nursing child on their backs. Most of the women, Falconbridge discovers, are attached as mistresses to the various English gentlemen, and their appearance of occupying "superior rank" stymies the conventional response of assuming their inferiority to her. Polygamy, she notes, "is considered honorable, and creates consequence" (77).

When faced with these naked women, Anna Falconbridge also records her frustration in attempting to convince Queen Clara, middle-aged, the first of the king's wives, to dress in the European manner. Instead she finds her "impetuous, litigious, and implacable" as Queen Clara tears the clothes off her back: "Finding no credit could be gained by trying to new fashion this *Ethiopian Princess*, I got rid of her as soon as possible" (62). Falconbridge, attempting to wash the Ethiop white, resists the recognition that her body resembles the body for which she has contempt; the bond of the female body which transcends race is instead made the unmistakable marker of conflictual difference. The European woman's Other cannot logically possess a female body so Falconbridge wishes to rid herself of its sight.

Lady Mary Wortley Montagu's Other is exotic and various in her *Letters during her TRAVELS in Europe, Asia, and Africa* (not published until 1763).[33] The preface by Mary Astell huffily dismisses men's travel narratives as inaccurate and "stuft with the same trifles." She mocks them: "They never fail giving you an account of the women, whom 'tis certain, they never saw." Instead, she offers "a new path." In Montagu's vision of the Other, a romantic vision of two hundred women of the Turkish baths, she admires their nude splendor and the nudity of the slaves who tend them, and they provoke her aesthetic and erotic pleasure:

> They Walk'd and mov'd with the same majestic Grace, which Milton describes of our General Mother. There were many amongst them as exactly proportion'd as ever any Goddess was drawn by the pencil of a Guido or Titian, and most of their skins shineingly white . . . perfectly representing the figures of the Graces.
>
> (I.314)

Her female vision leads her to admire the ladies' "finest skins and most delicate shapes," and she wishes for Mr Gervase [Charles Jervas the portrait painter] to share her voyeur's attitude and "to see so many fine Women naked in different postures, some in conversation, some working, others drinking Coffee." In bold contrast to usual notions of the female tea-party and other sites of private domesticity, Wortley Montagu remarks on the women's resistance to mutual disdain, to backbiting against each other: "In short, tis the Women's coffee house, where all the news of the Town is told, Scandal invented, etc." In spite of polygamy, she believes the Turkish women to be the "only free people in the Empire." The veil allows them the freedom to move invisibly, flitting from one scene to the next without detection: "This perpetual Masquerade gives them entire Liberty of following their Inclinations without danger of Discovery" (I.328). She goodhumoredly portrays herself as the one imprisoned, caught as she is in the "machine" the Turkish women assume her husband has locked her in, her stays. Yet there is also sameness: "Thus you see, dear Sister, the manners of Mankind doe not differ so widely as our voyage Writers would make us beleive [sic]" (I.329–30). Polygamy is synonymous here with female collectivity, female beauty, and sexuality, and in a magnificent reversal, *her body* is imprisoned rather than theirs. The Other – not racially different, but different in kind – is free, and polygamy represents liberty rather than restraint.

In sharp contrast, when she regards "the Companies of the country people" in North Africa "eating, singing, and danceing to their wild music" (I.425), class and race surface as more significant than gender. The creatures become animal-like instead of human, and their ugliness and exotic tattooed ornamentation safely distinguish them from European women:

> They are not quite black, but all mullattos, and the most frightfull Creatures that can appear in a Human figure. They are allmost naked, only wearing a piece of coarse serge wrap'd about them, but the women have their Arms to their very shoulders and their Necks and faces adorn'd with Flowers, Stars, and various sorts of figures impress'd by Gun-powder; a considerable addition to their natural Deformity.[34]

(I.425)

Later

> many of the women flock'd in to see me, and we were equally entertain'd with veiwing one another. Their posture in siting, the colour of their skin, their lank black Hair falling on each side their faces, their features and the shape of their Limbs, differ so little from their own country people, the Baboons, tis hard to fancy them a distinct race, and I could not help thinking there had been some ancient alliances between them.

(I. 427)

These North African women, like Queen Clara, refuse to wear the clothing of empire or to commodify themselves in its ideal of femininity

156

and virtue. Here the European woman narrator, Lady Wortley Montagu, sees herself in the face and body of the Other. She wishes to claim as female the exquisite naked beauty of the Turkish harem while rejecting any gender, class, or racial connection to the near-naked mulatto women. Their nakedness in her eyes is bestial rather than evoking the homoerotic sensuality of the harem. Wortley Montagu is not unlike the male traveler she scorns in pitting the "shineingly white" Turkish women against the tattooed African women.

Mary Wollstonecraft, adamant in her opposition to polygamy, established the European feminist position. "Polygamy," writes Mary Wollstonecraft in *A Vindication of the Rights of Woman* (1792) "is [another] physical degradation [of women by men]; and a plausible argument for a custom, that blasts every domestic virtue. . . . If polygamy be necessary, women must be inferior to man, and made for him."[35] She cites John Forster's *Observations Made During a Voyage Round the World* (1778), which claims that in Africa, polygamy enervates men while women

> are of a hotter constitution, not only on account of their more irritable nerves, more sensible organization, and more lively fancy; but likewise because they are deprived in their matrimony of that share of physical love which, in a monogamous condition, would all be theirs.[36]

Forster claims that this sexual deprivation for women leads to a hotter constitution, and the sex of the hotter constitution prevails in the population. In short, Africa is the torrid zone of sexuality where large numbers of passionately sexualized women roam unsatisfied. In a logical assumption which Wollstonecraft does not draw, the cold and less desirous European woman contrasts with her polygamous lascivious African counterpart.

It is rhetorically unclear whether Wollstonecraft believes that polygamy is justified in order to protect seduced women in countries where more women are born than men. Recognizing polygamy's social construction in the cause of women's collective interests and feminism, and arguing against those who find it arises to respond to some natural law, Wollstonecraft nevertheless obscures the situation of the African woman as she argues forcefully in behalf of European women.

The relation of feminism to polygamy and the Other woman is indeed a vexed one that is charged with unresolved issues. At the same time that European feminism emerges in the Enlightenment, differences among women make feminism's progress Western and exclusionary. European women supervise the Other woman abroad through their assumed dominance, taking on the position that Mr B occupied in the scene between Pamela and the Countess. The European interest in polygamy helps justify polygamy in slavery, pitting Englishwomen against African women, Other women against Other women – and men against English and African women as they lay claim to territory through the female body. Domestically, polygamy interferes with feminism's claims as women turn against each other. Heterosexual monogamy, with the support of feminism, is established as a national imperative; the Englishwoman is contained within the boundaries of marriage and nation.

European-American feminism may find in its eighteenth-century manifestations a harbinger of its current urgent need to find alternative trajectories when confronted with the problems that African-American and Third World feminist theorists in the USA and elsewhere aptly reveal. The Other is the self undressed, admired yet held fast in the male and white female gaze, freed within confinement, erotic, repulsive, excessive, a princess yet a slave, the noble female savage, superior yet inferior, multiple yet all the same. The Englishwoman abroad finds in the Other something which aids her in granting herself an identity and thus contributes to the now suspect liberal feminism, so closely bound with monogamous marriage and motherhood, of the later part of the century. The domesticated Other is fully articulated in *Pamela* II. But in postcolonial feminism, polygamy also maintains a potential subversive power and threatens to become radically uncontained. Contemporary feminist Trinh T. Minh-ha suggests that "difference" need not be opposed to "sameness, nor synonymous with separateness." She cautions against using difference as an attempt to locate racial essence:

> When women decide to lift the veil one can say that they do so in defiance of their men's oppressive right to their bodies. But when they decide to keep or put on the veil they once took off they might do so to reappropriate their space or to claim a new difference in defiance of . . . standardization.[37]

The Other woman of polygamy turns out to be, not surprisingly, both self and Other. What may be more surprising, less predictable, at home and abroad, is the way the Other woman's difference may instead be the occasion for unsettling "essences," sabotaging conflicts assumed because of those supposed essences, and preserving the enigma of speaking at once as the domestic woman, the Other woman at home, and the Other woman abroad. In the metaphor of *Pamela* II and the women's narratives of the Other, such a feminist position, a position of collective illusion, emanates from a hybrid subjectivity as it simultaneously regards itself and the world from one black eye and one blue eye, speaks from the mouth of Queen Clara and is embodied in the tattooed skin of the North African countrywomen. We may inhabit each other's bodies in a virtual reality of collective illusion which allows participation in a simulacrum and in the world at the same time. If we explore the permeable boundaries between virtual and real, between collective illusion and lived experience, we may begin to locate difference in such a way that we can move toward separating difference from domination and interrupt feminism's uneasy pluralist community with a contestatory collectivity of those who inhabit domestic spheres and torrid zones.

Part III

FEMALE AUTHORSHIP
AND
NEGOTIATING
DIFFERENCES

9

RE-READING
ELIZABETH CARY'S
THE TRAGEDIE OF MARIAM,
FAIRE QUEENE OF JEWRY

Dympna Callaghan

My own disappointment is that, as a group, we have been unable to address questions of race to any adequate degree in this book, and we are not exonerated in this deficiency by the most visible complexion of European Renaissance society. Rather, it is this very whiteness that we need to learn to see, as well as the ethnic and racial variety present within it. If feminists and postmodernists have taught us that what is absent from our perspective is precisely what our analyses must consider, then this collection asserts by its own omission the importance of addressing more fully the issue of race in Renaissance literature.

> (*The Matter of Difference: Materialist Feminist Criticism of Shakespeare*, ed. Valerie Wayne)[1]

[W]e should note . . . that the practice of including an inoculating critique of its own blind spots, so as to allow business to proceed as usual, has become a common tactic in contemporary political criticism.

> (Tania Modleski, *Feminism Without Women: Culture and Criticism in a "Postfeminist" Age*)[2]

The above juxtaposition of quotations foregrounds some of the problems both encountered and created by feminist critics who endeavor to address the question of "race." The first quotation marks and succumbs to one of the pitfalls of feminist criticism, namely its habitual tendency to take gender as the diacritical difference of culture, and in so doing to erase other systems of difference. It is the problematic structured by these quotations that I want to take as the context of this chapter. I will consider here the extent to which feminist criticism has proceeded with what Modleski calls "business as usual" even as it endeavored to change the structure of patriarchal canonicity by attending to the work of the first original play in English by a woman, Elizabeth Cary's closet drama,

The Tragedie of Mariam, Faire Queene of Jewry. The play has gained attention recently as a result of the feminist recognition that aesthetic value is not universal, that it does not reside within the text, but is historically and culturally specific and woefully subject to patriarchal biases.[3] But to change the canon is more than simply a matter of changing texts – it is to change the conditions and practices of reading all texts, and such changes, at least if they lay claim to political effectivity, must include "race" as a category of analysis.[4]

"Race" is actually part of the manifest content of *Mariam.* The play is set in Palestine among the Jews, who were highly racialized (as well as simultaneously demonized and criminalized) in Renaissance England and regarded as uniquely responsible for what was thought to be the most heinous act in human history – the crucifixion of Christ. Also, a conspicuously white female protagonist and a tawny female villain constitute the focus of the tragic action. So why has the play been read by critics as "obviously" – that is, with all the empiricist force of ideological recognition – "about" gender, not "race"? Why has *Mariam* been understood to speak univocally of gender? I want to argue here that suppression of "race" not only erases important thematic issues, but also impairs our understanding of gender within the play and the position of Cary as a Renaissance woman writer. Also, by setting Elizabeth Cary's destabilizations of "race" and its conventional oppositions (especially the black–white dichotomy) in an interpretive framework which assumes that "race" is already a power relationship inseparable from an analysis of gender, I hope to illuminate the ways in which "race" and gender figure in relation to one another in Renaissance culture and in Cary's text. For not only can we "justify" "race" as a crucial category of analysis in our own political moment, but also we can point to the way Elizabeth Cary herself deploys and manipulates the concept as a vital aspect of her construction and interrogation of femininity.

"RACE" AND RACIALIZATION

"Race" is not self-explanatory; it is currently the site of intense cultural contestation. The term merits quotation marks because, historically, racial marking functions as a denigratory process of cultural othering rather than a positive mode of self-definition.[5] That is, the concept of "race" is itself freighted with racism. (Objectively, there are no races, only racisms.) Yet feminism among other contemporary political discourses has sought to appropriate the category "race" so as to disclose how such marking has served as a mechanism of domination and oppression. Feminist use of "race" as a category of analysis in the triad gender, "race," and class has been concerned, then, not with establishing the pseudo-biological basis of racial characteristics, but with registering the history and material effects of "race" as a system of difference that is always imbricated with other modes of difference, especially gender. It is in this sense, as a fully historicized term of radical critique, that I will use "race" throughout.

In Renaissance studies, traditional scholarly resistance to the deployment of "race" as a category of analysis is based on its apparent invisibility in early modern England. This is wrong-headed (as the opening quotation indicates) because "white" is racially invisible only within the terms of the dominant ideology of white supremacy where only the other is racially marked.[6] (As we shall see, in Cary's *Mariam* the mark of whiteness, its de-racialization, far from being invisible, is vividly apparent.) Further, the argument that there is no empirical justification for an analysis of racial difference is a line of reasoning that ignores the (empirically verifiable) imperialist ventures in Ireland and the New World in the sixteenth and seventeenth centuries, which produced "race" as a category of difference as never before. This production entailed dual processes: the racialization of the other and the concomitant de-racialization of the self. Racially marked others in the English Renaissance included Africans and Celts, Jews, and the "wild Irish."[7] While the former are to our racial sensibility the hyper-visible others here, there is no reason to suppose that the racial otherness of Celts, Jews, and the Irish was not as indelible and irreducible according to Renaissance regimes of visible difference as the "fact" of "negritude" is for us.[8] This is so not only because "race" is a cultural construct rather than a natural category with no objective content, but also because there is a process of differentiation via the mark of blackness continually at work in Renaissance constructions of otherness.

"RACE" AND CARY CRITICISM

In current criticism of *Mariam*, "race" is a non-issue.[9] The overwhelmingly biographical emphasis of the few full critical essays we have is partly a consequence of the fact that current essays constitute the necessary work of feminist archeology; they are, therefore, concerned with the relation between the subject position of the woman writer and the literary text. These legitimate concerns, however, frequently degenerate into an apparently irresistible compulsion to explicate the play in terms of the female playwright, a tendency to displace the critical focus from the text onto the elusive and perhaps inscrutable woman who lurks seductively behind it. This propensity is perturbingly reminiscent of patriarchal reading strategies for women's texts and works in subtle but significant ways to make "race" irrelevant.

Some critical treatments verge on positing the play as an allegory of the events of Cary's rather turbulent life, especially the traumas of her marriage produced by her conversion to Catholicism (although most of the traumas, and probably the conversion, had not yet occurred when she wrote the play at seventeen): "Cary seems to have used the figures of the drama to represent some of the problems and contradictions which were surfacing in her early married life."[10] The principal characters, Salome and Mariam, have been read as Cary's personal psychomachia, and the play's themes have been addressed in terms of their "psychological roots" in the author's consciousness.[11] In a recent essay, the critic argues that in Mariam, Cary explores "an allegorical version of herself," and that Mariam's self-indictments, as well as the censoring power of Herod and the Chorus, must be read as "speaking, evidently, for an aspect of the author's own conscience or superego."[12] Another critic writes of *Mariam*: "This play is even more remarkable in the plight of its heroine, who, *like Lady Cary*, must come to terms with domestic and political tyranny in the form of her husband Herod, tyrant par excellence" [my emphasis].[13] Yet another feminist treatment asserts:

> Cary apparently entered into marriage with an impossible idealization of wifely behavior, which she expresses through Mariam, and with an even more impossible ideal of an independent, even rebellious, intellectual life, embodied in Salome. These deeply ambivalent attitudes shaped the remainder of her life.[14]

An enormously valuable (and less essentialist) aspect of feminist inquiry has been on the cultural contradiction produced by humanist valorization of eloquence, on the one hand, and on the other the tendency to regard publication as synonymous with a lack of chastity, which placed extraordinary constraints on the woman writer.[15] Margaret Ferguson observes:

> the question of a woman's right to assume a "public" voice is both central to the drama and unanswered within it. That unanswered question . . . is, moreover, central not only to the play but also to Renaissance debates about the nature and proper behavior of womankind.[16]

Similarly, Catherine Belsey notes:

> Women are entitled to speak and forbidden to speak, anxious to write and reluctant to be known to write. Ironically, there may be a sense in which the conditions of the production of this text re-enact the contradictions it so eloquently defines.[17]

Indeed, Cary invariably writes through the experience of woman as other, the self-alienation of the woman who takes up the position of the writing subject, which the culture defines as masculine. (In 1641, Edward Hyde, Earl of Clarendon, referred to her as "a lady of most masculine understanding, allayed with the passions and infirmities of her own sex".)[18] Ferguson's and Belsey's astute critical interventions explore vital issues regarding Cary's negotiations of patriarchal prohibitions on women's speech, writing, and agency. But of equal and perhaps greater importance is the *mode* via which these are negotiated. That is, there is a danger that the emphasis on the gender constraints placed upon Cary as a Renaissance woman writer and the concomitant biographical interest in her has only served, in some sense, to replicate rather than challenge the traditional terms of association between a woman's gender and her writing. As Ann Rosalind Jones shows, the expectation that women's "writing somehow still affirmed the silence enjoined upon them" is not borne out when those writings are "no longer assumed to be private confessions but recognized as maneuvers within the shared textuality of their time."[19] Similarly, I would argue that *Mariam* not only articulates but also *exceeds* in significant ways the constraints about speech and writing English Renaissance culture placed upon its female author.

That Cary does not simply replicate the condition of her own femininity is perhaps evinced by the vigorous critical suppression of historical sources occasionally required in order to assert the contrary: "She [Cary] may speak with liberty and impunity of an ancient queen of Judea . . . but the subject is ever herself." Cary is literally seen here to write veiled autobiography; her "real" subject (herself) is hid "under the cloak of true historical source."[20] By positing *Mariam* as frustrated self-expression, the critic entirely evacuates the specificity of the text and domesticates (by dismissing it) the play's radical otherness. Crucially, if unwittingly, then, the tendency to elide female author and text places "race" outside the sphere of feminist concern. The gynocritcal focus on reading Cary as a woman – the separation of gender from other systems of difference – tends to situate her curiously outside the material conditions in which she wrote and in relation to which she herself was placed as other.[21] This obscures the extent to which Cary took as her subject matter in *Mariam* the negotiation of conspicuously racialized otherness by writing a tragedy set in Palestine whose protagonist is no less than the Queen of the Jews.

A COUNTRY OF OTHERS

The principle of difference lies at the heart of the construction of cultural others, as feminist and postcolonial theory in coincident and parallel ways have shown.[22] Therefore, it is productive to examine Cary's otherness as a woman writer in relation to the racialized otherness of *Mariam* rather than to allow the former completely to subsume the latter. Importantly, these modes of cultural otherness (gender and

167

"race") are structurally connected aspects of the colonialist dialectic between self and other that emerged in the Renaissance:

> These encounters with the "other" . . . necessitated a concomitant confrontation with the self, provoking a re-evaluation of the known in relation to the newly discovered unknown. Significantly, and ironically . . . England's preoccupation with strangers and strange lands intensified the culture's re-examination of its own estranged others.[23]

There is no reason to suppose that Cary as a woman writer (herself an embodiment of otherness) was peculiarly exempt from the preoccupation with alterity that characterized the burgeoning imperialism of her milieu.[24] We know, for instance, that Cary had read Pliny, and would therefore be familiar with classical anthropology.[25] When Cary's former tutor, John Davies, begins his "The Muse's Sacrifice, Or Divine Meditations" (1612) with a dedicatory encomium to Cary and two of her female contemporaries, he depicts a writer singularly preoccupied with the intellectual exploration of linguistic and geographical otherness characteristic of the generic male humanist scholar, but uncharacteristic of women:

> With feete of State, *dost make thy* Muse to *mete*
> *the* scenes of Syracuse *and* Palestine.
> Art, Language; *yea; abstruse and holy* Tongues
> *thy* Wit *and* Grace acquir'd *thy* Fame *to raise.*[26]

There is good reason, then, not to dismiss the Palestine of Cary's *Mariam* as a mere backdrop, as a matter of incidental "local color." Rather, Palestine is the locus of complex racial and religious co-ordinates, at once the displaced center of Christianity and the home of the infidel. This setting is part of the way in which *Mariam* participates both in an aesthetic convention of otherness and in an intellectual fascination with Judaism which swept England from the reign of Henry VIII. The connection between the ancient Israelites and contemporary Jewry came under close scrutiny as the result of complex intellectual and political developments, which included the glorification of Hebrew, the interest in a universal language, the search for the lost ten tribes of Israel, and the belief that the conversion of the Jews was a necessary aspect of Christian eschatology. This occurred despite the fact that the Jews had been exiled from England in 1290 and were not readmitted (and then only on an unofficial basis) until the philo-semitic momentum reached its climax in the 1655 meeting with Rabbi Menasseh ben Israel at the Whitehall Conference.[27] Further, a connection had been firmly established between the Jews and the peoples of the New World. Explorers hoped to come upon the lost tribes, and Peter Martyr's

English translation of an account of the Spanish voyages of exploration, *The Decades of the New World* (1555), describes the Americas as a
"spirituall Israel." Indeed, the Native Americans actually encountered
were deemed to bear considerable resemblance to Jews since they practiced circumcision and spoke a language which, to the explorers' ears,
was reminiscent of Hebrew.[28] Both Cary's proficiency in Hebrew, undoubtedly one of the "abstruse and holy tongues" referred to by
Davies, as well as her reading Lodge's 1602 translation of Josephus's
Antiquities of the Jews (written in Greek), which is thought to be her
source for *Mariam*, are ways in which she participated in the intellectual ethos of her time.[29]

Yet, the negotiation of otherness, in English Renaissance culture as in
Cary's text, is conflicted because it entails simultaneously the impetus to
constitute and affirm self-identity via a relation with the other that can
manifest itself as either irresistible fascination, a disquieting sense of
affinity, or outright repulsion and denigration.[30] There are, for
example, anti-racist sentiments (sometimes alongside overtly racist ones)
in the discourses of Coryate, Purchas, and Sir Thomas Browne, who
occasionally attempt to establish the Jews as a "nation," rather than a
"race."[31] However, there coexisted with such notions, as with philo-
semitism more generally, a strong current of diabolization of the Jews.[32]
As David Katz points out in his book-length study of the subject: "These
English philo-semites wanted Hebrew without tears, philo-semitism
without Jews."[33] This renders the distinction between "theological" and
"racial" anti-semitism quite unfeasible.[34] The former is so virulent that it
far exceeds the bounds of the simply "religious" and is distinct from
other forms of religious intolerance such as that directed against
Catholics:

> . . . it is the demonological, supernatural element in the early
> modern attitude to the Jews which renders it quite different from
> other forms of opposition to religious minorities and outcasts. "Ye
> are of *your* father the devil," John admonished the Jews, "and the
> lusts of your father ye will do." . . . The Jews were thought to have
> some cosmic connection with the Antichrist. They were believed to
> carry a particular smell (*Foetor Judicus*), to poison Christians, desec-
> rate hosts, murder children and use their blood for ritual
> purposes.[35]

It is within this cultural frame, one where there was both reverence and
repulsion for Jews, that Cary's setting must be seen to signify. Palestine
provided an unusually suitable site for the depiction of male tyranny and
female resistance, and for a protagonist who embodies an unstable
mixture of antithetical elements – female virtue and rebellion. Both

fantasized and actual, Palestine is a place where Cary can unbalance the polarized binarisms which constituted the category "woman."

FEMALE RESISTANCE AND IRRESISTIBLE OTHERS

The play's production of femininity, alternatively vilified as wanton and valorized as virtuous, is crucially dependent upon "race." That is, the cultural polarization of the category "woman" is constructed via racial marking. Paradoxically, the stark coloration of virtuous femininity as white and licentious femininity as black is destabilized by the fact that these polarities are set in relation to one another amid Jews, peoples of an allegedly already compromised ethnicity. "Race" enables Cary to stage some of the contradictions that constitute the Renaissance condition of femininity, and by exploring femininity through it *The Tragedie of Mariam* gains a double focus on the otherness of woman. Racialized difference and geographical otherness, in fact, become preconditions of the representation of resisting femininity.

Yet "race" also works to make female resistance simultaneously possible and ethically insupportable. Mariam's ambivalent position in the play as stoic and virtuous, especially in death, but also as disobedient and vituperative is in part a function of her anomalous racial position. Within the conventions of Renaissance culture, Jewish women seem to be portrayed in a far more positive light – as literally less racialized – than the invariably patriarchal Jewish males. For example, Jessica, daughter of Shylock, who converts to Christianity in Shakespeare's *Merchant of Venice*, and Abigail, the daughter of Barabas, who flees to a convent in Marlowe's *The Jew of Malta*, are identified with Christianity rather than Judaism;[36] their fathers do not have the same propensity toward conversion and assimilation. The archetypal Jewish patriarch is Abraham, of course, to whom Gentiles bear an inescapably filial relationship. He is, as St Paul writes, "the father of us all."[37] Yet Abraham is hardly benevolent. He figures in Christian mythology as the murderous patriarch who circumcises Isaac and later ties him to the altar fully prepared to wield his knife, his hand stayed only by the timely intervention of the angel of the Lord.[38]

The significant parallels between Herod and the conventional, racialized representation of the Jew as the tyrannical patriarch (though he is not, of course, Mariam's father) make her insubordination quite legitimate (this is especially true when we recall that this same Herod is the notorious figure who massacred the innocents):

> Yet I rather much a milke-maide bee,
> Than be the Monarke of *Judeas* Queene.
> It was for nought but love, he wisht his end

170

Might to my death, but the vaunt-currier prove:
But I had rather still be foe than friend,
To him that saves for hate, and kills for love.
(I.i.59–64)[39]

Mariam here is very much constructed as the victim-subject of the jealous husband-monarch who "kills for love." Like Shakespeare's Cleopatra (IV.xv.73–5), she ponders the life of the milkmaid, a figure of essentialized, chaste femininity, the idealized lower-class virgin of pastoral convention, quite literally allied with the whiteness of milk, who is spared the onerous cares of women who associate with powerful men. But Mariam is not only a victim: in some sense, she is the rebellious figure who heralds the coming of Christ. As Elaine Beilin has noted, Lodge's translation of Josephus marks the events of Herod and Mariam's tumultuous marriage with a countdown to the birth of Christ in the margin.[40] For Mariam is also an amalgam figure of the apostate Jewish woman, based on the Virgin Mary, the eternal "daughter mother," "purged at once of the evil embodied in her ancestry."[41] Like Mary, Mariam represents the mercy of Christianity which again tempers the patriarchal rigor of the Old Testament.[42]

While earlier literary models had the Virgin Mary represent the advent of the New Law and the demise of the Old, Leslie Fiedler argues that the thematic fusion of the identity between the Virgin and the Jewish woman was a relatively new, Renaissance development. In the popular medieval ballad of *Hugh of Lincoln* a Gentile boy is slain for his devotion to the Virgin, but a beautiful Jewish girl helps her father ensnare the child. In contrast, in the Renaissance, Fiedler writes:

> By the time Shakespeare was dreaming Shylock and Jessica, there had begun to grow both in him and in his audience a longing – unsatisfied by either The Prioresses Tale or "Sir Hugh, or the Jew's Daughter," – for a representation of the female principle in Jewish form more human than the Blessed Virgin, yet, unlike the Jew's daughter of the ballad, benign and on the other side.[43]

This seems to indicate that an ever-increasing weight of the indictment for the killing of Christ is borne by the Jewish male, who is positioned as more racially debased than his female counterpart. Consider Thomas Adams's "defense" of women published in 1629:

> Though Christ honoured our sex, in that he was a man, not a woman: yet hee was borne of a woman, and was not begot of a man. And howsoever wicked women prove the most wicked sinners: yet the worst and greatest crime that ever was done, was committed by a man, not by woman; the crucifying of our Lord Jesus; not a woman had a hand in it.[44]

171

Here, men (irrespective of race) are marked by the crucifixion, while women are exonerated by virtue of the fact that they are seen as non-participants in the course of human history. Mariam is thus placed differently in relation to the racialization of Jews than Herod. This suggests a complex interrelation between gender and "race," and simultaneously endorses and interrogates Mariam's resistance to Herod.

For what is problematic about Mariam's rebellion against Herod, which is not so of Jessica's deception of Shylock or Abigail's disobedience to Barabas, is that, while daughters can refuse to obey Jewish fathers, wives are not permitted to disobey husbands, let alone forswear the marriage bed.[45] Cary deals with this by accentuating the production of racialized difference between Herod and Mariam and positing it as the circumstance of Mariam's wifely rebellion. Paradoxically, then, Herod becomes both more Jewish than Mariam and racially debased – an Edomite – while Mariam becomes both less Jewish than Herod and "pure" Jew. Mariam's mother, the ever-railing Alexandra, attacks her son-in-law in a fashion that constitutes Herod and Mariam's marriage as virtual miscegenation:

> Base *Edomite* the damned *Esaus* heire:
> Must he ere *Jacobs* child the crown inherit?
> Must he, vile wretch, be set in *Davids* chair?
> No, *Davids* soule within the bosome plac'te
> Of our forefather *Abram*, was asham'd
> To see his feat with such a toade disgrac'te,
> That seat that hath by *Judas* race been fain'd
> Thou fatall enemy to royall blood . . . .
> Was he not *Esaus* Issue, heyre of hell?
> Then what succession can he have but shame?
> Did not his Ancestor his birth-right sell?
> O yes, he doth from *Edoms* name derive,
> His cruell nature which with blood is fed:
> That made him me of Sire and sonne deprive,
> He ever thirsts for blood, and blood is red.
> (I.ii.89–111)

The differences of power and morality between Herod and Mariam presented here are overdetermined not only by gender, but also by "race," and class. The phrase "Judah's race" (which the printing produces as the racial epithet, "Judas race") is telling also because it extends beyond the parameters of our twentieth-century understanding of "race" into the realm of class and social hierarchy, which in the Renaissance is so thoroughly naturalized that it attaches to blood. In literal terms, "Judah's race" suggests the general sense of lineage as in "a race of kings" and refers to the long dynastic conflict between the descendants of Esau (Isaac's son who was tricked out of his inheritance by his twin, Jacob) and those of his brother. These Edomites were enemies to Israel until subdued by those of Mariam's blood, a history that would have been familiar to Renaissance readers.[46] Proper sovereignty, according to the voluble Alexandra, is deformed by the loathsome, reptilian Herod.

Although the question of lineage in terms of the contest for power is dealt with in Lodge's Josephus, it is not nearly so racialized as in *Mariam*, where Mariam's encounters with Salome leave us in no doubt about the fact that a specifically racialized difference is thought to exist between the Edomites and those of Jacob's line. Salome questions the logic of Mariam's attack by reference to well-nigh elemental human origins (a discourse to which Mariam herself resorts in more stoic terms when her own death is imminent):

> Though I thy brothers face had never seene,
> My birth, thy baser birth so farre exceld,
> I had to both of you the Princess bene.
> Thou partly Jew and partly Edomite,
> Thou Mongrell, issu'd from reiected race
> Thy Ancestors against the Heavens did fight,
> And thou like them wilt heavenly birth disgrace.

SALOME   Still twit you me with nothing but my birth,
> What ods betwixt your ancestors and mine?
> Both borne of *Adam*, both were made of Earth,
> And both did come from holy *Abrahams* line.

MARIAM   I favour thee when nothing else I say,
> With thy blacke acts ile not pollute my breath:
> Else to thy charge I might full iustly lay
> A shameful life, besides a husbands death.

(I.iii.240–54)

Crucially, Salome and Mariam, who are the central as well as the most sexualized female characters of the play (as opposed to Doris and Alexandra, who are so preoccupied with the advancement of their children that they become de-sexualized mothers), have their moral coloring reflected in the pigment of their skin. Mariam's diatribe, however, implies not merely that her antagonist's darkness is an accurate reflection of her "blacke acts," and base blood: "base woman . . . *Mariams* servants were as good as you / Before she came to be *Judeas* Queene" (II.iii.233–4). It also implies that her transgressions have their origins in her inferior heritage.

The racialization of Salome, then, permits the irresistible logic of her proto-feminist pronouncements about female desire and the injustice of divorce law: "Ile be the custom-breaker: and beginne / To show my Sexe the way to freedomes doore" (I.iv.319–20). As the stage villain, whose literary antecedents include the medieval Vice and the Renaissance Machiavel, Salome has a certain verbal license. However, these traditional and invariably male figures typically rail at women and indict them for concupiscence.[47] Salome constitutes a singular formal innovation. She is endowed with the license of the Vice–Machiavel but to reverse ends: she critiques male prerogative, articulates her outrageous sexual desires and asserts her will with impunity. In contrast, Mariam is ensnared in the Renaissance patriarchal trap, and her juxtaposition with Salome foregrounds and problematizes the cultural construction of female virtue and agency as mutually incompatible elements. Salome represents an unorthodox means of escaping Mariam's dilemma, namely the complete refusal of all the strictures men impose on female behavior; even while in typical Machiavellian form, she endangers the tragic protagonist.

Although Salome's uncensured enunciation of female rebellion is identified entirely as the discourse of unrestrained sexual appetite, "race," especially Mariam's attack on her caste, provides the motive for her vengeance:

> I scorne that she should live my birth t'upbraid,
> To call me base and hungry Edomite:
> With patient show her choller I betrayd,
> And watcht the time to be reveng'd by slite.
>
> (III.ii.1090–3)

The contrast between protagonist and antagonist is again racialized in a remarkable scene of sibling interaction when Salome wearies of Herod's endless and remorseful rhapsodizing about Mariam's beauty:

> SALOME Your thoughts do rave with doating on the Queen,
> Her eyes are ebon hewde, and you'll confesse,
> A sable starre hath beene but seldome seene
> Then speake of reason more, of *Mariam* lesse.
>
> HEROD Your selfe are held a goodly creature heere,
> Yet so unlike my *Mariam* in your shape,
> That when to her you have approached neere,
> My self hath often tane you for an Ape.
> And yet you prate of beautie: goe your waies
> You are to her a Sun-burnt Blackamore
>
> (IV.vii.1725–34)

Mariam is marked here as a racial other, an "ebon hewde," "sable starre." Her adversary reminds us (despite the doting Herod's immedi-

RE-READING *THE TRAGEDIE OF MARIAM*

ate de-racialization) that Mariam is not "white," so much as a de-racialized Jewess. Thus, Salome's exotic beauty, which has ensnared the likes of hapless Josephus, Constabarus, and Silleus, is produced as comically subhuman not against the beauty of an Anglo-Saxon princess, but against that of a black-eyed, Jewish queen. That is, the conventions of "race" here are produced as displaced conventions.

As Mariam progresses toward death and exoneration, she becomes whiter – more dazzlingly white than "fair" – and less sexualized (that is, within the dominant ideology of "race" she is de-racialized), while an increment of associations with voracious blackness accrue to Salome. Yet in a symptomatic erasure of "race," one feminist critic argues that Salome is imagistically based on the reference in Matthew's gospel to "a painted sepulcher, / That is both faire, and viley foule at once" and that "Mariam . . . is exempt from this portrayal. Part of her tragedy is the lack of whitewash: the beauty of Mariam is an indication of spiritual purity and innocence."[48] It is certainly true that Salome exhibits the glamor of evil, but the notion that she is "whitewashed," even though intended as a figurative rather than a literal description, betrays a singular inattention to the specifically racialized construction of feminine evil that Salome's character embodies. Far from being "white-washed," she is conspicuously dark and morally tarnished, while Mariam is insistently blanched and purified.[49]

In an early episode which demonstrates the play's investment in racialization and where gender difference becomes irrelevant in the face of bisexual desire, Alexandra laments having erred in trying to curry favor with Antony by presenting both her children to him, who are equally "fair": "The boyes large forehead first did fayrest seeme, / Then glaunsd his eye upon my *Mariams* cheeke" (I.ii.184–5). Unable to choose between Alexandra's equally pale and attractive offspring, Anthony espouses "the browne *Egyptian*," Cleopatra (who receives much worse treatment at Cary's hands than at those of Lodge and Josephus) and her artificially whitened ("wayned") face.[50]

Only when Herod repents her execution does Mariam's whiteness become unproblematic. The reiteration of de-racialized female beauty and morality is such that it signals that Herod has become unhinged by his malevolent uxoriousness:

> she was faire.
> Oh what a hand she had, it was so white,
> It did the whiteness of the snowe impaire
> I never more shal see so sweet a sight
> (IV.viii.2091–4)

He marvels that the sun can still shine when such a one is lost rather than "some *Egiptian* blows / Or *Æthiopian* doudy" (IV.viii.2136–7). "If she had

been like an *Egiptian* blacke, / And not so fair, she had bene longer lived"
(IV.viii.2181–2). Of course, Herod has had plenty of opportunity to
revoke the execution order before Mariam's death. He momentarily
repents his rashness by displacing the racialized/demonized difference
between his sister, "my blacke tormenter," and the luminous virtue of his
wife onto the primal distinction between dark and light:

> What meant I to deprive the world of light:
> To muffle *Jury* in the foulest blacke,
> That ever was an opposite to white.
>
> (IV.iv.1502–4)

These pervasive cultural elisions between darkness, black skin, evil, and
the "racialization" of femininity – especially the repeated vilification of
wanton femininity as black – were founded in the belief that Africans
and women were demonic and that the devil was black.[51] Such associations constitute not just the "imagery" of this text, but the conceptual
content of "race" in the Renaissance.

That Mariam's virtue is presented very traditionally in terms of whiteness should not cause us to dismiss the way in which beauty itself
becomes markedly de-racialized. Indeed, it precisely the fact that the
equation of beauty with whiteness is "conventional" that requires explanation. What is significant and remarkable is the way the racialization of
demonized femininity and the de-racialization of sanctified femininity,
as well as the preoccupation with moral difference as analogous to racial
difference, saturate this play. Cary manipulates the terms of the convention by making the culturally pervasive equation of inner purity with
whiteness work simultaneously to construct and problematize the conventional ideology of femininity. In a culture where femininity is polarized as literally black or white, women are still unstable signifiers. Cary's
use of the conventions for constructing gender virtues reveals them to be
dangerously dependent on a deracinated essentialism: virtue is white,
but white is really black. The text discloses female virtue as grounded
not in femaleness but in convention.

Nonetheless, Herod's misogynous ravings are lent a certain plausi-
bility by the fact that it is with a treachery of emotion, thought, and
speech rather than with actual infidelity that Mariam suffers both self-
recrimination and indictment by the play's Chorus. For Mariam, while
physically virtuous, has erred in her voluble upbraidings of Herod for
the murder of her grandfather and brother, and in her inability to set
her mind to perfect obedience once she discovers that he intended to
have her murdered had he failed to return from Rome. Herod charges:
"Foul pith contain'd in fairest rinde . . . thine eye / Is pure as heaven, but
impure thy minde" (IV.iv.1453–5). Similarly, Doris impugns Mariam's
physical purity for the years of adulterous "marriage" she has spent with

Herod: "In heav'n, your beautie cannot bring you, / Your soule is blacke and spotted, full of sinne" (IV.viii.1849–50). Doris's case against Mariam as the "other woman" is actually quite strong, and for a Renaissance audience, the outrageous cultural otherness of such marriage practices might well have sullied Mariam's protestations about her spotless virtue.

There is, in fact, no female subject position available in the play that is both viable and virtuous, except perhaps for the unsullied femininity of the dramatically insipid Graphina, servant lover of Pheroras. She is more virtuous than Mariam, whose racial characteristics she parallels by practicing that "fair virgin art" despite her inferior class position:

> For though the Diadem on *Mariams* head
> Corrupt the vulgar judgements, I will boast
> *Graphinas* brow's as white, her cheekes as red.
> (II.i.583–5)

Graphina represents the play's ostensible ideal of femininity (which, significantly enough, does not wholly comport with the cultural equation of female silence with chastity).[52] Like the humble milkmaid of Mariam's fantasy, Graphina is not presented with the obstacles to virtue that Mariam must endure. Once again lower-class femininity becomes a fantasized location, somewhere beyond the absolute and brutal power of Herod, which has impeded Mariam's path to perfect virtue.

In its complex imbrication with gender and class, we can begin to see how "race" shapes notions of female purity and beauty as well as the issues feminist criticism has shown to be the focal and contradictory concerns of *The Tragedie of Mariam*, namely wifely obedience versus female agency and autonomy.[53] For "race" is never a discrete entity; it is constituted by an inherent interrelatedness with other categories. Even the specular economy of the black–white dichotomy, the metaphysics of race on which much of the play's production of femininity relies, functions throughout as a fundamental binarism whose analogical extensibility encompasses gender, hierarchy, and morality as much as color. None of these categories, therefore, can be properly disarticulated from "race" understood in its non-positivist sense.

As I have tried to suggest, the discourse of "race" in *The Tragedie of Mariam, Faire Queene of Jewry* is a vital mechanism for the construction and negotiation of difference. In so doing, I have critiqued the effacement of "race" as a system of difference that has characterized feminist readings of the play. I have argued for this approach, however, not in the interests of "accuracy," but rather in the hope of pressuring our assumptions about the relation between current political concerns and the texts of the past and how we go about reading them. For as postcolonial theorists so eloquently and forcefully insist, the past must address its present.

10

"I RATHER WOULD WISH TO BE A BLACK-MOOR"

Beauty, race, and rank in Lady Mary Wroth's *Urania*

Kim F. Hall

In his 1551 handbook, *The Rule of Reason*, scholar-politician Thomas Wilson uses as an example of a "dilemma" an age-old male problem – how to handle a beautiful woman. Significantly renaming it a "horned argument," he goes on to describe a dilemma:

> when the reason consisteth of repugnant membres, so that whatso-ever you graunt you fall into the snare, and take the foile. As if I shoulde aske, whether it ware better to marie a faire womanne, or a fowle. If you saie a faire, then aunswere I, that is not good, for thei communely saie, shee will bee commune, and then I maie saie, ye are touched with the horned argument if that saiying be true. If you saie it were good to marie a harde fauored woman, then I aunswere, she wilbe lothesome, and so ye fall into an inconue-nience both waies.[1]

Wilson's example clearly demonstrates the ways in which rhetoric functions as an instrument of male contest and social control: throughout the text he posits a male subject, here caught in a verbal/social bind due to the alleged sexual unruliness of women.[2] Luckily, Wilson gives his reader the perfect escape from this logical stranglehold:

> And you maie confute the same by inversion, that is to saie, turnyng his taile cleane contrarie, as thus. As I shal marie a faire woman, I shal have great pleasure, and coumforte in her: If I marie a browne womanne, she shal not be commune to other, for fewe menne wil seeke after her. Therefore I shal haue comforte bothe waies.

Female desire, which leaves open the possibility of cuckoldry (either woman could seek other partners), is subsumed under male desire: the "faire" woman will increase his pleasure, the "browne" woman will serve no one's but his. Although the manifold issues of sexuality and reader identification in this passage beg for closer inspection, I would like to turn instead to the language of beauty in the text. The dilemma, first written as an almost painful restriction of male choice, is resolved by the revelation that the terms of beauty can be rewritten at will. Indeed, the expression of beauty changes in the writing of the proper retort. The first set of oppositions ("faire/harde fauored") refers more generally to features; these terms are then rewritten into a dark/light opposition ("faire/browne") which allows the male to have it "bothe waies." Such a variation alters the connotations of "faire"; redefined by its new relationship with "browne," it becomes a term both of beauty and of complexion.

Listing Wilson as its first example, the *Oxford English Dictionary* defines this use of *faire* as "Of complexion and hair: Light as opposed to dark." With some puzzlement, it states that this meaning is "apparently not of very early origin," therefore suggesting that this opposition between fair and dark, typical in discussions of beauty, happens only about the time of Wilson. This semantic shift is no accident, produced as it is at the moment of intensified English interest in travel and African trade.[3] The language of aesthetics is constitutive of the language of race in early modern England, the result of a number of forces which find expression later in the period, most notably in the "Dark Lady" sonnets and the English slave-trade.

A woman's text, Lady Mary Wroth's *The Countess of Montgomerie's Urania* (1621), clearly demonstrates how Wilson's early racial aesthetic is continually gendered. By the time of Wroth and Shakespeare, one can see a growing awareness of how the nexus of female beauty and male power, contained within the emerging language of race in early modern England, encompasses problems of public voice and literary authority. For a woman writer, struggling for a subject position from which to write, dark/light dichotomies become a key point of contest. This essay first examines the ways in which tropes of blackness in descriptions of beauty function as markers of race which work to differentiate between women. I then propose a reading of the *Urania* which suggests that Wroth and other women writers demonstrate a heightened sensitivity to difference and to the cultural implications of their own investment in the language of racial difference. However, like Wilson's hypothetical bachelor, women of the early modern period use the arbitrariness of this aesthetic to strengthen their own rhetorical and social positions at the expense of more marginalized groups.[4]

II

Wilson's *Rule of Reason* is typical of male-authored texts in that its construction of a male readership (and its use of women to empower men), as Mary Ellen Lamb argues, deprives women of "a primary source of subjectivity necessary for them to construct themselves as authors."[5] The intertwining of subjectivity and literary authority is central to tropes of blackness which are both racial and literary *topoi* as well as a product of patriarchal structures which manipulate and may preclude female subjectivity. In female-authored texts, the appearance of such tropes may represent women's attempts (as gender is not a privileged category for writing) to avoid the strictures of gender by borrowing authority from other categories reified by patriarchal structures: class, whiteness, and "Englishness."

English women's resistance to the exclusivity and hegemony of a patriarchal tradition is itself fraught with difficulty: in attempting to expose and escape destabilizing constructions of gender, these women position themselves at the site of other differences which further complicate the creation of "the" female subject. The complex interaction of race, class, and literary authority in these texts has powerful implications, both for the study of women in early modern England and for contemporary feminists. In her report on the 1982 National Women's Studies Association Conference, Chela Sandoval argues that white males achieve power by "othering" white women and people of color. Within this stratagem, white women always inhabit secondary positions:

> Interestingly, even though white women experience the pain of oppression they also experience the will-to-power. For while white women are "othered" by men and feel the pain of objectification, within this secondary category they can only construct a solid sense of "self" through the objectification of people of color.[6]

What we see in the early modern period is the paradigm forming in the constitution of a gendered subject position. Certain texts by women display in a like manner the simultaneous recognition of their own oppression and a will-to-power which helped shape women's experience.[7] From the moment of England's earliest colonial encounters, European women negotiate partriarchal discourses to construct a subject position for themselves, not only in relation to white male power, but also in relation to the "foreign" women coded as a threat to an already insecure, secondary position.[8]

Beauty, more than simply a matter of aesthetic pleasure, becomes a site of contest for women writers, who represent their own oppression and will-to-power in the intersections of gender, race, and empire formed by the language of Petrarchan beauty. Petrarchan poets provided Europe with a way of inscribing differences between women as well as with "the language of the discovery of a feminized new land."[9] The rhetoric of exploration describes the allure of foreign lands as the discovery of an unknown beauty and the language of beauty is itself grounded in a language of dark and light that already sets women against each other in competition for male favor. One manifestation of this language is the appearance of dark/light pairs of women in which one is "dark" and the other, golden blond. From Pamela and Philoclea in *The Countess of Pembroke's Arcadia* to Lucy and Mina in *Dracula*, to Joan Collins and Linda Evans in "Dynasty," such pairings are ubiquitous in Anglo-American culture. When women compete for the interest of a man, often one is made the black and demonized "other."

The languages of beauty and colonialism intersect when the ubiquitous "darkness" in these pairings comes to include foreign women who are posed to compete with fair, European women for male attention. Consequently, the "darkness" of the foreign "other" implicates all women.[10] One can see how the competition for male favor intensifies and is accentuated in Shakespeare's *A Midsummer Night's Dream*, when Lysander rejects his "dark" lover, Hermia, with the epithets, "Away you Ethiope" and "Out, Tawny Tartar."[11] Like Thomas Wilson, Lysander phrases his choice in terms of color and uses masculine "reason" to justify his completely arbitrary choice of Helena, "Who will not change a raven for a dove? . . . reason says you are the worthier maid" (II.ii.113–15). In the forest of Athens, Hermia's physical "darkness," her brunette hair, is changed to a sign approximating that of a racial distinction as she and Helena are pitted against each other for the attentions of Demetrius and Lysander. Such confrontations, provoked by the arbitrariness of male favor and desire, push women into inconsistent and unstable positions. Indeed, Helena bitterly rejects the label "fair" in her realization that she is not desired:

HERMIA God speed fair Helena! whither away?
HELENA Call you me fair? That fair again unsay.
Demetrius loves your fair, O happy fair!
(I.ii.180–3)

Helena's somewhat overwrought punning reveals a very real problem for the would-be female subject. As objects of male attention, no two women can be fair at the same time. When one is "fair" or desired, the other is almost as a matter of course "other" or dark.

Even when desired by different men, women are then placed into competitive positions, as men denigrate each other's mistress as "darker" or less beautiful than their own. Indeed, the language of beauty is one of the few ways in which men can make distinctions between women without compromising their own power. Unlike class or gender, color allows for the construction of woman as different while not necessarily establishing differences between men.[12] Indeed, Henry Louis Gates's assertion that race is a "dangerous trope" rather than an "objective term of classification" suggests that differentiation by beauty shares its arbitrariness – and power – with race:

Race is the ultimate trope of difference because it is so arbitrary in its application. The biological criteria used to determine "difference" in sex simply do not hold when applied to "race." Yet we carelessly use language in such a way as to *will* this sense of *natural* difference into our formulations.[13]

The racialization that permeates the language of beauty as exemplified by Wilson is one way in which the category of "race" is made to act as a "natural" difference. In a like manner, this "willed" sense of natural difference runs throughout the discourses of beauty in the early modern period as signs of racial difference are embedded in so-called "aesthetic" descriptions.[14]

Both economic and gender concerns are articulated through the arbitrary use of race. Racial "otherness" allows white men to lump all "others" (male and female) into another, less valued group. In the devaluing of dark-haired women as "Ethiopes" or "Tartars," all people of color are placed in secondary positions which reinforce European hegemony. Nevertheless, while the manipulation of gender inherent in formulations of beauty obviously puts women in very unstable positions, such a system does provide a basis for negotiation. Its hierarchical nature can be manipulated by a woman writer to create a more powerful position for herself. Thus, race as much as class becomes a crucial category as women writers differentiate between female characters.

The representation of Cleopatra in women's texts of the early modern period clearly displays the nexus of beauty, race, and empire in differentiation between women. Cleopatra's sexual allure seems as problematic as her political/erotic power is compelling. Unlike most male writers, women writers continually remind their readers of Cleopatra's darkness. They never forget the fact that her affair with Antony takes place in the shadow of an abandoned wife. In *Salve Deus Rex Judaeorum*, Emilia Lanier clearly identifies with the Roman Octavia, the wife abandoned through her husband's involvement with the "other." Consequently, Lanier emphasizes the blackness of the adulterous Cleopatra along with her beauty:

Great *Cleopatra's* love to *Anthony*,
Can no way be compared unto thine; . . .
No *Cleopatra*, though thou wert as faire
As any Creature in *Antonius* eyes;
Yea though thou wert as rich, as wise, as rare,
As any Pen could write, or Wit devise;
Yet with this Lady canst thou not compare,
Whose inward virtues all thy worth denies:
     Yet thou a blacke Egyptian do'st appeare;
     Thou false, shee true; and to her Love more deere.[15]

While not denying Cleopatra beauty, Lanier, "To take revenge for chast Octavia's wrongs," replaces Antony's right to make Cleopatra fair with her own judgment in favor of Octavia. So too, in Mary Sidney's *Antonie* (*c*.1590), a translation of Robert Garnier's *Marc Antoine*, Cleopatra's allure poses a problem when Sidney excises references to Cleopatra's beauty in an otherwise faithful translation.[16] Finally, Elizabeth Cary's *The Tragedie of Mariam* suggests an underlying competition between the "fair" Mariam and Cleopatra which feeds into Cary's striking use of blackness to accentuate status, cultural, and religious differences as the female characters compete, if not for Herod's amorous favor, then for access to his power. Beauty and race become contested categories which English females use to reveal their investment in the masculine engagement with foreign, female difference in imperial travel.

III

The Countess of Montgomerie's Urania uncovers the ways in which "literary" tropes of blackness shaped and articulated issues of gender and class for members of James I's court. In Wroth's life and her works, we have a clear example of the objectified and fetishized woman straining for a stable subject position. An intimate member of Anne of Denmark's circle, Wroth was deeply implicated in the Jacobean fascination with difference. She helped stage the mixture of transgressive sexuality and imperial desire in Ben Jonson's *The Masque of Blackness* and thus was present at a defining moment of the British empire which used blackness to privilege white beauty. In this masque the court women painted themselves black with the promise that they would later reappear, "turned" white by the power of the King, in *The Masque of Beauty*. Such fetishism of female skin serves to publicize the power of the King and the poet, but it also emphasizes the beauty and "whiteness" of the women's skins and, theoretically at least, draws attention to European female desirability.[17] While sent down from court, Wroth penned her own sonnet sequence which both demonstrates the problematic and powerful control tropes of blackness give the poet over his poetic subject and uses those tropes to refigure her own estrangement. The collision of the language of beauty with cultural difference in the *Urania* reveals Wroth's own complex – and often contradictory – engagement in the systems of power inherent in literary representations of blackness. Her awareness of the positioning of foreign women *vis-à-vis* European women is also intricately connected to her demonstration of how patriarchal systems work to objectify women and deny their subjectivity by creating differences between women that only enforce differences between men.[18]

Wroth's *Urania* opens with the shepherdess Urania, a woman not "certaine of mine own estate or birth," who has just been told by her country parents that she is a foundling. The wandering Urania meets the lovelorn knight Parselius and they, with other adventurers, sail to Naples to meet the famous knight Amphilanthus. This band of travelers is almost immediately blown off course to Venus' Isle (Cyprus) where they suffer their first trial by the House of Love. After drinking from a magic fountain, each character experiences an "enchantment" which creates illusions that propel the wómen into the House of Love. Notable among the illusions is the one suffered by Urania's maidservant and foster-sister, Limena, who sees her beloved, Allimarlus, embracing a black woman:

> *Urania's* maide beheld, *as she beleeu'd Allimarlus* in the second Towre, kissing and embracing a Black-moore; which so farre inraged her, being passionatly in love with him, as she must goe to revenge herselfe of that injurie.[emphasis added][19]

For a moment the reader sees what the maid fantasizes, a white man embracing a black woman. While this is an unusual (although not unprecedented) act in literature, we might question why the first dark "other" in the text is conjured up by this silent and almost forgotten character. This black figure, a vision entirely the product of the maid's imagination, is the locus of the varying concerns over status, beauty, race, and empire typical of the consistent use of tropes of blackness by women writers.[20]

The embrace of a black female by a white male, while not as common as the reverse pairing (black male/white female), is usually found in drama. In the seventeenth century, we see an emerging tradition of black maids beginning, most likely, with Zanthia in John Marston's *The Wonder of Women; or, The Tragedy of Sophonisba* (1606). These women commonly serve twin functions: a legitimate function as a maid and an illegitimate one as a bawd and/or whore.[21] Frequently, the two functions are assumed, if not actual. In *The White Devil*, Vittorina's maid, Zanche, is assumed to be her pander as well and is punished for the misdeeds of Flamineo, the actual pander. According to Anthony Barthelemy, in each appearance, the black woman "stands as a symbol of everything evil and low" and often serves as a metaphor for sexual evil. As he notes in his discussion of *Sophonisba*, these women are often embraced by a white, male character; at such times the black female "serves as a symbol of sin and love" and as an external representation of the spiritual state of the man who embraces her.[22] This dynamic works even when the women are not African characters. In Richard Brome's *The English Moore*, the villain, Nathaniel, rather than being repelled by the black-painted Millicent, is attracted to her, an attraction which is all the more proof of his villainy. The dramatic and metaphoric implications Barthelemy out-

184

lines are undeniably true on stage; however, the similarities of this moment only highlight the differences of the *Urania*.

Before reaching the enchanted fountain, the company is told by Venus's priest that lovers caught in the House of Love "suffer unexpressable tortures, in severall kindes as their affections are most incident to: as Jelousie, Despaire, Feare, Hope, Longings, and such like" (40). In other words, these visions in some way represent the innermost fears/ desires of the lovers. Interestingly, the maid's is the only fantasy which blocks the desires of the lover and repels rather than seduces or attracts her. Outraged at the sight, Limena rushes into the Tower of Desire intending to revenge herself against her rival:

> The shepherdesse her servant continuing her first passion got into that Tower too, where she stil saw her affliction, striving with as much spitefull jealousie, as that fury could vex her withall, to come at the *Moore* to pull her from her knight.
>
> (41)

The narrator tells us that this vision represents the "affliction" of the maid, jealousy, encouraging us to see the episode as an almost iconographic representation of jealousy. This is not an actual embrace, but the waiting-maid's fantasy and the embrace involves, not a villain, but the truly (and tediously) heroic Allimarlus. Absolutely no blame falls on Allimarlus himself, "being the onely sensible man left" (41); in fact he is the only one of the company who does not drink from the enchanted fountain that diverts them from their intended journey.

The narrative makes it quite clear that the Moor represents as well as kindles Limena's rage. However, we later see that the maid's jealousy was not unfounded and that this incident may in fact be a foreshadowing of Limena's marriage to Allimarlus. The subsequent unfolding of Limena's story suggests that the black woman also represents a problem in class or status. In Book IV the maid is beset with both jealousy and a sense of social inferiority. Knowing that Allimarlus is "a man fit for a greater womans love" (464), she accuses him of having an affair with a woman of greater rank. Not believing his denials, she becomes a trusted servant to the woman in order to catch her beloved. The maid's vision is not only another such projection of jealousy, it is also a desire: in fantasizing an African "other," this shepherdess/servant creates a privileged position for herself which does not affect the reader's view of Allimarlus. Thus, blackness only exists to make white that much more beautiful and acceptable, and Limena's class difference from Allimarlus is effaced under the more obvious racial difference of the "Black-moore."

In a larger sense, Allimarlus's embrace of the black woman represents female fears of the foreign difference that heroes – and travelers – encounter on these romantic adventures. The House of Love episode

foregrounds a gendered difference key to romance: men desire conquest while women desire men. The men abandon the women, fleeing
the House of Love in the hot pursuit of adventure and glory. When
Wroth conflates erotic passions and the passion for adventure in this
embrace, the resulting jealousy the black woman evokes may be as much
jealousy over male adventurism as jealousy over another woman. Wroth
demystifies a tradition of European male refusal to acknowledge that the
seduction of conquest and exploration and the seductiveness of native
women are often the same.[23] Women thus are always in subtle competition with the glory of travel and adventure that is the essence of male
romance.

The use of black to reify white, provoked in part by such contest, runs
throughout the *Urania* and is particularly noticeable in the sonnet cycle
Pamphilia to Amphilanthus (circulated in manuscript and published at the
end of the *Urania*). For example, in praising Pamphilia's verses,
Dolorinda claims that they only show Pamphilia "darkly," revealing her
actual fairness all the more: "that for any other, they might speake for
their excellencies, yet in comparison of their excelling vertues, they were
but shadows to set the others forth withall." In these verses, Wroth
evokes the arbitrary power of such binary thinking even as she rejects
the problematic subject position that it creates for women. Throughout
the sequence Pamphilia sees such divisions as dark and light, night and
day, as subject to the vagaries of "favor" and leading to uncertainty. In a
sonnet on suspicion, she shows how love is subject to change: "Noe little
sign of favor can I prove / Butt must be way'de, and turned to wronging
love, / And with each humor must my state begin" (4/P66.12–14).[24] In a
verse oddly evocative of both Dolorinda's judgment and Limena's view
of the "Blackamoor," Wroth shows how love's trials force an identification of white in relation to black: "Heere are affections, tri'de by loves
just might / As gold by fire, and black desernd by white, / Error by
truthe, and darknes knowne by light, / When faith is vallwed for love to
requite" (3/P79.5–8). In the next sonnet, Pamphilia wishes to escape the
trap of such oppositions: "Never to slack till earth noe stars can see, / Till
Sunn, and Moone doe leave us to dark night, / And Second Chaose once
again doe free / Us, and the world from all devisions spite" (4/P80.5–8).
As we shall see, Pamphilia reiterates this longing (albeit in a less apocalyptic vein) for the absolute destruction of these damaging encodings of
women throughout the *Urania*.

Beauty is one such value that Wroth simultaneously reasserts and
deconstructs. Carolyn Ruth Swift argues that Wroth uses stereotypes of
feminine charm "to reject masculine standards of female beauty and
virtue . . . heroines in *Urania* are beautiful because Wroth finds in
women a wit, courage, and spirit that create beauty."[25] Swift's reading
suggests that the *Urania* is an apolitical female world where women are

defined solely by virtue, but, as an examination of Wroth's use of blackness reveals, this world is not quite as "pure" as Swift's reading implies. While Wroth seems acutely aware of such tropes as signs of often-arbitrary male favor, she nonetheless does collude with masculinist scripts when she finds differences in women according to their rank and uses the language of beauty to reinforce distinctions in class. Thus it could be said that racial difference often subtends Wroth's emphasis on class differentiation, as in Limena's fantasy. While, as Swift suggests, Wroth's depiction of women is never as devastating as her uncle's depiction of a lower-class Mopsa in *The Countess of Montgomerie's Arcadia*, both Sidneys' evaluations of women are inextricably tied to their sense of class or rank.

Consequently rank and beauty both read very much the same throughout the romance. For example, when Wroth describes Lisia, "The lady was great, and therefore fair, full of spirit, and intising, pleasing and richly shee was attired, and bravely serv'd, an excellent hors-woman, and huntswoman she was" (414), she implies (albeit ironically) that for Lisia, as "great and *therefore* fair," fairness is dependent on her rank. In an earlier moment, the Duke Severus recognizes royalty by its complexion:

> The Duke all Supper time, curiously beholding the Knights, especially *Ollorandus*, who, he imagined by his complexion, and the favour of his face, to be the King, though it was long since he had seene him; but the ground he had in malice made him discerne that, which otherwise had laine hidden (envy having sharpnesse in discovering).
>
> (224)

Elsewhere, the shepherdess Allarina describes a May Day contest won by a woman who is beautiful in spite of her rank:

> . . . the rarest and the choycest beautyes came, among the rest one, who in truth I must confesse, was faire above the common beautyes in our time, but of the meanest parentage and ranke, being a servant to a Shepherdesse, who was of greatest place, for there is difference, and distinction made of their degrees, (though all below your sight) as well as in great ones, and as much curious choyce, and shame to match below their own degrees, as among Princes, whose great bloods are toucht, if staind with basenesse in the match they make.
>
> (184)

In a passage fascinating for its display of the niceties of rank, Allarina slights the beauty of a rival, not because of her virtue (or lack of it), but because of her rank. The shepherdess, while making the argument that

187

her rival is "meaner" than she and showing that shepherds are as sensitive to the nuances of rank and birth as lords, never loses sight of her audience, the Queen, who is really beyond such pastoral bickering. In parenthetically noting Pamphilia's alleged disinterest, Allarina forces a closer connection between herself and the Queen based on their distance from the status competition she outlines.

Status competition for men is more often located in knightly display and Wroth's portrayal of the chivalric code so integral to romance reveals most clearly the racial and patriarchal privileges generated by black/white oppositions. If, typically in this genre, the unidentified enemy, the unknown "other," is the Black Knight, the *Urania* demonstrates that this chivalric system, naturalized in romance, is in fact a highly artificial and male system of signification. Knights wear certain armors and emblems as signs of their status in erotic competition; however, this status is always defined by a knight, not imposed by a lady (although always ostensibly assumed *for* a lady). Knights often signal their romantic status through the use of colors in armor. This "dressing for success" occurs throughout the *Urania*. When Nereana, the "lady knight," signals her competition with Pamphilia by her attire, "for the kings being set, there entred a Lady of some beauty, attended on by ten knights, all in Tawny, her selfe likewise apparreld in that colour; her Pages and the rest of her servants having that liverie" (162), it is entirely possible that she has appropriated a system of signification seemingly only open to knights/males.

Unlike women, for whom color and complexion are constructed as "natural" effects rather than as subject positions assigned by men, men display for themselves their sense of being favored or disfavored through their chivalric garb, which can be removed at will. When planning their self-presentation, Steriamus and Amphilanthus disguise themselves in colored armor:

> . . . *Steriamus* desiring, that because his name was not yet knowne by desert, it might still be kept secret; and he most desired it, by reason of his vow. They agreed to it, and he was only call'd, The true despis'd, which was all the device in his shield. *Amphilanthus* did desire to be held unknowne too: but his reason was, that it was not so safe for so famous a man to be commonly knowne, in so great & imminent dangers. . . .
>
> (61)

Just as the two disguise themselves together, their disguises work as paired opposites: the unfavored one, Steriamius, is tawny and black and Amphilanthus, appropriately as the "never enough admired," wears red and white:

188

But then came the honour of his sexe, never enough admired, and belou'd *Amphilanthus*, his Armour was white, fillited with Rubies; his furniture to his Horse Crimson, embroydred with Pearle; his Shield with the same device, from which he took his name. *Steriamus* according to his fortune was in Tawny, wrought all over with blacke.

(62)

These passages visually recreate the red/white/black triad common to Petrarchan discourse. Nonetheless, these colors are not imposed upon the men; they are adopted in a manner as artificial as their armor. Furthermore, these "disguises" never seem to conceal an identity for very long and the men are never placed in the precarious subject positions of the women. Indeed, Amphilanthus's disguise is not a disguise at all, as a Gentleman approaches him, claiming, "My Lord, your worth cannot be hid, though you have obscured your name" (62).

This obvious use of armor as a system of self-signification in the pursuit of "amor" suggests an interesting gloss on a strange, masque-like episode in Book I which begins a new adventure. After Pamphilia assures her friend and rival, Antissia, that she has no romantic interest in Amphilanthus, they are greeted with a strange spectacle:

Tenne Knights comming in russet Armours, their Beaners up, their Swords in their hands; who comming more then halfe way to the State, making low reuerence, stood still, parting themselves to either side of the Chamber, to let the followers better be discerned. Then came tenne more, but in black Armours, chain'd together, without Helmets or Swords. After them came sixe armed like the first, three carrying Speares of infinite bignesse; one, the Sheild, and the other two the Sword and Helmet of a Knight, who for countenance seem'd no lover; his colour like a Moore; his fashion rude and proud, following after these sixe, who, as the first, divided themselves.

(79)

Coming so immediately after this picture of (albeit friendly) female rivalry, this alternating procession of red and black provides a visual analogue to the Pamphilia/Amphilanthus/Antissia triangle as well as an indication of Pamphilia's own ambivalence toward Antissia. It also presents a powerful convergence of jealousy, beauty, chivalric disguise, and race as the knights in "black Armours" are suggestively connected with a visual pun to the Knight who "seem'd no lover" because he has "colour like a Moore."

The rivalry between Antissia and Pamphilia provokes yet another extreme of color and, with the link between beauty and jealousy (which is so key to the Limena episode), underscores the competition between women that is at the heart of discourses of beauty. In an almost parodic glance at the artificiality of the trope, Wroth shows us Pamphilia's jealous reaction to Amphilanthus's praise of Antissia:

> But one day as they were alone together, some discourse falling out of the beautie of Ladies, *Amphilanthus* gave so much commendations of Antissia, as she betweene dislike, and a modest affection, answered, hee had spoke sufficiently in her praise: for truly my Lord, said she, me thinkes there is not that beautie in her as you speake of, but that I have seene, as faire and delicate as shee; yet in truth shee's very white, but that extreame whitenesse I like not so well, as where that (though not in that fulnesse) is mix'd with sweete lovelinesse; yet I cannot blame you to thinke her peerlesse, who views her but with the eyes of affection. *Amphilanthus* gave this reply; That hee till then had never seene so much Womanish dispostion in her, as to have so much prettie enuie in her, yet in his opinion (except her selfe) he had not seene any fairer, *Antisius* with that came to them, which brought them into other discourses, til they were forced to part.
>
> (50–1)

In her friendliness to Antissia, Pamphilia is not able to contradict Amphilanthus's judgment and make Antissia black to her "fair." Instead, she opposes his masculine word with her sight, thereby making the issue his authority in granting "whiteness" rather than her actual beauty. Thus the "extreame whiteness [she likes] not so well" is not so much Antissia's white complexion as it Amphilanthus's admiration of her. Of course, Amphilanthus's very nature (as the lover of many) makes it easy to see how unstable and arbitrary such male designations of fairness are. Part of Pamphilia's "womanish dispostion" is not only her jealousy, but her uncovering of Amphilanthus's masculine right to make women fair or black as he desires and her anticipation of Amphilanthus's inconstant reminder that both Antissia and Pamphilia are fair in his eyes.

It is in Pamphilia that Wroth locates resistance to the hegemony of male favor and color. After the conversation with Amphilanthus, Pamphilia expresses her sense of being stuck in this system of signification as she talks to the inconstant moon:

> Being heavie, she went into her bed, but not with hope of rest, but to get more libertie to expresse her woe. At last, her servants gone, and all things quiet, but her ceaselesse mourning soule, she softly rose out of her bed, going to her window, and looking out beheld the Moone, who was then faire and bright in her selfe, being almost

at the full, but rounded about with blacke, and broken clouds. Ah *Diana* (said she) how doe my fortunes resemble thee? my love and heart as cleare, and bright in faith, as thou art in thy face, and the fulnesse of my sorrowes in the same substance: and as thy wane must bee, so is my wane of hopes in my love; affections in him, being as cold to me, as thou art in comparison of the Sunnes heate: broken ioyes, blacke despaires, incirkling me, as those disseuered clouds do strive to shadow by straight compass-ing thy best light.

(51)

Here we see Pamphilia again recognizing that fairness is imposed, "affections in him, being as cold to me, as thou art in comparison of the Sunnes heat"; refusing to submit to Amphilanthus's inconstancy and thereby read herself as black/unfavored, she is only surrounded by blackness, "blacke despaires, incirkling me, as those disseuered clouds do strive to shadow by straight compassing thy best light" (51). It is at this moment, when she is least favored and, like the moon, not in the light of the sun, that the reader first sees her write.[26]

Of all the female characters, Pamphilia is the only one who continually wishes to be beyond such binary systems. Although it may be that her doubly secure rank as Queen of Pamphilia allows her this privilege, the wish is certainly in keeping with her constancy, as well as with her literary heritage: the reconciliation of the opposing virtues of the *Arcadia*'s Philoclea and Pamela.[27] Pamphilia's wish is, above all, to resist male inscriptions which may deny her subjectivity with their fickle inconstancy. At one such moment of resistance, she projects herself as a "Black-moore":

. . . torture me not with sorrowes, I will truly and religiously confesse, I am not worthy of you; but it is not my fault, I wish I were so fit, as you might ever love, and such an one as all the world might thinke fit for you, then I know you would be just: nor wish I this for any benefit, but for your love; for else in the comparison of other gaine unto my selfe, or any other then your loved selfe, I rather would wish to be a Black-moor, or any thing more dreadfull, then allure affection to me, if not from you; thus would I be to merit your loved fauour, the other to show my selfe purer, then either purest White or Black: but faith will not prevaile, I am forsaken and despised, why dye I not? it is not fit, no, tis not fit, I still must live, and feele more cause of woe, or better to say, to see my cause of woe.

(396)

This complex passage conflates many of the disparate and contradictory

191

strands of the discourse of blackness seen throughout early modern England. First, in wishing "to be a Black-moor, or any thing more dreadfull" rather than attract the other's desire, Pamphilia draws on an increasingly common Renaissance *topos* that black women are unattractive and repulsive. Even in the House of Love, Limena projects the undercurrent of that belief in seeing Allimarlus embracing a black woman. Paradoxically, this assumption almost never ends up as anticipated and men find themselves in the arms of black women in these texts, perhaps revealing that the male construction of black, female difference is a manifestation of desire complicated by the fear of difference. Hence, the dread inspired by Limena's "Black-moore" is merely an inversion of the desire evoked by a black Cleopatra. However, the wish and the punning desire to "dye" or change color (the latter a form of escape performed by Wroth in the *Masque of Blackness*) is a form of identification as Pamphilia implies that there is a strength in the outsider status of the black female; that is, in not being subject to the desires of males.

In Pamphilia's wish to be simultaneously "black" and beloved by Amphilanthus, Wroth draws on the Renaissance *topos* of impossibility and highlights the lack of subject position offered by the language of beauty which does not allow a woman the possibility of being both "black" and favored.[28] Pamphilia's subsequent claim recognizes the implications of her desire. In saying, "thus would I be to merit your loved fauour, the other to show my selfe purer, then either purest White or Black," she again wishes to have a stable – or "pure" – subject position beyond the objectification which accrues from being the focus of (inconstant) male desire. Like the author of her story, she readily acknowledges – and resists – her own subjection to the vagaries of male favor exhibited in the binarism of black and white.

IV

As women who by definition disobeyed (in the case of Wroth, with a vengeance) one or more strictures on being chaste, silent, and obedient, it is not surprising that women writers generally show a heightened awareness of the social (and therefore political) construction of difference.[29] However, as Lamb suggests, when "authors render visible the sites of resistance, the loopholes, the contradictions, the shiftings within gender ideology restricting women's language in the Renaissance,"[30] they also construct a system of power for themselves. Given that these women – "Shakespeare's sisters" – were writing in the formative years of English nationalism and empire, perhaps it is incumbent on those of us studying them to investigate their multifaceted roles in the development of colonialism in order to understand more fully the ways in which they appropriate patriarchal, imperial values even as they resist domestic ideologies.

Outlining women's position in the birth of England's empire is a difficult task. As sociologist Cynthia Enloe notes, much of the difficulty springs from a reluctance to acknowledge that colonialism was not a purely masculinist enterprise and to examine what may be unpleasant realities about women's roles:

> But in many arenas of power feminists have been uncovering a reality that is less simple. First they have discovered that some women's class aspirations and their racist fears lured them into the role of controlling other women for the sake of imperial rule. . . . To describe colonization as a process that has been carried on solely by men overlooks the ways in which male colonizers' success depended on some women's complicity.[31]

For feminists working on the Renaissance, this issue is further complicated by the still-tenuous nature of the study of women in early modern England. That women of the Renaissance were more restricted (as much by material conditions as ideology) certainly suggests that they had less influence in colonial thought than the more visible Victorian women travel writers and missionaries. Nonetheless, the women writers we are currently uncovering had their own engagements in foreign travel and empire and the implicit interracial rivalry between women was more than hypothetical. Wroth herself may have been present when Pocahontas was brought to court as the wife of John Rolfe and christened Rebecca. As an adolescent, Elizabeth Cary translated Abraham Ortelius's *Le Miroir du monde*, including such observations as, "[America] (except some little) is under the King of Spaine his Dominion" and "these saide countries be full of golde."[32] As an adult, she implemented her own plans to train Irish children in trades while her husband administered James I's colonial policy. Just like women in other ages, Renaissance women were not just passive observers of a male system, but were participants in and/or supporters of the new social order created by England's imperial imagination.

It may seem that locating (and thereby implicating) women in England's colonial project at the very moment when critics are recovering their voices from the depths of patriarchally induced obscurity is unfair. However, it is no less necessary than the recovery itself. As bell hooks argues:

> Only when we confront the realities of sex, race, and class, the ways they divide us, make us different, stand us in opposition, and work to reconcile and resolve these issues will we be able to participate in the making of a feminist revolution, in the transformation of the world.[33]

Feminists working on early women writers have a unique opportunity to begin a critical transformation at a relatively early stage. Coalitions built on false Edenic visions of the past are doomed to failure. In studying women's experiences of difference – even hegemonic ones – we can avoid the trap (epitomized in binary thinking) of attempting to resist patriarchy without the necessary resistance to racism, imperialism, and other forms of domination.

11

THE TENTH MUSE

Gender, rationality, and the marketing of knowledge

Stephanie Jed

In 1650, Anne Bradstreet's brother-in-law published her poetry in London under the title *The Tenth Muse, Lately Sprung Up in America*. In 1657, the volume was annotated in William London's *Catalogue [of] the Most Vendible Books in England* . . . as "Mrs. Bradstreet. The 10. Muse, a Poem. 8o." In 1668, a volume appeared in Mexico City celebrating and commemorating the completion of the cathedral. It included a sonnet of Juana Inés de Asbaje with an epigraph exalting her as "a glorious honor of the Mexican Museum" ("glorioso honor del Mexicano Museo"). In Madrid in 1689, the printer Juan García Infanzón published the first edition of the works of Sor Juana Inés de la Cruz, describing her on the title page as "the Tenth Muse . . . who in various meters, languages and styles fertilizes various issues" ("Musa Dézima . . . Que en varios metros, idiomas, y estilos, fertiliza varios assumptos"). Finally, in 1683, in Oxford, the Ashmolean Museum opened its doors to the public for the first time, charging admission to "peasants and women-folk who gaze at the library as a cow might gaze at a new gate with such noise and trampling of feet that others are much disturbed."[1]

My essay begins, against the background of this seventeenth-century compilation of "facts," to form an intuition and a question. The intuition is: that the category "Tenth Muse" was implicated in the European politics of constructing the "New World" as a museum. After all, institutions of knowledge and history-making, such as the Escorial, the British Museum, the Archivo de las Indias, the archives of the trading companies, "natural" histories and collections of travel narratives, were united by the common "museal" project of ruling new lands and peoples and making them "vendible."[2] The category "Tenth Muse," then, might provide an important interpretive key to the gender fictions implicit in these sixteenth and seventeenth-century institutions of classifying, knowing, and ruling. Indeed, the "evidence" for connecting the "Tenth Muse" to sixteenth and seventeenth-century European taxonomic

STEPHANIE JED

activities is abundant, but finding a rhetorical strategy for doing so is arduous. The question is: why?

THE "FACTS" OF THE TENTH MUSE

We might begin this investigation by looking at the fictional category "Tenth Muse" in the first published volumes of Anne Bradstreet and Sor Juana. In both cases, this fiction was the effect of social relations between men of letters and commerce for whom the idea of a woman writer made no sense. The epithet "Tenth Muse" thus provided a fiction to make sense of or explain the emergence of significant women writers in the colonial literature market. Taking on this explanatory function, the category "Tenth Muse" became a taxonomic "fact" which could account for the otherwise unintelligible appearance of women writers. As a fictional or constructed "fact," it provided a solution to the taxonomic impossibility of classifying Bradstreet and Sor Juana either as women or as writers. This "fact," moreover, had the function of commodifying these writers within a system of assumptions about authorship (men, inspired by Muses, did it) and gender (women did not write).[3] As a "fact" designed to account for and control any variance from the gender norm, the fictional classification "Tenth Muse" made these writers more intelligible, and thus more "vendible," in a taxonomic system which separated women from writers.

Anne Bradstreet's brother-in-law and promoter John Woodbridge carefully adhered to this taxonomic "fact," by introducing *The Tenth Muse* and her work of writing in the light of gender ambiguity. Fearing that the "excellency" of Bradstreet's poetry might make the (male) reader doubt that a woman wrote them, Woodbridge wrote: "the worst effect of his reading will be unbelief, which will make him question whether it be a woman's work, and ask, is it possible?" The two contradictory meanings of "whether it be a woman's work" – one being the question "could a woman have written such accomplished poetry?" and the other "should women be allowed to write poetry?" – were precisely those which characterized the difficulty of classifying the woman writer: if she were a writer, she could not be a woman, and if she were a woman, why wasn't she doing a woman's work? Given these two alternative taxonomies, Woodbridge chose them both: he classified Bradstreet as a woman "honoured and esteemed . . . [for] her exact diligence in her place," but he also classified her as a woman who wrote outside the time and space of "a woman's work," in the "few hours curtailed from her sleep and other refreshments." In this way, in Woodbridge's estimation, she was able to sustain the ambiguity of being both a woman and a writer. And so, she earned the classification "Tenth Muse," that "factual" category which marked her gender ambiguity. A "curious" kind of neutral, she occupied a category all her own.[4]

Bradstreet's own "Prologue" to her poetry adhered, in many ways, to this same taxonomic "fact." Citing the very convention that excluded women from writing, she excoriated the hypothetical critic "who says my hand a needle better fits." At the same time, however, she suggested that the Muse who inspired her poetry, unlike the female personifications who inspired male poets, was a neuter:

My foolish, broken, blemished Muse so sings,
And this to mend, alas, no art is able,
'Cause nature made it so irreparable.
                                        (l. 18–20)[5]

The syntax here is ambiguous enough to allow the "it" (of l. 20) to refer to either the Muse's song or to the "Muse" herself, made neuter for the occasion of inspiring a female poet. By interrupting the paradigm of the female muse who inspires the male writer, Bradstreet created a third space for herself, representing the taxonomic "fact" of her gender ambiguity as a woman writer and "Tenth Muse."

Sor Juana articulated a similar "fact" in her response to a Peruvian gentleman who suggested she become a man. The Muses, she implied, in their traditional function of separating women from writers, had exempted themselves from helping her to respond to his suggestion ("para responderos / todas las musas se eximen"). But, in any case, Sor Juana was uninterested in the prospect. She came to the convent, precisely "because there is no one to verify if I am a woman" and because there, her body could be "neuter or abstract" ("sólo sé que mi cuerpo / . . . / es neutro, o abstracto"). Indeed, the term "virgin," describing her sex, could be applied to either woman or man ("es común de dos lo virgen").[6] Given Sor Juana's insistence on transgressing gender categories and creating a gender fiction for herself, it is no wonder that the taxonomic "fact" of the "Tenth Muse" was invoked to classify and circumscribe her works in the literary market.

There are other interesting gender contradictions implicit in the "fact" of the "Tenth Muse," contradictions that seem to be at the heart of national and colonial projects. The titles of the works of both "Tenth Muses" included metaphors of generation which exceeded gender norms. Bradstreet's title, *The Tenth Muse, Lately Sprung Up in America*, evoked an image of parthenogenesis: this muse was not born from any inseminated figure of Mother America, but she sprang rather from the soil of New England, seemingly without the help of English seed. Here, the category "Tenth Muse," which accounted for Bradstreet's deviation from the Puritan sanctions against women making public statements,[7] also played an important role in English colonization. If the nine classical

Muses represented the power of English (and European) culture to dominate the world, a new category was required to assimilate new manifestations of this power in places far from London. The "Tenth Muse," a muse of commodification, incorporated Bradstreet's partheno-genetic verses into an English genealogy and continuity of power.

In like manner, Sor Juana was represented on her title page as "fertilizing" with her writings the colonial soil of New Spain. This title evoked an image of an androgynous muse, a female personification who could also perform the task of fertilization. In this case as well, the "fertilizing" verses, which accounted for Sor Juana's choice of the veil over marriage, illustrated the extent to which the "Tenth Muse," the muse of commodification, may have served Spanish colonial projects. Once again, the procreative capacity of her verses indicated the "Tenth Muse's" ability to reproduce Spanish and imperial power in places far removed from European museums.

Bradstreet and Sor Juana were constructed as "Tenth Muses" in a period in European cultural history which was dominated by the epis-teme of the museum.[8] And as Paula Findlen has so brilliantly shown, the museum, that dwelling-place sacred to the nine Muses, became the "axis through which all other structures of collecting, categorizing, and know-ing intersected."[9] In addition to being the epistemological institution which collected the "New World" for the purposes of ruling it, the museum also represented a space of social relations and activities. Reports from the "New World," promotional literature, "natural" histor-ies, editorial projects, and economic ventures provided the textual and relational ground for collecting, classifying, and knowing the "Tenth Muse" as a commodity and resource for cultural exploitation.[10] We might turn to this relational context to understand the production of the category "Tenth Muse."

"FACTS" PRODUCED IN THE CONTEXT OF RELATIONS

The construction of two eminent colonial poets as Tenth Muses in the latter half of the seventeenth century constitutes but one later episode in a long narrative of developing colonial economies. The earlier episodes of this narrative, I would like to suggest, may be found in the writings of collectors, natural historians, encyclopedists, and other culture brokers who were engaged in the separation of "knowledge" from colonial interests. In his book *The Old World and the New*, J. H. Elliott traces the route of New World objects and facts as they began to crowd the museums and studies of sixteenth-century European scholars.

At first, these objects and facts, collected indiscriminately and for curiosity's sake alone, were, Elliott says, "lumped together into an undif-ferentiated category of the marvellous or exotic." As such, they reinforced already existing European habits of thought and constructing knowledge. Later, as the desire to domesticate and appropriate the resources of the New World intensified, Europeans devised new methods to differentiate and rationalize the exotic in accordance with their goal of ruling and commodifying the new lands and peoples.[11] By the seventeenth century, questionnaires, travel narratives, encyclopedic compendia, museums, and libraries collected and classified "information" about places, plants, animals, and peoples, previously considered exotic, in such a way as to make them seem attractive to European investors and consumers. The construction of the category "Tenth Muse" can be understood in the context of this rationalizing program.

A "natural" historian's report about the iguana illustrates this relation between "facts," commodification, and reason. In Book 12, chapter 7 of his *Historia general y natural de las Indias*, Gonzalo Fernández de Oviedo (1478–1557), the official historiographer of Charles V and the military governor of the fortress of Santo Domingo, writes of the iguana, a creature then unknown in Europe.[12] He covers several points regarding the iguana, exemplifying the European concerns to classify New World knowledge and to exploit new commodities in commerce and trade. With regard to classification, Oviedo tells us that it is difficult to know if the iguana belongs to the category of animal or fish, and he warns us not to confuse the iguana with the crocodile, as many, including Pedro Martire, have done. He then goes on to treat the commodity side of knowledge, telling us that there are many ways to cook the iguana and its eggs, but that so far, the iguana's nourishment remains a mystery. In regard to this last point, the mystery of the iguana's nourishment, Oviedo writes:

> It is such a quiet animal, that it neither screams nor moans nor makes any sound, and it will stay tied up wherever you put it, without doing any damage or making any noise, for ten or twenty days and more without eating or drinking anything. Some say, on the contrary, that if you give the iguana a little cassava or grass or something similar, it will eat it. But I have had some of these animals sometimes tied up in my house, and I never saw them eat, and I had them watched day and night, and in the end, I never knew nor was able to understand what they were eating in the house, and everything that you give them to eat remains whole.[13]

At the end of the chapter, Oviedo connects his commodification of this creature to another kind of commerce, the European trade in exotic specimens and facts, a commerce that would enable Europe to secure cultural, and not just economic, domination over the newly encountered civilizations. Oviedo writes:

Having written the above, two of the bigger iguanas were brought to me, and we ate part of one in my house, and the other I had put away, tied up, to send to Venice to the Magnificent Mr. Joan Baptista [Ramusio], chancellor of the Signoria, and it was tied to a post on the patio of this fortress of Santo Domingo for more than forty days, during which time, it never ate any of the many things it was given; and I was told that these animals ate only earth, and I had a hundred pounds of dirt put in a barrel as the iguana's provisions, so that there would be no lack of it at sea. And I hope that while I am correcting these treatises, ships will arrive to let us know if the iguana arrived alive in Spain and with what nourishment.

When I arrived in Spain in 1546, however, I found out from the one who took the animal that it had died at sea.[14]

I am interested and intrigued by the tale of this ill-fated expedition for what it can reveal about how "social relations of domination are frozen into the logics" of taxonomies in the colonial period.[15] Once we start to examine the "rationality" of Oviedo's decision to send an iguana to Venice in a barrel of dirt, a whole series of relations emerges – social, cultural, and economic – to support this concept of reason. An analysis of the episode of the iguana will thus reveal some aspects of social organization underlying the construction and commodification of knowledge about the "New World." It can also point us to methods for analyzing the role of colonial women writers in this social organization.

Oviedo's account of the iguana is structured as a collection of taxonomic statements. For example, the discussion of whether the iguana should be classified as a "terrestrial animal" or fish has the effect of reifying those categories confounded by Oviedo's own contradictory understanding of the iguana, which "lives in both rivers and trees." In this way, Oviedo introduces the iguana to the European public more as an effect of his taxonomic prowess than as an effect of his inadequate eye. More important, however, is the function of this taxonomic prowess in the construction of a certain kind of rationality in Oviedo's account. Oviedo's ability to classify the iguana, with confidence, under the category "animal" serves as evidence that he knew enough about the iguana to believe that sending one in a barrel of dirt to Venice was a "rational" project.[16] Perhaps a similar line of reasoning was used to classify our "Tenth Muses" and to transport them to Europe.

Statements like "I never saw them eat" or "everything that you give them to eat remains whole" are selected by Oviedo, the "teller of the tale," to convince us, from his imperial point of view, of the rationality of his project.[17] It is a rationality which refers both to the rationale for colonial ventures and the relations of inequality and domination

200

required to sustain those ventures. And it is this concept of rationality which determines the selection and categorization of statements about the iguana's eating habits. Also informing this concept of rationality is Oviedo's relation to the Venetian statesman Ramusio; from the perspective of their common cultural and economic investment in New World taxonomies, this interested relation could indeed be seen as "rational." In his statements about the iguana, Oviedo, then, transposes a concept of rationality from his relations with Ramusio to the purported actuality of the iguana's nourishment. As we shall see later, a similar mechanism of transposed rationality might be investigated in relation to the construction of the Tenth Muse. It is important, in both cases, to examine how fictional categories and misguided observations can be generated from these "rational" relations.

Oviedo's relation with the Venetian Giovanni Battista Ramusio (1485–1557) was, in some ways, emblematic of the intercultural relations which sustained the dynamic of empire. This dynamic was characterized by a tension between the standardizing effects of the imperial bureaucracy and the economic and cultural differences within its jurisdiction. These cultural differences, rationalized and smoothed over by the bureaucratic structures of record-keeping and diplomatic networks, eventually produced the culture of national states. Ramusio's publication of Oviedo's works in Italian constitutes a chapter in that process. Oviedo informs us that when he sent off a live iguana to Venice in 1540, Ramusio was the secretary or chancellor of Venice's Council of Ten. He had come into contact with Oviedo through the official imperial network: Andrea Navagero, the official historiographer of the Venetian Republic, had established relations with Pietro Martire and with various members of the Council of the Indies in Seville and probably met Oviedo there in 1525 when Oviedo was preparing the abridged version of his *Historia natural*. Navagero, then, not only put Oviedo and Ramusio in contact with each other, but saw to it that Oviedo's *Sumario* or abridged version of his work would be published in Venice in Italian in 1534.[18]

The epistolary relation that ensued between Oviedo and Ramusio, who never met in person, was essentially one between an informant from the periphery and a metropolitan broker of knowledge. Because of his powerful position as knowledge-broker and important administrator of the Venetian State, Ramusio was sometimes better informed about New World developments than his informants and even provided information to Oviedo, at times, that helped him understand the "reality" he was living.[19] It is important to see Oviedo's production of facts about Hispaniola in relation to the interests of publishers like Ramusio who would market these facts in a particular ideological frame. And it is in this context of Ramusio's role as a broker of knowledge that the rationality involved in collecting facts about the iguana and sending one to Venice begins to emerge.

Ramusio had constructed and cornered a market of consumers of news about the New World which included not only traditional intellectuals but also merchants, bankers, and a general reading public in some way identified with the drama of New World encounters. In order to attract this general reading public, Ramusio organized his collection of New World accounts around the heroes and hopes of chivalry and conquest,[20] a cultural paradigm whose traditional function in European literature had always been to mystify the waging of war under the guise of epic poetry. Oviedo's literary talents and military role as governor of the fortress of Santo Domingo made him a perfect fit for this paradigm, whose function in the sixteenth century was to mystify the international economic partnerships, which would cause so much suffering throughout the world, under the guise of natural history. On January 1, 1538, two years before Oviedo attempted the expedition of the iguana, Oviedo and Ramusio entered into just such an economic partnership.

Signing a contract with Antonio di Priuli, the procurator of San Marco, Ramusio and Oviedo invested 400 gold ducats in an international business venture to which they committed themselves for six years. The 400 ducats were used to buy Italian and Venetian goods to send to Santo Domingo, where Oviedo sold them at a profit and used the money to buy liquors and sugars to sell in Cadiz, again, obviously, at a profit. This partnership, tracing the route of the infamous rum triangle, was among the first of its kind and provided a model for subsequent, larger-scale enterprises. Following this example, in 1560, the heirs of Tommaso Giunti, the publishers of Ramusio's collection *Navigazioni e viaggi*, invested a part of their publishing profits in a trading company that would take earnings from the selling of books and glass products and turn them into sugar and pepper for European markets.[21] If the trade in New World commodities and the trade in facts about natural resources had once served separate functions in the construction of imperial domination, now these two functions were completely intertwined. This network of economic/cultural relations constitutes a more pertinent signifier for Oviedo's descriptive statements about the iguana than any notion of what Oviedo may have actually observed. In the context of these relations, we can understand that it was reasonable and rational for Oviedo to ship off to Venice a live iguana in a barrel of dirt. Only by making visible and analyzing these relations are we able to challenge this concept of reason.

REORGANIZING KNOWLEDGE

The project of reconstructing an analogous context in which "facts" about the "Tenth Muse" were produced is a complex one. In the case of Anne Bradstreet, several circumstances surrounding the publication of *The Tenth Muse* point to a specific rhetorical context for her commodification as a poet.[22] Stephen Bowtell, for example, the publisher of *The Tenth Muse*, was a noted publisher of "political" materials.[23] In the context of England's civil wars, his investment in the commodity of a colonial "Tenth Muse" may be seen as a move to strengthen the image of the English nation in its Atlantic enterprise. William London's listing of *The Tenth Muse* in his 1657 *Catalogue [of] the Most Vendible Books in England* confirmed this function of Bradstreet's poetry as a "passive" item in an inventory of England's cultural merchandise.[24] Another London bookseller who collected and published Civil War books and pamphlets, George Thomason, included his copy of *The Tenth Muse*, purchased a few days after its issue, in a "secret" collection representing, in some sense, the interregnum state of the nation.[25] Here, the urgency with which Bradstreet's writings were acquired and collected may point to the crucial role played by cultural commodities in the formation of political ties. A further investigation of questions like these would put us on the path to interpreting the role of the "Tenth Muse" in constructing the "New World" as a museum.

The same kinds of textual relations might be researched in the case of Sor Juana. The political worlds which commodified her writings were those of the viceroys and the Church. It was the Countess of Paredes, wife of the Marquis de la Laguna (viceroy of New Spain from 1680 to 1686), who actually transported Sor Juana's writings to Madrid. And another imperial servant in New Spain, Juan Camacho Gayna, took the credit for preparing the first edition of Sor Juana's works. As Octavio Paz has suggested, it is likely that the Jesuit Diego Calleja had a more active role in the editing of this volume, as he had "a long-continuing interest" in Sor Juana.[26] For our purposes here, we might investigate rather what role these figures, and others associated with Sor Juana's writings, may have played in the administering of "New Spain" for a profit. What relations did these profits have to "facts" about the "New World" and categories for knowledge-making? The research and interpretation of texts representing these relations would provide a context for understanding the construction and promotion of Sor Juana as a "Tenth Muse."

My interest in these questions is twofold: first, I am interested in making the texts of publishers, bureaucrats, catalogue-makers, "natural" historians, investors, ethnographers, culture-brokers, and the like come together to tell us something about how the fiction of the "Tenth Muse" was produced as a "fact" within a particular concept of reason and taxonomy. The assembling of such texts would make visible, I believe, the way in which the "facts" of the "Tenth Muse" constituted a fiction related to the "I" who was ruling.[27] In the eyes of these producers of "facts," it would seem reasonable to make sense of a woman writer as a "Tenth Muse." The "Tenth Muse" was a packaging of knowledge that would sell, still another commodity to be exported and exploited in the metropolitan capitals of London and Madrid.

Second, I am interested in the "facts" of the "Tenth Muse" as a gender fiction, an "unreal" category which points to the constructed nature of all historical knowledge. Research libraries and archives, products of the same colonial relations which produced the "Tenth Muse," do not readily offer information about their own taxonomic fictions. The "Tenth Muse" and the various texts of culture-brokers, investors, "natural" historians, etc., which, coming together, construct her as a fiction, raise questions about the fictional structures in which we work. Perhaps Adrienne Rich was alluding to this fiction, when she wrote of Anne Bradstreet's place in a Women's Archive.

In her 1966 essay on the Puritan poet Anne Bradstreet, Adrienne Rich made a distinction between Bradstreet's earlier poems treating such themes as the Ages of Man and Assyrian monarchs and her later poems written "in response to the simple events in a woman's life." Characterizing Bradstreet's earlier poetry as "pedestrian, abstract, mechanical," Rich wrote: "Had she stopped writing after the publication of these verses, or had she simply continued in the same vein, Anne Bradstreet would survive in the catalogues of *Women's Archives*, a social curiosity or at best a literary fossil" (emphasis mine).[28] Rich went on to claim that the later, more personal poems "rescue Anne Bradstreet from the Women's Archives and place her conclusively in literature."[29] In her 1979 reflection on this essay, Rich regretted her "condescending references to 'Women's Archives,'" saying that such condescension exemplified "the limitations of a point of view which took masculine history and literature as its center and which tried from that perspective to view a woman's life and work."[30] No longer attempting to "rescue" Anne Bradstreet from the Women's Archives, Rich, in this reflection, rescues the Women's Archive as an important site of feminist research. To imagine a Women's Archive in which women writers share the shelf space in function of their relations with one another is to make visible the fictional categories and contradictions within which they wrote.

It is not clear, however, how we are to imagine this fictional Women's Archive and the fictional point of view which would take women's history and literature as its center. Are we to imagine a series of writings by individual women writers lying inert on a shelf in a vault, unable to be organized in the kind of organic relations from which most institutions of historical records were formed? Writers of the stature of Anne Bradstreet and Sor Juana, after all, never knew each other. Indeed, because the "facts" of conquest and colonialism implied a particular organization of social relations and knowledge, women writers in history could neither know each other nor form political or social ties. How then could a Women's Archive activate a relation which never existed in history? Would there be rearranging or more writing to be done?

In the histories of many archives and libraries, we find that generations of librarians and archivists have been arranging and rearranging historical materials to fit their own cultural needs. As the researcher walks into a library, archive, or museum, s/he is instantly aware of becoming part of this fiction. In a miscellany of sixteenth-century broadsheets in the Marciana Library in Venice, for example, we can read the notes of a nineteenth-century librarian who saw fit to extract materials pertaining to geography and the New World from their original context among chivalric verses and verses pertaining to European wars. We can see in these notes that in sixteenth-century Italy there was a social-historical connection between the literary *topoi* of chivalry and the conquest of the New World, a connection which, by virtue of the librarian's intervention, has been lost to the modern consciousness.[31] The feminist reader, reconstructing this connection, makes visible again the relations of sexual domination common to texts as diverse in time and kind as Ariosto's *Orlando furioso*, Vespucci's (in)famous letter of 1505, and the later abundance of English promotional literature highlighting the virgin, bride-like quality of the New World.[32] Understood as an intertext, these texts may be seen as one measure of the relation between women writers. Effecting a powerful relation of disconnection between women, this intertext can nonetheless be seen as one which bound women's writing together. In a Women's Archive, we might analyze the conditions under which this relation of disconnection in women's writing was produced instead of focusing on the images of disconnected women.

We might even rearrange materials to correspond to our interest in the appearance of women writers in relation to colonial representations of women. For how can we separate John Smith's representation of New England as a woman whose "treasures [have] yet never beene opened, nor her originalls wasted, consumed, nor abused" from the Muse who would soon after favor those treasures with her verses?[33] In the same way, it is difficult to separate the construction of Sor Juana as a "Tenth Muse" from the relations of ruling between Spain and New Spain and from the efforts of the Spanish kings to promote their cause of Christendom against the advance of Protestantism. The promotion of Bradstreet and Sor Juana as Muses in the literary marketplaces of London and Madrid, then, gives us some insight into the gendered construction of nationhood in these metropolitan capitals. These are some of the fictions whose records might be foregrounded in the Women's Archive, activating relations between those colonial women writers who never did, because they never could, relate to one another in institutional ways.

Nor should this kind of rearrangement of materials be seen as particularly radical or disrespectful of existing taxonomies. In the State Archive in Milan, where I have worked, archival materials have been disordered and reordered, dismembered and reclassified, according to the whims, logics, bureaucratic requirements, and scholarly exigencies of successive generations of archivists. The scholar is often reminded that archival reorganizations correspond to the establishment of new relations between citizens and the State, as well as to developments in scientific methods. We find, for example, that at the turn of this century, archival work, including reorganizations of materials, filing, and the making of catalogues and inventories, had come to a halt. The historian Nicola Raponi did not see this as a necessarily negative development. "It was," he wrote, "not a period of inertia but a rich and intense period of *methodological disorientation* . . . which was reflected in a kind of *eclectic* activity."[34]

I would like to suggest that we are currently living through a similar moment of disorientation, one which would favor making visible the constructed or fictional nature of "facts" and their classifications. Analysis of the rhetorical organization of inventories and catalogues of libraries, archives, and museums formed in the sixteenth and seventeenth centuries would be one way of dramatizing the fictional nature of colonial documentation projects.[35] Another way of dramatizing these rhetorics would be, of course, to write new fictions.

THE "TENTH MUSE" AT SEA

In the course of my search to understand the "Tenth Muse" syndrome in relation to colonial epistemologies, I was delighted to come upon the following account of Anne Bradstreet and Sor Juana Inés de la Cruz in a late seventeenth-century "natural" history of literature from the "New World." The hypothetical author of this history, perhaps one of Charles II's correspondents in Mexico City, had some familiarity with these women writers – both published and promoted as "Tenth Muses" in the metropolitan capitals of London and Madrid – and seemed anxious to represent them as potentially useful to culture-brokers at home. I report the passage in its entirety for the remarkable light it shines upon the space of "Tenth Musedom" in colonial economies and constructions of knowledge.

206

BOOK XII, CHAPTER VII

Concerning the woman or poet called Tenth Muse and the many commodities of this kind which exist in the New World.

This is a kind of commodity or woman who may be found in New England as well as in New Spain. In the first edition of my *General and Natural Literary History*, I put her in Book XIII, Chapter III (which deals with male writers), and now it seemed to me more appropriate to put her in this chapter which deals with women, in spite of the opinion of many that she could belong in either chapter, because many men do not know how to determine if she is a woman or a poet and they treat her as a neutral thing, thinking of her both as a woman and as a poet, because she is both, and both as a woman and as a poet, she exercizes and continues her life. She is called Tenth Muse.

I repeat that she is reputed to be a neutral animal, because she knows not only how to cook and sew but also how to write poetry better than many men. But I have decided to put her here in the category of women, because readers should not confuse the two categories women and poets, as many others have done.

I have visited Tenth Muses on several occasions, but I have never seen them write. The Tenth Muse is so quiet and diligent that she never neglects her womanly duties and so it is a mystery as to when she finds time to write. Perhaps she writes in the "few hours curtailed from her sleep and other refreshments," but I have never seen this happen. Moreover, she is content not to control the publication of her own work;[36] the vendibility of her writings, so favorable to the merchandizing of colonial projects, is completely out of her hands. Although the Tenth Muse performs many inspirational functions in culture and economy, the source of her own inspiration remains a mystery.

Having written the above, the published works of two Tenth Muses – Anne Bradstreet and Sor Juana – were brought to me, and we read part of the book by Sor Juana that afternoon, and the other I had put away, wrapped up, to send to London to the publishers of the Magnificent Thomas Heywood's *Generall History of Women* (1657) in the hopes that they would print an appendix regarding the Tenth Muse Anne Bradstreet. And I hope that while I am correcting these treatises, ships will arrive to let us know if the Tenth Muse's book arrived alive in London and in what condition.

When I arrived in London in 1700, however, I found out from the one who took the book that the Tenth Muse Anne Bradstreet would eventually end up in *The Norton Anthology of Literature by Women*.

Appropriating her fiction from the passage of Oviedo, this author made visible the implications and consequences of the category "Tenth Muse." She was interested in exploring not only what this classification might have meant for the two poets and for the reception of their works; but she was even more concerned to find a method for integrating the pervasive and gendered epistemology of the museum into her reading, one day, of these two poets' texts. For this reason, she defined the "Tenth Muse" as a taxonomic category to be classified in the same manner as all of the other categories of exotic curiosities which made their way, in the sixteenth and seventeenth centuries, from the "New World" to the cabinets of European men. She understood that seventeenth-century classifications of colonial women writers as "Tenth Muses" and the collection, for feminist purposes, of those same writers in *The Norton Anthology of Literature by Women* responded to markedly different historical and cultural pressures. But neither marketing project, she thought, found a place for women writers outside a system of male exchange. She wanted to suggest that part of the feminist project of producing new forms of relations and knowing might also include the dissolving of taxonomic "f-acts" into acts and relations of power. If the "Tenth Muse" was a taxonomic fiction, she wanted to write it for all to see.

12

JUGGLING THE CATEGORIES OF RACE, CLASS, AND GENDER

Aphra Behn's *Oroonoko*

Margaret W. Ferguson

Feminist literary scholars working in the field of Renaissance culture and trained mostly in US and Canadian universities have until recently defined their analytic focus more often with reference to problems of gender and class than with reference to race.[1] With some notable exceptions such as Karen Newman's recent essay on *Othello*, Laura Brown's study of Aphra Behn's *Oroonoko*, Ania Loomba's *Gender, Race, Renaissance Drama*, and the essays in the present volume, I know of little recent work by feminist students of early modern literature which directly attempts to *theorize* the relation between either historical or contemporary critical concepts of gender, race, and class.[2] Without claiming to untangle the various knots signaled by the conjunction of these terms in my title, I do want to reflect briefly on some of the questions that conjunction raises for feminist critical thinking now, before turning to Aphra Behn.

If feminist literary scholars of the Renaissance are at a relatively early stage in defining race as an analytic category and conceiving of research programs that would explicitly address its constellation of problems, we need, at the very least, to join Joan Kelly's famous question – Did women have a Renaissance? – with versions of that question for groups *other* than white European women, recognizing, however, that the different "versions" of the questions may not turn out to be neatly analogous.[3] Though analogies, even identities, may be a useful place to begin expanding a critical frame of reference – as I was reminded when an undergraduate in one of my classes on Behn's *Oroonoko* referred to the white female narrator of that work as a "member of the female race" – we need to work against as well as with the grain of our desire for parallels. We can see Joan Kelly herself trying to do this in a passage written in 1979, a passage which uses parenthetical phrases to signal both an awareness that the feminist scholar needs to constitute her object of study with reference to questions of race and an uncertainty about just *how* she should do so: "What we see are not two spheres of social reality but two (or three) sets of social relations. For now I would call them relations of work and sex (or of class and race, and sex/gender)."[4] Kelly's key dichotomies keep threatening to break into trichotomies, but they don't quite. A feminist-Marxist paradigm is clearly at work in her effort to define the object of study as a set of relations pertaining, broadly speaking, to the "parallel" realms of economic production, on the one hand – work – and the realm of the sex/gender system, on the other, that realm which feminist social scientists in the 1970s were defining in order to stress the cultural rather than biological determinations of "female nature."[5] But where does race fit into this paradigm? It doesn't, or doesn't very clearly. Why break the category of *work* down into "class" and "race," and what's the possible relation between these two subcategories and the apparently parallel subdivision Kelly parenthetically offers for sex, namely the two terms "sex/gender," separated however by a slash, not an "and"? Obviously, race doesn't stand in anything like the relation to class that gender, in Kelly's formulation, stands to sex.

I call attention to this formulation first because it's symptomatic of a continuing problem in Renaissance feminist studies and arguably in literary feminist scholarship by whites in the academy, more generally. I use Kelly also because her formulation points to a somewhat paradoxical and necessarily provisional solution that I want to propose, and briefly illustrate, in this chapter. The solution can be put first in a negative formulation: it is *not* to attempt to fix a definition of the terms or of their mode of correlation; such definitional work should not in any case be done in the abstract but rather with reference to specific historical instances. Just think, for example, of the complex ways in which the three categories are linked, conceptually and with material effects, in the well-known convention of American racial ideology whereby a white woman can give birth to a black child but a black woman cannot have a white child.[6] Another description of this convention stresses the idea of social status rather than gender: children of mixed marriages in twentieth-century US society are affiliated, regardless of their biological phenotype, with the racial group of the lower-ranking parent, Marvin Harris remarks in an encyclopedia article on "Race."[7] This consequential bit of ideology clearly solicits analysis with respect both to gender and to class, and indeed both categories, broadly construed, have interacted historically to shape, and sometimes abruptly alter, our culture's legal definitions of race. David Brion Davis notes, for instance, that the state of Maryland reversed the old convention of *partus sequitur ventrum* (the child follows the mother) in the late seventeenth century in order to "inhibit the lustful desires of white women."[8] Here white women as a group are characterized as prone to behavior that blurs socially important racial distinctions (the Maryland statute was generated by a discussion of how to classify mulattoes). An eighteenth-century document, however, displays a fear of female sexuality that is yoked with, or channeled through, an ideology of class: "The lower class of the women of England," wrote the noted historian of Jamaica, Edward Long, "are remarkably fond of the blacks, for reasons too brutal to mention; they would connect themselves with horses and asses, if the law permitted them."[9]

To illustrate the variability – across temporal and geographical boundaries – of ideological conceptions of race, the American historian Barbara Fields tells a lovely story about an American journalist who allegedly asked Haiti's Papa Doc Duvalier what percentage of his country's population was white. "Ninety-eight percent," Papa Doc responded.

> Struggling to make sense of this incredible piece of information, the American finally asked Duvalier: "How do you define white?" Duvalier answered the question with a question: "How do you define black in your country?" Receiving the explanation that in the United States anyone with any black blood was considered black, Duvalier nodded and said, "Well, that's the way we define white in my country."[10]

This anecdote leads me to a more positive formulation of my provisional solution: a plea to scholars to suspend their own assumptions about what a category like race means or meant to members of a different culture. Encountering the classic epistemological problem – which is also, inevitably, an ethical and political problem – of the "First World" anthropologist seeking to interpret a "native" cultural concept,[11] scholars who work with concepts of class, race, and gender might do well to keep all three terms floating, as it were, in an ideological liquid – a solution, I might venture to say – without assuming that we have any a priori understanding of what they mean even in our own by no means homogeneous academic subculture, much less what the terms may have meant for textual producers and receivers in different historical and cultural milieux than our own.

A certain kind of historicist scholar, of either the so-called "old" historicist or the radical Foucauldian "new" stripe, might object to my proposed (non) solution on the grounds that each of the categories of social thought I'm invoking here is in some sense anachronistic for Renaissance studies. While it is certainly true that the terms "race," "class," and "gender" had demonstrably different *dominant* meanings in Renaissance English than they do today, there are nonetheless significant areas of semantic overlap: Renaissance references to the "human" or the "English" race, for instance, don't entail the obsession with pigmentation differences typical of nineteenth- and twentieth-century notions of race, but the earlier usage does display the "ideological device," still common in many contemporary racial categorizations, of securing group identity by a (frequently mythical) set of genealogical rules.[12] The historicist objection against anachronism can be useful if it helps us avoid simplistic conflations, but the objection should not prevent us from seeking evidence pertaining to the *types* of systemic social inequities frequently signaled – whether inadvertently or critically – by the uses of one or more of these terms in post-Renaissance discourses. To stop the search for significant traces of such inequities is to accept an academic argument for hermeneutic "purity" that is arguably an ideological defense against seeing continuities between systemic injustices in past societies – including those partly shaped and largely represented by European intellectuals – and in our own. The effort of *interrogating* modern notions of race, class, and gender by comparing them (as it were) to earlier historical versions of these notions – and vice versa – seems to me crucial to the intellectual work of US feminism in the 1990s.

That work has been powerfully though also controversially begun by a number of recent scholars. Among them are Teresa de Lauretis in her book *Technologies of Gender* (1987), which argues that gender is a *representation*, not an essence fundamentally determined, for instance, by "sexual difference," and which further argues that "gender represents not an individual but a relation, and a social relation";[13] Barbara Fields, in the article from which I drew the Papa Doc story, an article entitled "Ideology and Race in American History" (1982), which argues provocatively for a demystified understanding of race as a category derived from historical circumstances and racist ideologies rather than from some imputed "reality" of biological fact; and the Marxist scholars Stephen Resnick and Richard Wolff, who argue for a non-essentialist conception of class in *Knowledge and Class* (1989). Defining class not primarily as a categorizing system for social groups but rather as a *process* by which "unpaid labor is pumped out of direct producers," they stress that this process is "overdetermined" (in a phrase they borrow, with caveats, from Louis Althusser, who borrowed it from psychoanalytic discourse) by other processes such as "labor transforming nature," "exerting and obeying authority among persons," "giving and gaining access to property," and, last but not least, language.[14] This approach to class is useful, first because it mitigates many of the problems raised by historians and literary scholars concerned with anachronism (i.e., should one speak of "classes" before the full development of capitalism and/or before class consciousness exists on the part of a given group?);[15] and second because it insists that any given individual may occupy more than one "position" relative to the "class process."

Let us look, now, at some of the ways in which the categories of race, class, and gender, understood as historically contingent and relational rather than foundational concepts, work in a mutually determining fashion in Behn's *Oroonoko* (1688) and in what we can reconstruct of the various historical discourses and shifting configuration of material life from which her book derives and to which it contributed substantially – most obviously by limning an image of the "Noble Negro" in ways that made it, as Laura Brown observes, "a crucial early text in the sentimental, antislavery tradition that grew steadily throughout the eighteenth century."[16]

Whatever the "facts" of Aphra Behn's birth (conflicting theories construct her as the illegitimate daughter of an aristocrat, male or female, or as the child of a barber or a wetnurse), the single most important determinant of her multiple class positions was arguably her access to, and later her deployment of, the skills of literacy.[17] Her lack of a classical education meant that she was not "fully" literate in her culture's terms, but her ability to read and write English and several other European languages nonetheless allowed her to earn her living by her pen, first as a spy for Charles II and later as the author of plays, poems, novellas, and translations. Though classic Marxist theory does not consider intellectual work "direct production," the writer in the early modern era, as a member of an emergent class or caste of secular intellectuals ambiguously placed between their sometimes relatively humble origins and the nobility whom they frequently served and with whom they often imaginatively identified, was in many cases a producer of commodities for the market. Indeed the energy with which many humanist writers sought to distinguish their labor from "merely" clerkly or artisanal work suggests how fraught with anxiety (then as now) was the self-definition of persons who occupied the ambiguous class position of intellectual worker.[18] If, from one perspective and in certain circumstances, the writer was himself (or much more rarely, herself) a worker from whose labor surplus was extracted by others (as, for instance, occurred when one worked for fixed wages as the secretary or accountant for an aristocratic plantation owner), from another perspective, the writer was often a (relatively) privileged beneficiary of the process whereby early capitalists profited from the forced labor (say) of indentured white servants or black or Indian slaves. My examples are of course chosen to highlight the multiple ambiguities that arise when one seeks to specify how a figure like Aphra Behn participated in the process of extracting surplus in Britain's early colonial economy. At this point, I will insist only on foregrounding the fact that she *did* participate, as a producer of verbal commodities who explicitly if intermittently defined herself as oppressed by and financially dependent on wealthy men, but also as a member of an English "family" of slave-owners (as it were) and as such, one who directly and "naturally" profited from others' labor.

The peculiarities of her multiple and shifting class positions are inextricably linked to, indeed partly determined by, the anomalies of her situation as a *female* writer, one who sold her wares to male patrons as a prostitute sells her body to clients. As Catherine Gallagher has brilliantly shown, Behn herself elaborated the prostitute–woman writer analogy along with an even more ideologically mystified one of the female writer as an absolutist monarch.[19] In *Oroonoko*, set in the early 1660s, before Behn's rather mysterious marriage to a Dutch merchant, but written in 1688, long after she had ceased to be a wife, she defines her status as formed in crucial ways by her gender; she refers explicitly to her "female pen," and frequently presents herself as a heroine with features drawn from literary codes of romance and Petrarchan lyric.[20] Lurking behind her portrait of the author as a young, unmarried lady with great verbal facility is a complex body of cultural discourse on Woman and the forms of behavior she should eschew (talking and writing in public, which behavior is often equated with prostitution) and embrace (obedience to fathers and husbands being a prime command).[21] An emerging cultural discourse about women who went to the colonies – often, allegedly, to acquire the husbands they'd not found in England, or worse, to satisfy their "natural" lust with men of color – also lurks behind Behn's self-portrait.[22] This cultural subtext, made into an explicit subplot of Thomas Southerne's 1696 stage version of *Oronooko*, seems particularly germane to Behn since, as Angeline Goreau has argued, her (adoptive?) father left her without a dowry when he died *en route* to Surinam.[23] Her novella at once partly reproduces the negative cultural subtext(s) of female gender and seeks to refute them.

Her social status is also defined as a function of her race, or, more precisely and provisionally, of her membership in a group of colonizing English white people who owned black slaves imported from Africa and who uneasily shared Surinam with another group of non-white persons, the native Indians. We can conveniently trace some of the contradictions in the narrator's social identity, with its multiple "subject positions" created in part by competing allegiances according to race, class, and gender, if we examine the narrative "I" in relation to the text's different uses of the pronoun "we." With whom does the "I" align itself?[24]

The first stage of an answer is to say that the "I" aligns itself sometimes with a "we" composed of women: in these cases the "I" is definitely a "she." At other times, however, the "I" aligns – or in political terms, allies – itself with a "we" composed of property-owning English colonists defending themselves against an "other" (a "them") composed of African slaves or of native Indians, and sometimes of both. In these cases, the gender of the "I" is evidently less salient than are nationality, membership in a surplus-extracting group, and color. Within these two basically contradictory subject positions, however, other configurations appear and disappear. "We" women, for instance, are sometimes opposed to cruel and powerful white men, and this opposition clearly participates in the interrogation of the institution of marriage which many of Behn's plays mount and which texts by other seventeenth-century Englishwomen pursue as well: Lady Mary Chudleigh, for instance, in a poem "To the Ladies," of 1703, wrote that "Wife and servant are the same, / But only differ in the name."[25] An opposition drawn along lines of gender within the British community allows – in the peculiar circumstances of colonialism – for an unusual alliance to flourish between white females, notably the narrator and her mother and sister, and the black slave Oroonoko: a community of the unjustly oppressed is thus formed, and indeed unjust oppression comes to be associated with a state of effeminacy figured, interestingly, as male impotence.[26]

The analogy between white women and Oroonoko, and particularly the alliance between the narrator and her hero, is, however, extremely volatile, partly because it posed an obvious double-pronged threat to the colonial social hierarchy in which white men occupied the top place. The narrator, as the unmarried daughter (so she claims) of the man who was supposed to govern the colony had he not died *en route* to his post, threatens the ideologies of patriarchy in some of the ways that Queen Elizabeth had done a hundred years before Behn wrote her book. To claim, as Behn does in her prefatory letter to an aristocratic patron, that there was "none above me in that Country," and to depict herself as living in "the best house" in the colony (p. 49), is to engage in imaginative competition with the man who actually stood in for Behn's father, one Colonel William Byam, who is painted as a brutal tyrant in the text and who cordially despised Aphra Behn, according to the historical record.[27] Wielding an instrument of writing which she and her society saw as belonging to masculine prerogative, the narrator courts notoriety by representing herself as the sympathetic confidante of a black male slave who had, in his native land, been a prince engaged in erotic and by implication political rivalry with his grandfather and king.[28] The narrator and Caesar are allied in a multifaceted league of potential subversion.

As if to defuse that threat, the narrative counters the "we" composed of white women and Oroonoko with a stereotypical configuration, familiar from the Renaissance drama, which pits sexually vulnerable (and valuable) Englishwomen against a black man imagined as a villainous rapist.[29] One can see the "we" shifting in a striking fashion between these two poles in a passage that occurs near the end of the tale immediately after a description of how Caesar – as the narrator announces she is compelled to call Oroonoko after he assumes his slave identity in Surinam (p. 40) – leads a slave rebellion, is deserted by all but one of the other slaves, and is recaptured and brutally punished by white male property-owners. The narrator interrupts the plot's temporal progression to return to a point in the just-recounted story when the outcome of Oroonoko's rebellion was still uncertain. That uncertainty is oddly preserved for Behn's readers by her shift from the simple past tense to a subjunctive formulation that mixes past, present, and the possibility of a different future:

> You must know, that when the News was brought . . . that Caesar had betaken himself to the Woods, and carry'd with him all the Negroes, we were possess'd with extreme Fear, which no Persuasions could dissipate, that he would secure himself till night and then, that he would come down and cut all our throats. This Apprehension made all the Females of us fly down the River to be secured; and while we were away, they acted this Cruelty; for I suppose I had Authority and Interest enough there, had I suspected any such thing, to have prevented it: but we had not gone many Leagues, but the News overtook us, that Caesar was taken and whipped like a common Slave.
>
> (pp. 67–8)

In this passage, the authorial "I" seems at once extraordinarily lucid and disturbingly blind about her own complicity in her hero's capture and humiliating punishment. Had she been present, she "supposes" she could have prevented the cruelty which "they" – white men – wrought upon the black male slave.[30] Her claim to possess some singular social authority, however, is belied by her representation of herself as part of a group of weak females, a passive group possessed – and the play on that word is rich – not by men, black or white, but rather by an agent named Fear and quickly renamed Apprehension. That oddly abstract agent, however, turns out, if we look closely, to be a product of something the passage twice calls "News" – a mode of verbal production that is often defined as unreliable in this text, and that belongs, significantly, to a semantic complex that names crucial features of Behn's own discourse in *Oroonoko*. The novella's opening pages announce that this is a "true eyewitness" account of things that happened in the "new Colonies," and the author advertising her wares, along with the lands her words represent, is well aware that she must offer "Novelty" to pique her English reader's interest, for "where there is no Novelty, there can be no Curiosity" (p. 3).[31] The author herself, it would seem, is both a producer and a consumer of "news," and in the passage about her roles in Oroonoko's aborted rebellion she represents her identity – and her agency – as an ambiguous function of the *circulation* of information.

Here, as in many other parts of the book, the narrative oscillates between criticizing and profiting from a "system" of circulation which includes not only words, among them the lies characteristic of male

216

Christian slave-traders, but bodies as well. In this disturbing oscillation, which has obviously contributed to the utter lack of critical consensus about whether Behn's book supports or attacks the institution of slavery, we can see the lineaments, I believe, of a more complex model of European colonization than Tzvetan Todorov posits in his book on *The Conquest of America*.[32] In contrast to Todorov's book and most instances of Renaissance travel literature I've read, Behn's novella construes the relation between Old World and New not only in terms of a binary opposition between self and "other" but also in terms of a highly unstable triangular model which, in its simplest version, draws relations of sameness and difference among a black African slave, a white Englishwoman, and a group of Native Americans who are described, in the book's opening pages, as innocents "so unadorned" and beautiful that they resemble "our first parents before the fall" (p. 3). Neither the white Englishwoman nor the black African man share the Indians' (imputed) quality of primeval innocence. The narrator and Oroonoko-Caesar have both received European educations, albeit less good, we may suppose, than those accorded to privileged white men; and both are at once victims and beneficiaries of socioeconomic systems that discriminate kings from commoners and support the privileges of the nobility with the profits of the slave-trade. Oroonoko is described as having captured and sold black slaves in African wars before he was himself enslaved by a dastardly lying Christian; and the narrator not only belongs to a slave-owning class but clearly supports the nationalistic colonizing enterprise which fueled and depended on the African slave-trade.[33] She laments the loss of Surinam to the Dutch a few years after the events of the novella take place (interestingly, the English traded that colony for New Amsterdam, in "our" America, in 1667) and even uses a lush description of a gold-prospecting river trip to suggest the desirability – in 1688, on the eve of William of Orange's accession to the British throne – of retaking the lost colony and its lost profits: "And 'tis to be bemoaned what his majesty lost by losing that part of America," she adds (p. 59).[34] By thus presenting a narrator and a hero who are both victims and beneficiaries of the international system of the slave-trade, and by contrasting and comparing both characters, at different moments, to the exotic and "innocent" Indians, Behn provides a perspective on "the Conquest of America" that complicates, among other binary oppositions, the ethical one, infinitely labile in the literature of the imperial venture, between "we" as "good" and "them" as "evil" – or vice versa.

What even this account of the complexity of Behn's novella leaves out, however, is the ideological force of the "other" black slave in the story – Imoinda, Oroonoko's beloved, whom the English rename Clemene. Imoinda is doubly enslaved – to the whites, male and female, who have bought her and also, as the narrative insists, to her black husband. In

striking contrast to the unmarried narrator, who stands, in relation to
Oroonoko, as a queen or Petrarchan lady-lord to a vassal – a "Great
Mistress" (p. 46) – Imoinda is an uncanny amalgam of European ideals
of wifely subservience and European fantasies about wives of "Oriental"
despots. She is thus the perfect embodiment, with the exception of her
dark hue, of an image of the ideal that the English author holds up to
this example of the "other"; such wives

> have a respect for their Husbands equal to what other People pay a
> Deity; and when a Man finds any occasion to quit his Wife, if he
> love her, she dies by his hand; if not he sells her, or suffers some
> other to kill her.
>
> (p. 72)

This passage occurs late in the tale, immediately after Oroonoko has
resolved to kill his pregnant wife for reasons that show him to be no less
obsessed than Othello by a sexual jealousy intricately bound up with
ideologies of property possession: "his great heart," the narrator
approvingly explains, "could not endure the Thought" that Imoinda
might, after his death, "become a Slave to the enraged Multitude," that
is, be "ravished by every Brute" (p. 71). So, with Imoinda's joyful consent
(she's considerably more compliant in her fate than Desdemona), he
"sever[s] her yet smiling Face from that delicate Body, pregnant as it was
with the fruits of tenderest Love" (p. 72).

Even this brief glance at Imoinda's death scene should suggest how
odd it is that Imoinda's specificity as a *black wife* should be effaced not
only from most critical narratives on Behn but also from the cover of the
only inexpensive modern edition of the text, the Norton paperback
edited by Lore Metzger. This object solicits the attention of potential
readers with a cover picture that evokes the titillating cultural image of
miscegenous romance in general and, in particular, the best-known
high-cultural instance of such romance for Anglo-American readers,
namely Shakespeare's *Othello*. The cover shows a black man on a tropical
shore holding a knife histrionically pointed toward the bare throat of a
white woman (figure 12.1). A note on the Norton edition's back cover
informs us that the frontispiece reproduces one from a 1735 edition of
Oroonoko – not, however, Aphra Behn's novella, but rather the play
published in 1696 by Thomas Southerne. Although some critics have
treated Behn's and Southerne's versions as interchangeable, there are in
fact crucial differences between them.[35] In addition to making his
Oroonoko a much less severe critic of slavery than Behn's hero is,
Southerne replaces Behn's idealized but distinctly black heroine with a
beautiful white girl. This change may perhaps be explained as
Southerne's bow to a strikingly gendered and also colored convention of
the Restoration stage which I'm still trying to understand, namely that

Figure 12.1 Frontispiece from *Oroonoko* by Thomas Southerne, London, 1735. Reproduced by permission of the Special Collections Office, New York Public Library.

male English actors could appear in blackface but actresses evidently could not.[36]

Whatever the reasons for Southerne's recoloring Behn's Imoinda, they can't be reduced to the exigencies of stage convention since he was criticized by contemporaries for not giving her a dark hue to match Oroonoko's – a hue the critic specifically terms "Indian" in a confusion typical of primitivist ideology.[37] Among Southerne's motives, I suspect, was a desire to capitalize on a rumor titillatingly mentioned and denied in the anonymous biography included in her 1696 *Histories* and *Novels*, a rumor that during her stay in Surinam Behn had a romance with Oroonoko.[38] The continuing circulation of this rumor through the medium of modern books, even though most critics don't credit it, is a commercial fact that needs more discussion than I have space for here. I do, however, want to open some questions about that fact, and our participation in it is as mostly First World-born and mostly white readers, or potential buyer-readers, of *Oroonoko*. Behn's text offers an ambiguous reflection on the role of intellectual producers and consumers in an expanding international market which included in the seventeenth century, as it still does in ours, books and bodies among its prime commodities. Behn's reflection on (and of) this market has many facets, one of which, uncannily but I think instructively, seems to anticipate the titillating representation of differently gendered and colored bodies that would advertise her story (but the possessive pronoun points to problems in the very conception of authorial "ownership") in the eighteenth century and again in the late twentieth.

The facet of Behn's "market representation" to which I'm referring is her textual staging of an implicit *competition* between the white English female author and the black African female slave-wife-mother-to-be. The competition is for Oroonoko's body and its power to engender something in the future, something that will outlive it. That power remains latent – impotent, one might say – without a female counterpart for which Behn offers two opposing images: Imoinda's pregnant body, holding a potential slave-laborer ("for," as the text reminds us, "all the Breed is theirs to whom the Parents belong"); and, alternatively, the author's "female pen," which she deploys to describe, with an unnerving blend of relish and horror, the scenes of Oroonoko's bodily dismemberment and eventual death following his leading of a slave revolt. She uses that pen also, as she tells the reader in the final paragraph, in hopes of making Oroonoko's "glorious Name to survive all Ages" (p. 78).

The narrator of course wins the competition. Through her pen flow at least some of the prerogatives of the English empire and its language, a language she has shown herself using, in one remarkable scene, as a potent instrument of sexual and political domination. In this scene, which explicitly pits an image of politically "dangerous" biological reproduction against an image of "safe" verbal production, the author presents herself most paradoxically as both a servant and a beneficiary of the eroticized socioeconomic *system* of domination she describes. When some unnamed English authority figures perceive that Oroonoko is growing sullen because of the "Thought" that this child will belong not to him but to his owners, the narrator is "obliged," she tells us, to use her fiction-making powers to "divert" Oroonoko (and Imoinda too) from thoughts of "Mutiny." Mutiny is specifically tied to a problem in population management, a problem about which Behn's text – like much colonialist discourse, including chilling debates on whether it is better to "buy or breed" one's slaves – is fundamentally, and necessarily, ambivalent.[39] Mutiny, the narrator observes, "is very fatal sometimes in those Colonies that abound so with Slaves, that they exceed the Whites in vast numbers" (p. 46). It is to abort the potential mutiny that the narrator is "obliged" to "discourse with Caesar, and to give him all the Satisfaction I possibly could" – which she does, entertaining him with stories about "the Loves of the Romans and great Men, which charmed him to my company." In an interestingly gendered division of narrative goods, she tells Imoinda stories about nuns.[40]

Playing a version of Othello's role to an audience comprised of her slaves, Behn dramatizes a complex mode of authorial "ownership" of characters cast in the role of enthraled audience. In so doing, she represents herself creating a paradoxical *facsimile* of freedom, for herself, her immediate audience, and by implication, her largely female English readers as well, in which servitude is rendered tolerable by being eroticized, fantasized, "diverted" from activities, either sexual or military, that might work to dislodge the English from their precarious lordship of this New World land. Just how precarious their possession was the narrative acknowledges by repeatedly lamenting their loss of the land to the Dutch; but the deeper problems of the logic of colonialism are also signaled, albeit confusedly, by the contrast between the description of slave mutiny quoted above and the explanation offered early in the story for why the British do *not* enslave the native Indians, a group which, like the Africans, are essential to the colonialists' welfare; "they being on all occasions very useful to us," the narrator says, "we find it absolutely necessary to caress 'em as Friends, and not to treat 'em as Slaves, nor dare we do other, their numbers do far surpassing ours in that Continent" (p. 5).[41] This passage sheds an ironic light on the later moment when the narrator uses stories to divert Oroonoko from thoughts of mutiny, for we see that one logical solution to the mutiny problem, a solution that her stories to Oroonoko suppress but which her larger narrative only partially represses, is the possibility of *not* enslaving a group of "others" who outnumber you. Such a solution, with respect both to Africans and to Indians, had been recommended by a few early critics of the colonial enterprise; but Behn is far from joining the tiny group who voiced criticisms of the whole system of international trade based on forced labor by persons of many skin colors including freckled Irish white.[42]

In its characteristically disturbing way, Behn's novel shows us just enough about the author's competition with Imoinda, and the enmeshment of that competition within a larger socio-sexual-economic system, to make us uneasy when we hold the book *Oroonoko* in our hands and realize that the text itself invites us to see the book as a safe-sex substitute for the potentially mutinous but also economically valuable black slave-child Oroonoko might have had with Imoinda. In a bizarre twisting of the old trope of book as child, Behn offers her contemporary English readers, and us too, a representation of an economy in which the white woman's book is born, quite starkly, from the death and silencing of black persons, one of them pregnant. Behind the scene of Oroonoko's final torture, which gruesomely anticipates Alice Walker's description, in her story of a cross-race rape during the US Civil Rights struggle, of "white folks standing in a circle roasting something that had talked to them in their own language before they tore out its tongue," is the murder-sacrifice of the black woman and her unborn child.[43] And the threat represented by the black woman, I would suggest, is obscurely acknowledged to be even greater than the threat represented by the black man, so that the text finally has to enlist him, through enticements of European codes of masculine honor and Petrarchan romance, to suppress the one character who actually uses physical force rather than words to attack the highest legal representative of the colonial system, namely the male Lieutenant-Governor. Reversing the Renaissance commonplace that defined deeds as masculine, words as feminine, Imoinda wounds Byam, the narrator tells us, with a poisoned arrow; he is saved, however – though the narrator clearly regrets this – by his Indian mistress, who sucks the venom from his wound. The white female narrator's own ambivalent relation to male English authority is figured here by the device of splitting "other" women into two roles: one rebellious and one erotically complicitous.

Imoinda's rebellious power – and the need to destroy it – are figured most strikingly, I think, in the two juxtaposed episodes where Oroonoko first kills a mother tiger and lays the whelp at the author's feet (p. 51) and then kills a property-destroying tiger – again female – and extracts her bullet-ridden heart to give to the English audience. At this moment Oroonoko is most transparently shown as a figure for the author of *Oroonoko*, a repository of novel curiosities which Behn offers to her readers as he offers the tiger's cub, and then its heart, to his owner-admirers:

This heart the conqueror brought up to us, and 'twas a very great curiosity, which all the country came to see, and which gave Caesar occasion of making many fine Discourses, of Accidents in War, and strange Escapes.

(p. 53)

Here Behn deliberately constructs her hero from echoes of Shakespeare; Oroonoko woos her and other British ladies as Othello wooed Desdemona with his eloquent story of his "most disastrous chances . . . moving accidents . . . hair breadth-scapes i' th' imminent deadly breach" (I.iii.134–6).[44] With respect to the power relation between a narrator and an audience, this scene offers a mirror reversal of the one in which the narrator entertains her sullen, potentially mutinous hero with *her* culture's stories of "great [Roman] men." We can now see even more clearly that the "ground" of both scenes, the "material," as it were, from which the production and reception of exotic stories derive, is the silent figure of the black woman – silent but by no means safe, as is suggested by the image of the female tiger and the narrative device of duplicating it.

Perhaps, then, the Norton cover is an ironically apt representation of the complex of problems centering on property – sexual, economic, and intellectual – that Behn's book at once exposes and effaces. For the white woman who stands in Imoinda's place might well be Behn herself, the literate white woman who spoke *for* some oppressed black slaves but who did so with extreme partiality, discriminating among them according to status (the novel sympathizes with *noble* slaves only, depicting common ones as "natural" servants and traitors to Oroonoko's cause) and also according to gender. Laura Brown has remarked that Behn's representation of Oroonoko is full of the ironies of the colonialist version of the self–other dialectic, in which the "other" can only be recognized as an image of the European self.[45] Brown does not, however, explore how Behn's narrative includes the "other other" of Imoinda in that dialectic, or rather, at once includes and occludes the multiple differences between the figure named Imoinda/Clemene and her black husband, her white "mistress," and, of course, her historical "self," the woman, or more precisely, women, who were Indians and Africans both and who did not speak English, much less the idiom of heroic romance Behn favors, until the Renaissance, as we call it, brought Europeans to African and American territories. The last word of Behn's book is "Imoinda." I want to suggest, by way of a necessarily open-ended conclusion, that a quest for the historical and contemporary meanings of that name – with its teasing plays on "I," "moi" [me], "am," "Indian" – will require more attention to modalities of identification and difference than most feminist, Marxist, deconstructionist, psychoanalytic, or new historicist critics have yet expended.

The importance of that task can perhaps be better appreciated when one thinks of how insistently the colonizing of the New World was figured as a project of erotic possession (as, for instance, in Donne's famous lines apostrophizing his naked mistress as "O My America, my New Found-land"), and, more specifically, as a project rife with fantasies of miscegenation – a mixing of ostensibly distinct categories that was just beginning, in the mid-seventeenth century, to be legally prohibited in the American colonies and which was for that reason acquiring a new erotic charge.[46] Indeed one might well want to pursue Imoinda's cultural significance by studying the odd symmetries and dissonances between the representations of both Africa and America as female bodies, the former repeatedly described as inaccessible, the latter as easily penetrable at first, but later often dangerous.[47]

If I end by suggesting that more work needs to be done on Imoinda's symbolic and material existences, I do so because I'm well aware that my own essay has only begun to formulate, much less answer, questions about the *blanks* on the maps which many of us use to explore the temporal and spatial terrain we term the Renaissance. In attempting a kind of interpretation that seeks to grasp relations of gender, race, and class through – and against – the material of a specific historical text read in a "context" impossible to delimit with certainty much less to master intellectually, I've sought to keep all three of my key category terms in play, not reducing any one to another, noticing how they sometimes supplement, sometimes fracture each other. I'm aware, however, that I'm a juggler who can't begin to handle enough balls: I've left out of this discussion many other categories of social thought that operate in Behn's text, among them religion and a powerful monarchist political ideology that arguably both drives and limits the story's investment in the oxy-moronic figure of the *royal* slave.[48] Despite the gaps in my narrative, I hope I've done enough to suggest not only the difficulties but some of the pleasures of working with conceptual categories that lie squarely in the center of battlefields, historical and contemporary. Working with such categories spurs me to think about my own implication in an economic and ideological system that has some salient continuities with the system inhibited and represented by Aphra Behn, a white woman writer whose gender allowed her to belong only eccentrically to the emerging caste of traveling intellectuals serving, representing, and sometimes critically anatomizing Europe's early imperial enterprises.

13

CIVILITY, BARBARISM, AND APHRA BEHN'S
THE WIDOW RANTER

Margo Hendricks

We have been unable to address questions of race to any adequate
degree in this book, and we are not exonerated in this deficiency by
the most visible complexion of European Renaissance society.
Rather, it is its very whiteness that we need to learn to see.[1]

As one of the small but growing number of scholars of color engaged
in the study of Renaissance English culture and colonialism, I am
heartened by the current attention being paid to early modern
European racialism and racism. Yet implicit in Wayne's comment cited
above is an uncomplicated assumption about what "race" means in the
early modern period. Intrinsic to this type of reasoning is a perception
that early modern English people equated "race" with color in the same
way that citizens of the United States currently do. In this presumption,
"race" is used as if it were a universal paradigm rather than a mediated
social practice.

In his introduction to *The Bounds of Race*, Dominick LaCapra obliquely
refers to this particular linguistic inflection, arguing that "race" has come
to be a "valorized and often unmarked center of reference"; and
consequently,

> [it becomes] decidedly difficult to overcome the tendency to privi-
> lege whiteness as the master-text . . . and to identify the nonwhite
> as "other" or "different." It is equally difficult to avoid the growing
> tendency to substitute a commercialized exoticism or an anodyne,
> commodified discourse on race for problems of racial stereotyping
> and oppression.[2]

Recognition of critical complicity in the transmission or reification of
such ideological tendencies has generated an incipient awareness of the
complex history of the idea that we call "race." To resist concomitantly
the "commercialized exoticism" attendant upon "race" *and* "make the
categories of race [as well as those of class and gender] . . . historically

contingent and relational rather than foundational concepts,"[3] feminist and cultural scholars cannot limit their readings to seeing the "whiteness" of Renaissance studies. Such a move will only make more precise the ideological binarism produced by racial categories, not undo it. Rather than marking "whiteness," the imperative that faces cultural and feminist scholarship is theoretically and historically to map the discursive and social practices that prompted seventeenth-century Englishmen and women to define themselves not only in terms of nationalism but also, increasingly, in terms of color.

This imperative, then, is the context of my reading of Aphra Behn's *The Widow Ranter*. One of the earliest professional women writers, Behn actively participated in the literary construction of late seventeenth-century English ideologies of cultural and social identity. Her relationship to the court of Charles II, as well as her own lived experiences, resulted in Behn's complex and often contradictory assumptions about race, class, and gender. Though she was politically conservative (Tory), Behn's writings reveal a social consciousness deeply affected by the colonial infrastructure of early modern capitalism. As a colonial subject and a writer complicitous in the production of English hegemonic discourses, Behn (and her writings) represents a particular resonance in early modern English culture. At a moment when "questions of race" were complicated by English overseas expansion, Behn dramatizes the politics of a particular notion of race and its effect on English colonialism.

Behn's play *The Widow Ranter* (*c*.1688–9) (despite, or perhaps because of its problematic idealization of American Indians) serves as a useful starting place to begin addressing the question of "race." The play is a tragi-comedy which comically maps the travails of impoverished gentlemen who travel to the Virginia colony in search of wealth, and the sexual relations which play a part in that process. *The Widow Ranter*, however, is an unusual text in that it is also a fictional revision of a historical event.[4] In 1676 Nathaniel Bacon, in defiance of the ruling oligarchy in the Virginia colony, organized a volunteer army of indentured English servants, African slaves, dissatisfied soldiers, and the laboring poor to wage war against the American Indians who resisted English hegemony. The success of Bacon's efforts to extirpate the American Indians created difficulties for the ruling council: his militarism was successfully containing the American Indian threat to English safety in the colony; yet Bacon's hubris in defying government orders to cease his activities could not be allowed to go unchecked. On October 26, 1676, Nathaniel Bacon died "of the 'Bloody Flux' and 'Lousey Disease,' only a month after having successfully captured Jamestown.[5] With his death, the rebellion collapsed and a number of Bacon's officers were put to death.

Aphra Behn's "dramatic revision" of Bacon's rebellion significantly rewrites the historical narrative: first, in its depiction of members of the Virginia Council the text inverts the class affiliation of the ruling oligarchy of Virginia; second, the text significantly marginalizes the brutality of Bacon's militarism; and third, Behn creates a tragic triangular relationship between Bacon and two American Indian monarchs. What is striking about this third "alteration" is that it displaces Bacon's relationship with his actual English-born wife, Elizabeth Duke, and constructs in its stead a fictional "star-crossed" miscegenous romance between Bacon and the American Indian Queen. In its integration of literary conventions, historical narrative, and the problematic sexual politics that seems to surface in much of Behn's canon, *The Widow Ranter* participates in what I shall call a racialized discourse of civility. The argument of this chapter, therefore, is that in its representations of the American Indians *The Widow Ranter* maps a central paradox of the concept of civility: the more the native becomes assimilated, the more her/his alienness becomes culturally reified. Essentially, though the American Indian may come to accept the values, customs, and ideologies of the English, ultimately and fundamentally s/he is not English; s/he will always be an Indian. Civility does not erase difference but, in fact, serves to emphasize difference. The play convincingly reminds its audience of what, in the last instance, links the English in Virginia – the perception of ultimately belonging to the same race.

THE IDEA OF CIVILITY

From its earliest engagement with the "New World," England strategically invoked the binarism of civility to carry out its imperial mission. In his study *Savagism and Civility*, Bernard Sheehan argues that, conceptually, this binarism construed a civilized society as definable by its sense of discipline, its religious morality, a legal system, and political authority.[6] Thus, as a value judgment, the discourse of civility always articulates a paradigm where native cultures exist as a "primal state" in which "savages might be either noble or ignoble, either the guardians of pristine virtue or the agents of violent disorder" but always different, always alien.[7]

In its articulation in English cultural discourses, the trope of civility draws upon very specific yet ambivalent ethnographic images of what English colonizers might expect to find in the New World.[8] On the one hand, these narratives represented the native peoples as treacherous, lazy, religious idolaters, ignorant of civil government, and sexually licentious. On the other hand, Arthur Barlow could write in 1584, "We found the people most gentle, loving, and faithful, void of all guile and treason and such as lived after the manner of the Golden Age."[9] It is Thomas

227

Harriot's view, however, which seems to reflect the habit of mind of the English who traveled to the New World:

> In respect of us they [the natives] are a people poor, and for want of skill and judgement in the knowledge and use of our things do esteem our trifles before things of greater value. . . . And . . . so much the more is it probable that they should desire our friend-ships and love and have the greater respect for pleasing and obeying us. Whereby may be hoped, if means of good government be used, that they may in short time be brought to civility and the embracing of true religion.[10]

The imposition of this value system, intricately intertwined with English imperial expansion, onto the native peoples of the English colonies was not without its contradictions. As Karen Kupperman writes,

> Discussion of the Indian character is complicated by the assump-tion that there was a native hereditary class system. The praise of Indian courtesy, dignity, and trustworthiness was often restricted to the Indian nobility. . . . What all this means is that status, not race, was the category which counted for English people of the early years of colonization. Put in its most direct form this means that it was not the case that the "savage" was forever set apart from civilized mankind by qualities which were peculiar to him. The "meaner sort," the low-born, whether Indians or English, were set apart by qualities peculiar to them.[11]

English attitudes toward the American Indians in the first few decades of the colonizing project (1580s to 1620s), according to Kupperman, were shaped by the class affiliation of the narrator; thus, the ability to "bring" the native to "civilization" was largely dependent upon the native's social position. Kupperman goes on to argue that this view linked "in roughly the same terms . . . English people of low status" and "the rank and file Indians."[12]

Though I am in general agreement with Kupperman's overall analy-sis, it seems to me that she ignores the centrality of "race" to discussions of status in England's colonial discourses. In his pioneering study *The Idea of Race*, Michael Banton observes that within Western history we can map the multiple ways in which "race" has been employed to describe personal identity – lineage, nation, typology, biology, and status. According to Banton, as a particular culture's social relations and prac-tices changed or as nation-states from Europe extended their territorial claims across oceans, "race" proved an effective polyseme in the process of constituting and authenticating an official explanation for social, cultural, and phenotypical differences. What becomes obvious, if the scholar steps outside her own particular historical consciousness, is the fact that a genealogy of "race" reveals that the concept has never had a fixed meaning, but has been variable.

In its conceptual shifts, "race" often leaves residues of previous significations to inflect current usage.[13] Kupperman's insistence that "status" was "the category which counted for English people," however, seems to elide the presence of these residues. Conceptually and politically, "race" permitted the English to explain hierarchies of lineage, status, or typology without changing the language. In other words, a writer could describe the inferiority of the Irish "race" and the superiority of the aristocratic "race" in the same text with little concern for conflicting meanings, since the text's audience would be expected to supply the requisite definition of the word "race." In this manner, the literary circulation of "race," unlike that of "status," infuses a more concrete and definitive resonance to the discourse of civility.

In a trenchant essay on "the other question," Homi K. Bhabha argues that it "is the force of ambivalence that gives the colonial stereotype its currency: ensures its repeatability in changing historical discursive conjunctures; informs its strategies of individuation and marginalization."[14] It is in the margins of such "ambivalence" that Behn locates her dramatic depiction of Bacon's rebellion. Though Behn ends with an image of a self-consciously unified English settlement, she begins with the drama of a class-based division among the English. And this "drama" is displayed along a familiar early modern racial grid – an anxiety about lineage.

For many of the characters in *The Widow Ranter*, arrival in Virginia necessitated a lineal history, a genealogy to authorize their new identity. Initially, especially among the lower-class immigrants, this was done by fabricating a gentry or aristocratic heritage out of the rubble of the English Civil War. For example, Mistress Flirt, in an effort to mute skepticism about Parson Dunce's lineage, claims, "but methinks Doctor Dunce is a very edifying Person, and a Gentleman, and I pretend to know a Gentleman; for I my self am a Gentlewoman: my Father was a Baronet, but undone in the late Rebellion" (I.i). The irony of this defense is that the very hierarchy which produced the social conditions that resulted in the parson's and Mistress Flirt's transportation to Virginia ends up being invoked in the construction of a new identity.

In the minds of the transported, the colonies represented an opportunity to "fashion" an identity. Behn captures this practice in her characterization of the Justices who share power in Virginia. Formerly men whose lives in England had resulted in their transportation for criminal activities, the Justices struggled to efface their past identities as "tinkers, excise-men, pickpockets, and farriers" – men of the "common Rank."[15] In an age preoccupied with identity, needless to say, the ability to "put on" an identity as easily as one puts on a coat is troubling. The success of men such as the Justices visibly undermines the class-based assumptions about who is capable of ruling. And, as if to militate against these early modern "Horatio Alger" narratives, Behn depicts these men as incompetent, foolish, cowardly, and driven by greed (this in stark contrast to the actual class origins of most of the Virginia oligarchy, a group of men with either aristocratic or gentry lineage).

Behn stages this heterogeneity to three effects: first, it individualizes her hero Bacon; second, it normalizes the class hierarchy which must accompany social order; finally, it harnesses racial consciousness against the threat posed by the American Indians. This final reason is the most significant in Behn's representation. If the English colonizers are to be successful in subjugating the American Indians, it can only happen under the administrative and military superiority of a particular form of English masculinity. The embodiment of "courtesy, liberality, decorum, . . . compassion," and honor, this man attests to the heroic ideal of Restoration militarism, the warrior prince.[16] In effect, Behn's text articulates a desire for a central figure to reaffirm the distance between the English and the "savages," as current English behavior seems dangerously close to denying any "difference."

In Behn's dramatic fantasy, Nathaniel Bacon, the embodiment of the warrior prince, points to the degeneracy, the barbarity, and thus the incivility of the "common Rank." He is a man who exercises power to sustain the authority of England's colonial project. Bacon is also an aristocratic figure who exudes a powerful romantic image in his respectful treatment of the women taken hostage, his solicitous concern for the wounded American Indian King, and his wooing of the American Indian Queen. Behn's depiction insists that the measure of English colonial masculinity is not acquired through wealth or social power but through birth.

In many respects, the contrast between Bacon and the ruling oligarchy stresses a conservative belief that the absence of aristocratic power in the colonies constitutes a significant threat to the entire project. Virginia is seen as a "Country . . . [that needs to be] peopled with a *well-born Race*, to make it one of the best Colonies in the World" (I.i. my emphasis). Like many of the reactionary narratives that emerged in the wake of the Civil War, Behn's rhetoric inextricably links the "race" problems surfacing within the colonial enterprise to the emergence of a powerful class that derives its wealth and power from trade and financial ventures, yet demonstrates little of the nobility fashionably expected of an early modern ruling class. Furthermore, in contrast to the Flirts, Parson Dunces, and Boozers, the truly "civilized" immigrants to Virginia have no need for a manufactured genealogy to explain their behavior. Clearly, the success of the American Indians' resistance arises from the dissension that marks English colonial society.

CIVILITY – RACE

In her explanation of what assumptions lay at the center of English colonialist discourse, Karen Kupperman writes that it "was a commonplace that the English would perform for the Indians the same function as the Romans once performed for the English – the bringing of civilization and Christianity."[17] What is often evident in the social and discursive practices of English colonists, however, is an ambivalence about the strategies of the mission to civilize the American Indian. In 1623 John Robinson wrote:

> Concerning the killing of those poor Indians, of which we heard at first by report, and since by more certain relation. Oh, how happy a thing had it been, if you had converted some before you had killed any! Besides, where blood is once begun to be shed, it is seldom staunched of a long time after. You will say they deserved it. I grant it. . . . Methinks one or two principals should have been full enough, according to that approved rule, The punishment to a few, and the fear to many.[18]

Thomas Morton, though criticized by the colonial oligarchy in Plymouth, Massachusetts, for his intimacy with the American Indians, shares this view – "I cannot deny but a civilized Nation, has the preheminence [sic] of an uncivilized, by means of those instruments that are found to be common amongst civile people. . . ."[19] While Morton views the American Indians as living a "contented life," he nonetheless perceives them to be an "uncivilized" people.

By 1676, this "civilized" ambivalence had erupted into full-fledged racism and genocide. Nathaniel Bacon, the heroic figure of *The Widow Ranter*, wrote in his "Manifesto" requesting a commission to wage war against the American Indians:

> Whether or no wee ought not to judge his Majesty's title prerogative good here, and his claime better than that of . . . all Indians whatsoever, and whether since his Majesty hath been possessed of this part of America, wee have not been invaded, and his Territories claimed, and his subjects barbarously murdered, his Lands depopulated and usurped by those barbarous Enemies, whose outrages, wrongs and violences offered to our Soveraigne and his subjects have been soe cunningly mixt among the severall Nations or familyes of Indians that it hath been very difficult for us, to distinguish how, or from which of those said Nations, the said wrongs did proceed.[20]

Though denied his commission, Bacon nonetheless embarked on his campaign.

The Widow Ranter assimilates much of this militaristic and polemical rhetoric in its characterization of Bacon: "Should I stand by and see *my* country ruin'd, my King dishonour'd, and his Subjects murder'd, hear the sad Crys of Widows and of Orphans?" (II.iv.). Yet, overall, Behn's treatment of Bacon is deliberately sentimentalized by his romantic attachment to Semernia, an American Indian woman. Furthermore, using the romantic escapade of the Widow Ranter (who boldly pursues and "captures" her man) as a parodic contrast to the relationship between the Englishman and the American Indian woman, Behn trivializes the genocidal implications of the use of the American Indian woman as a vehicle for the "bringing of the savages" to civility.

In their discussion of the English genocidal practices in Ireland, Ann Rosalind Jones and Peter Stallybrass observe that "civility . . . does not emerge through cultural evolution but through military conquest."[21] Nowhere is this hypothesis more acutely demonstrated than in the relationship between Bacon and the American Indian monarchs. In constructing this dramatic relationship, Behn directs attention away from the political drama taking place in Virginia, guiding the spectator's gaze through a sentimental lens of high romance. In this instance, Kupperman's reading (that the English viewed the American Indian through the spectrum of status and not race) appears valid; in a gesture of ideological elision, Behn rhetorically assimilates the characters Cavernio and Semernia into the civilized world of the English aristocracy. In almost every conceivable way, the Indianness of the monarchs is subsumed by their identification with Bacon.

Though at war, Cavernio and Bacon enact the ritualized discourse of aristocratic power:

KING   Yet though I'm young, I'm sensible of Injuries; and oft have heard my Grandsire say, That we were Monarchs once of all this spacious World, till you, an unknown People, landing here, distress'd and ruin'd by destructive Storms, abusing all our charitable Hospitality, usurp'd our Right, and made your Friends your Slave.

(II.i)

BACON   I will not justify the Ingratitude of my Fore-fathers, but finding here my Inheritance, I am resolv'd still to maintain it so, and by my Sword . . . defend each Inch of land, with my last drop of Blood.

(II.i)

Neither man will suffer a loss of honor; and as Cavernio recognizes, the differences between them are "better disputed in the Field."

As with Bacon, Cavernio's words and deeds are consistent with the heroic formulae Behn makes use of in her dramatic narratives. For example, in the duel that eventually costs him his life, Cavernio continually displays the honorable behavior of the "civilized" man: from his expressed concern that Bacon "bleed[s] apace" to his request that Bacon "Commend me to her [Semernia]" (IV.ii). Behn consciously manipulates the elision of difference between Cavernio and Bacon, making of both characters men who are "indeed above the common Rank, by Nature generous, brave, resolv'd and daring." (I.1) Thus, when Cavernio is murdered by Bacon, the audience is made witness to the death of a man who is "governed absolutely by [an] allegiance to the conventional aristocratic code of love and honor."[22] The mirroring of these two characters is consistent with Behn's dramatic technique. In her insightful analysis of *Oroonoko*, Laura Brown argues that "Oroonoko is . . . not only a natural European and aristocrat, but a natural neoclassicist and Royalist as well."[23] As Cavernio resists the invasion of his lands, he exemplifies the English warrior prince, and is an admirable match for his aristocratic counterpart, who "first taught . . . [Cavernio] how to use a Sword" (IV.ii).

Not until Act IV is there an explicit allusion to an inherent difference between the American Indian King and the Englishman. In the stage directions to a scene that can only be viewed as a stereotypical representation of the "barbaric" theology of the American Indians, Behn reminds her audience of the futility of any attempt to bring "civility" to the natives:

> *A Temple, with an Indian God placed upon it. . . . All bow to the Idol, and divide on each side of the Stage. Then the Musick playing louder, the Priests and Priestesses dance about the Idol with ridiculous Postures, and crying (as for Incantations) thrice repeated, Agah Yerkin, Agah Boah, Sulen Tawarapah, Sulen Tawarapah.*

(IV.i)

In evoking this image, Behn openly draws upon a cultural difference to mark racial inferiority. And, in this moment of non-Christian paganism, Cavernio and Semernia become visibly disengaged from the trope of civility.

Like Oroonoko, Cavernio falls victim to English imperialism and in the process his death, just as Oroonoko's, is linked to a classical heroic heritage – "He's gone – and now, like Caesar, I could weep over the Hero I my self destroyed" (IV.ii). What becomes obvious at this point is the paradox of the discourse of civility: to exercise an ideological strategy that erases all differences (i.e., makes of the American Indians "civilized" English) calls into question the continued immigration of English men and women. On the other hand, to abandon the ostensible "mission" of the colonizing project (i.e., "civilizing the savages") is to admit that territorial ambition and empire-building are the real motivation behind the English invasion of the American Indians' lands. In either case, the "civilized" American Indian remains a problem, since he poses untold legal and political contradictions for the English settlers, particularly in the acquisition of land. Once "civilized," the native becomes an equal competitor for property, and by extension control of the colony; and, given her/his a priori natal claim to the lands, such a competition is the last thing that imperialist hegemony desires. In the end, the English colonialists abandon the principle of bringing the American Indians, as a "race," to civility.[24] And despite his "civility," Cavernio dies alongside the other "savages" who "fall to massacring [the English] wherever [they] lie exposed to them" (I.i).

Before concluding my reading of *The Widow Ranter*, I want to look at the interlinking of miscegenation and the idea of civility in Behn's play.[25] Early in the play the audience learns that Bacon's "Thirst of Glory cherish'd by sullen Melancholy . . . was the first motive that made him in love with the young Indian Queen, fancying no Hero ought to be without his Princess" (I.i). On the one hand, literary convention can help us understand why Behn consciously elects not to represent Bacon's actual wife in the play: romantic love in Restoration comedy rarely takes place in marriage since the phenomenon is about courtship. On the other hand, however, literary convention cannot explain why Behn chooses to construct a miscegenous relationship. Behn's construction of the fantasy of Semernia, I believe, serves to deflect a very real anxiety in the racial ideology of English colonialism – unrestrained English female sexuality.

In an instance of form(al) mediation, Semernia, as an American Indian, displaces the unmarried upper-class English woman as the object of upper-class masculine erotic desire. In much of colonial English ethnography, American Indian women were stereotyped as sexually active and aggressive. In *A Map of Virginia*, one of the narrators reports that the women of Powhatan's nation "solemnly invited [John] Smith to their lodging; but no sooner was he within the house but all these nymphs more tormented him than ever with crowding and pressing and hanging upon him, most tediously crying, 'Love you not me?'"[26] William Strachey reported that American Indian men permitted their wives full sexual freedom, arguing "uncredible yt is, with what heat both Sexes of them are given over to those Intemperances, and the men to preposterous Venus, for which they are full of their owne country-disease (the Pox) very young."[27]

It is this "baggage" which Behn cannot displace in her representation of Semernia, though the Englishwoman tries. As Behn draws her, Semernia's "Indianness" is concealed by the rhetoric of a conventionalized version of English femininity. Semernia is virtuous, attractive, loyal, honorable, and she is in love with the heroic Bacon. Confiding in her servant Anaria, the Queen gives expression to the struggle between her passions and her reason: "Twelve tedious Moons I pass'd in silent Languishment; Honour endeavouring to destroy my Love, but all in vain" (V.iii). Though married to Cavernio, Semernia is not unaffected by the presence of Bacon. When the Englishman describes, with a "faltring" tongue, the effects of love – "It makes us tremble when we touch the fair one; . . . the Heart's surrounded with a feeble Languishment, the eyes are dying, and the Cheeks are pale" (II.i) – Semernia's reaction mirrors Bacon's words: "I'll talk no more, our Words exchange our Souls, and every Look fades all my blooming Honour" (II.i).

As a married woman, Semernia recognizes the "symptoms" as some-thing to fear, and she quickly seeks the protective standard of virtuous distance. In fact, to guard her "honour," Semernia exhorts Bacon to take "all our Kingdoms – make our People slaves, and let me fall beneath your conquering Sword: but never let me hear you talk again, or gaze upon your Eyes" (II.i). By the play's conclusion, Bacon's desire to possess Semernia does exact the enormous toll her prophetic words bespeak. In the end, her husband-king dead, her people dispossessed and slaugh-tered, Semernia's dilemma is resolved when Bacon mistakenly kills the Queen. The American Indian woman's body has channeled male inter-est until the Englishwomen can be safely engaged or wedded.

With Semernia's death, Behn effectively brings to closure her narra-tive of the romance. Bacon's death is somewhat anti-climactic: he com-mits suicide after successfully routing the Jamestown forces allied against him. Nonetheless, the play ends with two significant articula-tions. The first is the imposition of a class hierarchy among the English settlers. The army which pursued Bacon was composed of both gentry and lower-class men, and their class differences become resolved in pursuit of a common enemy. Even so, the play concludes with the Acting Governor dislodging Justices Whiff and Whimsey – "your Places in the Council shall be supplied by these Gentlemen of Sense and Honour" (V.v).

The second articulation of Behn's narration occurs just after Bacon slays Semernia. The General claims, "There ends my Race of Glory and of Life" (V.iii). Behn's ambiguous use of the word "Race" produces two parallel readings. In the first instance, "Race" straightforwardly signals the end of Bacon's ambitious endeavor. On a second and more ideologi-cal level, Bacon's words are much more revealing of a cultural anxiety about miscegenation if we read "Race" as a reference to lineage. In what follows I want to make a case for the second reading in light of the discourse of civility.

Bacon's rhetoric dramatizes the anxiety concerning the acquisition and transmission of property that circulates within the discourse of "race." In an earlier statement, Bacon declared that Semernia was "the dear Prize, for which alone he toil'd!" (V.iii). If we link his use of the word "toil'd" with his earlier declaration to "defend every inch of Land," Bacon's pursuit of Semernia takes on the rhetoric of property. Symbolically, Bacon's pursuit is about the English efforts to acquire American Indian lands. In a letter, John Winthrop argued, "That which lies common, and hath never beene replenished or subdued is free to any that possesse and improve it."[28] If we read Bacon's pursuit of Semernia as parallel to his efforts to possess American Indian lands, then it is not inappropriate to extrapolate a reading that sees both the woman and the lands as the "property" of another person, in this case Cavernio.

The acquisition of Semernia not only would signify Bacon's mastery of the American Indians (including their enslavement) and what they control but also the English man's right to lay claim to the American Indian female body. In Bacon's colonialist endeavors, Cavernio stands between the Englishman's accumulation of property – whether lands or the object of his erotic desire, Semernia. Given that Semernia is the wife of Cavernio and, in the context of early modern English ideologies regarding marriage, "belongs" to him, Bacon's actions represent an encroachment upon the property of the American Indian. The "warrior prince," far from being civilized, symbolizes social disorder and immorality. Yet from the English perspective, Bacon's position is typical of a general colonialist attitude.

It is this ambivalent racial inscription which makes Behn's *The Widow Ranter* a deeply troubling text. By framing the discourse of civility in a miscegenous romance, Behn doubly insures the eradication of the American Indians, but at the expense of obscuring the problematic paradox of Bacon's undertaking. Should Semernia become the "property" of Bacon (whether as his wife or his mistress), any offspring are of Bacon's "Race." What better way to shift the balance of power in the New World than by increasing dramatically the number of sympathetic natives who identify with a patrilineal authority and culture? More importantly, what better way to achieve this goal than through sexual and marital relations with American Indian women?

In her able study, Mary Dearborn argues that one of the "single most important received metaphor[s] of female ethnic identity" is "the story of Pocahontas."[29] This myth lies at the very center of Behn's depiction of Semernia, altered, however, to meet the objectives of the late seventeenth-century colonizing project. What this "metaphor of female ethnic identity" tells us is that, from the standpoint of the civilizing mission propounded by the English, miscegenation is both desirable *and* dangerous. And, given the overall objective of early modern English colonialism, the danger far outweighed the pleasures.

Miscegenation threatens the idea of assimilation that lies at the heart of civility. Unlike genocide, miscegenation can (and often does) result in the proliferation of "natives" who reject "civility."[30] What is more frightening, from the standpoint of the colonizers, is the possibility that the "savage" would come to dominate both in numbers and in culture.[31] If miscegenation could "civilize," could it not also create "savages" who preferred polygamy or a communal existence based on the absence of competition and greed?[32] Furthermore, if miscegenation erases the boundaries between the English and the American Indians, what then becomes of the ineradicable measure of "difference" required to justify the colonizing project?

Ultimately, it was the loss of "Englishness" within an erotic, miscegenous space of "civilized conquest" that most alarmed the colonizers. As Bacon pursues Semernia, is he civilized man or "savage" native? Do we excuse Bacon's blatant disregard of the Christian prohibitions against adultery, lust, and murder because the individuals who provoked this behavior were considered "savages"? Or, do we condemn him for his failure to remain a "true" Englishman? Finally, when Bacon takes his own life for love of an American Indian woman – "Come, my good Poison, like that of Hannibal; long I have born a noble Remedy for all the Ills of Life. I have too long surviv'd my Queen and Glory" (V.iv) – has he succumbed to "Indian savagism"? Or is his death the return of his "English civility"?

As Behn writes it, what seemed most important to the colonial project was unity among the English, as Bacon's last words indicate: "Now while you are Victors, make a Peace – with the English Council, and never let Ambition, – Love, – or Interest, make you forget, as I have done, your Duty and Allegiance" (V.v).

CONCLUSION

> I have sought to ensure that the integrity of the evidence was respected at all times, for this has always to be demanded from those who practise the writing of history. Beyond that, the interpreter is himself nothing but a spokesman for historical forces.[33]

Like others of her circle, Aphra Behn was deeply implicated in colonial politics; if Behn's account is to be believed, her father was, after all, appointed Lieutenant-Governor of the English Surinam colony. Yet there are clear traces of uncertainty in *The Widow Ranter* about the morality of English colonial actions in seventeenth-century Virginia. As Laura Brown and Margaret Ferguson have shown in their discussions of

Behn's *Oroonoko*, the historical does not easily coexist with the romantic idealization that Behn's discourse produces.[34] Despite the romanticization of both Cavernio and Semernia, their cultural identity is always inscribed by their Indianness. Even as Cavernio responds to Bacon's courtesy with courtesy, it is clear that even the aristocratic or royal American Indian is not (and cannot be) fully assimilable.

The discourse of civility allowed Behn to invent an "American Indian" who is both assimilable and unequivocally alien. Behn drew upon existing racialist ideologies and, in incorporating them into the discourse of civility, produced a new discourse that spoke to unalterable differences that were not easily exoticized. In creating *The Widow Ranter*, she unconsciously exposes the principal contradiction of her class-based discourse of civility: aristocratic civility is incompatible with colonialism and imperialism. However, when the discourse of civility is constructed upon a racialized binarism, as is the case with *The Widow Ranter*, then the justifications for genocide, cultural hegemony, and slavery become more easily enunciated and defensible.

Homi Bhabha argues, "the objective of colonial discourse is to construe the colonized as a population of degenerate types on the basis of racial origin, in order to justify conquest and to establish systems of administration and instruction."[35] As "race" becomes imbricated in the geopolitics of early modern England, then the moral impetus of ideologies such as civility becomes a sailor's knot, tightening its hold not on the American Indians but on the English immigrants. The "most visible complexion" of "race" in the early modern English discourse, to return to Valerie Wayne's observation, is indelibly etched not in color but in the paradox of civility. Only when the concept of civility proves to be an ideological contradiction in the colonial project does the idea of "race" shift its meaning.

In the end, while the African woman's body became the primary locus for the economic enactment of English imperialism in the Americas from the eighteenth century onward, the American Indian woman functioned as the initial register for a discourse of "race" where color fixed difference. Thus, while the phenotypical differences between the American Indians and the English, in the English racial consciousness, were not as stark as the differences between Africans and English, they were important to the construction of a newer racial ideology. Essentially, and this is where I diverge from scholars such as Kupperman, the differences were enough to produce a binarism of inferiority/superiority.

Ultimately, the task that faces Renaissance scholars is not just to make visible the "whiteness" that is presumed to be the center of the concept, as Wayne has argued. Rather, we must begin to question the implicit racial assumptions being reread as a homogeneous society attempts to

238

extend its hegemony beyond its own geographic boundaries. How does that society mark itself as different from the peoples it wishes to conquer? What effect does this marking have on the conquerors' own sense of identity? Only when we address these issues shall we begin to see the real property of the idea of "race." And perhaps, there will no longer be a need to "exonerate."

Part IV

GENDER, RACE, AND CLASS: COLONIAL AND POSTCOLONIAL

14

IROQUOIS WOMEN, EUROPEAN WOMEN

Natalie Zemon Davis

In the opening years of the seventeenth century in the Montagnais country, Pierre Pastedechouan's grandmother loved to tell him how astonished she had been at the first sight of a French ship. With its large sails and many people gathered on the deck, she had thought the wooden boat a floating island. She and the other women in her band immediately set up cabins to welcome the guests.[1] The people on a floating island appeared also to a young Micmac woman of the Saint Lawrence Gulf in a dream which she recounted to the shaman and elders of her community and which came true a few days later when a European ship arrived.[2]

Across the Atlantic, Mother Marie Guyart de l'Incarnation also first saw the Amerindian lands in a dream-vision, a vast space of mountains, valleys, and fog to which the Virgin Mary and Jesus beckoned her and which her spiritual director then identified as Canada. By the time she had boarded the boat in 1639, she hoped to "taste the delights of Paradise in the beautiful and large crosses of New France." Once at Québec, she and her sister Ursulines kissed the soil, Marie finding the landscape just like her dream except not so foggy. The Christianized Algonquin, Montagnais, and Huron girls, "freshly washed in the blood of the lamb, seem[ed] to carry Paradise with them."[3]

The similarities and differences in the situation and views of these women in the sixteenth and first half of the seventeenth centuries is my subject in this essay. I want to look at the Amerindian women of the eastern woodlands in terms of historical change – and not just change generated by contact with Europeans, but by processes central to their own societies. I want to insist on the absolute simultaneity of the Amerindian and European worlds, rather than viewing the former as an earlier version of the latter, and make comparisons less polarized than the differences between "simple" and "complex" societies. I want to suggest interactions to look for in the colonial encounter other than the necessary but overpolarized twosome of "domination" and "resistance," and attribute the capacity for choice to Indians as to Europeans. The

Amerindian case may also be a source of alternative examples and metaphors to illumine the European case. Indeed, an ideal sequel to this essay would be an inquiry about the history of European women that made use of Iroquois tropes and frames.

The term "Iroquois women" in my title is a shorthand for both the Hurons and the Iroquois among the nations speaking the Iroquoian languages, from whom many of my examples will be drawn, and in some instances for women of the groups speaking Algonquian languages, peoples from primarily hunting, fishing, and gathering communities such as the Montagnais, Algonquins, Abenakis, and Micmacs. On the whole, I will stay within the region penetrated by the French, though the woodlands Indians themselves ranged well beyond its reach. My sources are the classic travel accounts and the Jesuit and other religious relations from the eastern woodlands (including the writings of Marie de l'Incarnation and the women Hospitalers of Québec); ethnographic studies, including those based on archeological research and material culture; and collections of Amerindian tales and legends and customs made over the last 150 years and more.[4]

The Hurons and Iroquois alike lived from a digging-stick agriculture, gathering, fishing, and hunting.[5] The men opened the fields for cultivation, but the women were the farmers, growing maize, beans, squash, and in some places tobacco. The women also were the gatherers, picking fruits and other edible food and bringing in all the firewood. When villages changed their base, as they did every several years, it was sometimes in fear of their enemies, but ordinarily because the women declared the fields infertile and the suitable wood exhausted for miles around. The men were in charge of hunting, fishing, and intertribal trading, but the active women might well accompany their husbands or fathers on these expeditions when not held back by farming or cabin tasks. Along the way the women were expected to do much of the carrying, although if there were male prisoners with the band, their masters would have them help the women.[6] Warfare was in the hands of the men.

Responsibility for the crafts and arts was similarly divided. Men made weapons and tools of stone, wood, and sometimes bits of copper, carved the pipes, built the cabins, and constructed frames for canoes and snowshoes. Women were in charge of anything that had to do with sewing, stringing and weaving, preparing thread and laces by hand-spinning and winding, stringing snowshoes, and making baskets, birchbark kettles, nets, and rush mats. Once the men had made a kill at the hunt, the animal was the women's domain, from skinning and preparing the hide, softening and greasing the furs, to making garments and moccasins. The women were the potters, and also made all the decorative objects of porcupine quills, shells (including wampum necklaces and belts), beads, and birchbark. They painted the faces and bodies of their husbands and sons so that they would look impressive when they went visiting, and decorated each other for dances and feasts. As for the meals, the women took care of them all, pounding the corn into flour and cooking much of the food in a single kettle. (Similar work patterns were found among the Algonquian-speaking peoples, where horticulture was only occasionally practiced and where the women were thus on the move much of the time with the men.)

This division of labor looked very lopsided to the French men who first reported it, presumably contrasting it with European agriculture, where men did the ploughing, where women did the weeding and gardening, and where both did wooding and carrying, and with European crafts like leather and pottery, where men had a predominant role. "The women work without comparison more than the men," said Jacques Cartier of the Iroquois whom he had met along the Saint Lawrence in 1536; "the women do all the servile tasks, work[ing] ordinarily harder than the men, though they are neither forced or constrained to do it," said the Recollet Gabriel Sagard of the Huron women in 1623. "Real pack-mules," a Jesuit echoed a few years later.[7] Marie de l'Incarnation, in contrast, took the women's heavy work for granted, perhaps because she heard about it from the Huron and Algonquin women in a matter-of-fact way in the convent yard rather than seeing it, perhaps because she herself had spent her young womanhood in a wagoner's household, doing everything from grooming horses and cleaning slops to keeping the accounts.[8] In any case, Sagard noted that the Huron women still had time for gaming, dancing, and feasts, and "to chat and pass the time together."[9]

The differences that even Marie de l'Incarnation could not fail to recognize between her life in France and that of Huron and Iroquois women concerned property, kinship structures, marriage, and sexual practice. Whereas in France private or at least family property was increasingly freeing itself from the competing claims of distant kin and feudal lords, among both the Iroquois and the Hurons collective property arrangements – village, clan, band, or tribal – prevailed in regard to hunting and gathering areas and to farming plots. Matrilineality and matrilocality seem to have been more consistently practiced among the Iroquois than among the Hurons,[10] but for both societies the living unit was a long-house of several related families, in which the senior women had a major say about what went on. (The Algonquian-speaking peoples counted descent patrilineally and dwelt in smaller wigwams and summer lodges.)

Parents often suggested potential marriage partners to their children (among the Iroquois, it was the mothers who took the initiative), but then the younger generation had to act. A Huron youth would ask the permission of the parents of a young woman and give her a substantial present of a wampum collar or beaver robe; if, after a sexual encounter for a few nights, she gave her consent, the wedding feast took place.[11] As there was no dowry and dower but only a bride gift, so there was no property in the way of inheritance: the deceased took some of his or her mats and furs and other goods away to the other world, while the bereaved kin were given extensive gifts "to dry their tears" by the other members of their village and clan.[12]

Without property inheritance and without firm notions about the father's qualities being carried through sexual intercourse or the blood,[13] sexual relations between men and women were conducted without concern about "illegitimate" offspring. There could be several trial encounters and temporary unions before a marriage was decided on, and openly acknowledged intercourse with other partners was possible for both husband and wife. When a Huron father was questioned one day by a Jesuit about how, with such practices, a man could know who his son was, the man answered, "You French love only your own children; we love all the children of our people." When Hurons and Algonquins first saw the Québec Hospital nuns in 1639 – three women all in their twenties – they were astonished (so one of the sisters reported) "when they were told that we had no men at all and that we were virgins."[14]

Clearly there was room in the Iroquoian long-house and Algonquian wigwam for many quarrels: among wives at their different long-house fires, among daughters and parents about consent to a suitor,[15] among husbands and wives about competing lovers.[16] One Jesuit even claimed in 1657 that some married women revenged themselves on their husbands for "bad treatment" by eating a poisonous root and leaving the men with "the reproach of their death."[17] Much more often, an unsatisfactory marriage simply ended in divorce, with both man and woman free to remarry and the woman usually having custody of the children.[18]

In such a situation the debate about authority had a different content from that in Renaissance and early seventeenth-century Europe, where a hierarchical model of the father-dominated family was at best moderated by the image of companionate marriage or reversed by the husband-beating virago. Among the Amerindians, physical coercion was not supposed to be used against anyone within the family, and decisions about crops, food consumption, and many of the crafts were rightfully the women's. If a man wanted a courteous excuse not to do something, he could say without fear of embarrassment "that his wife did not wish it."[19]

When we leave the long-house fire and kettle for the religious feast or dance and council meeting, we have a different picture again. Religious belief among both the Algonquian- and Iroquoian-speaking peoples was diverse and wide-ranging, their high divinities, sacred manitous, and omnipresent lesser spirits remembered, pondered over, and argued about through decentralized storytelling. Recollets and Jesuits, hearing such accounts, would challenge the speakers: "How can the creator Yoscaha have a grandmother Aataentsic if Yoscaha is the first god?" they would ask a Huron. "And how could Aataentsic's daughter get pregnant with Yoscaha and his evil twin Tawiscaron if men had not yet been created?" "Was Atahocan definitely the first creator?" they would ask a Montagnais. Huron or Montagnais would then reply that he did not know for sure: "Perhaps it was Atahocan; one speaks of Atahocan as one speaks of a thing so far distant that nothing sure can be known about it." Or that he had the account from someone who had visited Yoscaha and Aataentsic or had seen it in a dream. Or, politely, that the French beliefs about "God" were fine for Europe but not for the woodlands. Or, defiantly, that he would believe in the Jesuits' God when he saw him with his own eyes.[20]

The Recollets and Jesuits reported such exchanges only with men, Father Lejeune even adding, "there are among them mysteries so hidden that only the old men, who can speak with credit and authority about them, are believed."[21] Marie de l'Incarnation, always attentive to women's roles and pleased that Abenaki belief included the virgin birth of the world-saver Messou, said only that traditional accounts of the "Sauvages" were passed on "from fathers to children, from the old to the young."[22] Women were certainly among the listeners to Amerindian creation accounts, for the "ancient tales" were told, for instance, at gatherings after funerals,[23] but were they among the tellers of sacred narratives? Speculation from the existing evidence suggests the following picture: during the sixteenth and early seventeenth centuries, men, especially older men, were the tellers of creation stories at male assemblies (as for the election of a chief)[24] and at mixed gatherings, but women recounted Aataentsic's doings along with many other kinds of narrative to each other and to their children.[25] If this be the case, then the situation of women in the eastern woodlands was rather like that of their Catholic contemporaries in Europe. There, for the most part, Catholic belief systems were formally taught by doctors of theology and male preachers and catechizers, and women reflected on such doctrine among themselves in convents and told Christian stories to their children.

To the all-important realm of dreams, however, Amerindian women and men had equal access. Huron and Iroquois notions of "the soul" and "the self" were more inflected, articulated, or pluralistic than Christian notions of the living person, where a single soul animated the body and where reason, will, and appetite were functions warring or collaborating within. Huron and Iroquois saw "the soul" as "divisible" (to use Father Brébeuf's term about the Huron), giving different names and some independence to different soul-actions: animation, reason, deliberation, and desire. The desiring soul especially spoke to one in dreams – "this is what my heart tells me, this is what my appetite desires" (*ondayee ikaton onennoncwat*); sometimes the desiring soul was counseled by a familiar *oki* or spirit who appeared in a dream in some form and told it what it needed or wanted, its *ondinoc*, its secret desire.[26] In France, dreams and the time between sleeping and waking were the occasion for extraordinary visits from Christ, the saints, the devil, or the ghosts of one's dead kin. In the American woodlands, dreams were a visit from part of oneself and one's *oki*, and their prescriptions had wider effect, forestalling or curing illness and predicting, sanctioning, or warning against future events of all kinds.

Amerindian women and men thus took their dreams very seriously, describing, evaluating, and interpreting them to each other, and then acting on them with intensity and determination. For a person of some standing, the village council might decide to mobilize every cabin to help fulfill a dream. So a woman of Angoutenc in the Huron country went outside one night with her little daughter and was greeted by the Moon deity, swooping down from the sky as a beautiful tall woman with a little daughter of her own. The Moon ordered that the woman be given many presents of garments and tobacco from surrounding peoples and that henceforth she dress herself in red, like the fiery moon. Back in her long-house, the woman immediately fell ill with dizziness and weak muscles, and learned from her dreams that only a curing feast and certain presents would restore her. The council of her birth-village of Ossassané agreed to provide all she needed. Three days of ritual action followed, with the many prescribed gifts assembled, the woman in her red garments walking through fires that did not burn her limbs, and everyone discussing their dream desires through riddles.[27] She was cured in an episode that illustrates to us how an individual woman could set in motion a whole sequence of collective religious action.[28]

Women also had important roles in dances intended to placate the *oki* spirits or to drive out evil spirits from the sick. Among the Hurons, a few women who had received a dream sign might be initiated along with men into a society whose curative dance was considered "very powerful against the demons"; among the Iroquois, women were received in several healing and propitiary societies.[29] To be sure, women were accused of witchcraft – that is, of causing someone's death by poisoning or charms – but no more than Huron and Iroquois men, and *okis* or *manitous* in mischievous action were not gendered female more than male.[30]

The major asymmetry in religious life in the sixteenth and seventeenth centuries concerned the shamans. The Arendiwane, as the Hurons called them ("sorcerers" or "jugglers" in the language of the

Jesuits), comprised the master shamans, who diagnosed and cured illness by dealing with the spirit world, and the lesser religious leaders,
who commanded winds and rains, predicted the future, or found lost
objects. The Jesuits scarcely ever described women in these roles among
either the Algonquian-speaking or Iroquoian-speaking peoples, and
Marie de l'Incarnation mentioned none at all. An Algonquin woman was
known "to be involved in sorcery, succeeding at it better than the men"; a
woman "famous" among the Hurons for her "sorcery" sought messages
from the *Manitou* about what kinds of feasts or gifts would cure an
illness; a Montagnais woman entered the cabin where the male shamans
consulted the spirits of the air and through shaking the tent-posts and
loud singing was able to diagnose an illness and foresee an Iroquois
attack.[31] Indeed, soothsaying seems to have been the one shamanic
function in which women were welcome, as with the old woman of
Teanaostaiaë village in the Huron country, who saw events in distant
battles with the Iroquois by looking into fires, and the Abenaki "Pytho-
nesses" who could see absent things and foretell the future.[32]

Most of the time, however, a woman was simply an aide, marking on a
"triangular stick" the songs for the dead being sung by a Montagnais
medicine man so their order would be remembered; walking around the
shaman and his male performers at a prescribed moment in a ritual to
kill a far-away witch.[33] Surely the herbal remedies known to be used by
later Amerindian women must have had their antecedents in the female
lore of the sixteenth and early seventeenth centuries,[34] and it is hard to
imagine that there were no religious specialists associated with the
menstrual cabins of the Iroquian communities and the Montagnais. It
may have been precisely the beliefs about defilement that barred women
from handling the sacred shamanic objects and rattle used in spirit
cures. Across the Atlantic, the powers and dangers of menstruation kept
European *religieuses* from touching altars and chalices too directly and
kept Catholic laywomen away from the mass during their periods.
Among the Hurons, the presence of a pregnant woman made a sick
person worse, but was required for the extraction of an arrow; among
the French Catholics, the glance of a post-partum woman brought
trouble to people in streets and roadways. Among the Amerindians,
medicine men were to abstain from sexual intercourse before their
ceremonies; among the Europeans, Catholic priests were to abstain from
sexual intercourse all the time.[35]

The most important asymmetry among Indian men and women was
political. In the female world of crops, cooking, and crafts, women made
the decisions; in lodge and long-house, their voice often carried the day.
Village and tribal governance, however, was in the hands of male chiefs
and councils, and, apart from the Iroquois, women's influence on it was
informal. (Only among the Algonquian peoples of southern New

England and the mid-Atlantic coast do we hear of women sometimes holding authority as sunksquaws along with the more numerous male sachems.)[36] Huron villages and Algonquin and Montagnais settlements often had two or more chiefs, their access to this honor partly hereditary but even more based on assessments of their eloquence, wisdom, generosity, or past prowess. The chiefs presided over frequent local council meetings, where women and young warriors were rarely present and where pipe-smoking men gave their views, the eldest among them being accorded particular respect. At larger assemblies of several clans and villages, the young men were invited as well, and sometimes the women.[37] When council or assembly decisions required embassies to other villages or nations – to seek support in war or to resolve disputes – the envoys were chiefs and other men.

In Iroquois communities, women had more formal roles in political decisions than elsewhere. Here, to women's advantage, succession to chieftancies was more strictly hereditary, passing matrilineally to a sister's son or another male relative named by the woman. Here among the Onondagas – so we learn from the pen of Marie de l'Incarnation – there were "women of quality" or "Capitainesses" who could affect decisions at local council meetings and select ambassadors for peace initiatives.[38] At least by the eighteenth century important women could attend treaty councils of the Iroquois nations, and perhaps they did so earlier.[39]

Now it is precisely in regard to this political life that major historical changes had occurred in the American/Canadian woodlands and villages from the fourteenth through sixteenth centuries. The evidence for these changes comes in part from archeologists: tobacco-pipes become more elaborate, pottery and sea shells are found further from their place of origin, and human bones in ossuaries show signs of being "cut, cooked and split open to extract the marrow."[40] The evidence comes also from the collective memory of Hurons and Iroquois after European contact and from Indian stories and legends.

A double picture emerges. First, warfare became more prevalent and intense, with the seizure of women as wives[41] and the adoption of some male captives and the torture and cannibalization of others. European contact then added to the complicated history of enmity and exchange between Iroquois and Hurons. As a Huron chief recalled to some Onondagas in 1652,

> Have you forgotten the mutual promises our Ancestors made when they first took up arms against each other, that if a simple woman should take it on herself to uncover the Sweat-house and pull up the stakes that support it, that the victors would put down their arms and show mercy to the vanquished?[42]

The two roles assigned to women by intensified warfare – the womanadoptor of an enemy and the woman-enemy incorporated as wife – must have had important consequences for consciousness. Let us consider here only the enemy wife, a position in which women living in Europe rarely found themselves (even though the foreign queens of Spain and France might have felt divided loyalties when their husbands went to war in 1635, the marriages had been made as peaceful alliance).[43] In the eastern American woodlands, Algonquin and Huron captives became Iroquois wives; Iroquois captives became Huron wives. Nor was their origin forgotten: Pierre Esprit Radisson among the Mohawks in 1652 discovered that his adoptive mother had been taken from the Huron country in her youth; Father Le Moyne among the Onondagas the next year was approached by a Huron wife who "wanted to pour out her heart to him."[44] This suggests that to the Amerindian habit of self-discovery through dream analysis was added for the enemy wife another source for self-definition: the experience of being forcibly transplanted, alone or with only a few of her kin, to a people who had a different language and burial ground from her ancestors. When the enemy wife was also a Christian in a non-Christian village, the impulse toward self-definition might be all the stronger, but the process predated conversion.

This setting for self-consciousness is rather different from those in which Renaissance historians usually locate the discovery of "the individual" or of a renewed sense of self among European Christians. There we stress how persons set themselves off against those whom they resembled, against their own kind and kin: some of Montaigne's best self-discovery occurred when he played himself off against his friend La Boétie and against his own father. The Amerindian enemy wife (and the adopted male enemy as well) represent a contrasting historical trajectory. Still, they should make us more attentive to European situations where the experience of "foreignness" and "strangeness" could prompt consciousness of self as well as of group. The emergence of Jewish autobiography by the early seventeenth century is a case in point.[45]

Along with intensified warfare, a second associated change took place in the eastern American woodlands in the fifteenth, sixteenth, and early seventeenth centuries: intertribal political federations appeared along with a new peacemaking diplomacy. The Huron League, or League of the Ouendats as they called themselves, was made up of four nations or tribes, two of them establishing themselves as "brother" and "sister" with a grand council in the fifteenth century, the other two being adopted, one in the last decades of the sixteenth century and the other in the early seventeenth century.[46] The Iroquois League of the Five Nations, the Houdénosaunee – three Elder Brothers and two Younger Brothers – was probably founded around 1500.[47] Its origin was memorialized in the Deganawidah Epic about a divine Iroquois seer, Deganawidah, who

preached peace, converted a Mohawk chief Hiawatha away from cannibalism, and then together with him transformed the wicked and obstruc-
tive Onondaga chief Thadodaho into a willing collaborator. (Women
enter the epic through Deganawidah's grandmother, who foresaw his
peace-bringing role in a dream; his mother, who received divine guidance in hidden seclusion and then gave birth to Deganawidah as a virgin;
and the daughter of Hiawatha, who died sacrificially in the encounter
with Thadodaho.)[48]

Among the many fruits of the League formation was the development
of a language of politics and diplomacy: a set of rules and styles of
communication that operated around the local council fire, on embassies
to rouse for war or make amends for a murder, at large assemblies, and
at general councils of the federation. At council meetings, where many
opinions were given, matters opened with the leader's appreciative
words about the men's safe arrival, no one lost in the woods or fallen in
the stream or slain by an enemy. A special tone of voice was used for all
the comments and opinions – the Hurons called it *acouentonch* – "a
raising and lowering of the voice like the tone of a Predicant à l'antique,
an old style Preacher," said a Jesuit in 1636.[49] Always the men spoke
slowly, calmly, and distinctly, each person reviewing the issues before
giving his opinion. No one ever interrupted anyone else, the rhythm of
taking turns aided by the smoking of pipes. No matter how bitter the
disagreement – as when some Huron villages wanted to rebury their
ancestors' bones in a separate grave – courteous and gentle language
was sought. The Hurons said of a good council, *Endionraondaoné*,
"even and easy, like level and reaped fields."[50]

In more elaborate public speeches, for example, as an envoy or at a
large assembly or to make a treaty, still another tone of voice was used –
"a Captain's tone," said a Jesuit, who tried to imitate it among the
Iroquois in 1654. Mnemonic devices were used "to prop up the mind,"
such as marked sticks and, for a major event, the ordered shells on a
wampum necklace or belt. Arm gestures and dramatic movements
accompanied the argument, and the speaker walked back and forth,
seeming "marvelous" to Jacques Cartier in 1535, and to the later Jesuits
"like an actor on a stage."[51] At the 1645 treaty between the Iroquois, the
French, the Algonquins, and the Montagnais, the tall Mohawk chief
Kiotseaeton arose, looked at the sun and then at all the company and
said (as taken from a rough French translation):

> "Onotonio [the French governor], lend me ear. I am the whole of
> my country; thou listenest to all the Iroquois in hearing my words.
> There is no evil in my heart; I have only good songs in my mouth.
> We have a multitude of war songs in our country; we have cast
> them all on the ground; we have no longer anything but songs of

rejoicing." Thereupon he began to sing; his countrymen responded; he walked about that great space as if on the stage of a theatre; he made a thousand gestures; he looked up to Heaven; he gazed at the Sun; he rubbed his arms as if he wished to draw from them the strength that moved them in war.[52]

Throughout, in all political speech, many metaphors and circumlocutions were used, which made it difficult to follow for anyone who had not learned the system. "Kettle" could denote hospitality ("to hang the kettle"), hostility or killing ("to break the kettle," "to put into the kettle"), and ritual reburial of ancestors ("Master of the Kettle," the officer for the Feast of the Dead).[53]

Meanwhile, the persons who were literally in charge of the kettle and who literally reaped the cornfields so that they were easy and even were not deliverers of this oratory. Women strung the shells for the wampum necklaces and belts used in all diplomacy, but they did not provide the public interpretations of their meaning. (Even the Algonquian sunksquaws of the central Atlantic coast are not known for their speeches, and it is significant that Mary Rowlandson, captive of the sunksquaw Weetamoo in 1676, said of her mistress only that "when she had dressed herself, her work was to make Girdles of Wampom and Beads.)"[54] To be sure, councils had to accede to the request of any woman to adopt a prisoner who would replace her slain or dead male relative, but this desire could be discovered by a word or gesture. Only one occasion has come down to us where a Huron woman gave a speech at an assembly: during the smallpox epidemic of 1640 at a large and tumultuous gathering of Ataronchronons, an older woman denounced the Jesuit Black Robes as devils spreading disease.[55] Even in the most favored case of the Iroquois, where the chiefs had been enjoined by Hiawatha to seek the advice of their wisest women about resolving disputes and where captains' wives might accompany an embassy, women never orated as ambassadors – the Five Nations never "spoke through their mouths" – and their opinion at treaty councils was given by a male Speaker for the Women.[56]

Indian men trained their sons in oratory: "I know enough to instruct my son," said an Algonquin captain in refusing to give his son to the Jesuits. "I'll teach him to give speeches." Huron men teased each other if they made a slip of the tongue or mistake, and accorded the eloquent speaker praise and honor. When the Mohawk chief Kiotseaeton wanted to persuade the Hurons to take part in a peace treaty with the Iroquois, he presented a wampum necklace "to urge the Hurons to hasten forth to speak. Let them not be bashful [honteux] like women." The Hurons "call us Frenchmen women," said the Recollet Sagard, "because too impulsive and carried away [*trop précipités et bouillants*] in our actions, [we] talk all at the same time and interrupt each other."[57]

It seems to me that connections between political change, eloquence, and gender can be similarly constructed in the North American villages and woodlands and in Western Europe in the fifteenth, sixteenth, and early seventeenth centuries. Renaissance political oratory, emerging in both republics and monarchies, and the art of formal diplomacy were part of a masculine political culture. As Leonardo Bruni said, "Rhetoric in all its forms – public discussion, forensic argument, logical fencing and the like – lies absolutely outside the province of women." The privileged few with a right to public pronouncement – the queens or queen regents and a rare learned woman – required exceptional strategies if their voice were to have an authoritative ring.[58]

Some European women sought the chance to speak publicly (or semi-publicly) in religion instead: members of radical and prophetic sects from the first Anabaptists to the Quakers; Protestants in the early days of the new religion, before Paul's dictum that women should not speak in church was strictly enforced; Catholics in the new religious orders, like Marie de l'Incarnation's Ursulines and the Visitation of Jeanne de Chantal, where women preached to and taught each other.[59]

Can we find evidence for a similar process in the eastern American woodlands, that is, did Amerindian women try to expand their voice in religious culture while Amerindian men were expanding political oratory? Conceivably, the role of women in dream analysis (which, as we have seen, involved describing one's dreams publicly and playing riddle games about them at festive fires) may have increased in the course of the sixteenth century. In 1656 an Onondaga woman used her dream-swoon to unmask the Christian Paradise to her fellow Iroquois: she had visited "Heaven," she announced to them, and had seen the French burning Iroquois.[60] Conceivably, the women soothsayers whom the Jesuits met were not simply filling a timeless function open to women, but were recent shamanic innovators. Conceivably, the Iroquois Ogiweoano society of Chanters for the Dead, described in nineteenth-century sources as composed of all or predominantly women, was not a timeless institution, but a development of the sixteenth and seventeenth centuries.[61]

The evidence we do have concerns Amerindian women who converted to Christianity. Some of them used the new religion to find a voice beyond that of a shaman's silent assistant, even while Jesuits were teaching them that wives were supposed to obey their husbands. Khionrea the Huron was one such woman, her portrait drawn for seventeenth-century readers by Marie de l'Incarnation. Brought to the Ursuline convent by her parents in 1640, when she was about twelve, Khionrea had been given the name Thérèse, Marie de l'Incarnation's favorite saint, and had learned to speak both French and Algonquin and to read and write. Two Huron men from her village came to the convent two years later and she preached to them through the grill:

> They listened to this young woman with unrivalled attention, and one day, when they were on the point of being baptized, one of them pretended no longer to believe in God and so she need no longer speak to him of faith or baptism. Our fervent Thérèse . . . became disturbed and said, "What are you talking about? I see the Devil has overturned all your thoughts so that you will be lost. Know you well that if you died today, you would go to Hell where you would burn with Devils, who would make you suffer terrible torments!" The good man laughed at everything she said, which made her think that he spoke with a spirit of contempt. She redoubled her exhortations to combat him, but failing, she came to us in tears. "Ah," she said, "he is lost; he's left the faith; he will not be baptized. It hurt me so to see him speak against God that if there had not been a grill between us, I would have thrown myself on him to beat him." We went to find out the truth . . . and the man affirmed that he had done this only to test her faith and zeal.[62]

Several months afterward Khionrea's parents came to take her back to her village to marry, expecting her to be "the example of their Nation and the Teacher (Maîtresse) of the Huron girls and women." Instead her party was captured by Iroquois, a number were slain, and Thérèse was married to a Mohawk. A decade later, in 1653, she was the mistress of the several families of her Iroquois long-house, still praying to her Christian God and leading others publicly in prayer.[63] Khionrea may have been placating *oki* spirits as well – though Marie de l'Incarnation would have hated to think so – and inspired non-Christian women in her village to experimental religious action. One thinks especially of how Christian forms and phrases could have been appropriated to elaborate and lengthen Indian propitiary prayer.

Cécile Gannendaris is another example of a Huron woman who found an authoritative voice through a new religious mix. Her biography was left by the Sisters of the Québec Hospital where she died at an advanced age in 1669, her Christian "virtue" being demonstrated not only by her fighting off "seducers" in her youth with smoldering logs and spanking her children "when they deserved it," but by giving spiritual guidance to her first and second husbands. Especially she taught and preached, "converting numerous Savages and encouraging them to live more perfectly."

> She was so solidly instructed in our mysteries and so eloquent in explaining them that she was sent new arrivals among the Savages

who were asking to embrace the faith. In a few days she had them ready for baptism, and had reduced the opinionated ones beyond defense by her good reasoning.

The French were impressed with her as well, the Jesuits learning the Huron language from her lips, the newly established Bishop of Québec coming to visit her in her cabin, and the Frenchwomen sending her gifts of food. The Hospital Sisters thought that Gannendaris's clarity of expression and discernment were a break with her Huron past, or, as they put it, "had nothing of the savage [*rien de sauvage*] about them." We would interpret these talents differently, as drawing on a Huron tradition of lucid male discussion around the council fire and on a long-house practice of women's teaching, here transformed by Christian learning and opportunity into a new realm of speech.[64]

When Iroquois women became interested in Christianity, the oratorical force of young converts struck them right away. In the fall of 1655, an Onondaga embassy came to Québec to confirm peace with the Hurons and their French allies and to invite the Black Robes to their villages. A chief's wife ("*une Capitainesse*," in the words of Marie de l'Incarnation) visited the Ursulines with other Onondagas several times and listened to the Huron Marie Aouentohons, not yet fifteen and able to read and write in French, Latin, and Huron. Aouentohons catechized her sister seminarians before the company and made a speech (*une harangue*) both to the chief and his wife:

> Send me as many of my Iroquois sisters as you can. I will be their older sister. I will teach them. I will show them how to pray and to worship the Supreme Parent of All. I will pass on to them what my teachers have taught me.

She then sang hymns in Huron, French, and Latin. The Capitainesse asked the Ursulines how long it would take their daughters to acquire such accomplishments.[65]

Religious eloquence was not, of course, the only kind of expressiveness that attracted some Indian women to Christianity.[66] The spirituality of the "Servant of God" Katherine Tekakwitha, daughter of a Mohawk chief and an enemy-wife Algonquin, was marked by heroic asceticism, intense female companionship, and absorption in mental prayer. Her holy death in 1680 at age 24 was followed by shining apparitions of her and by miracles at her tomb near Caughnawaga. But even Tekakwitha's life involved teaching, as she spoke to the women while they did their cabin tasks of the lives of the saints and other sacred themes and as, toward the end of her life, she instructed those drawn by her reputation on the virtues of virginity and chastity. As her confessor reported it, "At these times her tongue spoke from the depths of her heart."[67]

In one striking way, then, Iroquois and Huron women faced what European historians could call a "Renaissance" challenge in regard to voice and some of them made use of religious tools and the "Catholic Reformation" to meet it. But neither rebirth nor a return to a privileged past would be an image of change that came readily to them. In the thought of the Algonquian- and Iroquoian-speaking peoples of Marie de l'Incarnation's day, sacred time turned around on itself, but there was no historical golden age from which humankind had declined and to which it might hope to return. When people died, their souls divided into two, one part gradually moving toward the setting sun to the Village of the Dead, the other part remaining with the body "unless someone bears it again as a child."[68] There was no fully developed theory of reincarnation among the Hurons, however. Gaps were filled not so much by rebirth as by adoption: the adoption of the dead person's name, which otherwise could not be mentioned; the adoption of a captured enemy to replace a slain son. Things could be created anew, like wampum, which came from the feathers of a fierce and huge wampum bird, slain to win the hand of an Iroquois chief's daughter and then put to the new uses of peacemaking.[69] Institutions could be created anew by joint divine and human enterprise, as with Deganawidah and Hiawatha and the confederating of the Five Iroquois Nations.

Models for abrupt change were also available. One was metamorphosis, the sudden and repeatable change from bear to man to bear, from trickster to benefactor to trickster – changes emerging from the double possibilities in life, the ever-present destabilizing potentiality for twinning[70] (a potentiality that makes interesting comparison with the sixteenth-century fascination with Ovidian metamorphosis). A second model was the sudden fall to a totally different world. The first fall was at creation, when the pregnant woman Aataentsic plunged from the sky through the hole under the roots of a great tree (according to one version recounted to the Jesuit Brébeuf), landed on the back of a great turtle in the waters of this world, and after dry land had been created, gave birth to the deity Yoscaha and his twin brother. Falls through holes, especially holes under trees, are the birth canals to experiences in alternative worlds in many an Indian narrative.[71] A seventeenth-century Huron woman, describing Marie de l'Incarnation's life, might say that she tried to fulfill the promptings of a dream, as a person must always do, but what she thought would only be a boat trip turned out to be a fall down a hole. What that alternative world would become remained to be seen.

I hope that one of the Amerindian women in Marie's convent yard told her a seventeenth-century version of the Seneca tale of the origin of stories. We know it from the version told by the Seneca Henry Jacob to Jeremiah Curtin in 1883, where a hunting boy is its protagonist;[72] perhaps a woman's version 230 years before would have used a wooding girl instead. Set in the forest, the tale called to my mind Marguerite de Navarre's rather different storytelling field in the Pyrenees – a conjoining of alternative worlds. An Orphan Boy was sent each day into the woods by his adoptive mother to hunt for birds. One day he came upon a flat round stone in the midst of a clearing. When he sat upon it he heard a voice asking, "Shall I tell you stories?" "What does it mean – to tell stories?" the boy asked. "It is telling what happened a long time ago. If you will give me your birds, I'll tell you stories."

So each day the Orphan sat on the stone, heard stories, and left birds, bringing home to his mother only what he could catch on the way back. His mother sent other boys from the long-house and even men to follow him to find out why his catch had diminished, but they too were captivated by the stories and would say "haa, haa" with approval now and again. Finally, the stone told the Orphan Boy that he should clear a larger space and bring everyone in the village to it, each of them with something to eat. The boy told the chief, and for two days at sunrise all the men and women of the village came, put food on the stone, and listened to stories till the sun was almost down. At the end of the second day the stone said,

I have finished! You must keep these stories as long as the world lasts. Tell them to your children and your grandchildren. One person will remember them better than another. When you go to a man or a woman to ask for one of these stories, bring a gift of game or fish or whatever you have. I know all that happened in the world before this; I have told it to you. When you visit one another, you must tell these things. You must remember them always. I have finished.

15

ANDEAN WITCHES AND VIRGINS

Seventeenth-century nativism and subversive gender ideologies

Irene Silverblatt

The Spanish conquest of the Incas transformed the terrain of living, the shape of possibilities, of those who lived in the Peruvian Andes. And while the Spanish made the Inca empire into a colony through institutions of faith, power, and economy, they did so in gendered fashion. For gender ideologies – the broadly construed meanings implicated in the making of women and men – were intrinsic to the process of colony-building. Structures of colonial order were profoundly marked by gender, as were the thrusts of Andean resistance to them.

This essay will look at one aspect of the gendered dynamic of forces contouring colonial Andean life in the seventeenth century.[1] Specifically, I want to explore how Andean women, some called "witches," others "virgins," struggled to carve out a space of challenge to Spanish attempts to destroy their very senses of self and ways of being. Andean "virgins" and "witches" were key participants in nativist designs to keep colonial powers at bay – to limit Spanish distortions of what Andeans believed to be the basic moral grounding of social experience. Andeans met seventeenth-century campaigns to destroy their culture with a concerted effort to revitalize it; this essay explores the play of gender ideologies – and the play of women – at the heart of colonial Andean renewal.[2]

INDIAS IN THE SPANISH COLONY

Gender saturated the ordering of social experience in the Andean world under Inca rule: productive relations, the cosmos and its deities, strands of political domination were all highly marked by gendered structures and imageries. No single gender ideology characterized these representations; rather, multiple ideologies were contested, interpreted, and reinterpreted by the Inca empire's men and women, peasant and elite. Two gender models seem to stand out, however, for their impact on

Andean life-ways: gender parallelism and the conquest hierarchy. Both, albeit in different ways, were undermined and appealed to in the centuries' long process of Spanish colony-making and Andeans' challenges to it.

Norms of gender parallelism – the conceptualization of social relations in terms of parallel, gender-marked lines of descent (i.e., women stand as descendants in a line of women, and men in a line of men)[3] – molded Andean kin ties, land rights, and religious practice. Peasant women and men claimed use of particular fields through traditions of gender parallelism – as did women and men of Cusco's nobility. Similarly, women's religious organizations, responsible for the worship of female deities, were deeply entrenched features of *ayllu* (community/non-Inca polity) life, while analogous religious organizations, wedded to imperial politics, ordered relations of authority between Cusco and the provinces.[4]

In contrast, gender ideologies stipulating male dominance over women – expressed in metaphors of male conquest (marriage) of "native" women – also shaped social relations in the Incan Andes. The "conquest hierarchy," as Zuidema named it, was a social prism, a model of internal ranks between descent groups that constituted an *ayllu* or polity.[5] Although this frame used male and female images – in a discursive context of conquest and marriage – to mark social standing, it did not prescribe the direct manipulation of women by men.[6]

The association of men with conquest, however, did have repercussions for women and men as the Inca empire expanded. One striking example: the rights of Inca noblemen to survey and distribute women from vanquished polities became a basic structure of Inca empire-building. Transformed gender ideologies, embodied in novel state institutions, promoted a new category of "woman": the chosen women, or *aclla* – the wives of the Sun, the god of the conquering empire, or of his male descendent, the Inca. *Aclla*, alienated from conquered natal communities as the Sun's wives, became permanent retainers of the Inca state. Strikingly, of all the empire's subjects, only the *aclla* found their sexuality proscribed by norms of celibacy. They constituted a new class of women – one defined by its chastity – and irrevocably linked the sexual purity – virginity – of women with holiness and state power.[7]

Women experienced burdens as subjects of an Inca elite, but their experience as peasants under the Spanish state was profoundly different. One devastating change was effected as Spanish law joined with colonial tribute structures to undermine native social relations built around parallel descent. A case in point: the dramatic decline in population following the Spanish conquest made traditional norms of *ayllu* endogamy impossible to realize; native women married to men from foreign *ayllus* ended up bearing a double economic burden as they were tributed by their natal communities as well as by their husbands'.

Viceroy Toledo, confronted by the harmful consequences of this doubled tax on women, mandated that couples reside in the groom's *ayllu* and their children belong to his kin group.[8] Spanish policy, strengthening and encouraging patrilineal along with patrilocal ties, undermined parallel structures of descent and inheritance. It did not always succeed; nevertheless, colonial institutions pressured Andean gender relations, sapping parallel descent along with its implied potentialities for Andean women.

Spanish law considered women to be legal minors; and this evaluation of women's maturity permeated its caste-divided, two-tiered legal structure. Full privileges to enter contracts independently and enjoy title to property – privileges reserved for descendants of the Inca or provincial nobility – were limited to men; commercial activities of elite Indian women were constrained by tutelage laws. Their peasant sisters, on the same hand, found that colonial usufruct was granted to male household heads. Colonial tenure policy handicapped women, and the historical record shows that women, more than men, were apt to suffer the expropriation of their lands. Moreover, colonial administrators, landowners, magistrates, and clergy needed female labor for domestic service or for the production of goods, like cloth; and many succeeded in forcing native women – married, single, or widowed – to work under highly exploitative conditions.[9] In addition, chroniclers strongly suggest that native women bore the brunt of Spanish sexual abuse.[10]

In general, Andean women found themselves increasingly vulnerable in the colonial world as colonial pressures eroded the norms and institutions governing gender relations before conquest. Tragically, these forces could destroy the *ayni* (reciprocity) that traditionally marked the interaction of women and men in much of daily life. At their extreme they could promote a grotesque mockery of Western norms in which men "owned" their female relatives: some men, desperate to avoid forced service in the mines, even pawned female relatives to Spaniards.[11]

Colonial policies directed toward guaranteeing the orderly government of Indian communities also constrained women's direct, formal participation in *ayllu* political life. The colonial regime, in principal, sanctioned traditional customs regarding the selection of local chiefs; in practice colonial administrators did not recognize pre-Columbian structures of parallel hierarchies of authority. Although Andeans were quick to modify Spanish policies according to their own understandings of proper local government, the weight of Spanish gendered practices – inscribed in law, tradition, and expectations – left little room for the particularities of Andean gender norms affording women a public presence.[12] Certain elements of Spanish gender ideologies could not be broached: they included deeply entrenched convictions that by natural endowment men, and not women, were suited for public responsibilities.

Spanish gender ideologies were complex, harboring conflicting, yet integrally linked conceptions of and expectations about what women were supposed to be. Dominant notions moved around an axis in which women's sexuality played a crucial part: on the one hand, women, as a sex, were condemned for their alleged vulnerability to satanic advances; on the other hand, women, as the embodiment of family honor, found their lives, and their sexuality in particular, subjected to the vigilance of male kinsmen. European norms created female icons of the witch, the mortal enemy of man and God's kingdom, along with the virgin, idealized in the sacred figure of the Madonna, intercessor to God and Jesus. Both stereotypical ideals were carried to the Andes; both emerged, transformed, in seventeenth-century Andean communities.

Andean "witches" and "virgins" bore the gendered experience of Spanish colonization. Colonial Andean women found themselves multiply trapped. They could be hounded by colonial officials of the Church and State (including native office-holders) who wanted their labor, lands, or sex. Further, colonial politics denied women direct access to the official channels of authority regulating community life. No wonder some native women, firm in the belief that they were being persecuted, thought the world was "inside-out."[13] But if colonial structures of rule were gendered, so were the forms that resistance to them would take: and thus some Andean women, transformed into colonial witches and colonial virgins, tried to turn Spanish institutions and practices upside-down.

THE COLONIAL ANDEAN WITCH

From the fifteenth to the seventeenth centuries, European society was shaken by hunts for *alleged* witches, women consorts of the devil, whose satanic alliances were believed to threaten not only Christianity but the very fabric of civil and political life.[14] Spanish colonials – priests and bureaucrats – confronted by Andeans' very different customs and beliefs smelled devil worship: for it was the devil who had seduced *indios* into idolatrous ways; further, native religion was just one more weapon in the devil's arsenal to overthrow God's religion and the political order it supported.[15] By colonial rationale there was not a great leap from the discovery of idolatry to the discovery of witchcraft. Spanish expectations, contoured by the social stereotype of the European witch, framed colonial evaluations of pre-Columbian religion. And as we might expect, those witches responsible for and capable of performing the blackest of black magic were judged to be women, and following stereotype, particularly women who were old and poor.[16]

I would argue that a witchcraft-drenched portrait of indigenous religion was predominantly a figment of the Spanish imagination. It would have required that a notion kin to that of Europe's Satan – an entity embodying the forces of evil – figured prominently in Andean beliefs, and, moreover, that this representation of evil functioned on earth by making pacts with women perceived to be sexually lascivious, morally deficient, and thus easily swayed by diabolic promises.

But Andean cosmology did not harbor representations comparable to Western devils. Rather, Andean philosophy, conjuring the universe dialectically, saw opposing forces as reciprocal, complementary, and necessary for the reproduction of society and the universe as a whole. Native cultural ideals cherished maintaining a "balance" between dualist forces in the social, natural, and supernatural worlds; explanations of sickness, tied to this cosmovision, were rooted in the breakdown of "balance" between social groups, between society and nature, and between society and supernatural forces. Within this frame there was no conceptualization of women as inherently weak, morally shallow, dangerous beings who stood as the potential mortal enemies of man, civilization, and God. Andean understandings, to the contrary, placed them in a complementary relation to men, and acknowledged that their reciprocal interaction spurred the maintenance and reproduction of social existence.[17]

Spanish clergyman and bureaucrats, convinced of the substantiality of the devil and his consort the witch, believed Andean religious practice to be devil-inspired, and created witches where none existed before; yet, by the seventeenth century, some indigenous women did claim to be witches, engaged in satanic pacts and entertaining sexual liaisons with the devil. How can we make sense of these self-proclaimed Andean witches and their confessions?[18]

Records of native witches and their supposed powers are preserved in testimony accrued during the Church's infamous campaigns to "extirpate idolatry" in Peru.[19] These new battles against indigenous idol/devil worship, carefully described by Pierre Duviols[20] in his history of the extirpation campaigns, were waged by the Church with the backing of the Crown. Organized by Jesuits, the campaigns harbored conjoined political and religious motives. Colonial clerics and administrators shared the belief that the continued practice by *indios* of their traditional religion constituted a formidable weapon threatening both Christendom and colonial society as a whole: as devil worship, "idolatry" was one more facade used by Satan – the arch-enemy of Civilization – to further his designs.[21] Moreover, European preconceptions regarding women's innate susceptibility to diabolic influence seemed to influence how the idolatry campaigns were carried out: as in Europe, women, particularly, were hounded.[22]

Testimonies recorded in trials against women (and men) accused of idolatry reveal that some women confessed to knowing the "devil"; however, as we will see, the Andean devils, like the Andean witches, were not of the same piece as their European counterparts. The use of torture to force confessions was carried to the New World by colonial neo-Inquisitors, and while no doubt the content of many testimonies was the product of terrible, excruciating duress, factors which distinguished these witch-hunts from their European predecessors help account for significant differences in the nature of Andean confessions. Foremost, the social stereotype of the witch – so powerful and pervasive in the Old World that it shaped the charges levied by Inquisitors as well as the confessions wrung out of the accused – had only to some minimal degree permeated Andean thinking.

What might a confession mean, then, to a self-proclaimed Andean witch? To get a grasp on this question we have to recall both the dramatically transformed possibilities of living experienced by Andean women as a result of Spanish colonization along with the implosion of ideologies, generated by colonial rule, that provided a scaffolding of meanings through which Andeans attempted to make sense of their changing worlds. We have to look into the interplay between transforming, conflict-ridden, and gendered relations of political economy and the novel, hybridized, fused, and gendered symbols through which native women and men grasped and grappled with their contradictory colonial worlds. In the process we should glimpse how the changes institutionalized in the formation of a colonial society created arenas in which women began to exercise new "powers" – precisely because of their supposed diabolic pacts.

Juana Icha was brought to trial by priest-extirpators, accused of having made explicit pacts with the devil.[23] One of the chief witnesses against her, Felipe Curichagua – an "yndio" who lived in the same village as she – brought a range of charges. Curichagua claimed that Juana Icha acquired vast knowledge and powers from her devil, Apo Parato: she was a *curandera*, whose knowledge of healing included a profound understanding of herbal remedies; she also made offerings to various native deities, "she worships the earth and the stars and cries to the water," further proof, Curichagua argued, of Icha's diabolic pacts.

These accusations describe traditional Andean religious practice, which, of course, the Inquisitors would take to be heresy. However, Felipe Curichagua explicitly swore that Icha's powers were more pernicious, for they were derived from an alliance with the devil: "she sees Hell and forgives no one."[24] And the devil not only taught her how to heal; he instructed her in the black arts of harm. Juana Icha could foresee illness and misfortune; she could instill disease and even cause death.

264

Juana Icha was tortured and her Inquisitors pressured her to admit sexual liaisons with the devil. Ultimately, she did confess to a pact with the devil; but the devil of her dreams, his powers, and the powers with which he endowed his supposed acolyte did not fit the expectations of her accusers. Who was, then, Juana Icha's "devil"?

Her "devil," Apo Parato, appeared "in the form of an Indian man." However, while he would come to Juana Icha, he did not, contrary to his European counterpart and Spanish expectations, come with sexual demands. Rather, Apo Parato was hungry, and would arrive at night to be fed.[25]

Juana confessed to giving him food. She would arrange "*chicha* [maize beer], *coca*, black and white ground maize"[26] for him – offerings that Andeans traditionally gave to their gods. The diabolic pact uncovered by Spanish Inquisitors would seem to be infused by long-standing ritual practice governing native worship. But why would Apo Parato plague Juana Icha with demands for food? Native Peruvians expressed their devotion, their relations with the divine world, through the metaphor of "feeding." And ever since the Spanish conquest introduced Christian gods to the Andes, native gods were "hungry": the norms guiding ties between Andeans and their deities had not been fulfilled. Natives, neglecting traditional obligations to the sacred world, had starved their gods. And by not "feeding" them, Andeans had broken the balance of reciprocal duties and responsibilities binding humans and their divine representatives. Andean gods then, by the customary reckoning of Andean understandings, were no longer obliged to provide their human progeny with sustaining crops and herds. "Divine hunger" could explain the tremendous changes in living wrought by Spanish colonization.

But *indios* were not the only ones who broke covenants; native gods, even native "devils," found they could not appropriately return the gifts of mortals. Juana Icha also confessed to her Inquisitors that, at times, even when she "fed" Apo Parato, he did not have the powers to divinely reciprocate her offerings. For he was "stingy," Juana claimed. Hadn't she begged him for food, when desperately ill; and hadn't he replied that he didn't have the means to give her anything?[27]

Apo Parato does not fit the European stereotype imaged by priests/witch-hunters and confessed to by European witches. For the European devil was powerful, tantalizing women with his ability to provide them with food and clothing; instilling fear in the hearts of churchmen and noblemen with his ever-present threats to destroy God's kingdom. The Andean devil, on the contrary, was poor, stingy, without the means to provide for his acolytes. And even more telling, while Satan was willing to engage God in all-out battle, Apo Parato was scared, particularly of Spaniards and clerics.[28] Apo Parato, like his imaginers, sensed his limits.

But there were times when this Andean devil did seem to be effective; and Juana Icha testified to his powers and to their conjoined efforts. Against whom did they direct those acts that Spaniards and highly placed Indians called malevolent?

Apo Parato intervened in and terminated an affair that Icha's daughter was carrying out with a Spaniard; it appears that he did not approve of Indians mixing with their enemies. Another woman, hunted down by a lackey of the village priest, begged Juana Icha to call her devil for help; Apo Parato, according to Juana Icha's interior visions, promised that "this Spaniard would not pursue her."[29] Moreover, he successfully "bewitched" another Indian servant of the colonial regime: a native tribute-collector found himself unable to carry out his search for an Indian who had defaulted on tribute payments.[30] Indeed, Juana Icha, along with Apo Parato, seemed particularly incensed by these indigenous men who, taking advantage of their position in the colonial political apparatus, ended up abusing the Andeans they were supposed to represent.[31] The Andean devil, as described and confessed to by Juana Icha, might not have measured up to the expectations of colonial Inquisitors. Nevertheless, as an advocate – albeit constrained – of natives who felt unjustly put upon by the colonial regime, Apo Parato represented a symbolic force – a moral force – supporting Indian challenges to it.

Whether Juana Icha's abilities sprang from the devil or not, she could, in her limited way, challenge the official political establishment. Her success was tied to the "diabolic" powers attributed to her by both supporters and accusers. As a "witch" in native colonial society, Juana Icha became an advocate for village morality; and the standards she represented harkened to pre-Columbian understandings of the obligations of those in power to their community. Her fury was directed against Indian tax-collectors, assistants to village priests, mayors, and headmen who transgressed what she, and others, defended as customary limits of authority. We must remember that Juana Icha championed sentiments shared by her *ayllu*-mates. Let us return to Felipe Curichagua's testimony, lamenting her broad support:

> . . . and Don Francisco Poma Condor, mayor, apprehended Juana and then let her go . . . and then Don Pedro Yauri, an *Indio Principal* (headman or *curaca*) of this village recaptured her, but she still escaped, and Pedro de Zárate, the priest, ordered her arrest, but to no avail . . . because the Indians of the village support her.[32]

Francisca Cargua Chuqui was also accused of being the devil's consort, but like Juana Icha, her "witchcraft" took an Andean cast, and her powers were those that colonial society – both Spanish and Andean (in different ways) – bestowed on native (women) witches. Extirpators charged this elderly woman with various crimes involving pacts made with the devil: Cargua Chuqui was accused of being an adept healer; she was also accused of sowing chaos, damaging crops, decimating herds, spreading sickness, and killing at least five people.

Like Juana Icha, Francisca Cargua Chuqui was severely tortured, and much of her testimony was clearly obtained under terrible duress. Thus the tribunal heard confessions to a variety of diabolic encounters and diabolic murders. Yet the right to a defense/protector permitted Francisca Cargua Chuqui to testify on her own behalf and invalidate the extorted confessions: she bravely insisted that torture and fear had compeled her to admit what her Inquisitors wanted to hear.[33]

Nevertheless, she, again like Juana Icha, did acknowledge the powers of one "devil." And this "devil" was Cargua Chuqui's accomplice in her most heinous crimes – the murder of a priest and the death of a large landowner. Both the *hacendado* and priest were abusive to local Andeans; and both had treated Francisca Cargua Chuqui unfairly, physically punishing her and forcing her to work on their behalf. Similarly, Francisca Cargua Chuqui's "devil" did not meet European expectations, even as his guise might have deceived them; nor did he remain inalterably true to a pre-Columbian ideal: he simultaneously bore Andean and Spanish souls. Francisca Cargua Chuqui confessed to coplots with a devil, who took the form of a serpent: "a deformed serpent [encountered] by the mountain spring . . . with a beard that seemed like fire." And believing in the devil, she would worship it, "calling on it, in her soul, for aid and witchcraft."[34]

Now this confession would not surprise Spanish extirpators, for a devil-in-snake's clothing was a reasonable and expected guise for Satan to take. But in like and ironic fashion, nor would it surprise Andeans, for a snake-in-a-mountain spring was a reasonable and expected guise for the *amaru* to take. The *amaru*, a critical figure in Andean ways of thinking, could appear as a serpent, shooting out of mountain founts or headwaters. The *amaru* incorporated many and complex meanings in Andean symbology, and the concept of alliance or relation was a principal axis along which these meanings were situated. Frequently *amaru* embodied a force erupting when relations of balance or equilibrium were not attained within society, between society and nature, or between society and the supernatural world.[35]

Let's look again at the *amaru* whom Francisca Carhua Chuqui worshipped, at the "devil" whom she confessed to "feeding" and with whom she admitted to making pacts: the "deformed serpent . . . with a beard that seemed like fire." Perhaps Francisca Carhua Chuqui believed she could intercede and shape the direction of her life and that of her fellow villagers by adoring a devilish *amaru*. Sporting a blazing beard, the symbol of European manhood, this *amaru* embodied some of the dia-

bolic powers of her Spanish oppressors. But he also embodied the
powers of Andean serpents-in-springs: the eruptive energies unleashed
by severe social imbalance. "*Amaru*" charged revolt, even revolution, in
the Andes. Tupac Amaru, the last Inca King, led the armed resistance to
Spanish colonizing drives until his capture and execution, in 1572, forty
years after the European invasion. Two hundred years later, Tupac
Amaru was the name taken by the champion of the native rebellion
against colonial rule that rocked the Andes for over two years. So it
should not surprise us that Francisca Cargua Chuqui, persecuted by
colonial authorities, priests, and landowners, turned to the "devil"
amaru. By means of "witchcraft," an Andean "witchcraft," she was trying
to unleash those *amaru*-forces that would destroy the grotesquely distorted, unbalanced relations of living under colonial rule.

Andean "witches" were not the solitary old hags of European fame;
rather, they were actively sought by their fellows, turned to for advice and
comfort. Moreover, they were always present during the underground
religious gatherings that were condemned and persecuted by colonial
Church and State and that were devoted to the worship of Andean
divinities and to the dogged enactment of Andean ritual. Andean
"witches" were joined in their celebration of native tradition by another
gendered and hybrid category of colonial life, Andean "virgins."

ANDEAN VIRGINS

In the battle waged by the Church against Andean idolatry, condemned witches were not the only women persecuted by ecclesiastic
authorities. Women were also accused of being "priestesses" who
directed native religious practices, including community-wide celeb-
rations, outlawed by the colonial establishment. At the time of the
Spanish conquest women, as we have seen, commanded their own
religious organizations. Nevertheless, they were not, at least according
to most chronicle accounts, the principal officiants of their *ayllus'* inte-
grative religious cults; these positions tended to be reserved for men.[36]
By the seventeenth century, however, these gendered specifications
for Andean clergy no longer held. Women were "priestesses" to their
ayllus' gods.

Contradictions of Inca society and *ayllus*, expressed through conflicting gender ideologies, spawned women's exclusion from certain activities in Andean religious life; contradictions of colonial society, again
expressed in gender ideologies, offered novel possibilities for Andean
women. As colonial priestesses to their *ayllus'* gods, Andean women
became outlaws of the establishment and champions of Indian tradition.
Although men, too, were active leaders in Andean nativism, and all
priestesses were not chaste, now we find colonial "virgins" – indigenous

women who maintained celibacy – to be key participants in this Andean cultural revival.

The proceedings against idolatry abound with references to "virgins" – only women, no men among them – who devoted their lives to the worship of *ayllu* gods and goddesses. Some, through "marriage," became the sacred spokeswomen for gods in ways that harken to both the virgins of Inca fame and the virgin nuns introduced by the Spanish. In any case, these celibate women – mostly virgins but also widows who refused to remarry – were participating in an emerging, and apparently expanding, underground association. Like priestesses, they represented the growing and increasingly important role played by women in movements celebrating native culture and opposing anything Spanish.

Charges of idolatry and dogmatism were levied against Asto Mallao. Like other Andeans, she was accused of heretical practices, of worshipping *huacas* (divinities, shrines) along with her *ayllu*'s sacred ancestors. But unlike others, she was a *soltera* (unmarried, celibate woman) and had never been baptized. Thus, nearly eight decades after the Spanish invasion, Asto Mallao still carried only the traditional names used by her indigenous ancestors and had successfully avoided contamination by the Church. While most of her *ayllu* spent time in the colonial village center – the "*reduccion*," or forced settlement imposed by the Spanish, Asto Mallao lived in the *puna*, or high tableland, home to her *ayllu*'s divinities and home of her pre-Columbian progenitors.[37]

The campaigns against idolatry disclosed similar allegations throughout the northern and central highlands. Magdalena Antonia, for example, dedicated her life to the goddess Coya Guarmi. Witnesses affirmed that she remained a virgin throughout her life, and that her chastity was appropriate to the sacredness of her calling.[38] She came from a family of women devoted to Coya Guarmi; her aunt, one of Puquiian's most famed advocates of Andean religion, also dedicated herself to the goddess. Living in the high tablelands that housed Puquiian's traditional center of worship, only she could carry Coya Guarmi in pilgrimage from the *puna* to Puquiian's colonial *reducción*.

Another "pagan" virgin priestess, Francisca Guacaquillay, was close kin to the man who held political power in Otuco, her uncle and *curaca*, Don Alonso Ricari. Testimony again reflects the common pattern of colonial Andean purity with its mixing of female chastity and prohibitions against contamination by Church rites and doctrine.[39]

Guacaquillay's life history is emblematic of how colonial *ayllus*, under terrible pressure throughout the years of the extirpation campaigns, struggled to maintain their cultural integrity within the harsh constraints set by colonial rule. Francisca Guacaquillay began her training in nativist lore as a young girl when she was taken away from Otuco's *reducción* to live a celibate life in the *puna*. Guided by her mother, an infamous (by

269

Spanish reckoning) "idolator-confessor, who ordered her *ayllu* not to worship God,"[40] Guacaquillay learned early to challenge Spanish orthodoxy. As a religious outlaw, living in the tablelands far from the village centers of colonial influence, she was kept insulated from the polluting institutions and habits of Spain. And it was only with the support and connivance of a substantial body of *ayllu*-mates that she could have reached thirty-five without ever having been baptized, without ever having entered a church, without ever having had direct contact with Spanish society.

In the first decades of the seventeenth century, Francisca Guacaquillay was the only girl from her *ayllu* to be dedicated as a "virgin" to her gods. By 1656 four more were initiated into nativist service. All under ten years of age, they joined their mentor in the *puna* for training in Andean lore and ritual practice. María Francisca, María Micaela, María Cargua, and Francisca María – from the four *ayllus* which composed the village of Otuco – were being instructed in "the rights and ceremonies that the consecrated Indian [Francisca Guacaquillay] commands."[41] With virgin women as key participants, Andean nativism was taking deeper root.

Natives participating in the revival movements of the seventeenth century joined the sexual purity of virgin women with efforts to preserve the "purity" of what was conceived to be traditional Andean life. All consort with the world of the conquerors was condemned: "virgins" were not baptized, did not go to mass or catechism, never went to church. Coloring these prohibitions was the passion to live as "Andean" a life as possible, away from the contaminating influence of Spanish religion, Spanish government, Spanish men.

Colonial gender ideologies, highlighting "purities," rendered virgin women especially fit for ministering to native gods. Remember, Inca custom had also celebrated the chastity of *aclla*, who as wives of the Inca/Sun, were instrumental in construing imperial political order. So, perhaps Inca tradition, which melded political hierarchy with metaphors of virgin brides, bestowed an aura of power and appropriateness on the virgins of colonialism. Perhaps Christian ideology, with its flowering Marianist cults of the Renaissance, influenced Andean norms that so often named its virgins María.[42] In any case, sexual prohibitions had their practical consequences (intended or not). They protected these outlaw ministers from the vigilant eyes of colonial authorities (*solteras* did not constitute a significant category for colonial censuses); it shielded them from the lusts of Spanish men. Secluded in their *ayllu*'s remote tablelands, colonial virgins effectively disappeared from the cognizance of the Spanish world. What better protection for priestesses of an underground nativist revival?

The gendered institutions and ideologies of Spanish colonialism systematically eroded the life possibilities of most Andean women: before the Iberian conquest Andean women independently controled rights to their society's means of subsistence, held positions of authority in the *ayllu* and empire, and led their own religious organizations in honor of the Andes' goddesses. Colonial government privileged men as household heads, holders of civic offices, and officiants in the new state religion. In colonial irony, those same ravaging institutions and expectations provided Andeans – and Andean women in particular – with instruments to challenge culturally those structures that were so prejudicial to them. Although the seventeenth century was not an epoch of direct political assault on colonial rule, it was a time when a vigorous challenge to colonial intent was waged through vibrant and oppositional nativist movements. Just as they augmented the "aura" of virgin women in Peru, Spanish gender ideologies created witches where none had existed before. Church-extirpators, disparaging "the female sex," denounced these women as outlaws. They also helped transform them in the paradox of colonial cauldrons: in native eyes "witches" and "virgins" – the devil-inspired underminers of colonial disorder and the "pure," uncontaminated ministers of "idolatry" – became the legitimate champions of a contentious Andean culture.

16

INVADED WOMEN

Gender, race, and class in the formation of colonial society

Verena Stolcke

(Translated by Walden Browne)

> I am a man,
> And although of low birth,
> I am of pure blood,
> Never stained by Jewish or Moorish woman
>   (Lope de Vega (1562–1635), *Peribañez*[1])

Our memory is like a broken mirror. It does not reflect the world as it was, but our fragmented, partial, even personal reconstruction of it.[2] Something similar occurs with history. History is, in a way, a matter of perspective, and perspectives, in turn, are matters of values and politics. But precisely because of the fractures in the mirror of history we are also able to rearrange its fragments, seeking for those that were lost, and thus to recover the previously omitted or excluded from received accounts of historical events. Until recently, images of the conquest of America, including ones that saw themselves as critical, have systematically omitted the manner in which indigenous women and, shortly after, black women lived through the assault it made on their personal and cultural integrity. These images have also omitted the implications of the experience of women for colonial societies in the process of formation.

Certain chronicles – such as Guaman Poma de Ayala's *Nueva crónica y buen gobierno* – did denounce some of the most horrifying facts, including the humiliations indigenous women were submitted to. As in all wars, these women formed part of the booty coveted by the conquerors. The assault on indigenous women was not simply a matter of pleasure forced from the women of the vanquished; it was a definitive way of sealing the Spaniards' victory through the appropriation of that which, in the conquerors' reasoning, constituted the most valuable possession of the defeated. Nevertheless, historians have read these chronicles in a highly selective way. The conquest of America has therefore been presented as an affair between men, as an aggression

272

and dispossession realized by a few men (the Spaniards) against other men (the Indians).

The historiography of the conquest of course contains some images of its victims, but they are stereotypes that often mask what in reality occurred. One striking example is the Inca Garcilaso – the illegitimate son of an Inca princess and a *corregidor* in Peru. Even though his Spanish father married a Spanish woman who was presumably of "pure blood" instead of marrying his Inca mother, the father's acknowledgment of his son – a practice said to have been common among the colonizers – is in most historical accounts idealized or exalted. This interpretation, how- ever, disguises the fact that Garcilaso never could rid himself of the "stain" of his illegitimate and *mestizo* origin in order to accede to his father's nobiliary honors. Doña Marina, Cortés's interpreter and mis- tress, popularly known as La Malinche or La Chingada, is another emblematic case. The term "Chingada," ubiquitous in the Mexican lexicon, reflects the enormous ambivalence that surrounds the con- structed image of La Malinche. While recognized and represented as the victim of a rape, she is characterized as a consenting and useful tool for Cortés in the service of the conquest. Octavio Paz could thus describe her in *The Labyrinth of Solitude* as the quintessence of indigenous collaboratio- nism. Even today in Mexico the term "malinchismo" is used to speak of those who "sell out" their country. This interpretation of Doña Marina exempts the conqueror from all responsibility. The blame for the victim's misfortune is placed squarely on her own shoulders. Even though Cortés (already married to a Spaniard, as was Garcilaso's father) recognized the son of La Malinche as his own, he compelled her to marry one of his soldiers in exchange.

The attempt to reconstruct the relations that prevailed between women and men in pre-Colombian times, and hence to gauge the upheavals provoked by the conquest, is still riddled by blind spots. This is due in part to the cultural diversity of the subjugated peoples and the difficulty of interpreting the available sources or determining the mean- ings of the material realities described; but it is also not unrelated to the prejudices of those engaged in the task. It is, however, clear that the conquest not only brought to the indigenous population devastating diseases, a forced conversion to Christianity, new crops, stockbreeding, mining with its regime of forced labor, and the imposition of the Spanish language: it was also accompanied everywhere by violence against and the sexual abuse of indigenous women.

Through a critical rereading of the chronicles, Irene Silverblatt has proposed a correction of the "blind," distorted, or apologetic view of the experience of indigenous women in the case of Peru, showing how the violence of the conquest dramatically upset the relations between women and men that had prevailed under the Inca empire.[3] Women belonging to the Inca nobility were able to endure this experience in a less painful way, but for the majority of peasant women the conquest meant the loss of the material, political, and ritual prerogatives they had hitherto enjoyed. The conquest meant exploitation both of their labor and of their sexuality, not just by invading soldiers but by priests who crucified them in bed under the pretext of saving their souls. There were in fact many cases of such sexual "solicitation" concerning priests, though it was codified as a crime by the Inquisition, including the case narrated by Marcel Bataillon of a Jesuit said to have "solicited" more than one hundred women.[4]

In the early stages of colonization, noble Inca lineages were put on the same social level as the Spanish hidalgos. Nevertheless, over the course of time noble Inca women, including those women of rank whom the conquerors deigned to marry, lost their ancestral autonomy.[5] Inga Clendinnen has described the vicissitudes of the Maya women of Yucatán, the relocation of the villages by the missionaries in order to eradicate ancestral rituals and beliefs, the subjugation of women into forced labor for tribute and their sexual and other forms of exploitation in the homes of the conquerors.[6] There was always resistance on the part of these invaded women.[7] But in spite of this resistance, the Spanish invasion seems to have converted what had often been a complementary relationship between women and men into a bond of subjugation that meant – for indigenous women trapped between the sword and the cross – their subsequent material, cultural, spiritual, and sexual oppression.[8]

Instead of adding further detail to this tableau of sexual violence, I wish to focus attention on a more far-reaching, ideological dimension of the conquest. I hope to analyze ways in which social and racial conceptualizations brought over from the metropolis were disseminated through colonial elites in the society in formation, indicate how in the process these conceptualizations were reformulated, adapted to local circumstances with the end of legitimizing and perpetuating the new hierarchical social order, and finally how these values affected women in particular.

Until now scant attention has been paid to the dialectical interplay between the metropolitan culture transported to the colonies by the conquerors and the ideological organizing principles implanted in colonial society as it was forged in the centuries following the invasion. It is not my concern to analyze European fantasies about the "savage man"; I am concerned rather with investigating the influence of those ideological categories that structured Spanish society at the time. Some have sought to justify the conquest by alleging its civilizing mission. Others, more critically, have denounced the conquest as a political and economic project of colonization and spoilation. In any case, the colonial project involved, at enormous human cost, the imposition of the political prin-

ciples and spiritual and social values of the metropolis upon the autoch-
thonous population. Just *how* these cultural values were themselves
transformed in the process of colonization has, however, not yet been
sufficiently investigated.

An almost immediate consequence of the conquest was miscegenation
(*mestizaje*). Yet the fact that the sexual rapacity of the conquerors and the
concubinage of indigenous women produced a growing contingent of
mestizos need not in itself have implied the socio-racial disdain for the
mestizos that was to follow; nor need it have affected the structure of
colonial society. Perceived differences are always constructed historically. The very fact of the conquest, one of whose consequences was the
domination and exploitation of the local population, gave rise to a
profoundly unequal society. But this inequality could have been conceptualized and legitimated in various ways. A meritocratic principle, for
example, could have been adopted according to which a person's status
was determined by his or her achievements. The conquest did not occur,
however, in a historical and ideological vacuum. Quite the contrary: the
Crown, the Church and the conquerors, both secular and religious, with
the myriad of interests that motivated them, possessed (apart from their
greed) a world-view that mediated their project of colonizing and
exploiting the new territories and its peoples. There was an ideological
struggle surrounding both the status and the treatment of the indigenous peoples, over the question of whether they were human (essentially
equal to the conquerors and therefore capable of being converted to
Christianity) or whether on the contrary they were different by nature
and therefore inferior. If the second were the case, the question
remained of what criteria might be used to justify this inferiority.

The cultural and phenotypic diversity of the indigenous peoples
acquired in colonial America a profound social and political meaning
inspired by the contemporary metropolitan conceptualization of social
inequalities and the procedures institutionalized for their perpetuation.
Though metropolitan notions of social classification and segregation
may have been upset by the new socio-political reality, the cultural and
ideological burden transported by the conquerors to the so-called "New
World" played a decisive role in the construction of the political, social,
and economic inequalities of colonial society. I intend therefore to
analyze how the metropolitan doctrine of "limpieza de sangre" (purity of
blood) and the ideas of marriage and legitimacy it inspired acquired new
meanings when transferred to the American colonies – meanings that
had a special significance for women. My intent is to elucidate, in the
case of colonial society, the cryptic remark made by an English doctor in
the mid-nineteenth century, for whom "the uterus is to the Race what
the heart is to the Individual: it is the organ of the circulation to the
species."[9]

Modern racism – the attribution of socio-economic disabilities and inequalities to alleged racial and hence hereditary deficiencies – has frequently been interpreted as a perverse consequence of European colonial expansion. It has also been common to argue that racism as a doctrine dates from the nineteenth century only. These misconceptions are due in part to the fact that not enough attention has been paid to racialized ideological constructs in the metropolis that were put into service to justify the conquest and colonization of America.

The origins and etymological history of the term *raza* (race) are controversial. There are isolated cases of the use of the word *raza* in Spanish, *raça* in Portuguese, and *race* in French from the thirteenth century onward, though the term appears with greater frequency in the sixteenth century. Nevertheless, the connotations of the term seem to diverge depending on the political and geographical context in which it is used. According to some authors, the French term *race* initially referred to the members and ancestry of a family or "house" in the positive sense of "noble stock." *Stirpis nobilitas* (1512) is translated in 1533, for example, as "noblesse de sang." This meaning of *race* is lexigraphically cited as its primary definition until the nineteenth century: "il vient d'une noble race." *Raza* meant the succession of generations (*de raza en raza*) as well as all the members of a given generation. A close connection between "nobility" and "quality" was established by this term and because of its link with the idea of a hereditary community race was endowed with a political and social meaning from the start. It is noteworthy that this etymological origin of *raza* was the one picked up by a German author.[10] Corominas, however, derives the term from another Romance word that was confused in the middle of the fifteenth century with the old Castilian *raza* which meant "a patch of threadbare or defective cloth," or, simply, "defect, guilt." From the sixteenth century on, the term commonly appears in Castilian with a negative meaning in relation to "limpieza de sangre." Although the etymological origin of the Castilian *raza* seems to be multiple, Corominas concludes that

> when the foreign term "raza" in a biological sense or in its meaning of "species" entered Castilian, it was natural for the word to be contaminated by a pejorative connotation, even more so because its application to Moors and Jews lent itself to this pejorative sense on its own

even though this negative sense was not necessarily constant.[11] It is obvious that words are not neutral, but this etymological and political difference regarding the term *raza* is especially pertinent to the argument I wish to develop here. In effect, the criterion of *raza* was initially adopted in the metropolis in order to legitimate discrimination against and persecution of non-Christian communities and, later, of their newly converted Christian descendants on account of an original faith held to be hereditary.

The conquest of America coincided with the end of the so-called Spanish Reconquista and the politically and ideologically motivated expulsion or compulsory conversion of the Jews in 1492. A century later (1609–14), the Moriscos (converted Muslims) were also expelled from Spain. In the middle of the fifteenth century the Council of Toledo adopted the first "limpieza de sangre" statute. In 1480 the Spanish Inquisition was founded, and four years later it decreed in its constitution that those who had been sentenced for crimes against Christianity could not hold public office. Toward the end of the century various religious orders, military academies, universities, municipal councils, and cathedrals proceeded to adopt the "limpieza de sangre" statutes. These statutes were rules adopted by private associations and never formed part of Spanish imperial laws. The Inquisition was the sole court with immediate jurisdiction over purity of blood. Thus the Holy Office, as the ecclesiastical court charged with pursuing crimes against Christianity (principal among them Judaism and Islam), acted as mediator between theorists of exclusion and the people, popularizing the idea that all converts were suspect.[12]

In this manner, Catholicism, as a universalist religion, excluded nonbelievers from social honors, though conversion could initially remedy this deficiency. Through baptism, Jews and Muslims had the opportunity to become like Gentiles. This meant that in the beginning religious faith was not deemed an attribute of origin but one that could be acquired at will provided that the conversion was sincere. What started out as a religious and cultural discrimination around the middle of the sixteenth century, however, was transformed into racialist antagonism as the persecution of the *conversos* and the marginalization of the *moriscos* became more intense. What resulted was "a racist doctrine of original sin of the most repulsive kind."[13] Although there were those who agreed with the initial opinion that a baptized Jew could not be considered different from a baptized Gentile,[14] the *conversos* and *moriscos* as well as their forebears and offspring were quickly made the object of suspicion and discrimination based on the doctrine of "limpieza de sangre." Purity of blood was understood as the quality of having no admixture of the races of Moors, Jews, heretics, or *penitenciados* (those condemned by the Inquisition). According to this doctrine, non-Christian religious faith ceased to be a question of choice and was transformed into an inherent stain – inherited through "blood" and therefore indelible. As Henry Kamen notes: "many felt in the fifteenth century that the honor of the religion and the nation could only be conserved by assuring the purity of the lineage and by avoiding the mixture of Jewish or Moorish blood."[15] Once religion was converted into a natural – and hence, hereditary –

attribute, the zeal of those who sought to safeguard the prevailing religious-cum-racial hierarchy established a direct link between purity of blood, endogamic marriage, and (as proof of the former) legitimate birth. The Inquisition, examining genealogies for false declarations of purity, contributed to reinforcing these notions.

The introduction of the "limpieza de sangre" statutes did not, however, go uncontested. To the consternation of the Spanish nobility, who like the common people had in previous centuries widely intermingled with Moors and Jews, the only authentic "old" Christians turned out to be, in the end, very few. Faced with this classificatory paradox, the disputes amongst the elite and even within the Inquisition concerning this religious and racial doctrine intensified in the seventeenth century.[16] While on the one hand opposition to the ways jurists and theologians applied the doctrine grew, on the other the concept of purity gradually spread to include other "stains." These included "stains" of class such as those attributed to the exercise of servile trades. Thus the racialist doctrine of purity of blood adjusted to a changing socio-economic hierarchy. Finally, in the early nineteenth century the Holy Office was dissolved and, somewhat later, blood proofs for marriage were abolished. The notion that even before God some were more equal than others and that the distinction was racial was initially, therefore, a Spanish product intended for domestic consumption.

In colonial society, developments were different. For demographic and socio-political reasons, the "limpieza de sangre" doctrine was at its apogee by the eighteenth century just as it was losing force in the metropolis. From the beginning, neither

> Moors, Jews, their children, Gypsies, nor anyone not reconciled with the Church, nor child nor grandchild of anyone who had been publicly condemned to wear a sanbenito [a cloak worn by those condemned by the Inquisition]; nor child nor grandchild of anyone condemned or burned at the stake for heretical depravity or apostasy, be the relationship through the paternal or the maternal line[17]

were permitted to make the passage to the Indies, although this does not mean that some did not make their way to America. In a similar vein, the requirement of "limpieza de sangre" was progressively extended to new socially discriminated groups in the colonies. Until the sixteenth century, *mestizos* had not been differentiated from the pure Spaniards, with whom they enjoyed the same legal rights. Thereafter, however, *mestizos* and mulattoes were progressively made ineligible for the priesthood and public office.[18] In 1679, for example, the constitution of a seminary in Mexico prohibited the admission of sons who were not "pure and of pure blood without the race of Moors, Jews, those condemned by the

Holy Office, recent converts, mestizos nor mulattoes."[19]

The dramatic demographic collapse of the indigenous population was the first consequence of the conquest. There then followed a prolonged debate within the Church and the colonial bureaucracy about the quality and status of the survivors. In spite of attempts to establish a genealogical link between the indigenous population and the tribes of Israel, in the end the Crown conceded to the indigenous peoples the condition of "limpieza de sangre" except where they refused to be converted to Christianity.[20] Voluntary European immigration, the forced transport of African slaves, and miscegenation increased during the sixteenth and seventeenth centuries. A social hierarchization founded not upon religious but on explicitly racial criteria crystallized and social distinctions became progressively more scrupulous and subtle. On one side, there were free and enslaved blacks, mulattoes, *zambos* (part African, part indigenous), *zambaigos* (part African, part Asian),[21] "liquid" (pure) Indians, and *mestizos*; and on the other, poor, rich, Spanish-born, and Creole whites. The mulattoes, *mestizos*, and other mixed categories were the object of disdain and inspired profound distrust since they blurred racial boundaries and threatened the emerging racial hierarchy both conceptually and in practice. Toward the end of the seventeenth century royal decrees multiplied in an attempt to resolve doubts over the application of the doctrine of "limpieza de sangre," granting dispensation for entering the priesthood and for occupying public office as well as confirming cases of ineligibility on racial grounds. Finally, toward the beginning of the eighteenth century, for reasons still unclear, the indigenous population began to recover. The *mestizo* and mulatto population increased further – an increase due in general to the ubiquitous concubinage between white men and Indian or black women – as did the number of Spanish-born and Creole whites.[22]

Often the sexual excesses of the Spanish conquerors with Indian and later African women have been attributed to the sexual and emotional deprivations they suffered on account of a shortage of Spanish women in the colonies. Sexual abuses and forced cohabitation were in fact simply further demonstration of the conquerors' arrogance and disdain. In their eyes indigenous and African women were easy prey for sexual gratification. Right from the beginning of the colonization of America, the Crown promulgated a profusion of decrees and laws requiring all colonists with wives in Spain to have them sent over at the earliest opportunity. These laws, in effect until the eighteenth century, responded to a colonization policy that sought to safeguard the stability and security of the colonies through a genetic "whitewash."[23] There were, of course, difficulties in implementing this policy. Nevertheless, already in the sixteenth century there was no sign of a lack of Spanish women.[24] On the contrary, the middle of the century saw the foundation of the first convents destined for the daughters of legitimate Spaniards who had been unsuccessful in their search for suitable marriage partners.[25] Cortés's behavior in this respect was exemplary in its duplicity. At the same time that he was engaged in risky incursions into unknown territories in the company of Doña Marina, he stipulated that

> so as to make clear that the settlers of these regions intend to reside here permanently, I order that anyone who holds Indians or who was married in Castile or elsewhere send for their wives within a year and a half . . . under the penalty of losing their Indians and all else they have acquired or won.[26]

By the eighteenth century, colonial society had become a complex and multicolored human mosaic of inequalities – the result of the interaction between the criteria of class and race to the benefit of some (Creole and Spanish-born whites) and the detriment of everyone else. In the process the doctrine of "limpieza de sangre" was reinforced, lost any religious connotation, and became a purely racial notion. The Crown still insisted in 1734 that

> all distinctions and honors (be they ecclesiastical or secular) accorded to noble Castilians will be accorded to all caciques and their descendants; and to all less illustrious Indians or their descendants, who are "limpios de sangre" [of pure blood] without mixture or of a condemned sect will be accorded all the privileges, distinctions and honors that the "limpios de sangre" of this kingdom presently enjoy, called the general estate, by which royal determinations they are found to be qualified by Your Mercy for any honorific employ.[27]

In formal terms, therefore, the indigenous population still enjoyed certain privileges. In practice, by contrast, the indigenous population, along with the other non-white groups, had for a long time been the victims of socio-racial discrimination. And in most cases, they would lose what privileges they had with the arrival of the republic.

Colonial society was not, however, an impermeable and closed hierarchical order. On the contrary, the contradictions inherent in colonial society constantly threatened its stability and cohesion in various ways. Sporadic sexual unions and concubinage accounted to an important degree for miscegenation.[28] Ironically, however, the *mestizos* and mulattoes, offspring of the mostly extramarital sexual exploitation by white men of women they regarded as racially and hence socially inferior, tended to undermine the hierarchy predicated on alleged racial difference. Under these circumstances, legitimate marriage and legitimate birth acquired special importance for the elites and for those who sought to come close to them. Not only was legitimacy proof of the moral quality of the progenitors; it attested above all to their purity of blood. Illegitimate birth, on the other hand, was the sign of the "infamy, stain and defect" resulting from the mixture of races.[29] Still, economic success could compensate up to a certain point for one's racial condition,[30] and the Crown could grant dispensations of this "stain." This compensation for racially defined status contributed further to the society's openness.

As colonial society became more complex, however, contacts between the different social and racial categories increased and racism intensified. The fluidity of the colonial hierarchical order aggravated the obsession with the purity of blood amongst elites who were by definition white. The only guarantee of social prestige predicated on racial purity was marriage between racial equals. Paradoxically, the Church's marriage policy only served to heighten this tension by opposing a doctrine of spiritual equality to the racially based principle of the secular hierarchy. Until the eighteenth century, the Church held the exclusive prerogative to perform marriages. The doctrinal principle that governed ecclesiastical practice in the matter was freedom of marriage based on the consent of both parties. Canonical doctrine rejected any parental interference or opposition to a marriage for reasons of social or racial inequality. Ritual or blood kinship between the parties constituted the only important canonical impediment. For the Church, sexual virtue – virginity before marriage and chastity thereafter – was the highest good. These values were to prevail over any parental or social whims. Nevertheless, from the sixteenth century onward there were cases where parents tried to impede the marriages of their children for reasons of supposed social inequality.[31] In these disputes, the sexual virtue defended by the Church came up against paternal concern with protecting family purity.

In order to facilitate the Church's work in the colonies, the Crown went so far as to extend prerogatives to the local ecclesiastical courts so that these could pass sentence in the case of marital disputes. Through these courts the Church not only defended individual choice in marriage but also combated the many irregular sexual practices. Sexuality was to be confined to marriage among consenting partners and its only end was procreation. This canonical moral doctrine, which privileged sexual honor over social prestige and rejected any parental interference in marriages on the grounds of economic and social inequality, was nevertheless egalitarian in appearance only. The doctrine did ignore social inequalities but also imposed the strictest control over the sexuality of women in particular. Protection is often a hidden form of control. The other side of the Church's concern with protecting moral virtue was sexual control: the salvation of the soul depended upon the submission of the body. Nonetheless, the Church never succeeded in eradicating the sexual exploitation, outside of marriage, of the women held to be of low social and racial rank in the colonies. Interracial unions were mostly consensual – as they were euphemistically called at the time. In exalting sexual virtue, the Church therefore fomented discrimination between different categories of women in sexual terms: between women sexually abused by white men (generally those held to be of inferior socio-racial status and penalized because they supposedly lived in mortal sin) and virtuous women (white women from respectable families) who found their sexuality subjected to severe control.

Ecclesiastics in the colonies did not strictly comply with these precepts. The clergy were themselves notorious for sexual abuses. But the numerous prenuptial disputes that came before the ecclesiastical courts (either because the Church demanded that a couple marry after a seduction alleged to have occurred under promise of marriage, or because a marriage was celebrated in spite of parental opposition) indicate that the Church did threaten the temporal status interests of the elites. The parents' attempts to impede those marriages they considered socially unequal reveal a profound conflict between the Church's zeal for saving souls through the marriage of those already living in sin or who might end up doing so, regardless of the partners' respective social conditions, and the endeavors of the elites to safeguard their purity of blood as a prerequisite of social purity and privilege.

Toward the end of the eighteenth century the Church encountered increasing difficulties in defending its doctrine of freedom of marriage against prenuptial family interference. The Church's gradual loss of jurisdiction over marriage throughout this century has been attributed to the fact that its ability to defend moral and sexual virtue independent of any status concerns was being progressively undermined by growing parental obsession with social and racial purity.[32] This interpretation seems to be contradicted by the waning social relevance of the doctrine of "limpieza de sangre" in the metropolis at the time. The Church's loss of power over marriage may have been due instead to an increase in marriages deemed unequal by couples who followed the new spirit of individual liberty and equality of the times, which surely also had some impact in Spain and which caused profound dismay among both elite families and civil authorities.

Thus, in the second half of the eighteenth century the Church found itself fighting on two fronts. On the one hand it faced a State which was progressively cutting back the traditional powers of the Church in various political spheres. On the other, ecclesiastical authorities clashed with the Crown over which institution was to exercise jurisdiction over the civil effects of marriages deemed unequal. In 1775 the Crown requested an opinion of its Council of Ministers on measures to avoid unequal marriages given "the sad effects and most serious wrongs caused by marriages that are contracted by persons of very unequal circumstances and conditions." It argued that

> the excessive favor that the ecclesiastical ministers extend to the
> misconceived absolute and unlimited freedom of marriage, with no
> distinction made of persons and often against the just resistance of
> parents and relatives . . . has been the principal source from which
> has resulted for the most part the harmful effects that are suffered
> in Spain because of unequal marriages.[33]

In 1776, Charles III promulgated the Pragmatic Sanction in order to
avoid the abuse of contracting unequal marriages. Through this
Pragmatic Sanction, the State assumed jurisdiction over marriages. Free
choice in marriage was suppressed, and from this moment on marriage
could only be performed with paternal consent under the threat of
being disinherited.

Some historians have interpreted the Pragmatic Sanction as a reaction
on the part of Charles III against the marriage of his younger brother
with a woman of inferior social standing.[34] The Pragmatic Sanction was
promulgated during the Bourbon reforms at a time of political and
social transformation. On first sight it seems paradoxical that it was
during a period of political liberalization and modernization that the
Crown introduced severe controls over marriage. But laws are not
necessarily the direct legal expression of changes in social values; often
there is a dialectical relationship between the two. Hence it is more
plausible to see in the Pragmatic Sanction an attempt at social control at a
time when the new political climate, together with the Church's marriage
policy seemed to constitute a heightened threat to the established hierarchical order. As noted earlier, it was also during this period that the
"limpieza de sangre" doctrine lost validity in Spain. It is not at all atypical
for a reformist state, in no way committed to radical social change, to try
to overcome the contradictions generated by more liberal politics by
legally controlling its potential social consequences. The secularization
of marriage regulations resulted in the suppression of individual freedom to marry. Any marital dispute was thereafter to be decided by a civil
court. Various later royal decrees reinforced parental authority in matters of marriage.

The socio-political causes that gave rise to this marital legislation and
its consequences in Spain have still not been studied. However, in the
Indies the principle of "limpieza de sangre" underwent a late revival. In
1778, the King extended the Pragmatic Sanction to the Indies,

> bearing in mind that the same or more harmful effects are caused
> by this abuse [of unequal marriages] in my Realms and Dominions
> of the Indies on account of their size, diversity of the classes and
> castes of its inhabitants . . . and the serious harm that has been

283

experienced in the absolute and disorderly freedom with which marriage is contracted by impassioned and unfit youths of one and the other sex.[35]

Excluded from it were "mulattoes, negroes, coyotes and individuals of castes and races held and publicly reputed as such" who presumably did not hold honors needing protection. In all other instances parental consent was required. In cases of parental opposition, the civil authorities had the power to grant exemption. Nevertheless, the application of the Pragmatic Sanction in the colonies met with considerable difficulties. People with limited possessions had little to lose by marrying against their families' will. Even though these marriages were not frequent, there were those who wished to marry for love or in order to legitimize a premarital sexual relation in spite of social differences. The crucial problem, however, was posed by interracial marriages. Social and racial prejudices and reasons of state did not always succeed any more than ecclesiastical moral imperatives did in vanquishing passions that were, in any case, not just a characteristic of the young.

I will not analyze in detail the later legal developments concerning marriage nor their application in the colonies. I have done this previously in the case of Cuba.[36] But I wish to draw out some of the peculiarities that resulted from the special characteristics of colonial society and its consequences for women.

Several additional royal decrees concerning unequal marriage followed the one of 1778.[37] These subsequent decrees reveal significant disagreements over marriage policy between the Crown and colonial authorities. On the one hand, the Crown, on alleged demographic grounds, tended to look on marriage with favor even if parental opposition existed, whereas the civil authorities of the colonies tended to deny the required marriage licenses. On the other, there was considerable ambivalence regarding *interracial* marriage, and the colonial authorities expressed a renewed concern for the preservation of purity of blood at a time when this doctrine was rapidly losing ground in the metropolis.

It was not initially clear if only those of legal age and known nobility or those of pure blood in general were required to apply for official authorization to marry with "members of the castes." A decree of 1810 finally resolved the doubt by requiring all nobles *and* persons of known "limpieza de sangre" and of legal age who wanted to marry with negroes, mulattoes, and other castes to obtain a marriage license from the colonial civil authorities. This was not only equivalent to a virtual prohibition of interracial marriage: it also made clear that marriage was considered a matter of State. Both family interests and the stability of the social order were at stake. In the colonies, social stability also meant the preservation of the racial hierarchy. Cuba, one of the last Spanish colonies and in the nineteenth century at its economic peak as a sugar producer using a rapidly growing slave population, became the privileged site for the application of this marriage legislation.

What consequences did this new racist twist in marriage regulations have for women? Whenever social position in a hierarchical society is attributed to so-called racial and hence allegedly inherent, natural, and hereditary qualities, it is essential for an elite to control the reproductive capacity of its women in order to preserve its social pre-eminence. As a nineteenth-century Spanish jurist argued, only women can introduce bastards into the family. In institutionalizing the metaphysical notion of blood as a vehicle for family prestige and as an ideological instrument to guarantee the social hierarchy, the State in alliance with the families who were "limpios de sangre" subjected their women to renewed control of their sexuality while their sons took pleasure from those women regarded as being "without quality" (*sin calidad*) without thereby incurring any responsibility.

The Church had defended the freedom of marriage in order to protect sexual virtue as a moral value in itself. The State converted women's sexual virtue into an instrument to protect the social body. With this transformation, some women (the so-called daughters "of family") became the tools and others (those women deemed "without quality") became the victims of the racial and social hierarchy. In a hierarchical and racist society "the uterus is to the Race," in effect, "what the heart is to the Individual: it is the organ of the circulation to the species." But there is one more qualification to be made. As indicated above, colonial society was not a closed hierarchical order. On the contrary, the legal matrimonial paraphernalia were necessary precisely because there were always women and men ready to defy the politico-racial order and its social and moral values by wanting to marry against the grain.

It was this space for resistance against the social status quo which gave rise to racism in the first place. Modern Western society has been characterized from the start by a universalist and individualistic ethos according to which all humans are born equal and free. This doctrine is, however, permanently contradicted by really existing social inequality. Racism is an ideological sleight of hand which serves to neutralize the conflicts that result from this tension by naturalizing the socio-political order which produces them. In this sense racism is neither an outgrowth of colonial expansion nor is it simply in our own times an anachronistic historical residue. Significant socio-economic changes have, indeed, occurred since the colonial period but the basic economic and ideological logic has not changed. As inequality deepens "at home" as well as globally, the fact that some, the wealthy few, are more equal than others, the poor majority, continues to be justified by resorting to naturalizing doctrines in ways both old and new. The consequences of this for women involve persistent control of their sexuality as a means of controlling access to privilege. The issue is no longer who marries whom. The aging North attributes the growing North–South divide to the southern population "explosion." Simultaneously promoting pro-conception policies (such as *in vitro* fertilization) at home and aggressive population control abroad, it sidesteps the true reasons for inequality. In former times, marriage was the institutional framework within which socially appropriate procreation occurred. Today, procreation and social reproduction are controled even more directly by the State. Prosperous white women in the wealthier North are encouraged to procreate while those in the poor South are coerced into controling their reproductive capacities instead of having the means to decide for themselves. Paraphrasing the nineteenth-century utopian Fourier, the degree of freedom for women is indeed a symptom of the equality and freedom in the world.

17

OTHELLO'S IDENTITY, POSTCOLONIAL THEORY, AND CONTEMPORARY AFRICAN REWRITINGS OF *OTHELLO*

Jyotsna Singh

... it would be something monstrous to conceive this beautiful Venetian girl falling in love with a veritable Negro.

(S. T. Coleridge)

[there is] something extremely revolting in the courtship and wedded caresses of Othello and Desdemona.

(Charles Lamb)[1]

I accept!

And my special geography too; the world map made for my own use, not tinted with the arbitrary colors of scholars, but with the geometry of my spilled blood, I accept both the determination of my biology, not a prisoner to a facial angle, to a type of hair, to a well-flattened nose, to a clearly Melanin coloring, and negritude ... but measured by the compass of suffering and the Negro every day more base, more cowardly, more sterile, less profound, more spilled out of himself, more separated from himself, more wily with himself, less immediate to himself, I accept, I accept it all. ... And there are those who will never get over not being made in the likeness of God but of the devil, those who believe that being a nigger is like being a second-class clerk ... those who say to Europe: "You see I *can* bow and scrape, like you I pay my respects, in short, I am no different from you; pay no attention to my black skin: the sun did it."

(Aimé Césaire)[2]

At the end of Shakespeare's *Othello*, after the Moor murders Desdemona and recognizes his tragic error, he is concerned about how he will be remembered in Venice – and by implication, in history: "When you shall these unlucky deeds relate, / Speak of me as I am. Nothing extenuate, / Nor set down aught in malice."[3] A few moments later, Othello's firm claim to an identity is undermined, when he identifies with the "malignant and turbanned Turk," while "[dying] upon a kiss" as Shakespeare's tragic hero. Does the play's conclusion offer a clear, "moral" resolution to the tragedy, as critics have often suggested?[4] I would suggest that it simply lets the murderous deed "be hid," blocking off any further consideration of the social and psychic divisions which Othello experiences through the play, and which remain with him till the end, when he straddles contradictory roles – as "both infidel and defender of the faith."[5] Thus we cannot really "Speak of [Othello as he is]," for his "otherness" as a black man cannot be contained within the dominant, Western fantasy of a singular, unified identity.

From the opening scenes of the play, we quickly note how Othello experiences his identity in contradictory terms set by the Venetians. His belief in his own integrity ("My parts, my title, and my perfect soul / Shall manifest me rightly)" (I.ii.30–1) is predicated on the fact of his service to Venice: "My services which I have done the Signiory / Shall out-tongue his [Brabantio's] complaints" (I.ii.18–19). However, while the Venetians honor him for his military skills, they do not question the racist European ideology whereby Othello is variously marked as an "old black ram," "a barbary horse," and "a thing . . . to fear, and not to delight." So when the Duke of Venice defends Othello to Brabantio, he simply perpetuates the negative connotations of the word "black:" "Your son-in-law is far more fair than black" (I.iii.285). And it is also questionable whether Desdemona knows Othello any better when she declares that she sees his "visage in his mind" and binds herself to him for "his honors and his valiant parts" (I.iii.249–50). Desdemona's love for Othello comes to life in the stories he tells about his past. And who is Othello in these stories of slavery and adventure? He is simply a "character" in an imaginary landscape which viewers, then and now, recognize as a semi-fictional creation of colonialist travel narratives – from antiquity through the nineteenth century. These are accounts of "being taken by the insolent foe / And sold to slavery . . . [and of] anters vast and deserts idle, / Rough quarries, rocks, and hills whose heads touch / heaven, . . . And of Cannibals that each other eat, / The Anthropophagi, and men whose heads/ Grew beneath their shoulders" (I.iii.136–44). Thus, as some critics have suggested, Othello can only gain access to his own origins "through the ascriptions of European colonial discourses."[6] And these discourses do not so much reveal Othello's origins as they ideologically produce his "identity" as a black man within a configuration of familiar signifiers: slaves, "Cannibals," and "Anthropophagi." When Desdemona responds to these stories with "tears" and "pity" for "the dangers [he] had passed" (I.iii.166), she also, at least initially, loves Othello as a fictional character of these exotic narratives.

Generations of Western critics largely ignored these ideological underpinnings of Othello's identity and focused instead on the Moor's character in terms of psychological realism. However, in doing so, as the literary history of the play testifies, they had difficulty in reconciling Othello's role as a tragic hero with his blackness. Commentaries ranging from Coleridge's assertion that Othello was not intended to be black to A. C. Bradley's acknowledgment of the "aversion of our blood" to the sight of a black Othello ironically, and perhaps unwittingly, echo some of the Venetian voices in Shakespeare's play.[7] Like Brabantio and Iago, critics such as Charles Lamb, for instance, activate stereotypes of the Moor's "bestiality" *prior* to the murderous deed.[8] They rarely question Brabantio's view of Othello as a "civilized" Christian citizen in so far as he is the pliant servant of the Venetian State, though as Desdemona's husband he cannot escape the racist stereotypes pervasive in the culture. Overall, the Western literary tradition, until recently, has inevitably judged Othello as heroic only in terms of qualities that are considered Western, Venetian, Christian, and "civilized."

Today, in the postmodern, Anglo-American academy, most of us discount this earlier critical tradition as being implicitly racist and out-moded at best. Yet, because ideological divisions between the "civilized" West and "backward and uncivilized" non-Europeans continue to shape the popular imagination of the West, the old stereotypes sometimes reappear in contemporary discourses about the play. For instance, when undergraduates read the Introduction to the Signet Classic edition of *Othello*, they are introduced to the figure of the Moor as a stereotypical "character" within a "symbolic map" which naturalizes a division be-tween the Western "civilized" world and the "barbarian" non-Christians:

> Here then are the two major reference points on the map of the world of *Othello*: out at the far edge are the Turks, barbarism, disorder, and amoral destructive powers; closer and more familiar is Venice, the City, order, law, reason. . . . [in Cyprus] passions are more explosive and closer to the surface than in Venice, and here, instead of the ancient order . . . of the City, there is only one man to control violence and defend civilization – the Moor Othello, himself of savage origins and a converted Christian.[9]

While such a discourse is certainly not in the forefront of contemporary critical practices, and in this instance takes the form of an obligatory "innocuous" Introduction, it nonetheless reinforces essentialist cat-egories of difference between races that already exist in the minds of some in our society. It does so by reinscribing the map of a "symbolic geography" which continues to perpetuate racial divisions within today's postcolonial world. Before further examining the implications of these "symbolic" divisions, let us first turn to the political approaches to Shakespeare's *Othello* which, with the hindsight of history, have attempted revisionist readings that reveal the ideological underpinning of racist and sexist discourses of the play – and of its subsequent reproductions in the West.[10] For instance, Karen Newman, in an influential essay, shows us the relation between the play's racist discourses and the early phases of Western colonialism, examining the ways in which the play "stands in a contestatory relation to the hegemonic ideologies of race and class in early modern England."[11] She reads *Othello* in terms of an identification between black male sexuality and [white] femininity/female desire, both of which are perceived as a "monstrous" threat to the "white male hegemony" in the play – a threat that is expressed in the horror of miscegenation. Thus, Newman states:

> I want to argue . . . that femininity is not opposed to blackness and monstrosity, as white is to black, but identified with the monstrous, an identification that makes miscegenation doubly fearful. The play is structured around a cultural aporia, miscegenation.[12]

While the critic usefully points to certain parallels in the Renaissance attitudes toward racial and sexual difference, her conceptual scheme elides the condition of black masculinity with that of white femininity. Historically, we know that the taboo of miscegenation was not so much based on the fear of the femininity of white women as it was on the potential phallic threat of black men, who, incidentally, bore the brunt of the punishment for violating this taboo.[13] Newman's formulation suggests a seamless conflation of the different forms of prejudice when she conclusively defines her perspective:

> [it] seeks to displace conventional interpretations by exposing the extraordinary fascination with and fear of racial and sexual difference which characterizes Elizabethan and Jacobean culture. Desdemona and Othello, woman and black man, are represented by discourses about femininity and blackness which managed and produced difference in early modern England.[14]

This neat elision – of categories like "woman" and "black man," "femininity" and "blackness" – obscures the *specific* effects of stereotyping in the play, whereby Othello self-destructively internalizes the prevailing racism, while Desdemona does not enact or internalize the stereotypes of women's sexual "monstrosity." In fact, to the end, she remains an idealized, virtuous woman – keeping alive the image of a besieged, white femininity so crucial to the production of the black man as a "savage."

Overall, it seems, Newman's argument suggests a shared victimization of blacks and women, thus conflating the particular histories of white women's sexual oppression with the enslavement of black men. The scene of a "barbaric" black man evoked by the play's conclusion not only haunted the Western imagination in the Renaissance, but remains an integral part of postcolonial history; and the sexism suffered by European women does not necessarily or inevitably configure in the same history. Thus, while Newman's subtle, deconstructive reading of *Othello* in the context of ideological struggle offers useful insights into the relation between race and gender codes of the time, it also reveals a tendency in contemporary, Western feminist engagements with race which, in trying to chart the complexities of the relation between race and gender oppressions, implicitly *collapse* the categories of difference by assuming a common history of marginalization. Non-European or Third World readers, as we will see, do not reveal a similar investment in discursively eliding the different forms of victimization – of white women and blacks, for instance – because they have been participants in a long history of violent racial divisions that produced complex, and often confusing, sexual politics. African responses to Shakespeare's *Othello* during twentieth-century decolonization have radically resisted the image of Othello as a "barbarian," even while the generic conventions of tragedy, as well as the "civilizing" impulses of Western critics, have simply vindicated Othello as a tragic hero and "converted Christian" who temporarily succumbs to his "savage origins."[15] Thus, not surprisingly, a number of African readings and revisions of the play have attempted to alter the European ideological and cultural codes that have discursively and materially produced the black man as a violent "other" while marking the white woman as his innocent, and often idealized, victim. From their perspective, the end of Shakespeare's play *cannot foresee* the violence and conflict of colonial history, and even in his dying moments, Othello perpetuates the dichotomy between "civilized" Venetians and "barbaric" non-Europeans: for instance, he chastises himself as a "base Judean" who "threw a pearl away," and in stabbing himself ("I took the circumcised dog by the throat") he implicitly identifies with the "malignant and turbanned Turk." However, finally, he dies as a tragic hero within the "moral" resolution of the play, whereby the violence is displaced upon the demonized, "malignant" Turk, while Lodovico quickly hides the sin of murder that is also the sin of miscegenation on the marriage bed : "The object poisons sight; / Let it be hid" (V.ii.360–1).[16]

Europeans can turn their eyes away from this spectacle of violence – and from the "poisons" of racism in the play – through a disidentification with the black man, but for African viewers and readers, the deed cannot "be hid", as its image has proliferated through the centuries, making it a site for the production of troubled and contradictory colonial/postcolonial identities. Not surprisingly, then, the "new" literatures of Africa and the West Indies often have as their theme the divided subjectivity of the black man, aptly defined by Frantz Fanon as the "Black Skin, White Masks" syndrome.[17] Thus, while Alvin Kernan displaces the tensions of Othello's split identity – as both "the infidel and the defender of the faith" – onto a benign landscape of a "morality play, offering an allegorical journey between heaven and hell," African revisions historicize Othello's wrenching psychic conflicts within the violence of colonial/postcolonial history.[18] And when they read the play in the context of this revisionist history, they do not view the black man as a homogeneous, coherent subject, the universal "victim," but rather attempt to map the shifting boundaries of colonial identity – seemingly overdetermined by political forces and yet never statically held in place. One important effect of this historicization has been to *disarticulate* the connections between the victimization of black men and white women in ways that reveal the complexities of gender struggle within the patriarchy of European imperialism. There is, of course, a familiar tradition in Western scientific and social discourse of using analogies between females and people of "inferior" races and groups.[19] But these discursive analogies do not always conform to the material conditions within which different groups and races exist and which create different histories.

When Shakespeare's *Othello* – like other Western, canonical works – is read as a part of the "civilizing mission" of colonial history, then it tells a story of the empire's African subjects which is generally missing in critical accounts of the play. It is ironic that a work like *Othello* should have been part of a project by which English literary works were to aid in the manufacture of a native elite class, who would then be a "conduit of Western thought and ideas." Cultural values, as the colonists perceived them, moved downward from a position of power.[20] A number of postcolonial studies persuasively show how the British colonial administrators found an ally in English literature to support them in maintaining control over the natives under the guise of a liberal education. This was achieved by representing Western literary knowledge as universal, transhistorical, and rational and by disguising its hegemonic impulses as a humanizing activity that created a class of persons non-European "in blood and color, but English in tastes, in opinion, in morals and intellect."[21]

By all accounts, the success of empire depended on the production of the "mimic man" who was "whitewashed" by Western culture, and yet excluded from its full entitlements.[22] Postcolonial theorists like Frantz Fanon, and more recently Homi Bhabha, have identified "mimicry" as a crucial aspect of relations between the Europeans and non-Europeans in a colonial/postcolonial situation. For the black man, Fanon argues, pressures to imitate whites produce a pathological self-alienation: "He becomes whiter as he renounces his blackness, his jungle."[23] Bhabha theorizes the effects of mimicry to point to the ambivalences of colonial authority as it constructs the "other," whereby the colonial subject both resembles and differs from the master, "not quite/not white."[24] Those Africans or Indians who mediated between the imperial authorities and the native subjects were in certain ways to become "English," often Christianized, and yet, according to Bhabha, the creation of these mock

Englishmen was also troubling because "mimicry is at once a resem-blance and a menace."[25] Mimicry thus becomes a condition of the native's divided subjectivity and self-alienation as well as a means of resistance. It is on the nexus of this split between identity and difference that Africans have struggled to negotiate their identities through colonial/postcolonial history. The complex ironies of this dilemma are perhaps most vividly evoked by Aimé Césaire when his "Negro" defiantly "accepts" being "separated from himself" and yet parodies his own mimicry of Europeans: "You see I can bow and scrape, like you I pay my respects, in short, I am no different from you: pay no attention to my black skin, the sun did it."[26]

In this context, when Africans see themselves represented in the figure of Shakespeare's Othello – and in numerous Western interpret-ations of his character – they quite understandably resist the dichotomy of "civilization" and "barbarism" in terms of which Othello is judged. Recognizing that even in sympathetic readings, such essentialist cat-egories demonize the black races and occlude the material conditions of their struggle, African writers have sought to historicize the production of Othello's divided subjectivity as a "mimic man." In Murray Carlin's revision of Othello, Not now, sweet Desdemona, the playwright reminds us that Shakespeare's play as it exists today cannot escape the burden of history: "This play is not a critical essay on Shakespeare. . . . my play . . . is about the race conflict in the twentieth century."[27] This race conflict is articulated by a black actor playing Othello who rejects the image of Shakespeare's hero, "civilized" and Christianized by the Europeans. In the plot of the play, two actors, who are also lovers offstage, are rehears-ing for a production of Shakespeare's Othello in London. The male lead, known to us as "Othello," is a black from Trinidad and the woman, known as "Desdemona," is a white, South African heiress. The central question raised by both the playwright and his protagonist is "Why is Othello a black man?" This ironically refers to the frequent denial of Othello's real race in Western performance history when white actors played the role and usually not as "a Negro [but] done up – in a romantic, hawk-nosed sort of way, very reassuring to white audiences."[28] Questioning the cultural validity of this practice, Carlin's black actor wants to disrupt its signification when he suggests to "Desdemona": "Suppose I play Othello in white makeup? . . . white actors have always played Othello in blackface. Why shouldn't a black actor play him in whiteface?" (15). Mimicry, in this formulation, clearly scrambles and complicates colonial notions of difference where subjects were con-sidered mere imitations of the rulers.

In many instances, Carlin's actor from Trinidad recognizes his own colonized persona as he does Othello's: "I was born in the English language. . . . I was born in the language that William Shakespeare is talking" (31). Because of this awareness he resists an easy identity with Shakespeare's protagonist, who, in his eyes, is also represented as a European creation, "a black liberal" (44). The female lead, "Desdemona," however, denies the impact of colonial history and reads the play as a "universal" story of love and jealousy: "Othello is a jealous man. . . . She is a faithful, and loving innocent. And he's jealous. And there's your play" (28). Her lover, in contrast, seems self-righteously preoccupied with the Africans' historical struggle for identity. As a result he attempts to open the play to colonial history, and ironically does so by ascribing a transcendent vision to the bard:

> When the play was written the Age of Imperialism had already begun. . . . And Shakespeare . . . understood and foresaw all the problems of that Age. It is the first play about color that was ever written. . . . Here stands Othello, the negro, the black man – the only black man among hundreds of white people.
>
> (32–3)

Not only does Carlin's "Othello" articulate the alienation experienced by blacks through history, but he also attempts to revise the discursive configuration in which the black man is invariably cast as a sexual predator on innocent, white women. Challenging Shakespeare's image of a pure and devoted heroine, Carlin's "Othello" is obsessively preoccupied with Desdemona's power over the Moor. Repressing any empathy for her as a woman, he forces his co-star to confront Desdemona's dominant position within colonialist ideology:

> Desdemona is the first of the White Liberals. Yes she is a real white liberal. She wants power, through love – power, yes. They tell themselves they are on the side of the black man – they are fighting for him against the oppressors – but what they really want is to tell him what to do. That's your Desdemona. Othello is her personal black man. Hers because he is black – he's a slave. He must do what she says – and she won't leave him alone until he does.
>
> (37–8)

Carlin portrays his West Indian actor as a self-pitying neurotic, full of contradictions. He refuses to mimic the "White Liberals," and wants to transmute Shakespeare's Othello into "a passionate negro. All full of Bitterness and Suffering" (44). Yet, with some irony, the audience can also recognize his claims to the "authentic" "negro" identity of Othello simply as another pose of self-aggrandizement before his co-star. According to Fanon's theory of race and psychology in *Black Skin, White Masks*, the actor's attraction and hostility for the white woman is typical of the psychic divisions experienced by black men during colonial rule in places such as Fanon's native Martinique. According to Fanon, a

"Negro's" desire for a white woman is "a wish to be white. A Lust for revenge."[29] Thus, his sexism thrives on the fantasy of the European female's power over black men and, as Fanon suggests, he "enjoy[s] the satisfaction of being the master of a European woman . . . as a certain tang of proud revenge enters into it."[30] Clearly, then, gender struggle within European imperialism reveals a more complicated and often contradictory relation between discourses of race and gender than the standard feminist position allows in its frequent insistence upon the shared experiences of women and marginalized ethnic groups.[31]

Such complexities in the interplay of racial and sexual politics are more vividly and wrenchingly brought to life in another non-Western response to Shakespeare's *Othello*, the Sudanese author Tayib Salih's novel, *Season of Migration to the North* (1969). This work retells the story of a North African Othello, named Mustapha Sa'eed, tracing his journey from his poor and obscure origins in a village outside Khartoum to Cairo and then to London, where he wins acclaim as a scholar and economist, and back again to the Sudan where he lives as a humble farmer and a family man on the banks of the Nile. While in London, Mustapha spends seven years in prison for murdering his English wife, Jean Morris. Like Shakespeare's Othello and Carlin's West Indian actor, Salih's enigmatic hero is also caught up within the pressures of mimicry and self-alienation in a colonial/postcolonial society. Repeatedly, through the narrative, Mustapha Sa'eed self-consciously mimics Shakespeare's Moor though often through ambivalence and denial. For instance, before he meets Jean Morris, he seduces a number of European women by self-consciously enacting the sentimentalized stereotypes of Orientalism, often with starkly ironic, and sometimes parodic, results:

As we drank tea, she [Isabella Seymour] asked me about my home. I related to her fabricated stories about deserts and golden sands and jungles where non-existent animals called to one another. I told her the streets of my country teemed with crocodiles and lions and that during siesta time, crocodiles crawled through it. Half-credulous, half-disbelieving, she listened to me, laughing and closing her eyes. Sometimes she would hear me out in silence, a Christian sympathy in her eyes. There came a moment when I felt I had been transformed into a naked, primitive creature, a spear in one hand and arrows in the other, hunting elephants and lions in the jungles. Curiosity had changed to gaiety, and gaiety to sympathy. . . . when I stir the pool in its depths the sympathy will be transformed into a desire upon whose taut strings I shall play as I wish.[32]

According to Barbara Harlow,

the fantasies in which these women indulge, which Mustapha caters to consciously and provocatively, are so hackneyed and over-used as to be not only crude but trite . . . commonplaces of a romantic convention infatuated [with] . . . images conjured by the *Thousand and One Nights*.[33]

Such images of sensuality and violence are not unlike those with which Othello wins Desdemona, over the objections of her father, in Shakespeare's play. "My mother," Sheila Greenwood tells Mustapha, "would go mad and my father would kill me if they knew I was in love with a black man," and then declares, "how marvellous your black color is . . . the color of magic and mystery and obscenity" (139). And Ann Hammond sees in his eyes "the shimmer of mirages in hot deserts, . . . in [his voice] she hears the screams of ferocious beasts in the jungles" (145). The analogy with Shakespeare's protagonist is reinforced when Isabella Seymour asks him, "What race are you?" and Mustapha Sa'eed replies, "I am like Othello – Arab-African." In order to live the Western fantasy of Othello with a literal vengeance, Mustapha Sa'eed creates in his room in London a "den of lethal lies":

[with] the sandalwood and incense; the ostrich feathers and ivory and ebony figurines, the paintings and drawings of forests of palm trees along the shores of the Nile, boats with sails like doves' wings, suns setting over the mountains of the Red Sea, camel caravans wending their way along sand dunes. . . .

The stereotypical setting of the room, seemingly a self-parody, is in effect a site of contamination, as the protagonist tells us: "My bedroom was a well-spring of sorrow, the germ of a fatal disease. The infection had stricken these women a thousand years ago, but I had stirred up the latent depths . . . and had killed" (34). It is not incidental that images of disease and violence permeate these exotic fabrications that Mustapha Sa'eed enacts and encourages. In these Tayib Salih historicizes the cultural fantasies of the early travel narratives as they got transformed into the sentimental Orientalist myth by the nineteenth century. To some, this exoticism may seem benign, but at the time, with its heady mixture of intoxication and condemnation, it became a justification for continuing colonial domination, an excuse to "civilize" and rule over the Orientals.[34] And the European women in *Season of Migration to the North* are also, like Sa'eed himself, both the instigators and victims of this myth, replicating the conflicts of East and West. Thus, in contrast to Shakespeare, and like Fanon, Salih shows that sexual relations within a colonial struggle rarely produce idealized Desdemonas. If Mustapha Sa'eed, as a colonizer of European women, denigrates their identities as desiring subjects, they in turn only desire him in the context of racist fantasies. Thus, they cast an ironic light on Desdemona's "pity" and "tears" for Othello. In the case of Jean Morris, his wife, Salih further complicates the issue of gender struggle. Her fantasies of desire turn pathological as she takes a sadomasochistic pleasure in playing both predator and prey, finally and inexplicably begging her husband to kill her. Repeatedly, Salih manipulates and inverts the relations between colonizer and colonized, as a particular form of "revenge" that also shows, as Fanon has shown in *Black Skin, White Masks*, how political and racial power struggles produce psychic and sexual dislocations in gender relations.

Finally and inexorably, Tayib Salih makes Mustapha Sa'eed relive Othello's violent deed. When he kills his English wife, just as when he seduces the Englishwomen, he is aware of re-enacting Othello's life. Like Othello, he comes to Europe carried on the tide of colonial history and takes on an alien persona, but retrospectively he defines his cultural transformation as a European disease and repudiates not only his own resemblance to Othello, but also the Moor's very identity:

> They [the Europeans] imported to us the germ of the greatest . . . violence . . . the germ of a deadly disease that struck them more than a thousand years ago. Yes my dears, I came as an invader into your very homes: a drop of poison which you have injected into the veins of history. "I am no Othello. Othello was a lie."
>
> (95)

Such contradictions in the novel clearly make visible the complex production of a divided subjectivity in conditions in which it becomes impossible to "speak" of Othello as he is. Unlike Shakespeare's Othello, Mustapha Sa'eed is conscious of the way in which he is being defined by the West and he resists and manipulates the subject positions assigned to him within colonialist ideology. With some irony, Salih shows his protagonist willingly embracing the identity of a predator given to him by the British who initially "civilized" him. One of his professors at Oxford, who chooses to defend him at the trial, had earlier declared: "You Mr Sa'eed, are the best example of the fact that our civilizing mission in Africa is of no avail. After all the efforts . . . to educate you, it's as if you'd come out of the jungle for the first time" (94). To such assumptions, of which Sa'eed is keenly aware, his response is simply, "I am the intruder. . . . Yes my dear sirs, I came as an invader into your very homes" (94–5). While questioning Othello's identity as a "civilized" servant of the Europeans, Mustapha Sa'eed nonetheless draws an analogy between his sexual colonization of European women and the British takeover of the Sudan, especially when he identifies with Lord Kitchener:

When Mahmud Wad Ahmed was brought in shackles before Kitchener [in the Sudan], the intruder said to him, 'Why have you come to my country to lay waste and plunder?' It was the intruder who said this to the person whose land it was, and the owner of the land bowed his head and said nothing. So let it be with me.

(94)

Mustapha Sa'eed wants to rewrite the script of the colonial takeover of the Sudan. The period of the late nineteenth century into which he is born had already witnessed the consolidation of imperial power in North Africa. Thus, by playing the part of Lord Kitchener and others as an invader to England and a predator of English women, Mustapha Sa'eed feels he is reversing, in a way, "the rattle of swords in Carthage and the clatter of the hooves of Allenby's horses desecrating the ground of Jerusalem" (94–5).

As a "mimic man," and a violent, pathological reincarnation of Shakespeare's Othello, Mustapha Sa'eed is truly dangerous, both to himself and to his masters. If Othello was a man who "loved not wisely, but too well," and who temporarily allowed his baser, "savage" passions to overwhelm him, Salih's imitation of Shakespeare's hero incarnates a mind that never allows his feelings to overcome him – the "civilized" man of reason, his mind is "like a sharp knife, cutting with cold effectiveness."[35] Chameleon-like, he emulates and mimics his rulers, constantly displacing the binary relations of the colonizer and colonized, yet unable entirely to cast off his European identity even when he returns to the village on the Nile. Here, after Mustapha's disappearance, the narrator finds in a locked room a replica of an English drawing room, lined with books found in many traditional European libraries. Like his garish room in London, this setting also seems artificial – "a lie" that must remain hidden.

As a novel, a generic form imported by the Arabs from the West, *Season of Migration to the North* participates in what, by Arabic literary classification, is called a *mu aradeh*, literally "opposition," "contradiction," but meaning a formula whereby one person will write a poem, and another will retaliate along the same lines, but reversing the meaning."[36] The "symbolic geography" that Tayib Salih maps in this work points to complex interconnections between categories of difference that in Shakespeare's play, and in the old critical tradition, are represented as a simple division between the "malignant" Turk and the Christian Moor as the tragedy heads toward its conventional, moral, "resolution." Salih reminds us that Africans, Turks, Moors, among others, recognize Shakespeare's Othello as a "character" in a familiar, Orientalist landscape, both erotic and violent, a composite fantasy of the Europeans' "colonial harem."[37] As readers and viewers, they are drawn into both an identification with and disavowal of the Moor: living as "mimic men," they recognize that Othello's claims to *any* identity – either as a "savage" or as a Christian and a tragic hero – are tenuous and derivative. Clearly then, both *Season of Migration to the North* and *Not now, sweet Desdemona* remap the world of Shakespeare's *Othello*. Attempting to wrest it away from colonialist ideologies, they show how Shakespeare's play and its revisions are all inextricably tied to histories of racial conflict in the "new world" of the Renaissance, which is the "third world" of our postcolonial era.

Furthermore, it would be fair to suggest that these non-European, revisionist readings approximate what cultural theorists have called a counterdisciplinary practice whereby texts are read as multivocal sites of conflict and analyzed at the level of the *specific* historical struggles by which they are shaped.[38] Written in the 1960s, and in the wake of the African independence movements, these works clearly embody a call for cultural decolonization. However, their engagement with their own history is also complex, and often troubling, as they focus on the psychic self-divisions experienced by colonial subjects. Not surprisingly, then, the "characters" of Othello and Desdemona as incarnated by Carlin and Salih are caught up in a world of contradictory and complicated racial and sexual politics. And in this world, discourses of resistance to racism and sexism often work in *opposition* rather than in *collaboration* with one another: for instance, it is clear that these African readings of "race" in *Othello* and in colonial history deny white femininity its sanctified cultural space (there can be no virtuous and pure Desdemona), while disrupting the pervasive notion among feminists and other political critics in the West that victims of race and gender oppression are bound by a common struggle. Implicitly, at least, in their discursive configuration, Desdemona, like Miranda, colludes in creating the "otherness" of the black man.

To conclude, both *Not now, sweet Desdemona* and *Season of Migration to the North* question whether Shakespeare's *Othello* can be read and appreciated (as conservatives would insist) without the interventions of its non-European revisions. Of course, in terms of conventional reading practices, *Othello* remains an autonomous text, which is guaranteed its canonical status in the West. However, I would argue that it is crucial to expose the ideologies that secure the pleasure and "understanding" of most European audiences – an understanding that *separates* the play from our colonial legacy of continuing racial conflicts. Thus, to understand *Othello*'s place in the postcolonial moment is to open the play to the competing ideologies of multiple interpretations, some of which will enable Othello's descendants to claim their own histories and Desdemona's descendants to understand their complicity in the production of the "exotic" Moor.

NOTES

INTRODUCTION
Margo Hendricks and Patricia Parker

1 Valerie Wayne, ed., *The Matter of Difference: Materialist Feminist Criticism of Shakespeare* (Ithaca and London: Cornell University Press, 1991), p. 11.
2 Edited by Margaret W. Ferguson, Maureen Quilligan, and Nancy J. Vickers (Chicago and London: University of Chicago Press, 1986).
3 See, among others, Henry Louis Gates, Jr, ed., *"Race," Writing, and Difference* (Chicago: University of Chicago Press, 1986), the Introduction to Dominick LaCapra, ed., *The Bounds of Race: Perspectives on Hegemony and Resistance* (Ithaca and London: Cornell University Press, 1991), and the discussion of the history of the term in Michael Banton's *The Idea of Race* (London: Tavistock, 1977) and *Racial Theories* (Cambridge: Cambridge University Press, 1987).
4 See both the essays here and the discussion in Ann Rosalind Jones's and Peter Stallybrass's "Dismantling Irena: The Sexualizing of Ireland in Early Modern England," in Andrew Parker, Mary Russo, Doris Sommer, and Patricia Yeager, eds, *Nationalisms & Sexualities* (New York and London: Routledge, 1992) pp. 157–71, esp. pp. 159–60.
5 Chandra Talpade Mohanty, "Under Western Eyes," in Chandra Talpade Mohanty, Ann Russo, and Lourdes Torres, eds, *Third World Women and the Politics of Feminism* (Bloomington: Indiana University Press, 1991), pp. 51–80, esp. 51–2.
6 See *This Bridge Called My Back: Writings by Radical Women of Color* (Watertown: Persephone Press, 1981); *The Third Woman* (Bloomington: Third Woman Press, 1981); Amy Ling, *Between Worlds* (New York: Pergamon Press, 1990); Trinh T. Minh-ha, *Women, Native, Other: Writing, Postcoloniality, and Feminism* (Bloomington and Indianapolis: Indiana University Press, 1989); Audre Lorde, *Sister Outsider* (New York: The Crossing Press, 1984); Gloria Anzaldúa, *Borderlands, La Frontera: The New Mestiza* (San Francisco: Spinsters/ Aunt Lute, 1987); Paula Gunn Allen, "Some Like Indians Endure," in *Living the Spirit* (New York: St Martin's Press, 1987), p. 9.
7 See Sandra Gilbert, ed., *The Norton Anthology of Literature by Women* (New York: Norton, 1985), p. 252; bell hooks, *Ain't I a Woman: Black Women and Feminism* (Boston: South End Press, 1981); and Chela Sandoval, "U.S. Third World Feminism: The Theory and Method of Oppositional Consciousness in the Postmodern World," *Genders*, no. 10 (Spring 1991), pp. 1–24, esp. p. 9.
8 See bell hooks, *Feminist Theory from Margin to Center* (Boston: South End Press,

1984), p. 9; Gayatri Spivak, "Three Women's Texts and a Critique of Imperialism," *Critical Inquiry* 12 (Autumn 1985), pp. 243–61.

9 See her essay, along with that of King-Kok Cheung and others in *Conflicts in Feminism*, ed. Marianne Hirsch and Evelyn Fox Keller (New York and London: Routledge, 1990), and Valerie Smith, "Black Feminist Theory and the Representation of the 'Other'," in Cheryl A. Wall, ed., *Changing Our Own Words: Essays on Criticism, Theory, and Writing by Black Women* (New Brunswick: Rutgers University Press, 1989), pp. 38–57.

10 See Peter Hulme, *Colonial Encounters: Europe and the Native Caribbean 1492–1797* (London and New York: Methuen, 1986), and the discussions of Tzvetan Todorov, *The Conquest of America: The Question of the Other*, trans. Richard Howard (New York: Harper & Row, 1984) by, for example, Rolena Adorno, "Arms, Letters and Native Historians in Early Colonial Mexico," in René Jara *et al.*, eds, *1492–1992: Re/Discovering Colonial Writing* (Minneapolis: The Prisma Institute, 1989), pp. 201–24, and the review by Irma S. Majer in *MLN*, 98, no. 4 (May 1983), pp. 771–5, and Roberto Gonzalez-Echevarría in *The Yale Review*, 74, no. 2 (Winter 1985), pp. 281–90.

11 See variously the work of Annette Kolodny, discussed in chapter 5 of Patricia Parker, *Literary Fat Ladies: Rhetoric, Gender, Property* (London: Methuen, 1987); on Doña Marina, "La Malinche" or "La Chingada," both the essay by Verena Stolcke in this volume and, among other treatments, Américo Parédes, "Mexican Legend and the Rise of the Mestizo: A Survey," in W. Hand, ed., *American Folk Legend* (Berkeley: University of California Press, 1971), pp. 97–107; Adelaida R. De Castillo, "Malintzin Tenépal: A Preliminary Look into a New Perspective," in *Essays on La Mujer*, ed. Rosaura Sánchez and Rosa Martínez Cruz (Los Angeles: University of California Press, 1977), p. 125; Cherríe Moraga, "From a Long Line of Vendidas: Chicanas and Feminism," *Feminist Studies/Critical Studies*, ed. Teresa de Lauretis (Bloomington: Indiana University Press, 1986).

12 See Mary Louise Pratt, *Imperial Eyes: Travel Writing and Transculturation* (New York and London: Routledge, 1992).

13 See for example, Moira Ferguson's recent *Subject to Others: British Women Writers and Colonial Slavery 1670–1834* (London and New York: Routledge, 1992), which tracks the ways in which the very anti-slavery protest of British female writers that proved central to the security of British middle-class women's political self-empowerment contributed, in its "Eurocentric constructions of Africans and slaves," to the consolidating of imperialist and domestic racist ideologies.

14 See Judith Butler, *Gender Trouble: Feminism and the Subversion of Identity* (New York and London: Routledge, 1990); Valerie Traub, *Desire and Anxiety: Circulations of Sexuality in Shakespearean Drama* (New York and London: Routledge, 1992); Mary Nyquist, "'In the East My Pleasure Lies': Barbarism, Masculinism and Female Rule in Early Modern Republicanism," *Women's Studies* (forthcoming) with the discussion of the relation between Milton's Adam, the "rhetorics of property" that gendered the New World and discourses of discovery in chapter 5 of *Literary Fat Ladies*; Joan Pong Linton, "The Romance and Colonial Ideology 1575–1625" (work-in-progress); Margo Hendricks, "Obscured by Dreams: Race, Empire and Shakespeare's *A Midsummer Night's Dream*," forthcoming; Arthur Little, "'An Essence That's Not Seen': The Primal Scene of Racism in *Othello*," *Shakespeare Quarterly*, Fall 1993; Kim F. Hall, "Reading What Isn't There: 'Black' Studies in Early Modern England?" *Stanford Humanities Re/View* 3:1 (1993): 23–33; Paul

Julian Smith, *Representing the Other: "Race," Text, and Gender in Spanish and Spanish American Narrative* (Oxford: Clarendon Press, 1992).

1 THE COLOR OF PATRIARCHY
Critical difference, cultural difference, and Renaissance drama
Ania Loomba

I would like to thank Suvir Kaul, Sumit Guha, Lars Engle, and the editors of this volume.

1 Thomas Middleton, *The Changeling*, in *Thomas Middleton, Three Plays*, ed. Kenneth Muir (London and Melbourne: Dent, 1975), I.i.52.
2 See my "Teaching the Bard in India," *JEFL* (Special Issue on "Teaching Literature"), nos. 7 and 8, June and December 1991 (Hyderabad Central Institute of English and Foreign Languages), pp. 147–62.
3 Quoted by Joan W. Scott, "Deconstructing Equality-versus-Difference: or, the Uses of Post-structuralist Theory for Feminism," *Feminist Studies* 14, no. 1 (Spring 1988), p. 29. On the tensions between difference and equality see also Michèle Barrett, "The Concept of 'Difference'," *Feminist Review* 26 (Summer 1987), pp. 28–41.
4 See A. Loomba, "*Hamlet* in Mizoram," forthcoming in Marianne Novy, ed., *Cross-Cultural Performances: More Women's Re-Visions of Shakespeare* (Urbana-Champaign and Chicago: Illinois University Press) for discussions of this meeting ground, and an analysis of the political unconscious of the *Hamlet* performances.
5 Benita Parry, "Problems in Current Theories of Colonial Discourse," *Oxford Literary Review* 9, nos. 1–2 (1987), pp. 27–58.
6 Walter Cohen, "Political Criticism of Shakespeare," in Jean E. Howard and Marion F. O'Connor, eds, *Shakespeare Reproduced: The Text in History and Ideology* (New York and London: Methuen, 1987), pp. 37–8.
7 Carol Thomas Neely, "Constructing the Subject: Feminist Practice and the New Renaissance Discourses," *English Literary Renaissance* 18, no. 1 (Winter 1988), p. 7; see also Lynda E. Boose, "The Family in Shakespearean Studies; or – Studies in the Family of Shakespeareans; or – The Politics of Politics," *Renaissance Quarterly* 40, no. 4 (Winter 1987), pp. 707–42. All subsequent references to these essays have been incorporated in the text. See also Ann Thompson, "Are There Any Women in *King Lear*?" in Valerie Wayne, ed., *The Matter of Difference: Materialist Feminist Criticism of Shakespeare* (Ithaca: Cornell University Press, 1991), pp. 117–28.
8 Doubts about the political uses of poststructuralism are expressed by Perry Anderson, *In the Tracks of Historical Materialism* (London: Verso, 1980); Nancy Hartsock, "Rethinking Modernism: Minority versus Majority Theories," and Kumkum Sangari, "The Politics of the Possible," both in *Cultural Critique* 7 (Fall 1987), pp. 187–206 and 157–86 respectively; "Patrolling the Borders: Feminist Historiography and the New Historicism," *Radical History Review* 43 (1989), pp. 23–43. Postmodernism is usefully summarized by Jane Flax, "Postmodernism and Gender Relations in Feminist Theory," *Signs* 12, 4 (Summer 1987), pp. 621–43. Joan W. Scott, "Deconstructing Equality-versus-Difference," argues for the political potential of poststructuralism, as does Michael Ryan, *Marxism and Deconstruction: A Critical Introduction* (Baltimore: Johns Hopkins University Press, 1982). A sensitive account of both the overlaps and the differences between feminist historiography and new historicism is provided by Judith Newton, "History as Usual? Feminism and the

New Historicism," *Cultural Critique* 9 (Spring 1988), pp. 87–121. See also Leslie Wahl Rabine, "A Feminist Politics of Non-Identity," and Mary Poovey, "Feminism and Deconstruction," both in *Feminist Studies* 14, no. 1 (Spring 1988), pp. 11–31 and 51–65 respectively and "Critical Theory and the History of Women: What's at Stake in Deconstructing Women's History," dialogue section in *Journal of Women's History* 2, no. 3 (Winter 1991), pp. 58–108.

 9 Walter Cohen remarks, "the addition of race, sexuality, subjectivity, the body, or all of these issues to the list would only highlight the dilemma – the need for an account that overcomes both monistic reduction and pluralistic vacuity" ("Pre-revolutionary drama," in Gordon McMullan and Jonathan Hope, eds, *The Politics of Tragi-Comedy: Shakespeare and After* (London: Routledge, 1992), p. 146.

10 The centrality of Renaissance studies to new historicism and cultural materialism is evident from various recent discussions of these perspectives, especially Judith Newton, "Family Fortunes: 'New History' and 'New Historicism'," *Radical History Review* 43 (1989), pp. 5–22. See also various essays in H. Aram Veeser, ed., *The New Historicism* (New York: Routledge, 1989). Comparisons between the two analytical methods and their relationship to Renaissance studies have been widely commented on, including by Jonathan Dollimore, "Introduction: Shakespeare, Cultural Materialism and New Historicism," in Jonathan Dollimore and Alan Sinfield, eds, *Political Shakespeare: New Essays in Cultural Materialism* (Manchester: Manchester University Press, 1985), pp. 2–17, and "Shakespeare, Cultural Materialism, Feminism and Marxist Humanism," *New Literary History*, 21, no. 3 (Spring 1990), pp. 471–93; Walter Cohen, "Political Criticism of Shakespeare,"pp. 18–46; Don Wayne, "Power, Politics, and the Shakespearean Text: Recent Criticism of Shakespeare," in *Shakespeare Reproduced*, pp. 47–67; Louis A. Montrose, "Renaissance Literary Studies and the Subject of History," and Jean E. Howard, "The New Historicism in Renaissance Studies," both in *English Literary Renaissance* 16, no. 1 (Winter 1986), pp. 5–12 and 13–43 respectively. For the backlash against these perspectives see Edward Pechter, "New Historicism and its Discontents," *PMLA* 102, no. 3 (1987), pp. 292–303; Richard Levin, "Unthinkable Thoughts in the New Historicizing of English Renaissance Drama," *New Literary History* 21, no. 3 (Spring 1990), pp. 434–47 and various letters in the recent Bardbiz controversy in the *London Review of Books* – especially those by James Wood (March 22, May 24, and August 10, 1990).

11 Thompson, "Are There Any Women in *King Lear*?" is one recent attempt to reconcile feminist and materialist criticism of Shakespeare. Both Boose ("The Family") and Dollimore ("Shakespeare, Cultural Materialism") lament the fissured alliance, although Boose clearly does not regard it as having been a real possibility.

12 Boose, "The Family," p. 718.

13 Howard, "New Historicism," p. 31.

14 Don Wayne, "Power, Politics," p. 61. See also Valerie Traub, "Desire and the Difference It Makes," in Valerie Wayne, *The Matter of Difference*, p. 81.

15 Gayatri Chakravorty Spivak, "French Feminism in an International Frame," in *In Other Worlds: Essays in Cultural Politics* (New York: Methuen, 1987), p. 137.

16 Sandra Harding, "Introduction: Is There a Feminist Method?" in Harding, ed., *Feminism and Methodology* (Bloomington: Indiana University Press, 1987), p. 7. See also Gisela Bock, "Women's History and Gender History: Aspects of

an International Debate," *Gender and History* 1, no. 1 (Spring 1989), p. 11.

17 Susie Tharu and K. Lalita, eds, *Women's Writing in India*, vol. 1 (New York: The Feminist Press, 1990), pp. 30–1.

18 Gerda Lerner is quoted by Joan Kelly, *Women, History, Theory* (Chicago: University of Chicago Press, 1984), p. 6. In a recent article, "Reconceptualising Differences among Women," *Journal of Women's History* (Winter 1990), pp. 106–21, Lerner emphasizes that women cannot be treated as a unified category.

19 See Ania Loomba, *Gender, Race, Renaissance Drama* (Manchester: Manchester University Press, 1989), p. 56.

20 See, for example, Hazel V. Carby, "White Woman Listen! Black Feminism and the Boundaries of Sisterhood," in *The Empire Strikes Back: Race and Racism in Britian in the Seventies*, Center for Comtemporary Cultural Studies (London: Hutchinson, 1972), pp. 212–35, and Gloria Joseph, "The Incompatible *ménage à trois*: Marxism, Feminism, and Racism," in Lydia Sargent, ed., *Women and Revolution: A Discussion of the Unhappy Marriage of Marxism and Feminism* (Boston: South End Press, 1981), pp. 91–107.

21 See, for example, Angela Davis, *Women, Race and Class* (London: The Women's Press, 1982), and Patricia Hill Collins, *Black Feminist Thought: Knowledge, Consciousness, and the Politics of Empowerment* (London: Unwin Hyman, 1990).

22 Michèle Barrett, "Ideology and the Cultural Production of Gender," in Judith Newton and Deborah Rosenfelt, eds, *Feminist Literary Criticism and Social Change* (London: Methuen, 1986), pp. 70–102.

23 Dated July 12, 1990.

24 See my letter in *The London Review of Books*, August 15, 1991.

25 Stephen Greenblatt, *Learning to Curse: Essays in Early Modern Culture* (New York and London: Routledge, 1990), pp. 9–10.

26 See my "Overworlding the 'The Third World'," *Oxford Literary Review* 13 (1991), pp. 184–5.

27 See Loomba, *Gender, Race, Renaissance Drama* , ch. 2.

28 See Dollimore, "Shakespeare, Cultural Materialism," pp. 475–6.

29 Parry, "Problems in Current Theories,", p. 43.

30 John Webster, *The White Devil*, in Brian Gibbons, ed., *Elizabethan and Jacobean Tragedies* (Tonbridge, Kent: Ernest Benn, 1984), pp. 487–628.

31 Cedric Robinson, *Black Marxism: The Making of the Black Radical Tradition* (London: Zed Books, 1983), p. 27.

32 Peter Stallybrass, "The World Turned Upside Down: Inversion, Gender and the State," in Wayne, *The Matter of Difference*, pp. 201–2.

33 Arthur Brittain and Mary Maynard, *Sexism, Racism and Oppression* (Oxford: Basil Blackwell, 1984), pp. 5–6.

34 Quoted in Robinson, *Black Marxism*, p. 131.

35 In a 1952 article, "The Origins of Columbian Cosmography," Arthur Davies pointed to connections between Irish and blacks in colonial discourses. He is quoted by Robinson, who also notes that the Irish provided the prototype for the white servant (ibid., p. 104).

36 See Loomba, *Gender, Race, Renaissance Drama*, pp. 106–8.

37 See Robinson, *Black Marxism*, p. 121.

38 Jean-Louis Flandrin, *Families in Former Times: Kinship, Household and Sexuality*, trans. Richard Southern (Cambridge: Cambridge University Press, 1974), p. 4.

39 Quoted in ibid., p. 11.

40 Ibid., p. 47.

41 The interlocking of a variety of discourses that construct "woman" or otherness are, of course, starkly evident in plays such as *The White Devil*, and others where there is a central black presence and a deviant woman, such as *Othello*, *Titus Andronicus*, and *Antony and Cleopatra*. But it can also be detected elsewhere in interchanges or moments that are apparently more marginal to the vocabulary of blackness. In *Love's Labour's Lost*, extreme sexual adoration which is also a surrender of the self is expressed in the image of a "rude and savage man of Inde" who

> At the first op'ning of the gorgeous east,
> Bows not his vassal head and, strucken blind,
> Kisses the base ground with obedient breast.
>
> (IV.iii.217–21)

In the same play, since "Black is the badge of hell, /The hue of dungeons, and school of night," the ultimate test of love is its ability to remain unchanged even if the lover were black (IV.iii.250–75). By the same token, a repentant Claudio in *Much Ado About Nothing* expresses his new steadfastness by saying that he'll marry Hero, "were she an Ethiope" (V.iv.38). Citations from both plays are from *The Riverside Shakespeare* (Boston: Houghton Mifflin Co., 1974).

42 Thomas Dekker and Thomas Middleton, *The Roaring Girl*, in Russell A. Fraser and Norman Rabkin eds, *Drama of the English Renaissance* (New York and London: Macmillan 1976), pp. 334–68.

43 *Hic Mulier*, reprinted in Katherine Usher Henderson and Barbara F. McManus, *Half Humankind, Contexts and Texts of the Controversy about Women in England, 1540–1640* (Urbana and Chicago: University of Illinois Press, 1985), pp. 268–9.

2 "THE GETTING OF A LAWFUL RACE"
Racial discourse in early modern England and the unrepresentable black woman
Lynda E. Boose

1 The necessity may be especially acute when the dialogue takes place predominantly among Americans – heirs to the site where Europe's fantasies of ownership, power, and domination were deposited and have been played out in a history of racial violence. Especially for those who grew up in the United States, it may be nearly impossible to conceive of a time before what St Clair Drake calls "White Racism," a phenomenon which, unlike "less drastic forms of prejudice through which colored people were sometimes stigmatized," has been "sanctioned with a systematic ideology or embodied in institutional structures." St Clair Drake, *Black Folk Here and There*, 2 vols (Los Angeles: University of California Press, 1990), II: 13. Given White Racism's fantasy of "washing the Ethiop clean," "debriding" – a medical term for controlling infection and removing "foreign matter" by scrubbing away the upper layers of skin – seemed especially appropriate for an essay on race/gender. I have borrowed it from Susan Jefford's essay on "Debriding Vietnam: The Resurrection of the White American Male," *Feminist Studies* 14 (1988), 525–43.

2 Frank Reeves, *British Racial Discourse: A Study of British Political Discourse about Race and Race-Related Matters* (Cambridge: Cambridge University Press, 1983), 8.

3 Drake, *Black Folk Here and There*, II: 269.

4 Ibid., 269, 269–70.

5 Ibid., 271.

6 Ibid., 275.

7 James Walvin claims that in the early 1600s, blacks were "everyday sights" in Britain, employed as house servants, cooks, laborers, and clerks, and were "assimilated almost to the point of equality with white Englishmen particularly in religious and sexual matters." *Black and White: The Negro and English Society 1555–1945* (London: Allen Lane, Penguin Press, 1973), 10. See also Drake, *Black Folk Here and There*, II: 274.

8 On the links Webster forges between Venetians and the Irish, see especially Ann Rosalind Jones, "Italians and Others: Venice and the Irish in *Coryat's Crudities* and *The White Devil*," *Renaissance Drama* 18 (1987), 101–20.

9 Cited in L. P. Curtis, Jr, *Anglo-Saxons and Celts* (New York: New University Press, 1968), 84.

10 Quoted from Stephen Greenblatt, "Learning to Curse: Aspects of Linguistic Colonialism in the Sixteenth Century," in *First Images of America: The Impact of the New World on the Old*, 2 vols, ed. Fredi Chiappelli (Berkeley and Los Angeles: University of California Press 1976), II: 563.

11 The same constellated anxieties suggestively hint at an ur-location in those that form the narrative in Genesis of Jacob, his daughter Dinah, and the submission to circumcision that the men of Schechem all undergo in order that Prince Schechem's seizure of Dinah may be validated into marriage and future exchanges of women between the groups may become possible. Having deceptively agreed to the bond, the Israelites (led by Jacob's sons Simon and Levi) wait until the Schechemite men have submitted to the knife, then they renege on their bond, kill their incapacitated enemy, retrieve Dinah, and depart.

12 Winthrop Jordan, *White over Black* (Harmondsworth: Penguin, 1969), 20.

13 *Urania II* has never been published and is still in holograph manuscript at the Newberry Library; Josephine Roberts has been designated to transcribe it by EETS.

14 Cherrell Guilfoyle, "Othello, Otuel, and the English Charlemagne Romances," *Review of English Studies* 38 (1987), 50–5, 51.

15 Samuel Purchas, *Purchas His Pilgrimage, or Relations of the World and the Religions observed in all ages, And places discovered, from the Creation unto this present. . . .* (London: l6l3), VI: 14.545–6.

16 Purchas, *Purchas His Pilgrimage*, 546. This excerpt addresses an issue I raised earlier. Purchas constructs a taxonomy that groups "whiter Europeans" together and imagines the self as a part of that group.

17 Richard Hakluyt, *The Principal Navigations, Voyages, Traffiques & Discoveries of the English Nation* (1600), 12 vols, ed. Walter Raleigh (Glasgow: James MacLehose & Sons, 1903–5), VII: 261–71. My original connection to Best's essay comes from its citation in Karen Newman's fine essay, "'And wash the Ethiop white': Femininity and the Monstrous in *Othello*," in her book, *Fashioning Femininity and English Renaissance Drama* (Chicago: University of Chicago Press, l991), 78.

18 Janet Adelman, *Suffocating Mothers: Fantasies of Maternal Origin in Shakespeare's Plays, "Hamlet" to "The Tempest"* (New York: Routledge, 1992), 105.

19 Ibid., 106–7.

20 Drake, *Black Folk Here and There*, II: 34, 38, 199, 221, 224, 273.

21 Ibid., 210–13 and plates 7 and 8. *The Notre Dame Du Puy*, a 1622 painting by

Hieronymous Dumonteilh, represents a Negro Madonna holding a Negro Jesus.

22 Drake, *Black Folk Here and There*, II: 201.

23 Ibid., 193 and 346; see also *Morien, A Metrical Romance* (London: David Nutt, 1901), 1–16. The fact that the Black Knight survives in legend only in Germany and Holland perhaps is owed to the veneration of St Maurice, a Christianized African from Thebes who was martyred in the Swiss Rhône valley in AD 287 and who became symbolically associated with the Holy Roman Empire from AD 962 onward, when the Emperor Otto I of Saxony first marched under his banner (see Drake, *Black Folk Here and There*, II: 214–20).

24 *Morien*, 29, 41 (as quoted in Drake, *Black Folk Here and There*, II: 196, 198).

25 Drake, *Black Folk Here and There*, II: 348, n. 34. My thanks also to Monika Otter for providing me with the name of this son and its translation.

26 Jonathan Crewe, *Trials of Authorship: Anterior Forms and Poetic Reconstruction from Wyatt to Shakespeare* (Berkeley and Los Angeles: University of California Press, 1990), 120 and 183.

27 Stephen Orgel, ed., *Ben Jonson: The Complete Masques* (New Haven and London: Yale University Press, 1969), 46–7, 49–50, 51. All references to Jonson's masques are to this edition and are hereafter cited in the text.

28 Kim F. Hall, "Sexual Politics and Cultural Identity in *The Masque of Blackness*," in *The Performance of Power: Theatrical Discourse and Politics*, ed. Sue-Ellen Case and Janelle Reinelt (Iowa City: University of Iowa Press, 1991), 10.

29 Stephen Orgel points out in *The Jonsonian Masque* (New York: Columbia University Press, 1965; rpt 1981) that such a masque had been produced in 1551 at the court of Edward VI (34).

30 The December 29, 1604, dispatch of Nicolo Molin, the Venetian Ambassador, states that "When the festivities are over, which will be about Candlemass, the Queen will retire to Greenwich, nor will she leave it till her confinement" (*Calendar of Venetian State Papers* x, 312, cited in Charles Harold Herford and Percy Simpson, eds, *Ben Jonson* [Oxford: Clarendon Press, 1950], 446). According to P. M. Handover, *Arbella Stuart: Royal Lady of Hardwick and Cousin to King James* (London: Eyre & Spottiswoode, 1957), at the time the Queen played in *The Masque of Blackness*, she was nearly seven months pregnant with the Princess Mary (212).

31 On this aspect of the masque and the way the representation of female roles intensified as a political problem during the Jacobean and Caroline eras, see especially Suzanne Gossett, "'Man-maid, begone': Women in Masques," *English Literary Renaissance* 18 (1988), 86–113.

32 Hall shrewdly notes the various ways in which, by invoking the characterization of Anne as "an empty-headed spendthrift in endless pursuit of the unusual or the bizarre," critics have minimized, if not dismissed, the possibility of Anne's influence on the early stages of the masque genre ("Sexual Politics," 10, n. 16). When Herford and Simpson, for instance, quote Venetian Ambassador Zorzi Giustiniani's commentary on *The Masque of Beauty*, which includes praise for Anne's part in the creation of the masque and a comment on how "the mind of her Majesty, the authoress of the whole . . . reaped universal applause," the editors, bonding in fraternal familiarity with the two male artists, then immediately add the acerbic comment: "The fiction that the queen was 'authoress of the whole' masque was well kept up; one wonders what Ben and Inigo thought of it" (*Ben Jonson*, 457).

33 Hall, "Sexual Politics," 5.

34 *Winwood Memorials* ii, 44 (quoted in Herford and Simpson, *Ben Jonson*, 448).

35 *State Papers* 14, vol. xii, 6 (quoted in Herford and Simpson, *Ben Jonson*, 449).

36 From *Calendar of Venetian State Papers* xi (1607–10), 86 (quoted in Herford and Simpson, *Ben Jonson*, 457).

37 The child who had three years earlier danced as her mother's hidden partner beneath the Queen's subversively blackened disguise, the Princess Mary, had died just four months before Queen Anne appeared as Jonson's figure of contained feminine Harmony in his *Masque of Beauty*.

38 In its move to send the "Blackamoors" back, Jonson's *Masque of Blackness* acts out a deeply seated racist fantasy that continues to echo in American politics even in the 1990s.

39 Although statistics on how many such white-fathered children were born to slave-women are necessarily only guesses, the guesswork includes estimates ranging up to 50 per cent. Frederick Douglass, Booker T. Washington, and author William Wells Brown are all examples of unacknowledged sons fathered by white masters.

40 As part of the ritual of humiliation and repentance, persons guilty of a variety of sins in Elizabethan England were condemned by the Church courts to appear dressed in a white sheet and were made to read out a list acknowledging their various crimes. The punishment spanned civil and Church offenses, and records exist of white-sheeted penitents appearing at the crossroads to be whipped or in the church to confess in front of the congregation. Such an event involving Shakespeare's son-in-law occurred shortly before Shakespeare's death. On March 26, 1615/16, Thomas Quiney, married on February 10 to Judith Shakespeare, appeared in open court in the parish church and confessed his guilt in having impregnated one Margaret Wheeler, who, along with her child, had died in childbirth some two weeks earlier. Quiney was forced to face the "open shame of three days' penance open done." E. R. C. Brinkworth, in *Shakespeare and the Bawdy Court of Stratford* (Chichester: Phillimore & Co., 1972), speculates that the scandal surrounding the event may have resulted in the changes made in Shakespeare's will on March 25 and even to hastening his death (78–84).

41 My discussion of "the tragic mulatta" is deeply indebted to my colleague, Bill Cook, from whose insights and wealth of information I have profited immensely. As semantic marker and narrative inscription, the term "mulatto" recognizes an ideology of anxieties that were, by linguistic inference, pan-European in scope. Having first appeared in Spanish about 1588 (apparently indirectly received from the Portuguese via an Italian text), "mulatto" very quickly entered into English in 1595 through Drake's Voyage (Hakluyt Society, 22; see *OED*), and eventually became the French term as well for designating the progeny of "a European and a negro." But unlike the available word "mestizo" that had been applied to the racial mixture of European and native (Indian) groups in the Spanish New World, "mulatto" is not a neutrally descriptive term. "Mulatto" means little mule. And through that meaning not only is the black–white sexual act ideologically configured as the unnatural union of two separate animal species, it is also marked by the specific fear that hides behind its wishful fantasy that mulattoes – like mules – are by nature sterile. In an 1861 extension of the word into "mulattoism," the sheer tenacity of this fantasy – despite several centuries of observable evidence to the contrary – shines through the emphatic assertion cited from Van Evrie's *Negroes* that "The fourth generation of mulattoism is as absolutely sterile as muleism" (*OED*). But if the above hostilities embedded in "mulatto" seem to reflect anxieties more especially bred within and by the

New World enslavement of black Africans, those same anxieties of color-blending reappear, recycled as it were, in one very specific early nineteenth-century usage that is categorically and tellingly English. In it, the culture's sublimated anxieties over skin color appear projected back onto what was, for the English, more probably the site for their originary model of "a race apart." Amidst the more normative *OED* definitions of the word, an anomalous citation from 1816 and 1843 appears in which "Mulattoe" is said to refer to an "indurated greensand" or "an arenaceous stone, with . . . a speckled appearance (whence 'tis named)" peculiar to that favorite space of English anathema: Ireland. And thus, imprinted onto a semantic map that such circulation makes visible, New World anxieties about racial difference found their way back to their probable origin. There, they reattached themselves, illogically if predictably, to a site that non-Englishmen would find impossible to read in terms of racial difference. Nonetheless, that site still magnetized the racial term: after all, a variegated rock in Ireland was still a variegated signifier found within that particular place that, for the English, was already understood as the space of the Other.

42 See Dion Boucicault, *The Octaroon* in *Six Early American Plays, 1798–1890*, ed. William Coyle and Harvey G. Damaser (Columbus, Ohio: Charles E. Merrill, 1968), 178. Undoubtedly, the classic illustration is Dion Boucicault's wildly popular, mid-nineteenth-century melodrama, *The Octaroon*, which opened in New York December 6, 1859, four days after the execution of John Brown. But the tragic mulatta narrative also erupted onto Hollywood screens in especially intense bursts of life during the 1930s and 1950s, playing out, in the latter case, amidst the gathering crisis of public school integration. Yet even as Hollywood seized upon this titillating fiction, the format it devised – in which white actresses like Helen Morgan, Ava Gardner, Jeannie Crain, Yvonne de Carlo, Susan Kohner pass themselves as mulattas passing for white – itself revealingly attests to the unrepresentability of the black woman in systems of white desire.

3 THE FACE OF DOMESTICATION
Physiognomy, gender politics, and humanism's others
Juliana Schiesari

1 Ludovico Ariosto, "Satire C," in *Satire e Lettere*, ed. Cesare Segre (Turin: Einaudi, 1976), p. 64, II 260–1. On the dog as a fetish of domestication in Ariosto, see my "The Domestication of Woman in *Orlando Furioso* 42 and 43, or A Snake is Being Beaten," *Stanford Italian Review* X.1 (1991), pp. 123–43. Many thanks to Nancy Vickers, Paula Findlen, Georges Van Den Abbeele, and especially Ann Rosalind Jones for their helpful suggestions during the writing of this chapter.
2 Pico della Mirandola, "On the Dignity of Man," in *Renaissance Thought and Its Sources*, ed. Oskar Kristeller (New York: Columbia University Press, 1979).
3 Joan Kelly, "Did Women Have a Renaissance?," in *Women, History, and Theory: The Essays of Joan Kelly* (Chicago: University of Chicago Press, 1984).
4 Jacob Burckhardt, *The Civilization of the Renaissance in Italy*, trans. S. G. C. Middlemore (New York: Harper, 1958).
5 Kelly, "Did Women Have a Renaissance?," pp. 21–2.
6 Francesco Barbaro, "On Wifely Duties," in *The Earthly Republic: Italian Humanists on Government and Society*, ed. Benjamin G. Kohl and Ronald G. Witt, trans. Benjamin G. Kohl (Philadelphia: University of Pennsylvania Press, 1978), pp. 189–228; Leon-Battista Alberti, *I Libri Della famiglia*, trans-

lated as *The Family in Renaissance Florence*, trans. Renée Neu Watkins (Columbia, SC: University of South Carolina Press, 1969). On the commodification of women in Alberti's domestic politics, see Carla Freccero, "Economy, Woman, and Renaissance Discourse," in *Refiguring Woman: Perspectives on Gender and the Italian Renaissance*, ed. Marilyn Migiel and Juliana Schiesari (Ithaca: Cornell University Press, 1991), pp. 192–208.

7 On the history of the *querelle*, see Joan Kelly, "Early Feminist Theory and the *Querelle des femmes*," in Kelly, *Women, History, and Theory*, pp. 65–109; Constance Jordan, *Renaissance Feminism: Literary Texts and Political Models* (Ithaca: Cornell University Press, 1990), especially pp. 2, 86, 94, 100–1, 104–5, 191; Juliana Schiesari, "In Praise of Virtuous Women? For a Genealogy of Gender Morals in Renaissance Italy," in *Annali d'Italianistica* 7 (1989), pp. 66–87; also see the Introduction to *Rewriting the Renaissance: The Discourses of Sexual Difference in Early Modern Europe*, ed. Margaret W. Ferguson, Maureen Quilligan, and Nancy J. Vickers (Chicago: University of Chicago Press, 1986).

8 Leon-Battista Alberti, *Il Cavallo Vivo*, ed. Antonio Videtta (Naples: Stampa et Ars, 1981), p. 199.

9 Fernand Méry, *The Life, History, and Magic of the Dog* (New York: Grosset & Dunlap, 1970), pp. 45–63.

10 On the relation between femininity and animals, see especially Barbara Spackman, "*inter musam et ursam moritur*: Folengo and the Gaping 'Other' Mouth," in *Refiguring Woman: Perspectives on Gender and the Italian Renaissance* (Ithaca: Cornell University Press, 1991), pp. 19–34; and Marilyn Migiel, "The Dignity of Man," in *Refiguring Woman*, pp. 211–32.

11 Francesco Petrarca, "How a Ruler Ought to Govern His State," in *The Earthly Republic*, pp. 52–3 and 77–8.

12 Giovan Battista Della Porta, *Della fisionomia dell'uomo*, ed. Mario Cicognani (Parma: Ugo Guanda, 1988). See also Charles Le Brun, *La Physionomie humaine comparée à la physiognomie des animaux* (Paris: 1665). On the history of physiognomy, see Jean-Jacques Courtine and Claudine Haroche, *Histoire du visage: exprimer et taire ses émotions XVIe-au débout XIXe siècle* (Paris: Rivages, 1988). On the relation between Della Porta and Renaissance scientific literature see Paula Findlen, "Jokes of Nature and Jokes of Knowledge: The Playfulness of Scientific Discourse in Early Modern Europe," in *Renaissance Quarterly* 43: 2 (1990), pp. 292–331.

13 Renaissance physiognomy drew, of course, on the extensive medieval concern with the interpretation of visual features, from the superstititious fear that a pregnant woman who saw a wolf would give birth to a wolflike child to the abstract relation of beauty with honor and ugliness with evil. And in the aristocratic ideologies that reached full flower in the late Middle Ages and early Renaissance, the relation between noble birth and a given physical and moral disposition solidified in the assimilation of racial superiority to the specificity of a bloodline. See on this question, Arlette Jouanna, *Ordre Social: mythes et hiérarchies dans la France du XVIe siècle* (Paris: Hachette, 1977).

14 I wish to thank Ann Jones for pointing this interesting reversal out to me.

15 Ian Maclean, *The Renaissance Notion of Woman: A Study in the Fortunes of Scholasticism and Medical Science in European Intellectual Life* (Cambridge: Cambridge University Press, 1980).

16 See Manfred P. Fleischer, "'Are Women Human?' The Debate of 1595 Between Valens Acidalius and Simon Gediccus," *The Sixteenth Century Journal* 12: 2 (1981), pp. 107–20.

17 James S. Serpell, *In the Company of Animals* (London: Basil Blackwell, 1986),

pp. 122–3. See also C. W. Hume, *The Status of Animals in the Christian Religion* (Potter's Bar: Universities Federation for Animal Welfare, 1957), pp. 89–99.

18 See Tom Conley, "Montaigne and the Indies," *Hispanic Issues* 4 (1989), pp. 225–6. For a more detailed discussion of the debates, see Lewis Hanke, *All Mankind is One: A Study of the Disputation Between Bartolomé de las Casas and Juan Ginés de Sepúlveda in 1550 on the Intellectual and Religious Capacity of the American Indians* (DeKalb: Northern Illinois University Press, 1974).

19 René Descartes, *Discourse on Method*, in *Descartes's Philosophical Writings*, ed. Elizabeth Anscombe and Peter Thomas Geach (Indianapolis: Bobbs-Merrill, 1971), p. 41.

20 Descartes, *Meditations*, in *Descartes's Philosophical Writings*, p. 73.

21 Descartes, *Les Passions de l'âme*, in *Oeuvres philosophiques*, ed. Ferdinand Alquié (Paris: Garnier, 1963).

22 Marie de Rabutin-Chantal, Madame de Sévigné, *Correspondance*, ed. Roger Duchêne (Paris: Gallimard, 1972), 1: 337 and 464.

23 See Jean de La Fontaine, "Discours à Madame de La Sablière," in *Fables choisies mises en vers*, ed. Georges Couton (Paris: Garnier, 1962), pp. 266–70 and Couton's commentary, pp. 508–17; and François Bernier, *Abrégé de la philosophie de Gassendi* (Paris: 1674–82). On Madame de La Sablière and her salon, see Samuel, Vicomte Menjot d'Elbenne, *Mme de La Sablière* (Paris: Plon-Nourrit 1923), especially pp. 65–83.

24 Menjot d'Elbenne, p. 85. By "La Fontaine," Madame de La Sablière is referring to the person of the poet.

25 Menjot d'Elbenne, p. 241.

4 CANNIBALISM, HOMOPHOBIA, WOMEN
Montaigne's "Des cannibales" and "De l'amitié"
Carla Freccero

1 Louise Fradenburg, "Criticism, Anti-Semitism, and the Prioress's Tale," *Exemplaria* 1:1 (Spring 1989): 69–115, at 87, 76. I would like to thank Molly Whalen for her assistance in preparing this essay.

2 *Colonial Encounters: Europe and the Native Caribbean, 1492–1797* (London and New York: Methuen, 1986), 85.

3 Cited in Hulme, 17; from Christopher Columbus, *The Journal of Christopher Columbus*, trans. Cecil Jane, rev. and annotated by L. A. Vigneras (London: Hakluyt Society, Extra Series 38, 1960). See also B. W. Ife, ed. and trans., *Journal of the First Voyage* (Warminster: Aris & Philips, Ltd, 1990); Mauricio Obregòn, ed., Lucia Graves, trans., *The Columbus Papers: The Barcelona Letter of 1493, the Landfall Controversy, and the Indian Guides* (New York: Macmillan, 1991); Oliver Dunn and James Kelley, Jr, ed. and trans., *The Diario of Christopher Columbus' First Voyage to America 1492–1493* (Norman: University of Oklahoma Press, 1989); Samuel Eliot Morison, trans. and ed., *Journals and Other Documents on the Life and Voyages of Christopher Columbus* (New York: The Heritage Press, 1963).

4 See *Webster's Unabridged Third New International Dictionary of the English Language* and *Le Petit Robert 1: Dictionnaire de la langue française*; Hulme discusses the *OED* definitions in *Colonial Encounters*, 15–16.

5 See, for example, Gérard Defaux, "Un cannibale en haut de chausses: Montaigne, la différence et la logique de l'identité," *MLN*: French Issue 97: 4 (May 1982): 918–57; Edwin Duval, "Lessons of the New World: Design and Meaning in Montaigne's 'Des cannibales' (I: 31) and 'Des coches' (III: 6)," *Yale French Studies* 64, Special Issue: *Montaigne: Essays in Reading*, ed. Gérard

NOTES

Defaux (1983): 95–112; David Quint, "A Reconsideration of Montaigne's 'Des cannibales'," *Modern Language Quarterly* 51: 4 (December 1990): 459–89; Stephen Greenblatt, *Marvelous Possessions: The Wonder of the New World* (Chicago: University of Chicago Press, 1991); Michel de Certeau, *Heterologies: Discourse on the Other* (Minneapolis: University of Minnesota Press, 1986). It is worth mentioning that Montaigne's essay, as an early work of comparative anthropology, is extraordinarily progressive in its views. My argument is not designed to minimize this aspect of Montaigne's thought, but to discern a (psycho)analytics inhabiting his text.

6 "1580: Montaigne's 'Des cannibales': Cultural Anthropology and the Concept of the Other" (unpublished manuscript).

7 Donald Frame, ed. and trans., *The Complete Essays of Montaigne* (Stanford: Stanford University Press, 1957, repr. 1965), 262. All citations in English are taken from this edition. Michel de Montaigne, *Essais: Livre I*, ed. Alexandre Micha (Paris: Garnier-Flammarion, 1969), 158; page references to the French will follow the English throughout. As David Quint notes ("A Reconsideration"), the culture that the "cannibals" become signs of is indeed a warrior culture. Quint argues that Montaigne is conducting a sustained critique of warrior culture and compares the discussion in "Des cannibales" to Montaigne's portrait of gladiatorial Rome, as a culture where "honor" produces a Girardian "crisis of likeness" that ends in self-consumption and destruction. He relates this critique to Montaigne's concern about the destruction of the nation during the French (civil) wars of religion. Michel de Certeau, on the other hand, argues that Montaigne is nostalgically invoking a feudal culture of honor that is disappearing in contemporary France; see *Heterologies*, esp. 77.

8 On the question of European perceptions of the literacy of New World people, see Stephen Greenblatt, *Marvelous Possessions*, 9–12. These pages include a critique of Tzvetan Todorov's assertion that the technology of writing was indeed what constituted the Europeans as superior. See *The Conquest of America: The Question of the Other*, trans. Richard Howard (New York: Harper & Row, 1984).

9 "Montaigne's Readings for 'Des cannibales'," in George B. Daniel, Jr, ed., *Renaissance and Other Studies in Honor of William Leon Wiley* (Chapel Hill: University of North Carolina Press, 1968): 261–79. Léry, a Protestant, links the cannibalistic practices he observes to the religious practices of Roman Catholics in France. For a detailed discussion of the metaphoric continuum between Catholic religious practices and cannibalism, see Maggie Kilgour, *From Communion to Cannibalism: An Anatomy of Metaphors of Incorporation* (Princeton: Princeton University Press, 1990).

10 "'Eating Well,' or the Calculation of the Subject: An Interview with Jacques Derrida," in Eduardo Cadava, Peter Connor, and Jean-Luc Nancy, eds, *Who Comes after the Subject?* (New York and London: Routledge, 1991), 96–119, at 114.

11 For a beautiful and subtly ironic demystification of women's relation to polygamy, from a late twentieth-century point of view, see Mariama Bâ, *So Long a Letter*, trans. Modupé Bodé-Thomas (Oxford: Heinemann International, 1981, repr. 1989).

12 The only gender marker in the poem is "m'amie." Might Montaigne have heard this wrong? What language is being transcribed? Did an interpreter who knew French report these songs to Montaigne? Might that interpreter have said "mon ami?" These are some of the imaginary questions informing my argument about the love song.

13 "Shakespeare and the Cannibals," in Marjorie Garber, ed., *Cannibals, Witches, and Divorce: Estranging the Renaissance* (Baltimore: Johns Hopkins University Press, 1987), 40–66, at 41.

14 See Harry Levin, *The Myth of the Golden Age in the Renaissance* (London: Faber & Faber, 1970); Defaux mentions this aspect of "Des cannibales" in "Un cannibale en haut de chausses," 952. See also my discussion of utopia in relation to Rabelais's Abbaye de Thélème in *Father Figures: Genealogy and Narrative Structure in Rabelais* (Ithaca: Cornell University Press, 1991).

15 *Father Figures*, 90–133; see also "Politics and Aesthetics in Castiglione's *Il Cortegiano*: Book III and the Discourse on Women," in David Quint, ed., *Creative Imitation* (Binghamton: Medieval & Renaissance Texts & Studies, 1992): 251–71.

16 On the text as body, see Lawrence Kritzman, *The Rhetoric of Sexuality and the Literature of the French Renaissance* (Cambridge: Cambridge University Press, 1991), esp. 133–48; for the idealization of melancholia in the Renaissance as the cultural construct of masculine genius, see Juliana Schiesari, *The Gendering of Melancholia: Feminism, Psychoanalysis, and the Symbolics of Loss in Renaissance Literature* (Ithaca: Cornell University Press, 1992).

17 Sigmund Freud, "Mourning and Melancholia" (1917), trans. Joan Riviere, in Philip Rieff, ed., *General Psychological Theory: Papers on Metapsychology* (New York: Macmillan, 1963), 164–79, at 171.

18 Derrida says this at the end of a discussion about how an ethical relation to the other would be formulated; this is where the question, not of eating, but of eating well, comes up:

> If the limit between the living and the nonliving now seems to be as unsure, at least as an oppositional limit, as that between "man" and "animal," and if, in the (symbolic or real) experience of the "eat–speak–interiorize," the ethical frontier no longer rigorously passes between the "Thou shalt not kill" (man, thy neighbour) and the "Thou shalt not put to death the living in general," but rather between several infinitely different modes of the conception–appropriation–assimilation of the other, then, as concerns the "Good" (Bien) of every morality, the question will come back to determining the best, most respectful, most grateful, and also most giving way of relating to the other and of relating the other to the self. For everything that happens at the edge of the orifices (of orality, but also of the ear, the eye – and all the senses in general) the metonymy of "eating well" (bien manger) would always be the rule. The question is no longer one of knowing if it is "good" to eat the other or if the other is "good" to eat, nor of knowing which other. One eats him regardless and lets oneself be eaten by him.
>
> ("'Eating Well'," 114)

Metaphors of incorporation are standard *topoi* of such a discussion; Derrida's argument concerns precisely the philosophical genealogy of such a commonplace. I am not therefore suggesting that Montaigne's metaphors are novel, nor that there is a "proper" connection between the eating of friendship and the eating of cannibalism. I am arguing that the two are metaphorically related within the sacrificial structure, and thus the discourse of subjectivity Derrida describes.

19 Montaigne does not stop there; he continues, in a 1580 addition, to press the point with a rhetorical "and besides" that brings a certain insistence into the argument (see 138; 234). There is a tendency to misunderstand "homopho-

bia" because of its current use as a term of disapproval; I use it here in a more technical and descriptive, rather than evaluative, sense. In another passage, Montaigne describes two kinds of love ("affection [envers les femmes]" and "amitié") which, although presumably applicable to two difference kinds of objects (a woman and a man), seem rather to be two kinds of love experienced by the two subjects (Montaigne and Etienne) for the same kind of object (each other):

> During the reign of this perfect friendship those fleeting affections once found a place in me, not to speak of my friend, who confesses only too many of them in these verses. Thus these two passions within me came to be known to each other, but to be compared, never; the first keeping its course in proud and lofty flight, and disdainfully watching the other making its way far, far beneath it.

(137; 234)

20 *The Journal of Philosophy* 85: 11 (November 1988), 632–44, at 642. Derrida seems to ignore, or reclassicize, Montaigne's discourse here. Indeed it is the homophobic reaction to Greek love that makes of this a peculiarly "modern" text, that constitutes a rupture, along with the opening up of the eventual possibility of friendship between a man and a woman. It is interesting to note, in passing, that Derrida's essays, first on friendship, then on eating, sequentially twin Montaigne's "De l'amitié" and "Des cannibales."

21 Eve Kosofsky Sedgwick, *Between Men: English Literature and Male Homosocial Desire* (New York: Columbia University Press, 1985); Luce Irigaray, *This Sex Which Is Not One*, trans. Catherine Porter with Carolyn Burke (Ithaca: Cornell University Press, 1985), 193. Of the masculine economy of the same, Irigaray has this to say:

> Reigning everywhere, although prohibited in practice, hom(m)o-sexuality is played out through the bodies of women, matter, or sign, and heterosexuality has been up to now just an alibi for the smooth workings of man's relations with himself, of relations among men. Whose "sociocultural endogamy" excludes the participation of that other, so foreign to the social order: woman.

(172)

22 Derrida points out that there is "a friendship prior to friendships, an ineffaceable, fundamental, and bottomless friendship, the one that draws its breath in the sharing of a language (past or to come) and in the being-together that any allocution supposes, including a declaration of war" ("The Politics of Friendship," 636). See also on this subject Louise Fradenburg, "'Oure owen wo to drynke': Loss, Gender and Chivalry in *Troilus and Criseyde*," in R. A. Shoaf, ed., *"Troilus and Criseyde": Essays in Criticism: 'Subgit to alle poesye'* (Binghamton, N. Y.: MRTS, 1992), pp. 88–106, where she discusses the heroization of suffering "for" in the construction of the masculine chivalric subject.

23 When Defaux says that Montaigne is himself a cannibal and that cannibalism is "le geste culturel par excellence" ("Un cannibale," 954), he blurs the distinction between literal and symbolic upon which the construction of the sacrificial subject rests and thus does not recognize that the cannibal is the other of the same but a repudiated, disavowed, abjected other, and thus that the "subject" Montaigne is here split. Montaigne does not, after all, assert that he has cannibalized Etienne de La Boétie.

24 My discussion here, including the use of "rhetorical" questions, is indebted to

Judith Butler, *Gender Trouble: Feminism and the Subversion of Identity* (New York and London: Routledge, 1990), and to the Mrs William Beckman Lectures she delivered at UC Berkeley, February 6 and 13, 1992: "The Lesbian Phallus and the Morphological Imaginary" and "Phantasmatic Identification and the Question of Sex." I use the term "belatedly" not in its literal chronological sense, as there is no indication that Montaigne added the love song to his essay later, but rather in the sense of psychic belatedness. According to Pierre Villey, Montaigne composed "De l'amitié" in part before 1576, in part after that date. "Des cannibales," Villey argues, was for the most part composed around 1578. See Pierre Villey, ed., *Les Essais de Michel de Montaigne*, vol. 1, re-edited by V.-L. Saulnier (Paris: PUF, 1924, rev. 1978).

25 Carol J. Adams, *The Sexual Politics of Meat: A Feminist Vegetarian Critical Theory* (New York: Continuum Publishing Co., 1990). Derrida insists, however, that "Vegetarians, too, partake of animals, even of men. They practice a different mode of denegation" ("'Eating Well,'" 114–15).

26 "'Oure owen wo to drynke,'" 89; Schiesari, *The Gendering of Melancholia*.

5 FANTASIES OF "RACE" AND "GENDER"
Africa, *Othello*, and bringing to light
Patricia Parker

1 See Janis L. Pallister, trans., *On Monsters and Marvels* (Chicago: University of Chicago Press, 1982), pp. 188–9, and the text removed to Paré's *De l'anatomie de tout le corps humain* (1585), in Ambroise Paré, *Oeuvres complètes*, ed. J. F. Malgaigne (Paris: J. B. Baillière, 1840; Geneva: Slatkine, 1970), I: 168–9.

2 See Jean Céard, ed., *Des monstres et prodiges* (Geneva: Librairie Droz, 1971), pp. 26–7, on the reference to Africanus added to *Les Oeuvres de M. Ambroise Paré* (Paris, 1575), and Thomas W. Laqueur, "Amor Veneris, vel Dulcedo Appeletur," *Fragments for a History of the Human Body*, ed. Michel Feher *et al.*, Part 3 (New York: Zone, 1989), pp. 116–17, who cites the anecdote in the context of a different argument. On Africanus (baptized Giovanni Leone or "Leo" by Pope Leo X), see among others Eldred Jones, *Othello's Countrymen* (London: Oxford University Press, 1965), pp. 21–25, 27; and Christopher Miller, *Blank Darkness: Africanist Discourse in French* (Chicago: University of Chicago Press, 1985), esp. pp. 12–13.

3 On the titilating appeal of this "monster" literature, see Katharine Park and Lorraine J. Daston, "Unnatural Conceptions: The Study of Monsters in Sixteenth-Century France and England," *Past and Present* 92 (August 1981), 20–54. On European hunger for travel narratives, see Jones, *Countrymen*, ch. 1, and Winthrop D. Jordan, *White over Black* (Chapel Hill: University of North Carolina Press, 1968), pp. 1–63.

4 John Pory, trans., *A Geographical Historie of Africa* (London, 1600; rpt. Amsterdam: Da Capo Press, 1969), Book III, p. 122. The story of the "abominable vice" of the "Fricatrices" appears on pp. 148–9 here.

5 See Céard, ed., *Des monstres et prodiges*, p. 163.

6 See Marie Bonaparte, *Female Sexuality* (New York: International University Press, 1953), p. 203, with Laqueur, "Amor veneris," p. 121.

7 See Book 3, ch. xxxiv, "Of the Wombe," in *The Workes of that Famous Chirurgion Ambrose Parey*, trans. Thomas Johnson (London, 1634, p. 130): "*Cleitoris*, whence proceeds that infamous word *Cleitorizein*, (which signifies impudently to handle that part). But because it is an obscene part, let those which desire to know more of it, reade the Authors which I cited."

8 *Microcosmographia*, Book 4, ch. 16, "Of the Lap or Privities," p. 238.

9 On this Columbus, author of the *De re anatomica* (Venice, 1559), see Laqueur, *Making Sex* (Cambridge, Mass.: Harvard University Press, 1990), p. 64.

10 See *Microcosmographia*, Book 4, ch. xiii, p. 220; and, *inter alia*, John Minsheu's *Ductor in linguas* (London, 1617), "to Lappe, or fould up."

11 See Crooke (p. 239) on the female "privitie" as "too obscoene to look upon"; John Banister's *Historie of Man* (London, 1578), ch. 6, as to "Why the partes of women are here not spoken of"; and on Crooke's frontispiece, modestly shielding these female parts from view, Karen Newman, *Fashioning Femininity and English Renaissance Drama* (Chicago and London: University of Chicago Press, 1991), p. 3.

12 See *The History of Travayle*, trans. Richard Eden, augmented by Richard Willes (London, 1577), p. 6, a passage which depends on the figure of the "Eye" of God; and P. Ashton's translation of Joannes Boemus's *Omnium gentium mores* (1520), as *The Manners, Lawes and Customes of all Nations* (London, 1611), p. 470, on "God . . . to whom nothing is hidden." The phrase "ocularly recognizing" is applied to Marc Lescarbot's *Histoire de la Nouvelle France* (1609) in Alphonse Dupront, "Espace et humanisme," *Bibliothèque d'Humanisme et Renaissance* 8 (1946), 7–104.

13 See Luke Wilson, "William Harvey's *Prelectiones*: The Performance of the Body in the Renaissance Theater of Anatomy," *Representations* 17 (Winter 1987), 69–95, with *The Anatomical Lectures of William Harvey*, trans. G. Whitteridge (Edinburgh, 1966), 4[1v]. On science and the feminization of nature, see *inter alia* Evelyn Fox Keller, *Gender and Science* (New Haven: Yale University Press, 1985), pp. 33–65 and Carolyn Merchant, *The Death of Nature* (San Francisco: HarperCollins, 1980), and on Baconian science and New World "discovery," my *Literary Fat Ladies* (London: Methuen, 1987), p. 142. The quotation from Bacon is from *The New Organon and Related Writings*, ed. Fulton H. Anderson (Indianapolis: Bobbs–Merrill, 1960), pp. 13, 91, 89.

14 On "prodigies" and monsters linked with Africa (as in Massinger's "prodigy / Which Afric never equalled" and "Some monster, though in a more ugly form / Than Nile or Afric ever bred"), see Jones, *Countrymen*, pp. 126–7; Anthony Barthelemy, *Black Face, Maligned Race: The Representation of Blacks in English Drama from Shakespeare to Southerne* (Baton Rouge: Lousiana State University Press, 1987); and Newman, *Femininity*, ch. 5.

15 See pp. 57–8 of Pory's prefatory addition to Africanus's text.

16 "The Authors Preface to the Reader," *The Manners, Lawes and Customes of all Nations*.

17 *The Original Writings and Correspondence of the Two Richard Hakluyts*, ed. E. G. R. Taylor, Hakluyt Society, 2nd series, nos. 76–7 (London, 1935), vol. II, p. 333.

18 See Alison Plowden, *Danger to Elizabeth* (New York: Stein & Day, 1973), p. 226; and *The Elizabethan Secret Service* (New York: St Martin's Press, 1991), with R. A. Haldane, *The Hidden World* (New York: St Martin's Press, 1976), pp. 59–65, and Lowell Gallagher's *Medusa's Gaze: Casuistry and Conscience in the Renaissance* (Stanford: Stanford University Press, 1991).

19 See G. R. Elton, *Policy and Police* (Cambridge: Cambridge University Press, 1972), p. 329, on "delations and informations" in judicial "discovery," with my "'Dilation' and 'Delation' in *Othello*," in Patricia Parker and Geoffrey Hartman, eds, *Shakespeare and the Question of Theory* (London: Methuen, 1985), pp. 54–74, and "*Othello* and *Hamlet*: Dilation, Spying, and the 'Secret Place' of Woman," *Representations*, 44 (Fall 1993).

20 See, respectively, "Father Richard Holtby on Persecution in the North" (1593), in John Morris, ed., *The Troubles of Our Catholic Forefathers* (London:

Burns & Oates, 1877), vol. 3, p. 121; and Neville Williams, *Elizabeth I, Queen of England* (London: Sphere Books Ltd, 1971), p. 261.

21 Pory, trans., *Geographical Historie*, p. 58 of the prefatory material to Africanus's *Description*.

22 See, respectively, George Alsop, *A Character of the Province of Mary-Land* (London, 1666 edn), with *Literary Fat Ladies*, pp. 144–6; on the problem of testimony and evidence generally, Barbara J. Shapiro, *Probability and Certainty in Seventeenth-Century England* (Princeton: Princeton University Press, 1983); and on the Greek *arg* ("luster," as in "illustration") in *enargeia* and the Latin *vid-* as the root of "seeing" in *evidentia*, Terence Cave, *The Cornucopian Text* (Oxford: Clarendon Press, 1979), pp. 27–32, with *Literary Fat Ladies*, pp. 138–40.

23 On the Iberian resonances of Iago's name in relation to the "Portugals" named in Africanus as "the destroyers of Africa and her peoples," see Newman, *Femininity*, p. 164 n.31.

24 See Ashton's "To the Friendly Reader," in *The Manners, Lawes, and Customes of all Nations*.

25 See Pory's "To the Reader," and its defensive assurances that St Augustine and Tertullian were also "writers of Africa," with Emily C. Bartels, "Making More of the Moor: Aaron, Othello, and Renaissance Refashionings of Race," *Shakespeare Quarterly* 41, no. 4 (Winter 1990), 433–54, esp. pp. 437–38.

26 See Stephen Greenblatt, *Renaissance Self-Fashioning* (Chicago: University of Chicago Press, 1980), p. 237; Jones, *Countrymen*, pp. 21ff.; and Rosalind Johnson, "African Presence in Shakespearean Drama: Parallels between Othello and the Historical Leo Africanus," *Journal of African Civilization* 7 (1985), 276–87, with the critique of her emphases in Bartels, "Making More of the Moor," pp. 435–8.

27 On Desdemona's hunger for Othello's narrative, see Ruth Cowhig, "Blacks in English Renaissance Drama and the Role of Shakespeare's *Othello*," in David Dabydeen, ed., *The Black Presence in English Literature* (Manchester: Manchester University Press, 1985), pp. 1–25, esp. p. 8, with the addition that for her it would provide escape from a "claustrophobic patriarchal confine" in Ania Loomba's landmark discussion in *Gender, Race, Renaissance Drama* (Manchester: Manchester University Press, 1989), p. 55.

28 See, respectively, Erasmus, *De copia* Book II, in *The Collected Works*, ed. C. R. Thompson (Toronto: University of Toronto Press, 1978), vol. 24, p. 572; Henry Peacham, *The Garden of Eloquence* (1593), ed. William G. Crane (Gainesville: Scholars' Facsimiles & Reprints, 1954), pp. 123–4. Italics mine. Crooke not only displays the female "lap" or privity "dilated or laide open" to the eye but marks this "close" or secret place – "like the letter, o, small and wondrous narrow" – as capable of being "more open" or more contracted "according to a woman's appetite"; Columbus in the *De re anatomica* (p. 445) describes this female "opening" as "dilated with extreme pleasure in intercourse"; Crooke observes that in the sexual "opening" of virgins "the Membranes are dilated." But the possibility that a virgin could be sexually "opened" in this sense also introduced the possibility of a female sexuality out of control – that, as Othello puts it, "we can call these delicate creatures ours, / And not their *appetites*" (III.iii.269–70).

29 See Erik S. Ryding, "Scanning This Thing Further: Iago's Ambiguous Advice," *Shakespeare Quarterly* 40, no. 2 (Summer 1989), 195; on "occupy," *Literary Fat Ladies*, p. 132, with Marlowe's *The Massacre at Paris* ("whereas he is your landlord, you will take upon you to be his, and till the ground which he himself should oppupy"), and Peter Stallybrass, "Patriarchal Territories: The

Body Enclosed," in Margaret W. Ferguson *et al.*, eds, *Rewriting the Renaissance* (Chicago: University of Chicago Press, 1986), p. 128. On place-holding see Michael Neill, "Changing Places in *Othello*," *Shakespeare Survey* 37 (1984), 115–31, esp. p. 119; and Julia Genster, "Lieutenancy, Standing In, and *Othello*," *ELH* 57 (1990), 785–809.

30 See Michael Neill, "Unproper Beds: Race, Adultery, and the Hideous in *Othello*," *Shakespeare Quarterly* (Winter 1989), p. 394; Newman, *Femininity*, pp. 91–2. "Show," as in *Hamlet* (III.ii.139–46), or the pun on the "shoe with the hole in it" in *Two Gentlemen of Verona* (II.iii.14–18) resonates with overtones of female sexuality; see *Literary Fat Ladies*, p. 129. On the "act of shame," see Edward Snow's "Sexual Anxiety and the Male Order of Things in *Othello*," *English Literary Renaissance* 10 (1980), 384–412.

31 On this play in relation to the rise of pornography in the period, see Lynda E. Boose, "'Let it be hid': Renaissance Pornography, Iago, and Audience Response," in *Autour d'Othello*. Proceedings of conference sponsored by the University of Amiens and the University of Paris VII (Paris: Presses de l'UFR Clerc Université Picardie, 1987), 138–46.

32 "Othello's Handkerchief: 'The Recognizance and Pledge of Love'," *English Literary Renaissance* 5 (1975), 360–74.

33 See Book 24, ch. xlii of Johnson's English translation of Paré.

34 See Newman, *Femininity*, pp. 151–3; Stallybrass, "Patiarchal Territories," pp. 135ff.; and Bartels, "Making More of the Moor," pp. 450–1. Ania Loomba's revisionary account is particularly acute here. See n. 42, below.

35 For the complex of "Barber/Barbary" linked to a "common" female sexuality see *All's Well* II.ii.17 and Richard Burton's *Anatomy of Melancholy* III.iv.1.iii (1651 edn), p. 665; with *Antony and Cleopatra* II.ii.224 ("Our courteous Anthony . . . Being *barber'd* ten times o'er"), lines which link a "barbarous" nation, a "common" woman (though a queen), and implications of effeminacy.

36 See Ann Rosalind Jones, "Italians and Others: Venice and the Irish in *Coryat's Crudities* and *The White Devil*," *Renaissance Drama* (1987), NS 18 (Evanston: Northwestern University Press, 1988), pp. 101–19, esp. pp. 101–10 on Venice; on Cyprus, Neill, "Changing Places," p. 115, with Emrys Jones, "'Othello,' 'Lepanto' and the Cyprus Wars," *Shakespeare Survey* 21 (Cambridge, 1968), 47–52; S. Gosson, *A Shorte Apologie of the Schoole of Abuse* (London: Thomas Dawson, 1579), p. 83; on "Moor/More," Helge Kökeritz, *Shakespeare's Pronunciation* (New Haven: Yale University Press, 1953), p. 130. On the perceived excess of "Mores" in England as well as the image of the "lascivious Moor," see Jones, *Countrymen*, pp. 8, 12, with Ania Loomba, *Gender, Race, Renaissance Drama*, p. 43, who stresses the economic motive of controling or reducing their "populous" numbers in challenging G. K. Hunter's argument that Elizabethans had "no continuous contact" with black people and "no sense of economic threat from them," in his *Dramatic Identities and Cultural Tradition* (Liverpool: Liverpool University Press, 1978), p. 32.

37 See the text from Jean Bodin included in the frontal material to the Pory trans., p. 60.

38 See John M. Major, "Desdemona and Dido," *Shakespeare Quarterly* 10 (1954), 123–5; and *The "Aeneid" of Thomas Phaer and Thomas Twyne* (1573), ed. Steven Lally (New York: Garland Publishing, 1987), p. 82, which describes Dido as the Moorish Queen of "Moores, that have of dooble toong the name" (p. 24) and Carthaginians both as "Moors" and, in the Preface, "white Moors in Affrike" (p. 5). The overriding distinction throughout remains "Trojan/ Roman" as opposed to "Moor" and "Affrike." Sidonian-Carthaginian Dido is

318

clearly identified with the "Affrika" (p. 72) Aeneas is commanded to "for-sake" in Book IV; and Carthage is part of "Barbarie" as described at the opening of "Iohn Leo his First Booke" (Pory trans., p. 2). On the "Moor/white Moor" distinction in commentary on *Othello*, see especially Loomba, *Gender, Race, Renaissance Drama*, ch. 2, who also provides a critical overview of criticism linking "gender" and "race" in the play; on Carthago, Elizabeth, and Dido, see Stephen Orgel, "Shakespeare and the Cannibals," in Marjorie Garber, ed., *Cannibals, Witches, and Divorce: Estranging the Renaissance* (Baltimore: John Hopkins University Press, 1987), pp. 58–66. For the proclamation citing "the great number of Negroes and blackamours," *ca.* January 1601 (43 Elizabeth I), four years before the performance of *Othello* at the court of her successor, see Eldred Jones, *Countrymen*, plate 5, and Loomba, *Gender, Race, Renaissance Drama*, p. 43. According to *Thomas Clarkson's History of the Rise, Progress, and Accomplishment of the Abolition of the African Slave Trade* (1816), p. 30, Sir John Hawkins imported the first slaves into England from Africa in 1562. Contact with Africa, in other words, preceded the period of major English contact with the "New World." On Dido's effeminating effect, see William Caxton, trans., *Eneydos* (1490), sig. E$_4$ ("effemynate, wythout honour, rauysshed in to dileectacion femynyne"); Henry Howard, Earl of Surrey, trans., *Certain Bokes of Virgiles Aenaeis* (London, 1557), sig. E$_4$ ("wife-bound"). Phaer (sig. I$_3$v) translates Virgil's "uxorious" with "doting . . . / To pleas thy lusty spouse," and describes the effeminated Aeneas as made Moor-like through the "roabe of Moorishe purple" hanging from his shoulders in "Morisco gise," a "web" wrought by this Moorish queen. See also, on Dido and Cleopatra (linked with Africanus), Janet Adelman, *The Common Liar* (New Haven and London: Yale University Press, 1973), esp. pp. 71ff.; on Dido and Aeneas echoes surrounding Tamora and Aaron the Moor in *Titus Andronicus*, Bartels, "Making More of the Moor," p. 445; on the "monstrous" rule of women, John Knox, *The First Blast of the Trumpet Against the Monstruous regiment of women* (Geneva: J. Poullain, 1558); for one self-styled Aeneas sailing upon England as the realm of a new Dido, Gallagher, *Medusa's Gaze*, p. 79; on the complexities of English/Spanish as well as Roman/Carthaginian relations in respect of the racial and gender stereotypes activated by Marlowe's Dido, see Margo Hendricks, "Managing the Barbarian: *The Tragedie of Dido Queene of Carthage*" (*Renaissance Drama* forthcoming). The "liberal" reception of a stranger that opens this queen of "Barbarie" to the *double entendres* surrounding "widow Dido" in *The Tempest* (II.i.77–82) makes her an even more ambiguous parallel for the Venetian daughter who welcomes another "extravagant . . . stranger" and then appears to become a uxorious "general's general."

39 I stress the importance of asymmetry and of misplacement/displacement within this apparent chiasmus for the reasons that Loomba's reading of these crossings and splits elicits (p. 54) in applying to *Othello* Homi Bhabha's gloss on Frantz Fanon's split subject, in his Introduction to *Black Skin, White Masks*, trans. Charles Lam Markmann (London and Sydney: Pluto Press, 1986), p. xvi: "black skins, white masks is not . . . a neat division; it is a doubling, dissembling image of being in at least two places at once which makes it impossible for the devalued . . . to accept the colonizer's invitation to identity." As Loomba points out, it is not simply that "Othello's colour and gender make him occupy contradictory positions in relation to power" (p. 41) but that his shift to the position of Venetian husband also involves his increasing racial isolation and differentiation (pp. 48, 50, 54, 60). Desdemona, con-demned as "black" when sexuality is figured by color, both appears to occupy

the place of a woman of "Barbary" and yet retains the position of white insider that Iago can use to unsettle the confidence of the Moor. It is crucial to recognize the coexistence in *Othello* of separate narratives which cannot be conflated or symmetrically analogized and of different kinds of oppression, objectification, and projection.

40 See *The Merchant of Venice* V.i.9–12 ("In such a night / Stood Dido with a willow in her hand / Upon the wild sea-banks, and waft her love / To come again to Carthage"). Though there is no space to develop this here, it is crucial to note that the phrase "My mother had a maid call'd Barbary" (IV.iii.26) suggests not just an association with Desdemona but the class and racial overtones of a servant to a Venetian matron, either literally a woman of "Barbarie" or bearing a name evocative of it.

41 See Dympna Callaghan, pp. 163–77, and *The Tragedy of Mariam Fair Queene of Jewry* by Elizabeth Cary, Lady Falkland, with *The Lady Falkland: Her Life*, ed. Barry Weller and Margaret Ferguson (Berkeley and Los Angeles: University of California Press, 1993).

42 See Guido Ruggiero, *The Boundaries of Eros: Sex Crime and Sexuality in Renaissance Venice* (Oxford: Oxford University Press, 1988), ch. 6 ("Sodom and Venice"); and the entries for "Barber," "Buggery," "Servant, Serving-man," and "Turk," in Frankie Rubinstein, *A Dictionary of Shakespeare's Sexual Puns and Their Significance* (London: Macmillan, 1984). "Bugger" is of course a contraction of "Bulgarian." On "fallow/follow" see Herbert A. Ellis, *Shakespeare's Lusty Punning in Love's Labour's Lost* (The Hague: Mouton, 1973), pp. 132–5.

43 On Iago's penetration/insemination of Othello through the "ear," see, *inter alia*, John N. Wall, "Shakespeare's Aural Art: The Metaphor of the Ear in *Othello*," *Shakespeare Quarterly* 30, no. 3 (Summer 1979), 358–66, esp. p. 361.

44 The King James (1611) version of 1 Corinthians 6 speaks of "abusers of themselves with mankind." See, on "monster" in this sense, Alan Bray, *Homosexuality in Renaissance England* (London: Gay Men's Press, 1982), pp. 13ff., with his discussion (pp. 71–6) of the cultural othering of sodomitical practices, including the English case of Domingo Cassedon Drago (a "negar" accused of "buggery"); on transvestite theater, Laura Levine, "Men in Women's Clothing: Anti-theatricality and Effeminization from 1579 to 1642," *Criticism* 28, no. 2 (Spring 1986), 121–43, and Stephen Orgel, "Nobody's Perfect: Or Why Did the English Renaissance Stage Take Boys for Women?" in Ronald R. Butters *et al.*, eds, *Displacing Homophobia* (Durham, N.C.: Duke University Press, 1989), pp. 7–30; on the "open secret," Jonathan Goldberg's *Sodomitries: Renaissance Texts, Modern Sexualities* (Stanford: Stanford University Press, 1992), ch. 3; on the contradictions between denunciation of sodomy among unforgivable "crimes" (James I, *Basilicon Doron*) and the practices of figures as prominent as Francis Bacon and the King himself, see Bruce R. Smith, *Homosexual Desire in Shakespeare's England* (Chicago: University of Chicago Press, 1991), esp. pp. 14, 26, 176; on visibility in relation as well to sexual acts between women and on the differences between England and the continent, see Valerie Traub's important discussion in *Desire and Anxiety* (London: Routledge, 1992), esp. pp. 106–13.

45 For readings of *Othello* in relation to fears of invasion and "the enemy within," see Richard Marienstras, *New Perspectives on the Shakespearean World*, trans. Janet Lloyd (Cambridge: Cambridge University Press, 1985), chs 5 and 6, and Jonathan Dollimore, "The Cultural Politics of Perversion: Augustine, Shakespeare, Freud, Foucault," *Genders* 8 (July 1990), 1–16; on the "Turk" as uncomfortably close double of the European, see Timothy J. Hampton,

"Turkish Dogs: Rabelais, Erasmus, and the Rhetoric of Alterity," *Representations* 41 (Winter 1993), 58–62.

6 AN ENGLISH LASS AMID THE MOORS
Gender, race, sexuality, and national identity in
Heywood's *The Fair Maid of the West*
Jean E. Howard

I wish to thank Kim Hall and John Archer for rigorous and generous readings of this essay.

1 *Nationalisms and Sexualities*, ed. Andrew Parker, Mary Russo, Doris Sommer, and Patricia Yaeger (New York: Routledge, 1992), p. 2.
2 For the importance of recognizing the ways in which sexuality and gender are distinct if interrelated phenomena, see Gayle Rubin, "Thinking Sex: Notes for a Radical Theory of the Politics of Sexuality," in *Pleasure and Danger*, ed. Carole S. Vance (Boston: Routledge & Kegan Paul, 1984), pp. 267–319; Eve Sedgwick, *Epistemology of the Closet* (Berkeley: University of California Press, 1990), pp. 27–35; and Valerie Traub, *Desire and Anxiety: Circulations of Sexuality in Shakespearean Drama* (London: Routledge, 1992).
3 Perry Anderson, *Lineages of the Absolutist State* (1974; rpt. London: Verso, 1986), pp. 15–59 and 113–42.
4 Benedict Anderson, *Imagined Communities: Reflections on the Origin and Spread of Nationalism* (London: Verso, 1983), esp. pp. 25–8.
5 As Benedict Anderson emphasizes, pre-modern states quite unselfconsciously extended their sovereignty over heterogeneous peoples and "absorbed" them (ibid., p. 26). With the emergence of nationalism came an insistence on the particularity of peoples and their non-assimiliability. As Richard Helgerson has argued, this preoccupation with the nation as a bounded territory manifested itself in sixteenth- and seventeenth-century projects to map the land of England and in investigations of the topography and local histories of England's discrete regions. Paradoxically, regionalism thus could be part of the development of a nationalism focused more on the land of England than on the body of the monarch. See "The Land Speaks," ch. 3 of *Forms of Nationhood: The Elizabethan Writing of England* (Chicago: University of Chicago Press, 1992), pp. 105–47.
6 In *Middle-Class Culture in Elizabethan England* (1935; rpt. Ithaca: Cornell University Press, 1958), Louis B. Wright was one of the first to single out Heywood as "the greatest theatrical spokesman of the bourgeois ideals of his age" (p. 650), including a self-consciously nationalistic patriotism.
7 I agree with Martin Orkin that what he terms "color prejudice" existed in early modern England as well as opposition to the supposed barbarism of African people (*Shakespeare Against Apartheid* [Johannesburg: A. D. Donker Ltd, 1987], p. 60). Nineteenth-century notions of racial difference had obviously not been elaborated, and terms such as *Moor* had notoriously unstable meanings, indicating, variously, monstrousness or evil, a follower of Islam, an inhabitant of the New World, a black inhabitant of Africa, or a white or tawny inhabitant of Africa (Anthony Gerard Barthelemy, *Black Face, Maligned Race: The Representation of Blacks in English Drama from Shakespeare to Southerne* [Baton Rouge: Louisiana State University Press, 1987], pp. 1–17). Nonetheless, skin color served in many texts, including *The Fair Maid of the West*, as a defining marker of difference between peoples and a basis for denigration and exploitation. Rather than seeking out some other language

by which to talk about these phenomena, I speak in this paper of an emergent discourse of race in early modern England and attempt to map the complexities of one of its manifestations.

8 There is now a considerable literature about the gender and sexual implications of crossdressing on the Renaissance stage. I summarize much of that literature in my essay "Crossdressing, the Theatre, and Gender Struggle in Early Modern England," *Shakespeare Quarterly* 39 (1988), pp. 418–40.

9 For important discussions of Elizabeth's manipulations of her gender and sexuality to serve the ends of power see Winfried Schleiner's "*Divina Virago*: Queen Elizabeth as an Amazon," *Studies in Philology* 75 (1978), pp. 163–80; Louis Montrose, "'Shaping Fantasies': Figurations of Gender and Power in Elizabethan Culture," *Representations* 2 (1983), pp. 61–94; and Leah Marcus, "Shakespeare's Comic Heroines, Elizabeth I, and the Political Uses of Androgyny," in *Women in the Middle Ages and the Renaissance: Literary and Historical Perspectives*, ed. Mary Beth Rose (Syracuse: Syracuse University Press, 1986), pp. 135–53.

10 Helgerson, "The Land Speaks," pp. 105–47.

11 For a good discussion of the patriarchalism underlying early modern English monarchical theory see Marie Axton, *The Queen's Two Bodies: Drama and the Elizabethan Succession* (London: The Royal Historical Society, 1977), and Gordon Schocket, *Patriarchalism in Political Thought: The Authoritarian Family and Political Speculation and Attitudes, Especially in Seventeenth-Century England* (Oxford: Basil Blackwell, 1975).

12 For an interesting discussion of competing meanings of the family in sixteenth- and seventeenth-century England see Catherine Belsey, "Disrupting Sexual Difference: Meaning and Gender in the Comedies," in *Alternative Shakespeares*, ed. John Drakakis (London: Methuen, 1985), pp. 166–90.

13 It is interesting to note Bess's command of the pen in this play, a control evident in the will she has drawn up in IV.ii.28–42, the articles for control of her ship she reads out in the same scene (IV.ii.72–84), and the written conditions she puts before Mullisheg before she will converse with him (V.i.51–8). This is one more indication of Bess's potentially subversive appropriation of traditional male prerogatives and instruments.

14 For a careful discussion of patterns of private charity in Elizabethan London see Ian Archer, *The Pursuit of Stability: Social Relations in Elizabethan London* (Cambridge: Cambridge University Press, 1991), pp. 163–82.

15 The negative associations of the color black in the West are discussed by G. K. Hunter in "Othello and Colour Prejudice" in *Dramatic Identities and Cultural Tradition* (New York: Barnes and Noble, 1978), pp. 31–59.

16 Barthelemy, *Black Face, Maligned Race*, p. 165.

17 John Hawkins probably had the dubious distinction of being the first Englishman to trade in slaves. As Jack D'Amico notes in *The Moor in English Renaissance Drama* (Tampa: University of South Florida Press, 1991), p. 14, Hawkins plied this trade as early as the 1560s.

18 For a good discussion of the way the English attempted to differentiate themselves from the Spanish in writings about the New World and in their encounters with American Indians see Louis Montrose, "The Work of Gender in the Discourse of Discovery," *Representations* 33 (1991), pp. 1–41.

19 D'Amico, *The Moor in English Renaissance Drama*, pp. 7–40.

20 Leo Africanus, *The History and Description of Africa*, 3 vols (London: The Hakluyt Society, 1896), vol. II, p. 409.

21 John Pory, who translated Leo Africanus into English in 1600, speaks in his introductory "A Generall Description of All Africa" of there being two kinds

of Moors, "namely white or tawnie Moores, and Negros or blacke Moores" (ibid., vol I, p. 20). Leo Africanus himself seems to indicate that the North African region of Barbarie is inhabited by people of "a browne or tawnie colour" (vol. I, p. 123) and assigns "the Negros or blacke Moores" to the more southern regions (vol. I, p. 130).

22 For a reproduction of an illustration of this proverb in Geoffrey Whitney's *A Choice of Emblems* (1586) and a discussion of its significance, see Karen Newman, "'And wash the Ethiop white': Femininity and the Monstrous in *Othello*," ch. 5 of *Fashioning Femininity and English Renaissance Drama* (Chicago: University of Chicago Press, 1991, pp. 76–7.

23 For an excellent discussion of the fear of miscegenation in *Othello* see Newman, pp. 71–93.

24 Ania Loomba, *Gender, Race, Renaissance Drama* (Manchester: Manchester University Press, 1989), p. 52.

25 For a comprehensive history and discussion of English Renaissance dramatic depictions of Muslims see Samuel Chew, *The Crescent and the Rose: Islam and England during the Renaissance* (New York: Oxford University Press, 1937), ch. 11, "Moslems on the London Stage," pp. 469–540. See also Robert Schwoebel's *The Shadow of the Crescent: The Renaissance Image of the Turk (1453–1517)* (Nieuwkoop: B. de Graaf, 1967) for a general history of anti-Turkish and anti-Islamic sentiment in Western Europe in the fifteenth and sixteenth centuries.

26 Chew, *The Crescent and the Rose*, p. 340.

27 Traces of a hatred of the Muslim Turk appear in this play when the Chorus before Act V relates that Bess has become famous as a privateer. "The French and Dutch she spares, only makes spoil / Of the rich Spaniard and the barbarous Turk" (IV.v.7–8). England's European allies are exempt from attack, but the Catholic Spaniard and the Muslim Turk are fair game.

28 D'Amico, in *The Moor in English Renaissance Drama*, p. 78, argues that the Christian West often portrayed Islam "as fabricated revelation set up to allow indulgence, like the polygamy dictated by the false prophet's incontinence."

29 When I have taught this play, students are always confused as to whether Clem actually is castrated or only frightened by the sight of the razor. In *Part II*, written approximately thirty years later, Clem repeatedly refers to his castration in a way that makes it seem indisputable that he really *has* lost his "best jewels." There is no doubt, however, that matters are more ambiguous in *Part I* because the effects of castration are presented so unrealistically. For example, Clem comes running on stage after the event has supposedly occurred. Alev Croutier, in *Harem: The World Behind the Veil* (New York: Abbeville Press, 1989), graphically describes various methods for castrating those selected to be eunuchs. Elaborate procedures for preventing hemorrhage were devised, including burial for three days in desert sand or very tight bandaging (pp. 130–1). No one would run anywhere after such an experience. Castration is obviously as much a fantasy and fear as a fact in Heywood's text.

30 In "Dismantling Irena: The Sexualizing of Ireland in Early Modern England," *Nationalisms and Sexualities*, pp. 157–71, Ann Rosalind Jones and Peter Stallybrass discuss a similar process by which the English effeminated the Irish male and erased the Irish female to secure their own gender dominance (p. 168). In Heywood's text, no Moorish women are actually seen on stage in *Part I*.

7 AMAZONS AND AFRICANS
Gender, race, and empire in Daniel Defoe
Laura Brown

This essay was originally published in *Ends of Empire: Women and Ideology in Early Eighteenth-Century English Literature*, pp. 135–69. Copyright © 1993 by Cornell University, used by permission of the publisher, Cornell University Press.

1 I would like to thank the graduate students in "Colonialism and Eighteenth-Century Literature" (Cornell, Spring 1988) for numerous insights on the materials here, and especially Sheila Lloyd and Ben Halm for their invaluable help.

2 For example, Page duBois, *Centaurs and Amazons: Women and the Pre-History of the Great Chain of Being* (Ann Arbor: University of Michigan Press, 1982); Abby Wettan Kleinbaum, *The War Against the Amazons* (New York: McGraw-Hill, 1983); Sharon W. Tiffany and Kathleen J. Adams, *The Wild Woman: An Inquiry into the Anthropology of an Idea* (Cambridge, Mass.: Schenkman Publishing Co., 1985); William Blake Tyrrel, *Amazons: A Study in Athenian Mythmaking* (Baltimore: Johns Hopkins University Press, 1984); Julie Wheelwright, *Amazons and Military Maids* (London: Pandora Press, 1989).

3 See Simon Shepherd, *Amazons and Warrior Women: Varieties of Feminism in Seventeenth-Century Drama* (New York: St Martin's Press, 1981); Stephen Orgel, "Jonson and the Amazons," in *Soliciting Interpretation: Literary Theory and Seventeenth-Century English Poetry*, ed. Elizabeth D. Harvey and Katharine Eisaman Maus (Chicago: University of Chicago Press, 1990), pp. 119–39.

4 For example, the work of Stephen Greenblatt, Walter Michaels, Louis Montrose, John Bender, and Leonard Tennenhouse.

5 See Donna Landry, *The Muses of Resistance: Laboring-Class Women's Poetry in Britain, 1739–1796* (Cambridge: Cambridge University Press, 1990); Peter Hulme, *Colonial Encounters: Europe and the Native Caribbean, 1492–1797* (New York: Methuen, 1986); Felicity A. Nussbaum, *The Brink of All We Hate: English Satires on Women, 1660–1750* (Lexington: University of Kentucky Press, 1984); Nancy Armstrong, *Desire and Domestic Fiction: A Political History of the Novel* (New York: Oxford University Press, 1987).

6 John Dryden, "The Sixth Satyr of Juvenal," II. 350–70, in *The Poems of John Dryden*, vol. 2, ed. James Kinsley (Oxford: Clarendon Press, 1958).

7 This is Peter Green's translation of Juvenal's lines 355–6 in *Juvenal: The Sixteen Satires* (Harmondsworth: Penguin, 1967).

8 Juvenal, I. 113.

9 Dryden, II. 157–8.

10 Dryden, I. 855–7.

11 Dryden, II. 828–32.

12 Dryden, II. 405–8.

13 See Nussbaum, *The Brink of All We Hate*, p. 78.

14 Henry Fielding, "Juvenalis Satyra Sexta," in *Miscellanies by Henry Fielding, Esq:*, vol. 1, ed. Henry Knight Miller (Oxford: Clarendon Press, 1972), p. 111, II. 364–7.

15 *Miscellanies*, p. 111, n. 4. See William B. Boulton, *Amusements of Old London* (London: Nimmo, 1901), pp. 30–1.

16 Joseph Addison, *Spectator*, ed. Donald F. Bond (Oxford: Clarendon Press, 1965), vol. 4, no. 434, July 18, 1712, pp. 24–6.

17 Nussbaum, *The Brink of All We Hate*, p. 44.

18 Dianne Dugaw, *Warrior Women and Popular Balladry, 1650–1850* (Cambridge: Cambridge University Press, 1989).

19 *The Female Soldier: Or, The Surprising Life and Adventures of Hannah Snell* (1750), intro. by Dianne Dugaw, Augustan Reprint Society, no. 257 (William Andrews Clark Memorial Library, University of California, Los Angeles, 1989), pp. 1–2.

20 Dugaw, *Warrior Women*, pp. 213–15.

21 Alexander Pope, *The Rape of the Lock*, in *The Rape of the Lock and Other Poems*, ed. Geoffrey Tillotson (London: Methuen, 1940), I.139. Subsequent references to this poem will be to this edition and will be cited parenthetically in the text.

22 John Dryden, *Aeneid*, in *The Poems of John Dryden*, XI.937–44, and X.698–9.

23 Daniel Defoe, *Review*, I [i.e. IX], no. 43 (January 8, 1713), in *Defoe's Review, Reproduced from the Original Editions*, intro. by Arthur Wellesley Secord (New York: Columbia University Press, 1938), facs. book 22, p. 85.

24 Daniel Defoe, *Roxana*, ed. Jane Jack (Oxford: Oxford University Press, 1981), pp. 70–3. Subsequent references will be to this edition.

25 Aphra Behn, *Oroonoko: or, The Royal Slave*, intro. by Lore Metzger (New York: Norton, 1973), p. 2.

26 James Ralph, *Clarinda, or the Fair Libertine: A Poem in Four Cantos* (London, 1729), pp. 37–8. Quoted in Louis A. Landa, "Pope's Belinda, the General Emporie of the World and the Wondrous Worm," *South Atlantic Quarterly* 70 (1971), 223.

27 See also Soame Jenyns, *The Art of Dancing. A Poem* (1730), in *Poems* (London, 1752), p. 7; and J. D. Breval, *The Art of Dress. A Poem* (London, 1717), p. 17. Also cited in Landa, "Pope's Belinda," p. 232.

28 In Marxist thought, the "mystical character of the commodity" arises with the generalization of commodity exchange. This substitution occurs because, under an advanced system of exchange, products acquire their value not from their utility, but through their potential for exchange with other products. Under these conditions,

> the commodity reflects the social characteristics of men's own labour as objective characteristics of the products of labour themselves, as the socio-natural properties of these things. Hence it also reflects the social relation of producers to the sum total of labour as a social relation between objects, a relation which exists apart from and outside the producers.

The "secret" that the fetishism of the commodity always conceals is the real structure of human relationships underlying those values dictated by exchange, "the definite social relation between men themselves which assumes . . . the fantastic form of a relation between things." This period in English history is characterized by precisely that extension of exchange – in the form of mercantile capitalism – that Marx describes as the condition for the fetishism of commodities. See Karl Marx, *Capital*, trans. Ben Fowkes, vol. I (New York: Random House, 1977), p. 164.

29 See James Thompson, "Dryden's *Conquest of Granada* and the Dutch Wars," *The Eighteenth Century: Theory and Interpretation* 31 (1990), 218.

30 For example, Shirlene Mason, *Daniel Defoe and the Status of Women* (St Albans, Vt. and Montreal: Eden Press, 1978); Katherine Rogers, "The Feminism of Daniel Defoe," in *Women in the Eighteenth Century and Other Essays*, ed. Paul Fritz and Richard Morton (Toronto: Hakkert, 1976), pp. 3–24; Sudesh Vaid, *The Divided Mind: Studies in Defoe and Richardson* (New Delhi: Associated Publishing House, 1979); Paula Backscheider, "Defoe's Women: Snares and Prey," *Studies in Eighteenth-Century Culture* 5 (1976), 103–20.

31 *Review*, 107 (December 1705), V, pp. 425–6.
32 See Defoe's *Review*, January 8, 1713; February 3, 1713.
33 "Reading Race and Gender: Jonathan Swift," *Eighteenth-Century Studies* 23 (1990), Special issue *The Politics of Difference*, ed. Felicity Nussbaum, pp. 424–43.
34 Alison Dale Taufer, "From Amazon Queen to Female Knight: The Development of the Women Warrior in the Amadis Cycle" (dissertation, UCLA, 1988), pp. 38–47.
35 Samuel Purchas, *Hakluytus Posthumus or Purchas His Pilgrimes* (Glasgow: James MacLehose, 1906), vol. XVI, "The Admirable adventures and strange fortunes of Master Anthonie Knivet . . . 1591," pp. 177–289; also "A Description and Discoverie of the River of Amazons, by William Davies Barber Surgeon of London," pp. 413–16.
36 Richard Hakluyt, *The Principal Navigations Voyages Traffiques and Discoveries of the English Nation* (Glasgow: James MacLehose, 1904), vol. 10, "The discoverie of the large, rich, and beautifull Empire of Guiana . . . by Sir Walter Ralegh," pp. 366–7.
37 Purchas, vol. VII, "The Voyage of Sir Francis Alvarez, a Portugall Priest, made into . . . Ethiopia, *Continued*," pp. 205–6. See also Taufer, "From Amazon Queen," p. 36.
38 Purchas, vol. VI, "A report of the Kingdome of Congo, a Region of Affrica, gathered by Philippo Pigafetta, out of the discourses of Master Edward Lopes a Portugell," pp. 407–516, this quote p. 508.
39 Purchas, vol. VII, "A Brief Relation . . . which . . . John Bermudez brought from . . . Ethiopia," pp. 319–78. This quote p. 363.
40 Daniel Defoe, *Captain Singleton*, ed. Shiv K. Kumar (Oxford: Oxford University Press, 1973), pp. 86–7. Subsequent references will be to this edition.
41 See Samuel Kwaku Opoku, "The Image of Africa, 1660–1730 (Defoe and Travel Literature)" (dissertation, Princeton University, 1967), p. 4.
42 James Thompson provides a useful definition of this phenomenon:

> The Dutch wars were fought over trade, and they should be seen as an official extension or a systematic venture above and beyond ordinary competition and the normal preying upon shipping and one another's outposts in the East and West Indies and along the West African coast. An analogy can be drawn here between the last phase of enclosure, as E. P. Thompson presents it in *Whigs and Hunters, the Origins of the Black Act*, and the struggle over navigation, maritime law, and fishing rights – the official pretexts for the Dutch wars . . . ; in both cases, what we see is a bourgeois process of systematizing exploitation by legitimating it. The same process is at work in the struggle over the use of privateers and pirates: colonization is the legitimating and the systematizing of a formerly episodic rapine.
>
> ("Dryden's *Conquest of Granada*," p. 218)

8 THE OTHER WOMAN
Polygamy, *Pamela*, and the prerogative of empire
Felicity Nussbaum

1 *Horace Walpole's Correspondence with Sir Horace Mann*, ed. W. S. Lewis, Warren Hunting Smith, and George L. Lam (New Haven: Yale University Press, 1967), 24: 21. Mungo Park's *Travels in the Interior Districts of Africa: Performed*

under the Direction and Patronage of the African Association, in the Years 1795, 1796, and 1797 (London, 1799). For a publication history, see Kenneth Lupton, *Mungo Park the African Traveler* (Oxford: Oxford University Press, 1979), esp. 109.

2 *Records of the African Association 1788–1831*, ed. with an intro. by Robin Hallett for the Royal Geographical Society (London: Thomas Nelson & Sons, Ltd, 1964), 10. The African Association, a group of wealthy aristocratic men, grew to 109 members by 1791.

3 *Records of the African Association*, 31.

4 William Smith, *A New Voyage to Guinea: Describing the Customs . . . Appointed by the Royal African Company to survey their settlements, etc.* (London, 1744), iii. The Preface to this volume is apparently not written by Smith.

5 Willem Bosman, *A New and Accurate Description of the Coast of Guinea. Divided into the Gold, the Slave, and the Ivory Coasts*, trans. from the Dutch (London, 1705), Preface.

6 Captain Philip Beaver, *African Memoranda: Relative to an Attempt to Establish a British Settlement . . . on the Western Coast of Africa, in the Year 1792* (London, 1805), writes that "slaves are the money, the circulating medium, with which great African commerce is carried on; they have no other," 395. For a discussion of the parallel commodification of the novel, see Terry Lovell, *Consuming Fiction* (London: Verso, 1987).

7 Jean Baptiste Labat, *Voyages and Travels along the Western Coast of Africa, from Cape Blanco to Sierra Leone* (1731), vol. II in *A New General Collection of Voyages and Travels: Consisting of the most Esteemed Relations, which have been hitherto published in any Language; comprehending every thing remarkable in its Kind in Europe, Asia, Africa, and America . . .*, [complied by John Green?] 4 vols (London, 1745–7); and Francis Moore and Captain B. Stibbs, *Travels into the Inland Parts of Africa: Containing a Description of the Several Nations . . .* (London, 1738). See also *Records of the African Association*, 25.

8 Ignatius Sancho, *Letters of the Late Ignatius Sancho, an African to which are prefixed Memoirs of his Life*, 2 vols (London, 1782), 2: 4–5.

9 Michele Wallace uses this term in reference to all black women in *Invisibility Blues: From Pop to Theory* (London and New York: Verso, 1990).

10 Caleb Fleming, *Oeconomy of the Sexes, or the Doctrine of Divorce, the Plurality of Wives, and the Vow of Celibacy Freely Examined* (London, 1751), 32.

11 Homi K. Bhabha, "The Other Question: Difference, Discrimination and the Discourse of Colonialism," in *Literature, Politics and Theory: Papers from the Essex Conference 1976–84*, ed. Francis Barker *et al.* (London and New York: Methuen, 1986), 148–72, 156. For the concept of "consolidating the imperialist self," see especially Gayatri Spivak, "Three Women's Texts and a Critique of Imperialism," in *Race, Writing, and Difference*, ed. Henry Louis Gates, Jr (Chicago: University of Chicago Press, 1986), 262–80, and Aihwa Ong, "Colonialism and Modernity: Feminist Representations of Women in Non-Western Societies," *Inscriptions* 3/4 (1988): 79–93.

12 See Figure 8.1, Frontispiece to *A New General Collection of Voyages and Travels*, vol. 2.

13 Sylvana Tomaselli, "The Enlightenment Debate on Women," *History Workshop* 20 (Autumn 1985), 101–24.

14 A. Owen Aldridge's articles, "Polygamy and Deism," *JEGP* 48 (1949), 343–60, and "Polygamy in Early Fiction: Henry Neville and Denis Veiras," *JEGP* 65 (1950), 464–72, remain the definitive studies.

15 P. Dubliniensis, *Reflections upon Polygamy, and the Encouragement given to that Practice in the Scriptures of the Old Testament* (London, 1737), 1. This treatise

also argues that in polygamous relationships women are deprived of their natural right, sufficient sexual gratification. This defense of women's sexuality as a natural right appears in several of Madan's antagonists, including T. Hawkes, *A Scriptural Refutation of the Argument for Polygamy Advanced in a Treatise entitled Thelyphthora* (London, [1781]), 101. Bigamy was apparently common practice. According to Lawrence Stone, *The Road to Divorce: England 1530–1987* (Oxford: Oxford University Press, 1990), 191,

> The most common reason in the late seventeenth and early eighteenth centuries for declaring a marriage intrinsically void was bigamy arising from a previous marriage. . . . The Act followed custom in exempting persons whose spouses had been overseas or absent without news for seven years or more.

Legal cases of multiple marriages, often involving a wife from another country or religion, considered the status of the marriage under English law. *Warrender v. Warrender* (1835) rules that

> Marriage is one and the same thing substantially all the Christian world over. Our whole law of marriage assumes this: and it is important to observe that we regard it as a wholly different thing . . . from Turkish or other marriages among infidel nations, because clearly we never should recognize the plurality of wives, and consequent validity of second marriages . . . which . . . the laws of those countries authorise and validate.
>
> (J. H. C. Morris, *The Recognition of Polygamous Marriages in English Law* [Tübingen: J. C. B. Mohr], 291)

16 John Millar, *The Origins of the Distinctions of Ranks: or, an Inquiry into the Circumstances which give rise to the Influence and Authority in the Different Members of Society*, 3rd edn (London, 1781), 124.

17 Olaudah Equiano, *The Interesting Narrative of the Life of Olaudah Equiano or Gustavus Vassa, the African*, in *The Classic Slave Narratives*, ed. Henry Louis Gates, Jr (New York: New American Library, 1987), 13.

18 For these references to polygamy, see Jerom Merolla da Sorrento, *A Voyage to the Congo and Several other Countries* (1682) in *A General Collection of the Best and Most Interesting Voyages and Travels in all Parts of the World*, ed. John Pinkerton, 17 vols (London, 1814), 16: 213; Francis Moore and Captain B. Stibbs, 133; John Barbot, *A Description of the Coasts of North and South-Guinea, and of Ethiopia Inferior, Vulgarly Angola* (1732), in Awnsham and John Churchill, *A Collection of Voyages and Travels*, 6 vols (London, 1732), 5: 240; J. Gazilhier *Voyages and Travels to Guinea and Benin* (1699) in *New General Collection* [compiled by John Green, reprinted Frank Cass & Co (London, 1968)], 3: 113; and William Smith, *New Voyage*, 26, 102.

19 Paul Lovejoy, "Concubinage in the Sohoto Caliphate 1804–1903," *Slavery and Abolition* 11.2 (1990), 158–89, esp. 180. He adds, "Concubinage is virtually ignored in the literature on slavery, yet it was the central mechanism for the sexual exploitation of women in Islamic societies" (159). Alexander Falconbridge, *An Account of the Slave Trade on the Coast of Africa* (London, 1788), for example, maintains that women slaves seldom exceeded a third of those transported (12). Claire Robertson, "The Perils of Autonomy," *Gender and History* 3.1 (Spring 1991), 91–6 convincingly suggests that transporting more males than females was due to African "desire to retain women slaves, *not* to European's preference for male labor. Women slaves were kept primarily because of their agricultural labor value and secondarily due to

their reproductive capabilities that were useful for expanding African lineages" (95).

20 Harriet Jacobs's *Incidents in the Life of a Slave Girl: Mrs. Harriet Brent Jacobs, Written by Herself* (1861) (New York: AMS Press, 1973), 57. The narrative by "Linda Brent" was edited and framed by white women.

21 Henry Neville, *The Isle of Pines, or A Late Discovery of a fourth Island near Terra Australis, Incognita by Henry Cornelius Van Sloetten* (London, 1668).

22 Martin Madan, *Thelyphthora: or, a Treatise on Female Ruin in its causes, effects, consequences, prevention, and remedy; considered on the basis of the Divine Law*, 2 vols (London, 1780). One of Madan's most unusual arguments is that polygamy is justified because Christ was born of a polygamous relationship. See John Towers, *Polygamy Unscriptural: or Two Dialogues Between Philalethes and Monogamus* (London, 1780), 8.

23 Richard Hill, *The Blessings of Polygamy Displayed, in an Affectionate Address to the Rev. Martin Madan occasioned by his late Work, entitled Thelyphthora, or A Treatise of Female Ruin* (London, 1781), 39; and Martin Madan, Letter 4 to Rev. Mr G (April 14, 1781), *Letters on Thelyphthora: with an Occasional Prologue and Epilogue by the Author* (London, 1782).

24 Saunders Welch, *A Proposal to Render Effectual a Plan to Remove the Nuisance of Common Prostitutes from the Streets of the Metropolis* (London, 1758), 7.

25 John Matthews, *A Voyage to the River Sierra-Leone, on the Coast of Africa* (1788), 99.

26 David Hume, "Of Polygamy and Divorces" (1742) reprinted in *Essays Moral, Political and Literary* (Oxford: Oxford University Press, 1963), 185–95. Hume believed that blacks were "naturally inferior to the Whites. There scarcely ever was a civilised nation of that complexion. . . . Such a uniform and constant difference could not happen, in so many countries and ages, if nature had not made an original distinction between these breeds of men" ("Of National Characters," 213 n. 1). Hume, in charge of the British Colonial Office from 1766, added this note to the 1753–4 edition, and it was later used as a basis for scientific racism. See Richard H. Popkin, *The High Road to Pyrrhonism* (San Diego: Austin Hill Press Inc., 1980), 251–66.

27 Mungo Park, 268. According to Frances Moore and Captain Stibbs, Mumbo Jumbo is a cant language spoken exclusively by men (40). Mumbo Jumbo was impersonated as a folkloric invention dressed in a long coat and a tuft of straw on top who kept women in awe of masculine authority. Women flee when Mumbo Jumbo arrives.

28 T. C. Duncan Eaves and Ben D. Kimpel, *Samuel Richardson: A Biography* (Oxford: Clarendon Press, 1971), 135.

29 Terry Castle, *Masquerade and Civilization: The Carnivalesque in Eighteenth-Century English Culture and Fiction* (Stanford: Stanford University Press, 1986), 132. Though she does not mention polygamy, Castle richly describes the way the sequel to *Pamela* must "be different, but also *exactly the same.*"

30 *Pamela; or, Virtue Rewarded* in *The Works of Samuel Richardson*, ed. Leslie Stephen (London: Henry Southeran & Co., 1893), III.53. For a subtle analysis of Pamela's double jeopardy as wife and mother, see Ruth Perry, "Colonizing the Breast: Sexuality and Maternity in Eighteenth-Century England," *Journal of the History of Sexuality* 2.2 (October 1991), 204–34.

31 Fatna A. Sabbah, *Woman in the Muslim Unconscious*, trans. Mary Jo Lakeland, (New York: Pergamon Press, 1984), 25, discusses the way that Muslim women's visible physical attributes are openly interpreted as indicators of veiled sexual organs.

32 A[nna] M. Falconbridge, *Narrative of Two Voyages to the River Sierra Leone*

during the Years 1791–2–3, 2nd edn (London, 1802). Falconbridge despised colonial policies but equivocated about abolishing the slave-trade.

33 Lady Mary Wortley Montagu, *Letters of the Right Honourable Lady M–y W–y M–e: Written during her TRAVELS in Europe, Asia, and Africa*, 2 vols (London, 1764). I have cited the modern edition, *The Complete Letters of Lady Mary Wortley Montagu*, ed. Robert Halsband (Oxford: Clarendon Press, 1965), 2 vols. See also Joseph W. Lew, "Lady Mary's Portable Seraglio," *ECS* 24.4 (Summer 1991), 432–50. Lew believes that Lady Mary "subverts both Orientalist discourse and eighteenth-century patriarchy itself."

34 On tattooes, see Harriet Guest, "Curiously Masked: Tattooing, Masculinity, and Nationality in Late Eighteenth-Century British Perceptions of the South Pacific," in John Barrell, ed., *Painting and the Politics of Culture* (Oxford: Oxford University Press, 1992).

35 Mary Wollstonecraft, *A Vindication of the Rights of Woman*, ed. Miriam Kramnick (Harmondsworth: Penguin, 1975), ch. IV.

36 John Reinold Forster, *Observations Made During a Voyage Round the World on Physical Geography, Natural History and Ethic Philosophy* (London, 1788), 425–6.

37 Trinh T. Minh-ha, "Not You/Like You: Post-Colonial Women and the Interlocking Question of Identity and Difference," *Inscriptions* 3/4 (1988), 71–7, esp. 73. For a discussion of the use of the veil in protest against the Shah of Iran, see Nayereh Tohidi, "Gender and Islamic Fundamentalism," in *Third World Women and the Politics of Feminism*, ed. Chandra Talpade Mohanty, Ann Russo, and Lourdes Torres (Bloomington: Indiana University Press, 1991), 251–67.

9 REREADING ELIZABETH CARY'S *THE TRAGEDIE OF MARIAM, FAIRE QUEENE OF JEWRY*
Dympna Callaghan

This essay was written while I was a Monticello College Foundation Fellow at the Newberry Library. I am grateful to members of the Fellows' Seminar, especially Val Flint, Mary Beth Rose, and Susan Rosa, for stimulating discussion of the issues presented here. For earlier inspiration, I thank my graduate class at Syracuse University, especially Roxann Wheeler. I am also indebted to Peggy McCracken and Jim Shapiro for their valuable comments.

1 Valerie Wayne, ed., *The Matter of Difference: Materialist Feminist Criticism of Shakespeare* (Ithaca: Cornell University Press, 1991), p. 11.

2 Tania Modleski, *Feminism Without Women: Culture and Criticism in a Postfeminist Age* (New York: Routledge, 1991), p. 6.

3 Bill Ashcroft, Gareth Griffiths, and Helen Tiffin, *The Empire Writes Back: Theory and Practice in Post-Colonial Literatures* (New York: Routledge, 1989), p. 175.

4 Ibid., p. 176.

5 On "Othering," see Gayatri Chakravorty Spivak, "The Rani of Simur," in Francis Barker *et al.*, eds, *Europe and Its Others*, vol. I (Colchester: University of Essex Press, 1985).

6 See Ann Russo, "'We cannot live without our lives': White Women, Antiracism, and Feminism," in Chandra Talpade Mohanty, Ann Russo, and Lourdes Torres, eds, *Third World Women and the Politics of Feminism* (Bloomington: Indiana University Press, 1991), pp. 297–313.

7 All of these groups were present in the British Isles in the English Renaissance. We know, for example, that there were Africans in England

because Elizabeth tried to exchange them for English people held captive in the Netherlands. See Karen Newman, "'And wash the Ethiop white': Femininity and the Monstrous in *Othello*," in Jean E. Howard and Marion F. O'Connor, eds, *Shakespeare Reproduced: The Text in History and Ideology* (New York: Methuen, 1987), p. 148.

Despite the expulsion of Jews from England in 1290 there remained a small Jewish presence, and the Lopez affair and the presence of a number of Hebrew scholars at Oxford and Cambridge made the Jewish presence more visible. See Frank Marcham, ed., *Lopez the Jew* (1594) by Gabriel Harvey (London: Waterlow & Sons, 1927) and Jacob Lopez Cardozo, *The Contemporary Jew in the Elizabethan Drama* (Amsterdam: H. J. Paris, 1925).

On the Irish, see Ann Rosalind Jones, "Italians and Others," in David Scott Kastan and Peter Stallybrass, eds, *Staging the Renaissance: Reinterpretations of Elizabethan and Jacobean Drama* (New York: Routledge, 1991), p. 257. On the racialization of Jews in the nineteenth and twentieth centuries, see Sander L. Gilman, *The Jew's Body* (New York: Routledge, 1991).

8 The complexity of this issue is apparent in contemporary US culture where it seems appropriate to differentiate racism from anti-semitism precisely because Jews are not now usually considered as racial others. Racial otherness is now principally defined in terms of African descent. (Indians and Asians are not nearly so racialized as Africans.) See Frantz Fanon, "The Fact of Blackness," in David Theo Goldberg, ed., *Anatomy of Racism* (Minneapolis: University of Minnesota Press, 1990), pp. 108–26.

9 Betty S. Travitsky, "The Feme Covert in Elizabeth Cary's Mariam," in Carole Levin and Jeanie Watson, eds, *Ambiguous Realities: Women in the Middle Ages and Renaissance* (Detroit: Wayne State University Press, 1987); Elaine V. Beilin, *Redeeming Eve: Women Writers of the English Renaissance* (Princeton: Princeton University Press, 1987), pp. 157–76; Sandra K. Fischer, "Elizabeth Cary and Tyranny, Domestic and Religious," in Margaret Patterson Hanney, ed., *Silent but for the Word: Tudor Women as Patrons, Translators, and Writers of Religious Works* (Kent, Ohio: Kent State University Press, 1985), pp. 225–37; Margaret W. Ferguson, "The Spectre of Resistance: The Tragedy of Mariam (1613)," in Kastan and Stallybrass, eds, *Staging the Renaissance*, pp. 235–50; Margaret W. Ferguson, "Running on with Almost Public Voice: The Case of E.C.," in Florence Howe, ed., *Tradition and the Talents of Women* (Chicago: University of Illinois Press, 1991), pp. 37–67. See also Nancy Cotton, *Women Playwrights in England c.1363–1750* (Lewisburg: Bucknell University Press, 1980), pp. 31–8; Catherine Belsey, *The Subject of Tragedy: Identity and Difference in Renaissance Drama* (New York: Methuen, 1985), pp. 164–5, 171–5; Betty Travitsky, ed., *The Paradise of Women*, pp. 209–12; Mary R. Mahl and Helene Koon, *The Female Spectator: English Women Writers Before 1800* (Bloomington: Indiana University Press, 1977), pp. 99–102; Germaine Greer *et al.*, eds, *Kissing the Rod: An Anthology of Seventeenth Century Women's Verse* (New York: Farrar, Straus, Giroux, 1988), pp. 54–5; Angeline Goreau, "Two English Women in the Seventeenth Century: Notes for an Anatomy of Feminine Desire," in Philippe Ariès and André Béjin, eds, *Western Sexuality: Practice and Precept in Past and Present Times*, trans. Anthony Forster (Oxford: Basil Blackwell, 1985), esp. p. 105; Angeline Goreau, *The Whole Duty of a Woman: Female Writers in Seventeenth-Century England* (Garden City: Doubleday, 1985). Of related interest: Alexander Maclaren Witherspoon, *The Influence of Robert Garnier on Elizabethan Drama* (New Haven: Yale University Press, 1924).

10 Beilin, *Redeeming Eve*, p. 164.

11 Ibid., pp. 164, 174.
12 Ferguson, "Running on," pp. 43, 49.
13 Fischer, "Elizabeth Cary," p. 227.
14 Cotton, *Women Playwrights*, pp. 34–5.
15 See Ann Rosalind Jones, *The Currency of Eros: Women's Love Lyric in Europe, 1540–1620* (Bloomington: Indiana University Press, 1990), p. 1.
16 Ferguson, "Spectre of Resistance," p. 236. See also Ferguson, "Running on," p. 38.
17 Belsey, *Subject of Tragedy*, p. 175.
18 Quoted Beilin, *Redeeming Eve*, p. 157.
19 Jones, *Currency of Eros*, p. 2.
20 Fischer, "Elizabeth Cary," pp. 228, 231.
21 For a critique of the gynocritical approach to Renaissance women writers, see Jones, *Currency of Eros*, p. 6.
22 Ashcroft *et al.*, *Empire Writes Back*, p. 175.
23 Emily C. Bartels, "Malta, the Jew, and the Fictions of Difference: Colonialist Discourse in Marlowe's *The Jew of Malta*," *ELR* 20: 1 (1990), p. 2.
24 See Margaret T. Hodgen, *Early Anthropology in the Sixteenth and Seventeenth Centuries* (Philadelphia: University of Pennsylvannia Press, 1964).
25 See Lady Georgiana Fullerton, *The Life of Elisabeth Lady Falkland, 1585–1639* (London: Burns & Oates, 1883), p. 266. See also *The Lady Falkland: Her Life*, ed. Richard Simpson (London: Catholic Publishing & Bookselling Co., 1861), p. 113. For further biographical information, see Kenneth B. Murdoch, *The Sun at Noon: Three Biographical Sketches* (New York: Macmillan, 1939).
26 Alexander B. Grosart, ed., *The Complete Works of John Davies of Hereford*, 2 vols (n.d.; repr. New York: AMS Press, 1967), vol. 2, p. 5.
27 Jews were expelled from Spain in 1492 and from Portugal in 1497. See Jonathan I. Israel, *European Jewry in the Age of Mercantilism, 1550–1750* (Oxford: Clarendon Press, 1985); John Edwards, *The Jews in Christian Europe 1400–1700* (New York: Routledge, 1988); David S. Katz, *Philo-semitism and the Readmission of the Jews to England 1603–1655* (Oxford: Clarendon Press, 1982).
28 See Katz, *Philo-semitism*, p. 134.
29 The Beinecke Library at Yale University has the 1602 edition of Lodge, but I have consulted the Newberry Library's 1620 edition. Flavius Josephus, *The Famous and Memorable Works*, trans. Thomas Lodge (London: Simon Waterson, 1620). Dunstan makes the case for Cary's use of Lodge. Elizabeth Cary, Viscountess Falkland, *The Tragedy of Mariam* (1613), ed. A. C. Dunstan, The Malone Society Reprints (Oxford: Horace Hart for Oxford University Press, 1914), pp. xiii–xix.

There is an earlier version of the Herod–Mariam story translated into English, which indicates something of the extent of contemporary interest in this aspect of Jewish history. Joseph Ben Gorion, *A Compendium and Most Marvellous History of the Latter Times of the Jewes Common Weale*, trans. Peter Morwyn (1575; London: Colophon, John Wallie, 1579).

Fullerton claims that Cary "perfectly understood" Hebrew in her youth (Fullerton, *The Life*, p. 7; Simpson, *Lady Falkland*, p. 4). There has been far less interest in Cary's intellectual endeavors than in recovering her emotional traumas. The biography of Cary written by her daughter is largely about her conversion to Catholicism, which critics tend to read primarily as a matter of "personal experience," the limits of which have been well established in feminist critiques of essentialism. At a time when intellectual and political thought was virtually synonymous with theological doctrine, conversion to

Catholicism was an intellectual position on contemporary texts and arguments arrived at only after intense study, not just a matter of private soul-searching. See Kenneth L. Campbell, *The Intellectual Struggle of the English Papists in the Seventeenth Century: The Catholic Dilemma*, Texts and Studies in Religion, vol. 30 (New York: Edwin Mellen Press, 1986); Peter Milward, *Religious Controversies in the Jacobean Age* (Lincoln: University of Nebraska Press, 1986); George H. Tavard, *The Seventeenth-Century Tradition: A Study in Recusant Thought* (Leiden: E. J. Brill, 1978). Cary's interest in the Jews is clearly part of an intellectual and theological interest, one she shared with English Protestants, who were after all responsible for convening the Whitehall Conference.

30 The trope of foreignness applied to other nations, "another country, a country of others," where it was possible to explore what was forbidden in the domestic environment (Jones\ "Italians and Others," p. 251).

31 See James Finn, *Sephardim: Or the History of the Jews in Spain and Portugal* (London: Gilbert & Rivingto, 1841), p. vi; Katz, *Philo-semitism*, pp. 170–1. Sir Thomas Browne inquires into the "vulgar and common error" "That Jews stink." This turns out to be a meditation on whether Jews constitute a nation or whether they have distinct, physiologically based, racial characteristics. He concludes that a "metaphorical expression" has been transformed into a "literal construction" and that it is dangerous to "annex a constant property unto any nation" (Thomas Browne, *The Works of the Learned Sir Thomas Browne* [London: Thomas Basset, Richard Chiswell, Thomas Sawbridge, Charles Mearn, & Charles Brome, 1686], p. 169). Coryate describes Jews of different nationalities in Venice:

> I observed some fewe of these Jewes especially some of the Levantines to bee such goodly and proper men, that then I said to my selfe our English proverbe: To look like a Iewe (whereby is meant sometimes a weather beaten warp-faced fellow, sometimes a phrenticke and luna-ticke person, sometimes one discontented) is not true.
> (Thomas Coryate, *Coryats Crudities* [London: W. S[tanby], 1611],
> p. 232.)

Spelling of the authors' names in these entries conforms to the title-pages of the works consulted.

32 Katz, *Philo-semitism*, pp. 2–3.

33 Ibid., p. 244.

34 G. K. Hunter has argued that in Elizabethan England Jews were regarded as theologically and morally wanting rather than as racially other. He bases his argument on the possibility of conversion. Yet historical evidence shows that conversion did not secure a Jew's freedom from anti-semitism. Since they were regarded as innately treacherous, it was felt that one could never be sure about the authenticity of Jews' conversion. G. K. Hunter, "The Theology of Marlowe's *The Jew of Malta*," *Journal of the Warburg and Courtauld Institutes* 27 (1964), pp. 211–40. See also Michael Ferber, "The Ideology of *The Merchant of Venice*," *ELR* 20: 3 (1990) p. 441. *The Merchant of Venice* and *The Jew of Malta* are examples of this stereotyped representation from the drama. We also know that Stephen Gosson wrote a play called *The Jew* which was performed at the Bull in 1579, recorded as "representing the greediness of wordly chusers, and bloody mindes of Usurers" (N. W. Bawcutt, ed., *The Jew of Malta* by Christopher Marlowe [Baltimore: Johns Hopkins University Press, 1978], p. 4). On the distinction between anti-Catholicism and anti-semitism, see Katz, *Philo-semitism*, p. 162.

35 Katz, *Philo-semitism*, pp. 3–4. Purchas notes that Papists are "the common adversarie" of both Jews and Protestants. He writes of the "Partition-wall which separateth Jew and Catholike" on grounds of the Jewish intolerance for idolatry, and fulminates against Catholics who seem rather further from conversion to true Christianity than Jews. Samuel Purchas, *Purchas His Pilgrimage, Or Relations Of The World And The Religions Observed In All Ages and places discovered, from the Creation unto this Present*, vol. I (London: William Stansby for Henrie Fetherstone, 1613), p. 184.

36 Even this view must be tempered by Sir Thomas Browne's proposition that the Jews were an impure race because of the strong sexual desire Jewish women had for Christian men. See Katz, *Philo-semitism*, p. 170.

37 Leslie A. Fiedler, *The Stranger in Shakespeare* (1973; London: Paladin, 1974), p. 99.

38 There are also medieval legends about Jewish fathers who kill their children when they become converts to Christianity (Bawcutt, *Jew of Malta*, p. 9).

39 All play quotations are taken from Dunstan's *Mariam*. In the interests of readability, I have emended "v" to "u" and "f" to "s" throughout.

40 See Beilin, *Redeeming Eve*, p. 165. Ferguson notes that Mariam's beheading conjures up the ghosts of Mary Queen of Scots and of Christ's harbinger, "John the Baptist, beheaded by Herod's servants at Salome's request," "Spectre of Resistance," p. 245. This is, of course, a different Herod (Antipas) and a different Salome (the daughter of Heroditas), but Valency has observed that all the Herods were so evil that they became a sort of historical amalgam, so that the wickedness of one Herod invariably summons up the deeds of the others (Maurice J. Valency, *The Tragedies of Herod and Mariamme* [Morningside Heights: Columbia University Press, 1940], pp. 19–67).

41 Fiedler, *Stranger in Shakespeare*, p. 99.

42 This phenomenon has its literary antecedents in the Virgin's intervention in Chaucer's *The Prioress's Tale* and in the ballad of *Hugh of Lincoln* where a Gentile child is slain for his devotion to the Virgin. See Fiedler, *Stranger in Shakespeare*, p. 98.

43 Fiedler, *Stranger in Shakespeare*, p. 101.

44 Quoted Charles H. and Katherine George, *The Protestant Mind of the English Reformation 1570–1640* (Princeton: Princeton University Press, 1961), p. 282.

45 See Fiedler, *Stranger in Shakespeare*, p. 106. Obviously, in terms of the plot, actual conversion is not a choice available to Mariam, even though, as we have seen, she is symbolically marked by Christianity.

46 Ferguson suggests that the marriage of Herod and Mariam is an "interfaith union" ("Running on," p. 43). It is not clear that English Renaissance Christians were particularly aware of any religious difference between Edomites and Jews. Purchas writes:

> Idumaea lyeth Southward from Judea: It had the name of *Edom*, the surname of *Esau*, sonne of *Isaak*. . . . It was subdued by David, according to the Prophecie, *The elder shall serve the younger*. They rebelled under *Ioram* the sonne of *Jehsophat*; as *Isaak* had also prophecied. From that they continued bitter enemies to the people of God, till Hircanus, the sonne of Simon compelled them to accept both the Jewish Dominion and Religion: after which they were reckoned among the Jews.

He also remarks, in a chapter entitled "Of the divers Sects among the Jewes,"

> The *Herodians* were Jewes, otherwise agreeing with the rest; but they

334

thought *Herod* to be the Messias, moved by *Jacobs* prophecie falsely interpreted, *That the Scepter should not depart from Juda till Shilo came.* When as therefore they saw *Herod* a stranger to possesse the kingdome, they interpreted as aforesaid.

(Purchas, *Pilgrimage*, pp. 83, 128)

Similarly, the issue of "colonization" tends to strike modern readers of the play as a relevant theme given the relation between Palestine and Rome. However, Renaissance culture's interest in the Jews does not take this form.

47 See my *Woman and Gender in Renaissance Tragedy: A Study of Othello, King Lear, The Duchess of Malfi and The White Devil* (Atlantic Highlands: Humanities Press, 1989), pp. 123–39.

48 Fischer, "Elizabeth Cary," p. 235.

49 On the question of Mariam's execution see Frances Dolan, "'Gentlemen, I have one thing more to say': Women on Scaffolds in England, 1563–1680," *Medieval and Renaissance Drama in England* (forthcoming).

50 On Alexandra see Mary Beth Rose, "Where Are the Mothers in Shakespeare? Options for Gender Representation in the English Renaissance," *Shakespeare Quarterly* 42: 3 (1991), p. 314. On Cleopatra, see Travitsky, "Feme Covert," p. 189.

51 See Harry Levin, *The Power of Blackness* (New York: Alfred Knopf, 1958) and Winthrop Jordan, *White over Black* (Chapel Hill: University of North Carolina Press, 1968).

52 For a splendid analysis of Graphina as an instance of appropriate but restrained female utterance see Ferguson, who reminds us that *graphesis* means Writing ("Running on," p. 47).

53 Feminist critics have noted that this is what is unusual about Cary's treatment of her theme, in comparison with both her source and with other Renaissance dramatic treatments of the Herod–Mariam story. For example, Beilin comments "Cary structures the play to make Mariam's conflict between obedience to and rebellion against Herod's authority the central concern" (*Redeeming Eve*, p. 166).

10 "I RATHER WOULD WISH TO BE A BLACK-MOOR"
Beauty, race, and rank in Lady Mary Wroth's *Urania*
Kim F. Hall

This essay owes much to conversations with Gwynne Kennedy, who unselfishly shared with me her research on Mary Wroth, particularly her unpublished paper, "'She thinckes she daunces in a net': The Reception of Lady Mary Wroth's *Urania*." I am also grateful to Margreta de Grazia, Lucy Maddox, Maureen Quilligan, Phyllis Rackin, and Susan Zlotnick for their many helpful comments and suggestions.

1 Thomas Wilson, *The Rule of Reason, Conteinying the Arte of Logique*, ed. Richard S. Sprague (Northridge: San Fernando State College Foundation, 1972), 84–5.

2 Frank Whigham, *Ambition and Privilege: The Social Tropes of Elizabethan Courtesy Theory* (Berkeley: University of California Press, 1984), links Elizabethan courtesy literature to changing formations of aristocratic identity and argues that Wilson's *Arte of Rhetorique* "makes possible a new conception of the hierarchical social order" (3). While Whigham primarily emphasizes rank and social order as a site of struggle, Patricia Parker, *Literary Fat Ladies:*

Rhetoric, Gender, Property (New York and London: Meuthuen, 1987), argues for the centrality of gender in the "problematics of ordering" (98) demonstrated in rhetorical treaties.

3 Although William Hawkins completed the first English trading voyage to West Africa in 1530, the decade of the 1550s is typically used to date the beginnings of the English experience with Africa. In 1551, Thomas Wyndham returned two North African Moors to their country from England. 1554 saw the first West Africans brought to London to learn English and to act as interpreters in African trade as well as the publication of William Prat's *Description of the Country of Aphrique*. Richard Eden's translation of Peter Marytr's *Decades of the New World*, which included the first published accounts of two actual voyages to Africa (Thomas Wyndham to Guinea in 1553 and John Lok to Elmina in 1554–5), was published in 1555 with William Waterman's adaptation of Boemus, *The Fardle of Fashions*. A translation of Pliny, *A Summary of the Antiquities and Wonders of the World* . . . appeared in 1556. See Eldred Jones, *Othello's Countrymen: The African in English Renaissance Drama* (Oxford: Oxford University Press, 1965); Winthrop Jordan, *White over Black: American Attitudes toward the Negro 1550–1812* (Chapel Hill: University of North Carolina Press, 1968) and James Walvin, *The Black Presence: A Documentary History of the Negro in England* (New York: Schocken Books, 1972).

4 This is not to argue that women construct themselves as men, but to suggest that they similarly borrow from patriarchal categories in order to empower themselves as white females.

5 Mary Ellen Lamb, *Gender and Authorship in the Sidney Circle* (Madison: University of Wisconsin Press, 1990), 9.

6 Chela Sandoval, "Feminism and Racism: A Report on the 1982 National Women's Studies Conference," in *Making Face/Making Soul = Haciendo Caras: Creative and Critical Perspectives by Feminists of Color*, ed. Gloria Anzaldúa (San Francisco: Aunt Lute Books, 1990), 64. See also Marilyn Frye, in *The Politics of Reality: Essays in Feminist Theory* (Trumansburg: The Crossing Press, 1983), 114–21, who argues that whiteness is a male construct that offers the illusion of power to white women,

> Since white women are *almost* white men, being white, at least, and sometimes more-or-less honorary men, we can cling to a hope of true membership in the dominant and powerful group, we can be stuck in our ignorance and theirs all our lives.

7 For what are probably the best-known expressions of resistance to this dynamic see bell hooks, *Ain't I a Woman: Black Women and Feminism* (Boston: South End Press, 1981). See also *All the Women Are White, All the Men Are Black, but Some of Us Are Brave: Black Women's Studies*, ed. Gloria T. Hull, Patricia Bell Scott, and Barbara Smith (New York: The Feminist Press at the City University of New York, 1982).

8 I should add here that I see these women, particularly Wroth, as having what Ann Rosalind Jones, *The Currency of Eros: Women's Love Lyric in Europe, 1540–1620* (Bloomington and New York: Indiana University Press, 1990), terms a "negotiated viewer position" in relation to discourses of race and beauty. She adopts this term from feminist film criticism and suggests that "a 'negotiated' viewer position is one that accepts the dominant ideology encoded into a text, but particularizes and transforms it in the service of a different group" (4).

9 In her investigation of the connections between rhetorical display and prop-

erty, Patricia Parker, *Literary Fat Ladies*, finds in travel narratives "a link in the discourse itself between the blazon and its form of rhetorical display, the tradition of opening the 'bosom of nature' to view, and the language of the discovery of the feminized new land, opened to its developer" (142). For more on the language of the blazon and control over the female body, see Nancy Vickers's influential essay, "Diana Described: Scattered Women and Scattered Rhyme," in *Writing and Sexual Difference*, ed. Elizabeth Abel (Chicago: University of Chicago Press, 1982), 95–110 and her "'The blazon of sweet beauty's best': Shakespeare's *Lucrece*," in *Shakespeare and the Question of Theory*, ed. Patricia Parker and Geoffrey Hartman (New York: Methuen, 1985), 95–115.

10 See Catherine Belsey's deconstructive argument on binary oppositions, "Disrupting Sexual Difference: Meaning and Gender in the Comedies," in *Alternative Shakespeares*, ed. John Drakakis (London and New York: Methuen, 1985), 166–90. Although Belsey does not include dark/light or black/white in her list of oppositions, it is obviously as fundamental as the others she does include and "white" is privileged with black, the term that is "always other, always what is *not* the thing itself" (185). In her discussion of stereotypes of black women, Patricia Hill Collins, *Black Feminist Thought: Knowledge, Consciousness and the Politics of Empowerment* (Boston: Unwin Hyman, 1990, 68–70), identifies black/white as a fundamental dichotomy in "the process of oppisitional difference" linked to the objectification of black women.

11 *The Riverside Shakespeare* (Boston: Houghton Mifflin, 1972), III.ii.257. All references to Shakespeare's plays are to this edition, hereafter cited in the text.

12 My argument here responds to Peter Stallybrass's discussion of the contradictory formations of women within categories of gender and class ("Patriarchal Territories: The Body Enclosed," in *Rewriting the Renaissance: The Discourses of Sexuality in Early Modern Europe*, ed. Margaret W. Ferguson, Maureen Quilligan, and Nancy J. Vickers [Chicago and London: University of Chicago Press, 1986], 133), in which he argues that "the differentiation of women simultaneously establishes or reinforces the differentiation of men."

13 Henry Louis Gates, Jr, ed., *"Race," Writing, and Difference* (Chicago: University of Chicago Press, 1986), 5.

14 Certainly the heated arguments against cosmetics in anti-feminist and anti-matrimonial literature might suggest both the arbitrariness of the "beautiful" and a recognition that women's use of cosmetics simultaneously denies the existence of "natural" beauty and usurps the male prerogative to create and manipulate the category.

15 A. L. Rowse, *The Poems of Shakespeare's Dark Lady: Salve Deus Rex Judaeorum by Emilia Lanier* (London: Cape, 1978), 123. The poem is also available in a modernized version from the Brown Women Writers' Project.

16 Alexander MacClaren Witherspoon, *The Influence of Robert Garnier on Elizabethan Drama* (New Haven: Yale University Press, 1924), 86, somewhat patronizingly notes one of the few changes in Mary Sidney's translation:

> Virtuous lady as she was, she did not think it needful or edifying to dwell on the charms of Cleopatra, and where the Frenchman had written with some animation, "*la singulière beauté de Cléopatre, Reine d'Egypte, arrivée en Cilice en royal magnificence*," she dismisses the fair Egyptian with the curt phrase, "Cleopatra Queene of Ægypt."

17 For more on *The Masque of Blackness* and its role in reconciling English nationalism and Jacobean designs for empire see my essay, "Sexual Politics

337

and Cultural Identity in *The Masque of Blackness*," in *The Performance of Power: Theatrical Discourse and Politics*, ed. Sue-Ellen Case and Janelle Reinelt (Iowa City: University of Iowa Press, 1991), 3–18.

18 I argue for a slightly more complex version of identity formation than that offered by Naomi J. Miller, "'Nott much to be marked': Narrative of the Women's Part in Lady Mary Wroth's *Urania*, *Studies in English Literature: 1500–1900* 29 (Winter 1989), 121–38, who argues "that Wroth's women more consistently realize their identities through affirmations of their relatedness rather than through assertions of difference" (126). While Wroth's primary emphasis is on connections between women, that very emphasis seems to provoke a set of tensions about difference.

19 Mary Wroth, *The Countess of Montgomerie's Urania*, STC 26051, p. 40. All references to the *Urania* are to this edition, hereafter cited in the text.

20 In her discussion of this figure, Josephine Roberts, "Labyrinths of Desire: Lady Mary Wroth's Reconstruction of Romance," *Women's Studies* 19: 2 (1991), 183–92, argues that the figure is a dream symbol which "serve[s] physically as a double for the maid, allowing her to view her subservience from the outside and eventually to become conscious of her own self-abnegation" (199). Robertson makes the maid and the "black-moore" part of a shared sameness, whereas my argument is to highlight blackness as a difference that helps constitute whiteness as a value.

21 Anthony Gerard Barthelemy, *Black Face, Maligned Race: The Representation of Blacks in English Drama from Shakespeare to Southerne* (Baton Rouge and London: Louisiana State University Press, 1987), 123.

22 Ibid., 126.

23 For a complete discussion of the gendering of racial difference in English travel narratives, see my dissertation, "Acknowledging Things of Darkness: Race, Gender, and Power in Early Modern England" (University of Pennsylvania, 1990).

24 Mary Wroth, *The Poems of Lady Mary Wroth*, ed. Josephine Roberts (Baton Rouge and Louisiana: Louisiana State University Press, 1983). All references to Wroth's poems are to this edition; hereafter cited in the text.

25 Carolyn Ruth Swift, "Feminine Identity in *The Countess of Montgomerie's Urania*," *English Literary Renaissance* 14 (Autumn 1984), 332–3.

26 Ann Rosalind Jones suggests that in *Pamphilia to Amphilanthus*, Wroth finds much of her authority in her identification with Night: "many of the more forceful poems in the sequence establish Night as a feminine figure with whom Pamphilia identifies and through whom she can prove her merit" (*The Currency of Eros*, 146).

27 See Elaine V. Beilin, *Redeeming Eve: Women Writers of the English Renaissance* (Princeton: Princeton University Press, 1987), 215.

28 The emblem of the impossible in the Renaissance, "washing the Ethiop white," also speaks to this desire as it both evokes and precludes the possibility of whiteness and favor existing simultaneously with blackness. For a discussion of this trope, see Karen Newman's essay, "'And wash the Ethiop white': Femininity and the Monstrous in *Othello*," in *Shakespeare Reproduced: The Text in History and Ideology*, ed. Jean Howard and Marion O'Connor (New York and London: Methuen, 1987), 143–62.

29 Wroth had two illegitimate children by her first cousin and wrote her romance after being sent down from court. For Wroth's biography, see Roberts's introduction to *The Poems of Lady Mary Wroth*. For a discussion of the *Urania* poems as Wroth's response to the ideologies restraining Stuart women, see Maureen Quilligan, "The Inconstant Subject: Instability and

Authority in Wroth's *Urania* Poems," in *Soliciting Interpretations: Essays in Seventeenth-Century Poetry*, ed. Elizabeth Harvey and Katherine Maus (Chicago: University of Chicago Press, 1990), 274–307.

30 Lamb, *Gender and Authorship*, 10.

31 Cynthia Enloe, *Bananas, Beaches, and Bases: Making Feminist Sense of International Politics* (Berkeley and Los Angeles: University of California Press, 1989), 16.

32 Kenneth B. Murdoch, *The Sun at Noon: Three Biographical Sketches* (New York: Macmillan, 1939), 10.

33 bell hooks, "Feminism: A Transformational Politic," in *Talking Back: Thinking Feminist • Thinking Black* (Boston: South End Press, 1989), 25.

11 THE TENTH MUSE
Gender, rationality, and the marketing of knowledge
Stephanie Jed

I want to emphasize that this essay is a theoretical reflection on the construction of the "Tenth Muse" in relation to history and history-making institutions; it is not an essay on Anne Bradstreet and Sor Juana. I hope I will not seem arrogant by using and developing the construction of these writers as examples. For relevant bibliography, I refer the reader to Raymond F. Dolle, *Anne Bradstreet: A Reference Guide* (Boston: G. K. Hall & Co., 1990) and to the important collection of essays edited (and authored) by Stephanie Merrim, *Feminist Perspectives on Sor Juana Inés de la Cruz* (Detroit: Wayne State University Press, 1991).

Many people have helped me to work out the ideas in this essay. The students in my Gender Studies class (Spring 1991) explored the possibilities of a Women's Archive in their construction of a historicizing, fictive relationship between Sor Juana and Anne Bradstreet. Bett Miller's dissertation in progress on the works of Nicole Brossard has challenged me to explore alternative spatial constructions and genealogies of women's writing. I would like to express appreciation to Eduardo Garcia for his stimulating feedback and support. I would like to express special gratitude to my colleagues who have read and generously discussed with me countless drafts of this essay: Judith Halberstam, Nicole Tonkovich, Beth Holmgren, and Pasquale Verdicchio.

1 Concerning the early publication and promotion of Anne Bradstreet's works, see *The Tenth Muse (1650) and, From the manuscripts, Meditations Divine and Morall Together with Letters and occasional Pieces by Anne Bradstreet*, facsimile reproductions with an intro. by Josephine K. Piercy (Delmar: Scholars' Facsimiles & Reprints, 1978); Dolle, *Anne Bradstreet*, 1–4; Pattie Cowell, "The Early Distribution of Anne Bradstreet's Poems," in *Critical Essays on Anne Bradstreet*, ed. Pattie Cowell and Ann Stanford (Boston: G. K. Hall & Co., 1983), 270–9; Elizabeth Wade White, *Anne Bradstreet "The Tenth Muse"* (New York: Oxford University Press, 1971), 251–92. Concerning the early publication of the works of Sor Juana, see *Sor Juana Inés de la Cruz ante la historia*, A compilation by Francisco de la Maza (Mexico City: Universidad Nacional Autónoma de México, 1980), 35; Ludwig Pfandl, *Sor Juana Inés de la Cruz, La Décima Musa de México: Su vida, su poesía, su psique*, ed. Francisco de la Maza (Mexico City: Universidad Nacional Autónoma de México, 1983), 83–6. Pfandl notes that Lope de Vega, in 1624, had referred to Marcia Leonarda as the "tenth muse." Indeed, many other cases of "Tenth Muses" might be cited. Finally, the episode of the Ashmolean Museum is reported in Paula Findlen's important essay, "The Museum: Its Classical Etymology and Renaissance

Genealogy," *Journal of the History of Collections* 1, no. 1 (1989), 72.

2 Findlen, "The Museum," 68.

3 I am indebted to my colleague Nicole Tonkovich for helping me to clarify these gender norms with respect to literary production. For an important treatment of the same gender contradiction in the history of science, see Londa Schiebinger, "Feminine Icons: The Face of Early Modern Science," *Critical Inquiry* 14, no. 4 (1988), 661–91; and *The Mind Has No Sex? Women in the Origins of Modern Science* (Cambridge, Mass., and London: Harvard University Press, 1991).

4 John Woodbridge, "Epistle to the Reader," *The Works of Anne Bradstreet*, ed. Jeannine Hensley (Cambridge, Mass., and London: Harvard University Press, 1967), 3.

5 Anne Bradstreet, "The Prologue," ibid., 15–17.

6 *A Sor Juana Anthology*, trans. Alan S. Trueblood (Cambridge, Mass., and London: Harvard University Press, 1988), 26–33 (poem no. 48).

7 Susan Howe, "The Captivity and Restoration of Mrs. Mary Rowlandson," *Temblor*, no. 2 (n.d.), 118; Annette Kolodny, *The Land Before Her: Fantasy and Experience of the American Frontiers, 1630–1860* (Chapel Hill: University of North Carolina Press, 1984), 17.

8 The work of Michel Foucault has, of course, been fundamental to the understanding of this episteme. See, in particular, *The Order of Things: An Archeology of the Human Sciences* (New York: Vintage Books, 1973).

9 Findlen, "The Museum," 63.

10 Daniel Defert, "Collecting the World: Accounts of Voyages from the Sixteenth to the Eighteenth Centuries," *Dialectical Anthropology* 7, no. 1 (September 1982), 11–20. For a related study, may I refer the reader to my "Making History Straight: Collecting and Recording in Sixteenth-Century Italy," *Bucknell Review* 35, no. 2 (1992), 104–20.

11 J. H. Elliott, *The Old World and the New: 1492–1650* (Cambridge: Cambridge University Press, 1970), 32–8.

12 Gonzalo Fernández de Oviedo, *Historia general y natural de las Indias*, vols. 117–21 in the series Bibiloteca de Autores Españoles (Madrid: Ediciones Atlas, 1959), vol. 118 (vol. 2 of the *Historia general*), 32–5. Cf. Elliott's brief reference to the episode in *The Old World*, 37.

My own research (limited as it is to events and developments on or emanating from the Italian peninsula) has led me to think about the "Tenth Muse" in relation to Oviedo. Remote in time and place from the construction and promotion of the "Tenth Muse," this text nonetheless provides a jarring (and, I believe, productive) context for making visible the relation of taxonomies and "facts" to gender, rationality, and the marketing of knowledge. It is my hope that scholars who specialize in Sor Juana and Anne Bradstreet will think of other texts more pertinent to this argument.

13 Oviedo, *Historia*, 32. Translations are my own.

14 Ibid., 35.

15 Donna Haraway, "Teddy Bear Patriarchy: Taxidermy in the Garden of Eden, New York City, 1908–1936," *Social Text*, vol. 11 (Winter 1985), 52. See also Margaret Hodgen, "The Place of the Savage in the Great Chain of Being," in her *Early Anthropology in the Sixteenth and Seventeenth Centuries* (Philadelphia: University of Pennsylvania Press, 1964), 386–430.

16 My analysis of this episode is indebted to the feminist sociological methods articulated by Dorothy E. Smith in her books: *The Everyday World as Problematic: A Feminist Sociology* (Boston: Northeastern University Press, 1987); *The Conceptual Practices of Power: A Feminist Sociology of Knowledge*

(Boston: Northeastern University Press, 1990); *Texts, Facts, and Femininity: Exploring the Relations of Ruling* (London and New York: Routledge, 1990).

17 Smith, *Texts*, 21–8.

18 Marica Milanesi, "Introduzione," in Giovanni Battista Ramusio, *Navigazioni e viaggi*, 6 vols (Turin: Einaudi, 1978–85), vol. 1, xxi. (Oviedo's *Sommario* and *Della naturale e generale istoria dell'Indie* may be found in vol. 5 of this edition.)

19 Ibid., xix–xx.

20 Defert, "Collecting the World," 16.

21 Milanesi, introductory note to Ramusio's "Discorso sopra varii viaggi . . ." in *Navigazioni*, vol. 2, 961–2.

22 This section of my essay is especially indebted to Patricia Parker's essay "Rhetorics of Property: Exploration, Inventory, Blazon," in *Literary Fat Ladies: Rhetoric, Gender, Property* (London and New York: Methuen, 1987), 126–54. Parker's brilliant analysis of the figure of inventory illuminates the way in which the promotion of a woman writer can become a way of making her "a passive commodity in a homosocial discourse or male exchange in which the woman herself does not speak" (131).

23 White, *Anne Bradstreet*, 252.

24 Parker, "Rhetorics of Property," 131.

25 Cowell, "The Early Distribution," 272 n. 11; White, *Anne Bradstreet*, 251–2. The place of this copy of the 1650 edition of *The Tenth Muse* in Thomason's collection of Civil War and Commonwealth period books and pamphlets now residing in the British Museum is dramatically inviting of rhetorical analysis.

26 See bibliography in n. 1 and Octavio Paz, *Sor Juana or, The Traps of Faith*, trans. Margaret Sayers Peden (Cambridge, Mass.: Harvard University Press, 1988), 199. For an important analysis of the political context in which Sor Juana wrote, see Jean Franco, "Sor Juana Explores Space," in *Plotting Women: Gender and Representation in Mexico* (New York: Columbia University Press, 1989), 23–54.

27 Haraway, "Teddy Bear Patriarchy," 52.

28 Adrienne Rich, "Anne Bradstreet and Her Poetry," in *The Works of Anne Bradstreet*, xiii. This essay was written for the first printing of this edition in 1967.

29 Ibid., xvii.

30 Adrienne Rich, "Postscript," ibid., xxi.

31 Biblioteca Marciana, Misc. stampe 2088.

32 "Lettera di Amerigo Vespucci delle isole nuovamente trovate in quattro suoi viaggi" (Florence, 1505). On the subject of gender in English promotional literature, see Kolodny, Parker, 141–6, and especially the essay of Louis Montrose, "The Work of Gender in the Discourse of Discovery," *Representations* 33 (1991), 1–41.

33 John Smith, "The Description of New England," in *Tracts and Other Papers relating principally to the Origin, Settlement and Progress of the Colonies in North America*, collected by Peter Force (Gloucester, Mass.: Peter Smith, 1963) vol. 2, 9. Cited also by Parker, "Rhetorics of Property," 140.

34 Nicola Raponi, "Per la storia dell'Archivio di Stato di Milano: Erudizione e cultura nell'*Annuario* del Fumi (1909–1919)," *Rassegna degli Archivi di Stato* 31, no. 2 (1971), 316.

35 Here, I would like to suggest that Parker's analysis of the figure of inventory in literary and political texts might be transposed to the actual instruments of historical research.

36 Franco, "Sor Juana," 25.

12 JUGGLING THE CATEGORIES OF RACE, CLASS, AND GENDER
Aphra Behn's *Oroonoko*
Margaret W. Ferguson

Many colleagues and students have helped me with this essay; I owe special thanks to Judy Berman, Ann R. Jones, Mary Poovey, David Simpson, Valerie Smith, and Liz Wiesen. An earlier version of this essay was written for a special issue of *Women's Studies: An Interdisciplinary Journal* (Spring 1991) edited by Ann R. Jones and Betty Travitsky. I am grateful to Wendy Martin, editor of *Women's Studies*, for allowing me to reuse materials that originally appeared in that special issue.

1 For cogent, bibliographically useful discussions of the historical and conceptual problems implicit in the varying popular and academic understanding of each of these terms see Henry Louis Gates, Jr, "Writing 'Race' and the Difference it Makes," pp. 1–20 and Anthony Appiah, "The Uncompleted Argument: Du Bois and the Illusion of Race," both in *"Race," Writing, and Difference*, ed. Henry Louis Gates, Jr, *Critical Inquiry* 12 (Autumn 1985); Joan Wallach Scott, "Gender: A Useful Category of Historical Analysis," in her *Gender and the Politics of History* (New York: Columbia University Press, 1988), pp. 28–50; Raymond Williams's discussion of ambiguities in both Marxist and non-Marxist notions of class in *Keywords* (New York: Oxford University Press, 1976), pp. 51–9; Constance Jordan, "Renaissance Women and the Question of Class," in *Sexuality and Gender in Early Modern Europe*, ed. James G. Turner (Cambridge: Cambridge University Press, 1993), pp. 90–106; and Stephen A. Resnick and Richard D. Wolff, *Knowledge and Class* (Chicago: University of Chicago Press, 1987).

2 See Karen Newman, "'And wash the Ethiop white': Femininity and the Monstrous," in *Fashioning Femininity and the English Renaissance Drama* (Chicago: University of Chicago Press, 1991); Laura Brown, "The Romance of Empire: *Oroonoko* and the Trade in Slaves," in *The New Eighteenth Century*, ed. L. Brown and Felicity Nussbaum (New York: Methuen, 1987), pp. 40–61; and Ania Loomba, *Gender, Race, Renaissance Drama* (Manchester: Manchester University Press, 1989).

3 See Joan Kelly, "Did Women Have a Renaissance?" (1977); rpt. in *Women, History, and Theory: The Essays of Joan Kelly* (Chicago: University of Chicago Press, 1984), pp. 19–50.

4 Kelly, "The Doubled Vision of Feminist Theory," in *Women, History, and Theory*, pp. 51–64; the quotation is from p. 58.

5 For a pioneering effort to define a "sex/gender" system (a phrase she prefers to "patriarchy" or "mode of reproduction"), see Gayle Rubin, "The Traffic in Women," in *Toward an Anthropology of Women*, ed. Rayna R. Reiter (New York and London: Monthly Review Press, 1975), pp. 157–210, esp. pp. 159, 167. More recently, some feminists have criticized this concept as granting an overly "transparent" determination to the body (what Rubin calls "anatomical sex difference"); see, e.g., Moira Gatens, "A Critique of the Sex/Gender Distinction," in *Beyond Marxism?*, ed. J. Allen and P. Patton (Leichhardt, NSW: Intervention Publications, 1985), pp. 143–60; and also Teresa de Lauretis, *Technologies of Gender: Essays on Theory, Film, and Fiction* (Bloomington: Indiana University Press, 1987), p. 9 (on why she prefers the term *gender* to sex/gender system).

6 See Barbara Fields, "Ideology and Race in American History," in *Region, Race*

and Reconstruction, ed. J. Morgan Kousser and James M. McPherson (New York: Oxford University Press, 1982), p. 149.

7 *International Encyclopedia of Social Sciences*, ed. David L. Sills (New York: Macmillan, 1968), 13: 264.

8 David Brion Davis, *The Problem of Slavery in Western Culture* (Ithaca: Cornell University Press, 1966), p. 277.

9 Edward Long, *Candid Reflections upon the Judgement Lately Awarded by the Court of King's Bench . . . on What is Commonly Called the Negro Cause* (London, 1772; cited in Davis, *The Problem of Slavery*, p. 277); see also Natalie Zemon Davis's discussion of the ideological and sometimes political associations between "unruly" women and lower-class men during the Renaissance, in "Women on Top," *Society and Culture in Early Modern France* (Stanford: Stanford University Press, 1975), pp. 124–51.

10 Fields, "Ideology and Race," p. 146.

11 For an interesting discussion of this problem see Wendy James, "The Anthropologist as Reluctant Imperialist," in *Anthropology and the Colonial Encounter*, ed. Talal Asad (New York: Humanities Press, 1973), pp. 41–69, and other essays in that volume, including Asad's Introduction.

12 The *OED* gives numerous illustrations from Renaissance texts of the definitions of race as "Mankind" (1.5a) or as "A limited group of persons descended from a common ancestor" (1.2), though it cites no examples of meanings stressing physical differences and a general taxonomic division of all humans according to race (1.2d: "One of the great divisions of mankind, having certain physical differences in common") until 1774; the first reference to race as a liability (implicitly) of dark color is Emerson's remark, in *English Traits* (1856), that "Race in the Negro is of appalling importance" (1.6b). It is instructive to read the *OED*'s highly selective diachronic narrative on race in conjunction with Marvin Harris's discussion of the synchronically various uses of the term and its "ethnosemantic glosses," which are applied "to human populations organized along an astonishing variety of principles." To illustrate that variety, he remarks that in some societies where the group identity is not secured through the "ideological device" of genealogical rules, categorizations will tend to rely *more* on visible signs of difference such as skin color than they do when "the idea of descent" is paramount. In Bahia, for instance, where descent rules are absent, "full siblings whose phenotypes markedly differ from each other are assigned . . . to contrastive racial categories" and "pronounced disagreements concerning the identity of individuals frequently occur" ("Race," *International Encyclopedia of Social Sciences* 13: 263, 264).

13 See de Lauretis, *Technologies of Gender*, pp. 2–3.

14 Resnick and Wolff, *Knowledge and Class*, pp. 115, 117.

15 In *Keywords* Raymond Williams suggests that the term "class" acquired its modern sense designating divisions of social groups (in contrast to divisions among things like plants) during the period between 1770 and 1840 (p. 61). For a discussion of the problems of using "class" in analyzing early and premodern social formations, see E. P. Thompson, "Eighteenth-Century English Society: Class Struggle Without Class?" *Social History* 3 (1978), 133–65. See also Constance Jordan's important recent essay "Renaissance Women and the Question of Class" (cited above, n. 1).

16 Brown, "The Romance of Empire," p. 42.

17 According to Behn's first biographer, she was a "Gentlewoman, by Birth, of a good Family in the City of Canterbury in Kent" (*Memoirs on the Life of Mrs. Behn. Written by a Gentlewomen of her Acquaintance, in Histories and Novels*,

London: printed for S. Briscoe, 1696, sig. A₇v, quoted from the British Library copy). Not until the late nineteenth century did anyone seek publicly to refashion Behn's biography; Sir Edward Gosse then lowered her social status on the evidence of a scribbled note, "Mrs Behn was daughter to a barber," in the margin of a recently discovered MS by Anne Finch, the Countess of Winchelsea. Goreau provides an account of Gosse's "discovery" (given authority in his *Dictionary of National Biography* article on her) and subsequent biographical arguments on pp. 8–10 of *Reconstructing Aphra: A Social Biography of Aphra Behn* (New York: The Dial Press, 1980). For further discussions of the "mystery" of Behn's birth and the manifold speculations it has engendered, see Goreau, pp. 11–13, 42–3; Sara Mendelson, *The Mental World of Stuart Women: Three Studies* (Brighton: Harvester, 1987), pp. 116–20; and Maureen Duffy, *The Passionate Shepherdess: Aphra Behn, 1640–89* (London: Cape, 1977), ch. 1. See Goreau, *Reconstructing Aphra*, pp. 12–13, for a discussion of the importance of Behn's (anomalous) education for her social status.

18 See Wlad Godzich, "The Culture of Illiteracy," *Enclitic* 8 (Fall 1984), 27–35, on humanist intellectuals as servants of the emerging nation states and the expanding international market of the early modern era. See also the chapter on Joachim de Bellay in my *Trials of Desire: Renaissance Defenses of Poetry* (New Haven: Yale University Press, 1983).

19 I am grateful to Catherine Gallagher for letting me see her chapters, "Who Was That Masked Woman? The Prostitute and the Playwright in the Comedies of Aphra Behn" and "The Author Monarch and the Royal Slave: *Oroonoko* and the Blackness of Representation," in her forthcoming book *British Women Writers and the Literary Marketplace from 1670–1820*. A version of "Who Was That Masked Woman?" appears in *Last Laughs: Perspectives on Women and Comedy* ed. Regina B. Barecca (New York: Gordon & Breach, 1988).

20 For the date of *Oroonoko*'s composition see George Guffey, "Aphra Behn's *Oroonoko*: Occasion and Accomplishment," in *Two English Novelists: Aphra Behn and Anthony Trollope*, co-authored with Andrew White (Los Angeles: William Andrews Clark Memorial Library, 1975), pp. 15–16. All quotations from *Oroonoko* are from the text edited by Lore Metzger (New York: W.W. Norton & Co., 1973). The reference to the female pen is from p. 40. See Laura Brown, "The Romance of Empire," esp. 48–51, for a discussion of the story's debt to the traditions of heroic romance and, in particular, coterie aristocratic drama.

21 For an excellent account and bibliography of the Renaissance ideology of normative femininity, see Ann Rosalind Jones, *The Currency of Eros: Women's Love Lyric in Europe, 1540–1620* (Bloomington: Indiana University Press, 1990), ch. 1.

22 For examples of this gendered "colonial" cultural discourse see the passages cited above from Davis, *The Problem of Slavery*, and Goreau, *Reconstructing Aphra*, pp. 48–9 (on the fears of "sodomy" that kept one lady living in Antigua housebound, and on the repercussions of the fact that men in the colonies greatly outnumbered women).

23 On Behn's situation after her father died, impoverished but also freer of paternal constraint than was thought proper, see Goreau, *Reconstructing Aphra*, p. 42.

24 My account of the multiple alignments of the "I" is indebted to questions prepared by Judy Berman for a graduate seminar at the University of California, Berkeley, in the spring of 1988.

25 Chudleigh's text, from her *Poems on Several Occasions* (London, 1703), is quoted from *First Feminists: British Women Writers 1578–1799*, ed. Moira Ferguson (Bloomington and Old Westbury: Indiana University Press and the Feminist Press, 1985), p. 237. Cf. the statement in a famous pamphlet entitled *The Levellers*, also from 1703, that "Matrimony is indeed become a meer Trade [.] They carry their Daughters to *Smithfield* as they do Horses, and sell to the highest bidder." Quoted in Maximillian E. Novak and David Stuart Rodes's edition of Thomas Southerne's *Oroonoko* (Lincoln: University of Nebraska Press, 1976), p. xxiv.

26 Behn offers a more literal and comic representation of impotence in the first part of the novella, where Imoinda is taken from Oroonoko by his tyrannical but impotent grandfather; she also represents male impotence in many of her plays and in her witty poem "The Disappointment."

27 The quotation is from the "Epistle Dedicatory" to Lord Maitland, included in the edition of *Oroonoko* by Adelaide P. Amore (Washington, DC: University Press of America, 1987), p. 3, but not in the Norton edition. See Goreau, *Reconstructing Aphra*, pp. 68–9, for Byam's reasons for disliking Behn and his snide reference to her as "Astrea" in a letter to a friend in England.

28 See her Preface to *The Lucky Chance*, where she requests "the Priviledge for my Masculine Part the Poet in me (if any such you will allow me) to tread in those successful Paths my Predecessors has so long thriv'd in" (*The Works of Aphra Behn*, ed. Montague Summers, 6 vols [1915; rpt. New York: Benjamin Blom, 1967], 3, p. 187).

29 For a fine discussion of this stereotypical confrontation across color and gender lines, see Anthony Barthelemy, *Black Face, Maligned Race: The Representation of Blacks in English Drama from Shakespeare to Southerne* (Baton Rouge: Louisiana State University Press, 1987), esp. ch. 4. Behn herself, in *Abdelazar; Or the Moor's Revenge* (1677), her adaptation for the Restoration stage of Dekker's *Lust's Dominion*, exploits the conventional image of the threateningly sexual black man.

30 Note that the most logical syntactic antecedent of "they" would be a group of *black* men composed of Oroonoko and his band, perpetrating the rape which one might easily construe as the referent for "this cruelty." The grammatical ambiguity arguably points to the struggle between the narrator's original perception of danger and her "corrected" but guiltily impotent retroactive perception that the white men, not the black ones, were her true enemies.

31 Cf. the passage where the white male character Trefry is said to be "infinitely well pleased" with the "novel" of Oroonoko's and Imoinda's reunion (p. 44).

32 See, for instance, the diametrically opposed interpretations of George Guffey and Angeline Goreau on the issue of Behn's representation of black slaves. For Guffey, who reads confidently "through" the sign of Oroonoko's blackness to an English political subtext, the novella's ideological argument is not anti-slavery but against the enslavement of *kings*, specifically the Stuart King tenuously on England's throne in 1688 ("Aphra Behn's *Oroonoko*: Occasion and Accomplishment," pp. 16–17). Goreau, in contrast (and equally confidently), sees Behn's "impassioned attack on the condition of slavery and defense of human rights" as "perhaps the first important abolitionist statement in the history of English literature" (*Reconstructing Aphra*, p. 289). See Tzvetan Todorov, *The Conquest of America: The Question of the Other*, (New York: Harper, 1984).

33 The text is, however, significantly ambiguous about whether Behn could or did own slaves in her own right, as an unfathered, unmarried woman. In her prefatory letter to Maitland, she refers to Oroonoko as "my Slave," but she

suggests, in the course of the story, that she lacked the power to dispose of her chattel property: she relates that she "assured" him falsely, as it turns out, that he would be freed when the governor arrived (p. 45).

34 Cf. p. 48, where the narrator laments that "certainly had his late Majesty [Charles II], of sacred Memory, but seen and known what a vast and charming World he had been Master of in that Continent, he would never have parted so easily with it to the Dutch"; the passage goes on to advertise the natural riches of the (once and future) colony. On the British loss of Surinam in exchange for New York, see Eric Williams, *From Columbus to Castro: The History of the Caribbean* (1970; rpt. New York: Vintage, 1984), p. 81.

35 See, for example, Lore Metzger's introduction to the Norton *Oroonoko*, pp. ix-x and Eric Williams, *From Columbus to Castro*, p. 207: "Oroonoko opposed the revolts of the slaves as did his creator, Mrs. Behn." That statement seems to rely more on Southerne's version, where Oroonoko is made to speak in favor of the institution of slavery and lead a revolt only with great reluctance, than on Behn's, where the hero passionately leads the slaves to revolt and defends their right to regain their liberty (p. 61).

36 In *Guinea's Captive Kings: British Anti-Slavery Literature of the XVIIIth Century* (Chapel Hill: University of North Carolina Press, 1942), p. 21, Wylie Sypher suggests that it was more acceptable for theater audiences that Imoinda be white. Queen Anne and her ladies had been criticized for wearing blackface in Jonson's *Masque of Blackness*, but Englishwomen representing Moors had evidently worn black masks and make-up in the Lord Mayor's pageants in London after the Restoration; see Anthony Barthelemy, *Black Face, Maligned Race*, esp. ch. 3.

37 For the poem attacking Southerne for failing to give Imoinda an "*Indian hue*," see Maximillian E. Novak and David S. Rodes's Introduction to their edition of Southerne's *Oroonoko*, p. xxxvii. In *The Problem of Slavery*, Davis discusses the tendency to conflate Amerindians and African blacks in a discourse of "primitivism" (p. 480).

38 See *Memoirs on the Life of Mrs. Behn* (cited above, n. 17), sig. B_1r; The rumor is also mentioned by Lore Metzger in her Introduction to *Oroonoko*, p. x; most modern biographers prefer another story (which has some documentary support) that Behn had an affair with a white Republican, William Scott, during her stay in Surinam (see Goreau, *Reconstructing Aphra*, pp. 66–8).

39 On the "buy or breed" debates, see Daniel P. Mannix in collaboration with Malcolm Cowley, *Black Cargoes: A History of the Atlantic Slave Trade 1518–1865* (New York: Viking, 1962), p. 52.

40 See Amore, "Introduction" to *Oroonoko*, for the hypothesis that this detail testifies to Behn's piety and possible Catholicism. Accepting the likelihood that she was indeed a Catholic, I wouldn't assume that the stories designed for Imoinda by the narrator are any more pious than Behn's own racy stories about nuns; indeed there may well be a bit of authorial self-reference (or even witty self-advertisement) here. See Behn's *History of the Nun, or, The Fair Vow Breaker* and *The Nun, or The Perjur'd Beauty*, both in *The Works of Aphra Behn*, ed. Montague Summers, vol. 5.

41 Since the blacks also greatly outnumbered the whites in the colony, Behn's explanation for the distinction in the English treatment of the two non-white groups is clearly problematic. The matter continues to be a site of debate in modern histories of slavery in the New World, for even though Indians *were* frequently enslaved, all of the colonial powers came, eventually, to prefer African to Amerindian slaves for reasons that confusingly blended economic,

theological, and cultural explanations. Some modern historians, for instance Winthrop Jordan, in *White over Black: American Attitudes toward the Negro, 1550–1812* (Chapel Hill: University of North Carolina Press, 1968), invoke color difference as an explanation for why Africans came (eventually) to be seen as better (more "natural") slaves than Indians, but this view, cited and refuted by Fields, p. 11, seems anachronistic and reductive. More satisfactory discussions are given by Davis, *The Problem of Slavery*, who sees the distinction as an "outgrowth of the practical demands of trade and diplomacy" (p. 178) bolstered by ideological fictions about blackness (the biblical color of evil) and "noble savages"; and by William D. Phillips, Jr, *Slavery from Roman Times to the Early Transatlantic Trade* (Minneapolis: University of Minnesota Press, 1985), who, in discussing the commonly cited adage that "one Negro is worth four Indians" in terms of labor power, suggests that the difference between the Africans' experience in agricultural societies and the Amerindians' in mainly hunting-gathering cultures helps account for this sobering ideological distinction (p. 184) that makes a person's *economic* value stand in antithetical relation to his or her *moral* value (in European eyes, at least, which equated freedom with "natural" nobility).

42 For discussions of early critics of slavery such as Las Casas (who came only late in life to decry the enslavement of blacks as well as Indians) and Albornoz, see Davis, *The Problem of Slavery*, p. 189 and *passim*; Eric Williams, *From Columbus to Castro*, pp. 43–4; and Goreau, *Reconstructing Aphra*, p. 289 (on the Quaker George Fox's opposition to the system of slavery).

43 Alice Walker, "Advancing Luna – and Ida B. Wells," in *You Can't Keep a Good Woman Down* (New York: Harcourt Brace Jovanovich, 1981), p. 93.

44 Quoted from *Othello*, ed. Alvin Kernan (New York: New American Library, 1963), p. 55.

45 See Brown, "The Romance of Empire," pp. 47–8, where she comments astutely on Behn's description of Oroonoko as a perfect European hero ("his nose was rising and Roman, instead of African and flat," Norton edn, p. 8).

46 Elegy 19, "To his Mistris Going To Bed," quoted from *John Donne: Poetry and Prose*, ed. Frank Warnke (New York: Random House Modern Library, 1967), p. 96. See Mannix and Cowley, *Black Cargoes*, p. 60, on the Maryland Assembly's early (1663) law against racial intermarriages, a law specifically directed against Englishwomen; cf. Davis's observation, in *The Problem of Slavery*, that the North American colonies adopted "harsh penalties for whites who had sexual relations with Negroes, and the punishments were usually more severe for white women" (p. 277, n. 27).

47 See Barthelemy, *Black Face*, ch. 3, for a rich account of personifications of Africa on English maps and in pageants; and see also Louis Montrose, "The Work of Gender in the Discourse of Discovery," *Representations* 33 (Winter 1991), 1–41.

48 See Maureen Duffy and George Guffey for different versions, both I think reductive, of a topical interpretation of *Oroonoko* which takes Behn's hero as an allegorical figure for various Stuart monarchs, especially the "martyred" Charles I and the soon-to-be-deposed James II. Catherine Gallagher offers a more nuanced reading of the novella in terms of absolutist political ideology in her forthcoming *British Women Writers and the Literary Marketplace*.

13 CIVILITY, BARBARISM, AND
APHRA BEHN'S *THE WIDOW RANTER*
Margo Hendricks

1 Valerie Wayne, ed., *The Matter of Difference: Materialist Feminist Criticism of Shakespeare* (London: Harvester Wheatsheaf, 1991), 11.

2 Dominick LaCapra, ed., *The Bounds of Race: Perspectives on Hegemony and Resistance* (Ithaca: Cornell University Press, 1991), 2.

3 Margaret Ferguson, "Juggling the Categories of Race, Class, and Gender: Aphra Behn's *Oroonoko*," ch. 12, this volume.

4 One of the primary texts Behn may have used was *Strange News From Virginia: Being a full and True Account of the Life and Death of Nathanael Bacon Esquire, Who was the only Cause and Original of all the Late Troubles in that Country. With a full Relation of all the Accidents which have happened in the late War there between the Christians and Indians*. The pamphlet narrates Bacon's lineage, his settlement in the Virginia colony, his anger at the Virginia Council's refusal to grant him a commission, the ensuing discord between Bacon and the Council, his death, and the sentences meted out to his principal followers.

5 Wilcomb E. Washburn, *The Governor and the Rebel: A History of Bacon's Rebellion in Virginia* (Chapel Hill: University of North Carolina, 1957), 85.

6 Bernard W. Sheehan, *Savagism and Civility: Indians and Englishmen in Colonial Virgina* (Cambridge: Cambridge University Press, 1980), 2.

7 Sheehan, *Savagism and Civility*, 2.

8 See Ann Rosalind Jones and Peter Stallybrass, "Dismantling Irena: The Sexualizing of Ireland in Early Modern England," in *Nationalisms and Sexualities*, ed. Andrew Parker, Mary Russo, Doris Sommer, and Patricia Yaeger (London: Routledge, 1992), 157–71.

9 Louis B. Wright, ed., *The Elizabethans' America: A Collection of Early Reports by Englishmen on the New World* (Cambridge, Mass.: Harvard University Press, 1965), 109.

10 Thomas Harriot, *A Brief and True Report of the New-Found Land of Virginia*, in *The Elizabethans' America*, ed. Louis B. Wright (Cambridge, Mass.: Harvard University Press, 1965), 129–30.

11 Karen Ordahl Kupperman, *Settling with the Indians: The Meeting of English and Indian Cultures in America, 1580–1640* (New Jersey: Rowman & Littlefield, 1980), 121–2.

12 Kupperman, *Settling with the Indians*, 122.

13 See Michael Banton's *The Idea of Race* (London: Tavistock, 1977) and *Racial Theories* (Cambridge: Cambridge University Press, 1987) for an incisive analysis of the history of "race." See also *Anatomy of Racism*, ed. David Theo Goldberg (Minneapolis: University of Minnesota, 1991).

14 Homi K. Bhabha, "The Other Question: Difference, Discrimination and the Discourse of Colonialism," in *Out There: Marginalization and Contemporary Cultures*, ed. Russell Ferguson, Martha Gever, Trinh T. Minh-ha, and Cornel West (New York: MIT Press, 1990), 71.

15 Aphra Behn, *Five Plays* (London: Methuen, 1990). All references to *The Widow Ranter* are to this edition, hereafter cited in the text.

16 Marvin B. Becker, *Civility and Society in Western Europe, 1300–1600* (Bloomington: Indiana University Press, 1988), xiii.

17 Kupperman, *Settling with the Indians*, 113.

18 John Robinson, "How Happy a Thing Had It Been, if You had Converted Some before You Had Killed Any!" in *The Indian and the White Man*, ed. Wilcomb E. Washburn (New York: New York University Press, 1964), 176–7.

19 John Morton, *New English Canaan*, in *The Indian and the White Man*, ed. Wilcomb E. Washburn (New York: New York University Press, 1964), 37–8.
20 Morton, *New English Canaan*, 37.
21 Jones and Stallybrass, "Dismantling Irena," 160.
22 Laura Brown, "The Romance of Empire: *Oroonoko* and the Trade in Slaves," in *The New Eighteenth Century*, ed. Laura Brown and Felicity Nussbaum (New York: Methuen, 1987), 48.
23 Brown, "The Romance of Empire", 58.
24 Sheehan, *Savagism and Civility*, 3.
25 *Webster's New Collegiate Dictionary* defines miscegenation as the "marriage or interbreeding of different races." Usage of the word occurs for the first time in 1863 specifically to describe sexual and marital relations between "whites" and "blacks." Thus, for me to employ the term to describe such relations between American Indians and Europeans is, of course, problematic given the linguistic history of the word. However, lacking a better descriptive term and believing that similar assumptions inform resistance to intermarriages or sexual relations, I feel justified in expanding the definitional boundaries of miscegenation to include sexual and marital relations between American Indians and English immigrants.
26 Wright, *The Elizabethans' America*, 185.
27 Quoted in Kupperman, *Settling with the Indians*, 59.
28 John Winthrop, cited in *The Invasion Within: The Contest of Cultures in Colonial North America* (Oxford: Oxford University Press, 1985), 137. What is not clear in this declaration is the English attitude toward cultivated "Indian" lands.
29 Mary Dearborn, *Pocahontas' Daughters: Gender and Ethnicity in American Culture* (New York: Oxford University Press, 1986), 97.
30 Here I am thinking of the literary and film trope of the "half-breed" who self-consciously rejects "white" culture for American Indian culture.
31 For example, the Maryland colony enacted one of the earliest prohibitions against English–African miscegenation: "any White man that shall beget any Negroe Woman with Child whether Free Woman or Servant, shall undergo the same Penalties as White Women." These penalties included indentured servitude for seven years for the man or woman and thirty-one years for the child(ren) of such unions. Occurrences of English–African miscegenation in the Virginia colony in the first half of the seventeenth century were also generally punished. There is, however, no record of legal opposition to marital relations between Englishmen and American Indian women in the early stages of English colonialism in the Virginia colony. See William Browne *et al.*, eds, *Archives of Maryland* (Baltimore, 1883–1912), vol. 1.
32 See Felicity Nussbaum, "The Other Woman: Polygamy, *Pamela*, and the Prerogative of Empire," ch. 8, this volume.
33 Walter Rodney, *A History of the Upper Guinea Coast 1545 to 1800* (New York: Monthly Review, 1970), ix.
34 See Laura Brown, "The Romance of Empire," and Margaret W. Ferguson, "Whose Dominion, or News from the New World: Aphra Behn's Representation of Miscegenous Romance in *Oroonoke* and *The Widow Ranter*," in *The Production of English Renaisance Culture*, eds. David Lee Miller, Sharon O'Dair, and Harold Weber (Ithaca: Cornell University Press, 1994).
35 Bhabha, "The Other Question," 75.

14 IROQUOIS WOMEN, EUROPEAN WOMEN
Natalie Zemon Davis

An initial version of this essay was given on May 2, 1992, at the University of Chicago Centennial Colloquium "Do We Need 'The Renaissance'?" A somewhat different version will appear in the papers of the conference, edited by Philippe Desan, Richard Strier, and Elissa Weaver.

1 Paul Le Jeune, *Relation de ce qui s'est passé en la Nouvelle France en l'année 1633* (Paris, 1634) in Reuben Gold Thwaites, *The Jesuit Relations and Allied Documents* (henceforth *JR*), 73 vols (Cleveland, Ohio: Burrows Brothers, 1896–1901), 5: 118–21, 283 n. 33. Pierre Pastedechouan was born about 1605 and taken to France around 1618 by the Recollet brothers, then returned to Canada in 1625, living sometimes with the Jesuits and much of the time with the Montagnais. See also Gabriel Sagard, *Le Grand Voyage du pays des Hurons* (1632), ed. Réal Ouellet (Quebec: Bibliothèque québécoise, 1990), 58.

2 "The Dream of the White Robe and the floating island/Micmac," in Ella Elizabeth Clark, *Indian Legends of Canada* (Toronto: McClelland & Stewart, 1991), 151–2; also Silas Rand, *Legends of the Micmac* (New York: Longmans Green, 1894). For another Amerindian telling of the floating island and the coming of Europeans, see the excerpt from William Wood (1634) in William S. Simmons, *Spirit of the New England Tribes. Indian History and Folklore* (Hanover, NH: University Press of New England, 1986), 66. For a use of the floating island to describe origins of the Amerindians from a race of white giants, see "The Beginning and the End of the World (Okanogan of the Salishan Languages)," in Paula Gunn Allen, ed., *Spider Woman's Granddaughters. Traditional Tales and Contemporary Writing by Native American Women* (Boston: Beacon Press, 1989), 106–7. For references to the motif-type "Island canoe," see Stith Thompson, ed., *Tales of North American Indians* (Cambridge, Mass.: Harvard University Press, 1929), 275 n. 14.

3 Marie de l'Incarnation and Claude Martin, *La Vie de la vénérable Mère Marie de l'Incarnation première supérieure des Ursulines de la Nouvelle France* (Paris: Louis Billaine, 1677; facsimile ed. Solesmes: Abbaye Saint-Pierre, 1981), 228–30, 400, 408. Marie de l'Incarnation, *Correspondance*, ed. Dom Guy Oury (Solesmes: Abbaye Saint-Pierre, 1971), no. 28, 64–5, no. 41, 91.

4 General bibliographical orientation can be found in Dean R. Snow, *Native American Prehistory. A Critical Bibliography* (Bloomington: Indiana University Press for the Newberry Library, 1979); Neal Salisbury, *The Indians of New England. A Critical Bibliography* (Bloomington: Indiana University Press for the Newberry Library, 1982); James P. Ronda and James Axtell, *Indian Missions. A Critical Bibliography* (Bloomington: Indiana University Press for the Newberry Library, 1978). The writings of James Axtell have been pioneering in the study of the American Indians in their encounter with Europeans: *The European and the Indian: Essays in the Ethnohistory of Colonial North America* (Oxford and New York: Oxford University Press, 1981); *The Invasion Within. The Contest of Cultures in Colonial North America* (New York and Oxford: Oxford University Press, 1985); *After Columbus. Essays in the Ethnohistory of Colonial North America* (New York and Oxford: Oxford University Press, 1988); *Beyond 1492. Encounters in Colonial North America* (New York and Oxford: Oxford University Press, 1992). A general historical and ethnographical orientation to the Amerindian peoples of Canada is R. Bruce Morrison and C. Roderick Wilson, eds, *Native Peoples. The Canadian*

Experience (Toronto: McClelland & Stewart, 1986). Bruce G. Trigger's *Natives and Newcomers. Canada's "Heroic Age" Reconsidered* (Kingston and Montréal: McGill-Queen's University Press, 1985) is an excellent presentation of both archeological and historical evidence. Important studies of Iroquoian-speaking peoples include Elisabeth Tooker, *An Ethnography of the Huron Indians, 1615–1649* (Washington, DC: Smithsonian Institution for the Huronia Historical Development Council, 1964); Conrad Heidenreich, *Huronia. A History and Geography of the Huron Indians* (Toronto: McClelland & Stewart, 1971); Bruce G. Trigger, *The Children of Aataentsic. A History of the Huron People to 1660*, new edn (Kingston and Montréal: McGill-Queen's University Press, 1987) [with much archeological material from before the seventeenth century]; Lucien Campeau, *La mission des Jésuites chez les Hurons, 1634–1650* (Montreal: Editions Bellarmin, 1987), especially 1–113 on the pre-contact Hurons); Francis Jennings, *The Ambiguous Iroquois Empire. The Covenant Chain Confederation of Indian Tribes with English Colonies from Its Beginnings to the Lancaster Treaty of 1744* (New York: W. W. Norton, 1984); Francis Jennings, William Fenton, Mary Druke, and David R. Miller, eds, *The History and Culture of Iroquois Diplomacy. An Interdisciplinary Guide to the Treaties of the Six Nations and Their League* (Syracuse: Syracuse University Press, 1985); and Daniel K. Richter, *The Ordeal of the Longhouse. The Peoples of the Iroquois League in the Era of European Colonization* (Chapel Hill: University of North Carolina Press for the Institute of Early American History and Culture, 1992). Important studies of Algonquian-speaking peoples include Alfred Goldsworthy Bailey, *The Conflict of European and Eastern Algonkian Cultures, 1504–1700*, 2nd edn (Toronto: University of Toronto Press, 1969); Simmons, *Spirit of the New England Tribes*; Colin G. Calloway, ed., *Dawnland Encounters. Indians and Europeans in Northern New England* (Hanover, NH and London: University Press of New England, 1991); W. Vernon Kinietz, *The Indians of the Western Great Lakes, 1615–1760* (Ann Arbor: University of Michigan Press, 1965); Richard White, *Indians, Empires, and Republics in the Great Lakes Region, 1650–1815* (Cambridge: Cambridge University Press, 1991). Penny Petrone provides an introduction to Amerindian literary genres in *Native Literature in Canada. From the Oral Tradition to the Present* (Toronto: Oxford University Press, 1990). A major study of the art and material culture of Amerindian peoples, with much early historical evidence, is *The Spirit Sings. Artistic Traditions of Canada's First Peoples. A Catalogue of the Exhibition* (Toronto: McClelland & Stewart for the Glenbow-Alberta Institute, 1988). Special studies of Iroquois women have a long history behind them: a collection of essays from 1884 to 1989 is W. G. Spittal, ed., *Iroquois Women. An Anthology* (Ohsweken: Iroqrafts, 1990). Marxist and feminist approaches opened a new chapter in the study of Indian women of northeastern America in the work of Judith K. Brown, "Economic Organization and the Position of Women among the Iroquois," initially published in *Ethnohistory*, 17 (1970) and reprinted in *Iroquois Women*, 182–98, and Eleanor Leacock, "Montagnais Women and the Jesuit Program for Colonization," in Mona Etienne and Eleanor Leacock, eds, *Women and Colonization. Anthropological Perspectives* (New York: Praeger, 1980), 25–42. Karen Anderson's recent *Chain Her by One Foot. The Subjugation of Women in Seventeenth-Century France* (London and New York: Routledge, 1991) does not carry the conceptual argument beyond Leacock's pioneering essay. A new historical and ethnographical study of Iroquois women is under way by Carol Karlsen. An introduction to the history of Amerindian women of many regions is Carolyn Niethammer, *Daughters of the Earth. The Lives and Legends of American Indian*

Women (New York: Macmillan, 1977). Paula Gunn Allen has published several works that draw on a mix of historical examples, legends, and women's values and lore in her own Lakota family in order (as she says in the subtitle to *The Sacred Hoop*) "to recover the feminine in American Indian traditions": *The Sacred Hoop: Recovering the Feminine in American Indian Traditions*, 2nd edn (Boston: Beacon Press, 1992); *Spider Woman's Granddaughters*; and *Grandmothers of the Light. A Medicine Woman's Sourcebook* (Boston: Beacon Press, 1991).

5 Among many primary sources for this information on the division of labor: Sagard, *Grand Voyage*, Part 1, ch. 7 and passim, and *JR*, 5: 132–3.

6 On women being assisted in carrying tasks by male prisoners, see Marc Lescarbot, *The History of New France*, trans. W. L. Grant, 3 vols (Toronto: Champlain Society, 1907–1914), Book 6, ch. 17, 3: 200, 412.

7 Jacques Cartier, "Deuxième voyage de Jacques Cartier (1535–1536)," ed. Théodore Beauchesne in Charles A. Julien, ed., *Les Français en Amérique pendant la première moitié du 16e siècle* (Paris: Press Universitaires de France, 1946), 159. Sagard, *Grand Voyage*, 172. Sagard applied to the Huron women what Lescarbot had said in his *Histoire de la Nouvelle France* (1609), about women of the Micmacs and other Algonquian-speaking groups:

> J'ay dit au chapitre de la Tabagie [on banquets] qu'entre les Sauvages les femmes ne sont point en si bonne condition qu'anciennement entre les Gaullois et Allemans. Car (au rapport même de Iacques Quartier) "elles travaillent plus que les hommes," dit-il, "soit en la pecherie, soit au labour, ou autre chose." Et neantmoins elles ne sont point forcées, ne tourmentées, mais elles ne sont ni en leurs Tabagies [at their banquets], ni en leurs conseils, et font les oeuvres serviles, à faute de serviteurs.

Lescarbot, *New France* 3: 411. *JR*, 4: 204–5 ("ces pauvres femmes sont de vrais mulets de charge").

8 Marie de l'Incarnation, *Correspondance*, no. 97, 286; no. 244, 828–9. Marie de l'Incarnation and Claude Martin, *Vie*, 41–3, 54–5.

9 Sagard, *Grand Voyage*, Part 1, ch. 7, 172.

10 Heidenreich (*Huronia*, 77) gives two sources for Huron matrilineality. First, a single sentence from Samuel Champlain where, after noting that Hurons are not always sure of the father of a child because of permitted sexual promiscuity in marriage, he goes on,

> in view of this danger, they have a custom which is this, namely that the children never succeed to the property and honors of their fathers, being in doubt, as I said, of their begetter, but indeed they make their successors and heirs the children of their sisters, from whom these are certain to be sprung and issued

(*The Works of Samuel Champlain*, trans. H. P. Biggar, 6 vols [Toronto: Champlain Society, 1922–1936], 3: 140). Second, an unclear description of cross-cousin marriage by Sagard (*Grand Voyage*, Part 1, ch. 11, 199) that could apply to either a patrilineal or matrilineal situation. Elsewhere Sagard, said that after divorce Huron children usually stayed with ther father (201). Heidenreich concluded that matrilocality was sometimes practiced, sometimes not (77). In *Children of Aataentsic*, Trigger talks of a "matrilineal" preference among the Iroquoians more generally, but adds that their "kinship terminology and incest prohibitions seem to reflect a bilateral ideal of social organization." He suggests that Huron boys in the lineages of chiefs lived with their mother's brother, and that when they married their wives came to live with them rather than following the matrilocal principle (55, 100–2). See also Trigger's *Natives and Newcomers*, 117, 208 and Richter, *Ordeal of the Longhouse*, 20. Lucien Campeau shows from evidence about specific Huron families described in the *Jesuit Relations* that the Hurons were not consistent in matrilocal living arrangements nor in the matrilineal passing of chiefly honors (*Mission des Jésuites*, 54–8). Karen Anderson takes Huron matrilineality and matrilocality for granted, but does not review the Jesuit evidence or mention Campeau's book (*Chain Her by One Foot*, 107, 193). A mixed practice in regard to lineage and dwellings creates an interesting and variegated situation for Huron women.

11 Sagard, *Grand Voyage*, Part 1, ch. 11, 198–9; *JR*, 14: 18–19; 27: 30–1; 30: 36–7; Claude Chauchetière, *The Life of the Good Katharine Tegakoüita, Now Known as the Holy Savage* (1695) in Catholic Church, Sacred Congregation of Rites, *Positio . . . on the Introduction of the Cause for Beatification and Canonization and on the Virtues of the Servant of God Katharine Tekakwitha, the Lily of the Mohawks* (New York: Fordham University Press, 1940), 123–5; Pierre Cholenec, *The Life of Katharine Tegakoüita, First Iroquois Virgin* (1696) in Catholic Church Sacred Congregation of Rites, *Cause fir Beatification*, 273–5. Tooker, *Ethnography*, 126–7; Trigger, *Children of Aataentsic*, 49.

12 Sagard, *Grand Voyage*, Part 1, ch. 1, 291–2. *JR*, 10: 264–71. The remaining goods of the deceased were not given to his or her family, but after the burial were given to "recognize the liberality of those who had made the most gifts of consolation" at the funeral (*JR*, 43: 270–1).

13 Intercourse itself as the sole source of conception was problematized in folktales in which females get pregnant from passing near male urination or scratching themselves with an object used by a male (Claude Lévi-Strauss, *Histoire de lynx* [Paris: Plon, 1991], 21–2). Among some Amerindian peoples today, pregnancy is believed to occur only through many occasions of intercourse (Niethammer, *Daughters of the Earth*, 2). Among the Hurons in the seventeenth century, it was believed that the body-soul of a deceased person might sometimes enter the womb of a woman and be born again as her child (*JR*, 10: 285–7). When an adult male died, and especially an important male, such as a chief, his name was given to another person, not necessarily kin to the bereaved, and he then took up the deceased person's role and attributes (*JR*: 10: 274–7, 23: 164–9; Alexander von Gernet, "Saving the Souls: Reincarnation Beliefs of the Seventeenth-Century Huron," in Antonia Mills and Richard Slobodin, *Amerindian Rebirth: Reincarnation Belief among North American Indians and Inuit* [forthcoming Toronto: University of Toronto Press, 1993]). These adoptive practices carry with them a very different sense of the succesion of qualities from that current in sixteenth- and seventeenth-century Europe, where lineage and stock were so important.

14 *JR*, 6: 254–5. Jeanne-Françoise Juchereau de St Ignace and Marie Andrée Duplessis de Ste Hélène, *Les Annales de l'Hôtel-Dieu de Québec, 1636–1716*, ed. Albert Jamet (Québec: Hôtel-Dieu, 1939), 20.

15 Sagard reported a "grande querelle" between a daughter and a father who refused to give his consent to the suitor she desired, so the latter seized her (*Grand Voyage*, Part 1, ch. 11, 199–201; this story was already recounted by Lescarbot, ibid., 203 n. 4). Marie de l'Incarnation, *Correspondance*, no. 65, p. 163.

16 In addition to occasional reports in the *Jesuit Relations* of jealousy among spouses are the legends about a wife who goes off with a bear lover and the husband's efforts at retrieval or revenge. Lévi-Strauss, *Histoire de lynx*, 146;

"The Bear Walker (Mohawk)," in Herbert T. Schwarz, ed., *Tales from the Smokehouse* (Edmonton, Al.: Hurtig Publishers, 1974), 31–5, 101. A similar theme with a buffalo lover in "Apache Chief Punishes His Wife (Tiwa)," in Richard Erdoes and Alfonso Ortiz, eds, *American Indian Myths and Legends* (New York: Pantheon Books, 1984), 291–4.

17 *JR*, 43: 270–1.

18 *JR*, 8: 151–2; 23: 186–7; 28: 50–3 ("en leurs mariages les plus fermes, et qu'ils estiment les plus conformes à la raison, la foy qu'ils se donnent n'a rien de plus qu'une promesse conditionelle de demeurer ensemble, tandis qu'un chacun continuera à rendre les services qu'ils attendent mutuellement les uns des autres, et n'offensera point l'amitié qu'ils se doivent; cela manquant on iuge le divorce estre raisonnable du costé de celuy qui se voit offensé, quoy qu'on blasme l'autre party qui y a donné occasion"). On women ordinarily having custody of the children, *JR*, 5: 136–9; Marie de l'Incarnation, *Correspondance*, no. 52, 123 ("c'est la coûtume du païs que quand les personnes mariées se séparent, la femme emmène les enfans").

19 *JR*, 5: 172–3, 180–1. For an example of a wife using the need for her husband's assent to allow her infant to be baptized (possibly an excuse to cover her own reluctance), see *JR*, 5: 226–9.

20 Sagard, *Grand Voyage*, Part 1, ch. 18, 253–7; *JR*, 5: 152–7, 6: 156–63, 7: 100–3, 8: 118–21, 10: 128–39, 144–8. Marie de l'Incarnation, *Correspondance*, no. 270, 916–17. Tooker, *Ethnography*, 145–8 and Appendix 2; Elisabeth Tooker, ed., *Native North American Spirituality of the Eastern Woodlands. Sacred Myths, Dreams, Visions, Speeches, Healing Formulas, Rituals and Ceremonials* (New York: Paulist Press, 1979); Campeau, *Mission des Jésuites*, ch. 7; Axtell, *Invasion Within*, 13–19.

21 *JR*, 8: 117–19. *JR*, 30: 60–1, for an evidently all-male gathering to elect a new captain among the Hurons:

> Ils ont coustume en semblables rencontres de raconter les histoires qu'ils ont appris de leurs ancestres et les plus éloignées, afin que les ieunes gens qui sont presens et les entendent, en puissent conserver la memoire et les raconter à leur tour, lors qu'ils seront devenus vieux.

Creation accounts were among the tales told at the gathering.

22 Marie de l'Incarnation, *Correspondance*, no. 270, 917–18. Also, Jean de Brébeuf on the Hurons: "Or cette fausse creance qu'ils ont des ames s'entretient parmy-eux, par le moyen de certaines histoires que les peres racontent à leurs enfans" (*JR*, 10: 148–9).

23 *JR*, 43: 286–7.

24 *JR*, 30: 58–61: Paul Ragueneau describes the telling of creation stories by men at meeting for the election of a chief, where "les anciens du païs" were assembled.

25 Women storytellers are documented among the Amerindians in the early nineteenth century (Clark, *Indian Legends of Canada*, x–xi; Jeremiah Curtin, ed., *Seneca Indian Myths* [New York: E. P. Dutton, 1922], 243, 351; Marius Barbeau, ed., *Huron-Wyandot Traditional Narratives in Translations and Native Texts* [Ottawa: National Museum of Canada, 1960], 2–3), and individual women can be traced back to the eighteenth century (e.g., the Seneca grandmother of Johnny John, who told her grandson "A Man Pursued by his Uncle and by His Wife" and whom John described in 1883 as having lived "to be one hundred and thirty years old" [Curtin, *Seneca Indian Myths*, 307]; the Huron-Wyandot Nendusha, who lived to a hundred and told the traditional tales to her grandson, an elderly man in 1911 [Barbeau, *Huron-Wyandot*

Narratives, 2]). According to Penny Petrone, herself an honorary chief of the Gulf Lake Ojibway and specialist on Amerindian tales, some oral narratives were the "private property" of certain tribes, societies within tribes, or of particular persons and families. These could be told and heard only by certain persons (*Native Literature in Canada*, 11). Petrone does not mention gender as a factor in these exclusions and has herself collected sacred tales from Tlingit women; but the cultural habit of restricting the pool of tellers for certain narratives might account for the fact that formal recitals of creation accounts were attributed by the Jesuits and even by Marie de l'Incarnation to men. On the other hand, these sacred stories could not have been successfully passed on if the women with good memories and narrative skills had not also told them on many occasions. (For a woman with evident storytelling skills, see *JR*, 22: 292–5: the blind woman's story about how her grandfather got a new eye.) Petrone thinks my speculation about different settings in which men and women told the sacred stories in the early period is plausible (phone conversation of January 18, 1993). Paula Gunn Allen maintains that Amerindian stories about "women's matters" were for the most part told by women to other women (Allen, ed., *Spider Woman's Granddaughters*, 16–17).

26 *JR*, 8: 22–3; 10: 140–1, 168–73; 17: 152–5; 33: 188–91. Tooker, *Ethnography*, 86–91 and Iroquois evidence, 86, n. 62, 87, n. 63. Dreams could also involve the departure of the rational soul from the body to observe distant events or places.

27 *JR*, 17: 164–87.

28 *JR*, 43: 272–3 for an Iroquois woman who came to Québec to get a French dog of which her nephew had dreamed, and discovering the dog had been taken elsewhere, took a voyage of over four hundred miles through snow, ice, and difficult roads to find the animal.

29 *JR*, 30: 22–3. On the Huron "confraternities," Campeau, *Mission des Jésuites*, 105. Brébeuf's description of a special dance group for curing a man of madness had 80 persons in it, 6 of whom were women (*JR*, 10: 206–7). Games of lacrosse were also ordered for healing purposes (10: 184–7), but this would be only for men. Shafer, "The Status of Iroquois Women," (1941) in Spittal, ed., *Iroquois Women*, 88–9. For an early eighteenth-century picture of Iroquois women and men doing a curing dance together, see the illustration to *Aventures du Sr. C. Le Beau* reproduced by Ruth Phillips, "Art in Woodlands Life: the Early Pioneer Period," in *The Spirit Sings*, 66.

30 *JR*, 10: 222–3, for the Amerindian definition of *sorciers*: "ceux qui se meslent d'empoisonner et faire mourir par sort," who, once declared as such, can have their skulls smashed by anyone who comes upon them without the usual amends for a murder (compensatory gifts to the bereaved kin). For old men accused and punished as sorcerers: *JR*, 13: 154–7, 15: 52–3. Tooker, *Ethnography*, 117–20. The Jesuits also use the word "sorcerer" as one of several perjorative terms for all the various medicine men and shamans among the Amerindians, though there was some uncertainty among the fathers about whether they were actually assisted by Satan (*JR*, 6: 198–201; 10: 194–5, Brébeuf: "Il ya donc quelque apparence que le Diable leur tient la main par fois").

31 *JR*, 14: 182–3; 8: 26–61; 9: 112–15. A Montagnais *sorcière* recieved messages from the Manitou (*JR*, 31: 242–3). Huron women were prepared to blow on a sick person when no medicine man was around to do it (*JR*, 24: 30–1).

32 *JR*, 8: 124–7; 38: 36–7. The Huron soothsayer is the only reference given to women shamans in Tooker, *Huron Indians*, 91–101. Leacock's statement that

"Seventeenth-century accounts . . . referred to female shamans who might become powerful" ("Montagnais Women," 41) gives as supporting evidence *JR*, 6: 61, which includes no reference whatsoever to this topic, and 14:183, the woman "involved in sorcery," mentioned in my text. Robert Steven Grumet gives seventeenth-century evidence for women "powwows" or "pawwaws" among the central coast Algonquians of southern New England ("Sunksquaws, Shamans, and Tradeswomen: Middle Atlantic Coastal Algonkian Women during the 17th and 18th Centuries," in Etienne and Leacock, eds, *Women and Colonization*, 53).

33 *JR*, 6: 204–7. On sticks as mnemonic devices, see William N. Fenton, "Structure, Continuity, and Change in the Process of Iroquois Treaty Making," in Jennings, ed., *Iroquois Diplomacy*, 17. *JR*, 6: 194–9: at this ceremony, intended to make a distant enemy die, all the women were sent from the cabin but one, who sat next to the shaman and moved around the backs of all the men once during a specified point in the ceremonies. A similar ceremonial role in the sacrifice of the corpse of a person dead by drowning or freezing (*JR*, 10: 162–5). To appease the sky's anger, the body is cut up by young men and thrown into the fire. Women walk around the men several times and encourage them by putting wampum beads in their mouths. Among the Hurons, if a pregnant woman entered the cabin of a sick person, he or she would grow sicker (*JR*, 15: 180–1). By the presence of a pregnant woman and the application of a certain root, an arrow could be extracted from a man's body. In all of these examples, it is the female body, pregnant or not-pregnant, which is the source of power or danger.

34 Niethammer, *Daughters of the Earth*, 146–63 on herbal medicine and medicine women. Her examples of women shamans come from a later period and, except for the Menominee story about Hunting Medicine (collected 1913), are all from regions other than those of the Algonquian- and Iroquoian-speaking peoples. In *Grandmothers of the Light* and *The Sacred Hoop*, Paula Gunn Allen develops a modern medicine woman's culture based on Amerindian values and tales of goddesses. Her examples of women shamans are all from the late nineteenth and twentieth centuries (*Sacred Hoop*, 203–8). On the earlier period: "Pre-contact American Indian women valued their role as vitalizers because they understood that bearing, like bleeding, was a transformative ritual act" (ibid., 28).

35 Champlain, *Works*, 3: 97–8; Sagard, *Grand Voyage*, Part 1, ch. 4, 132–3. The critical issue may be the menstrual taboos, which would allow women to deal with certain matters, but, as Niethammer points out, would prevent women from handling "the sacred bundle" of the shaman (*Daughters of the Earth*, xii). Pregnant women: *JR*, 15: 180–1; 17: 212–13. Sexual restraint for men before shamanic ceremonial: *JR*, 15: 180–1. Menstrual separation and the power of the glance of the menstruating woman: *JR*, 29: 108–9; 9: 122–3. Separation of post-partum women among Algonquian peoples: Nicholas Perrot, *Memoir on the Manners, Customs, and Religion of the Savages of North America* (c. 1680), in Emma Helen Blair, ed. and trans., *The Indian Tribes or the Upper Missippi Valley and Region of the Great Lakes*, 2 vols (Cleveland, Ohio: Arthur Clark, 1911; New York:Klaus Reprint, 1969), 1: 48.

36 The best study is Grumet, "Sunksquaws, Shamans, and Tradeswomen," 46–53. See also Niethammer, *Daughters of the Earth*, 139–41; Carolyn Thomas Foreman, *Indian Women Chiefs* (Muskogee: Hoffman Printing Co., 1966); Samuel G. Drake, *The Aboriginal Races of North America*, 15th edn (Philadelphia: Charles Desilver, 1860), Book III, chs 1, 4 on the Wampanoag sunksquaws Weetamoo and Awashonks.

37 Descriptions of government and councils from Champlain, *Works*, 3: 157–9; Sagard, *Grand Voyage*, Part 1, ch. 17, 229–32; Brébeuf in *JR*, 10: 229–63; Bailey, *Algonkian Cultures*, 91–2; Heidenreich, *Huronia*, 79–81; Campeau, *Mission des Jésuites*, ch. 5; Fenton, "Iroquois Treaty Making," 12–14. Evidence in regard to women: Champlain on men's conduct on council meetings: "ils usent bien souvent de ceste façon de faire parmy leurs harangues au conseil, où il n'y a que les plus principaux, qui sont les antiens: Les femmes et enfans n'y assistent point" (1: 110); Sagard, 230–1, talking about local council meetings: "Les femmes, filles et jeunes hommes n'y assistent point, si ce n'est en un conseil général, où les jeunes hommes de vingt-cinq à trente ans peuvent assister, ce qu'il connaissent par un cri particulier qui en est fait" 230–1); Brébeuf, on the council chamber:

> la Chambre de Conseil est quelque fois la Cabane du Capitaine, parée de nattes, ou ionchéés de branches de Sapin, avec divers feux, suivant la saison de l'année. Autrefois chacun y apportoit sa busche pour mettre au feu; maintenant cela ne se pratique plus, les femmes de la Cabane supportent cette dépense, elles font les feux, et ne s'y chauffent pas, sortant dehors pour ceder la place à Messieurs le Conseillers. Quelquefois l'assemblée se fait au milieu du Village, si c'est en Esté [this may have been the time when women could most easily attend and listen, NZD], et quelquefois aussi en l'obscurité des forests à l'ecart, quand les affaires demandent le secret.
>
> (*JR*, 10: 250);

Paul Le Jeune on the Huron community of both "pagans" and Christians at Saint Joseph (Silléry): The Christian elders decided

> d'assembler les femmes pour les presser de se faire instruire et de recevoir le sainct Baptesme. On les fit donc venir, et les ieunes gens aussi. Le bon fut qu'on les prescha si bien que le iour suivant une partie de ces pauvres femmes, rencontrant le Pere de Quen, luy dirent, "Où est un tel Pere, nous le venons prier de nous baptiser, *hier les hommes nous appellerent en Conseil, c'est la premiere fois que iamais les femmes y sont entrées*"
>
> (italics mine; *JR*, 18: 104).

Drawing from a general description of Huron civility, in which Brébeuf talks of marriages, feasting, and other kinds of sociability and comments

> Ce qui les forme encor dans le discours sont les conseils qui se tiennent quasi tous les iours dans les Villages en toutes occurrences: et quoy que les anciens y tiennent le haut bout, et que ce soit de leur iugement qui dépende la decision des affaires; neantmoins s'y trouve qui veut et chacun a droit d'y dire son advis
>
> (*JR*, 10: 212),

Karen Anderson assumes that women could be present at any Huron council meeting and speak whenever they wanted (*Chain Her by One Foot*, 124). But this is in contradiction to other evidence, including more specific evidence given some pages later by Brébeuf himself. Brébeuf was following the usual practice in men's writing in the sixteenth and seventeenth centuries and using "chacun" (and other general nouns and pronouns) to refer to men; the paragraph in question is describing male civility.

38 Marie de l'Incarnation, *Correspondance*, no. 161, 546, September 24, 1654 ("Ces capitainesses sont des femmes de qualité parmi les Sauvages qui ont

voix delibérative dans les Conseils, et qui en tirent des conclusions comme les hommes, et même ce furent elles qui déléguèrent les premiers Ambassadeurs pour traiter de la paix"); no. 191, 671. In 1671, Father Claude Dablon said of Iroquois women of high rank that they

> are much respected; they hold councils, and the Elders decide no important affair without their advice. It was one of these women of quality who, some time ago, took the lead in persuading the Iroquois of Onnontagué, and afterward the other nations, to make peace with the French.
>
> (JR, 54: 280–1).

This is surely the same Onodaga "capitainesse" who visited the Ursuline convent during the embassy of 1654. In contrast, in the early eighteenth century Pierre-François-Xavier de Charlevoix claimed of the Iroquois that "the men never tell the women anything they would have to be kept secret, and rarely any affair of consequence is communicated to them, though all is done in their name" (quoted in W. M. Beauchamp, "Iroquois Women," *Journal of American Folklore*, 13 [1900], reprinted in Spittal, ed., *Iroquois Women*, 42–3). Carol Karlsen, currently engaged in a study of Iroquois women, says she has found considerable variation from period to period and nation to nation: in some instances, women attend council, in some they have meetings of their own and their views are communicated to the council (Lecture at Princeton University, March 25, 1993). Daniel Richter, in his important recent study *The Ordeal of the Longhouse*, describes women's roles in naming which man in a hereditary chiefly family would assume the role of leadership, and concludes that there "appears to have been a form of gender division of political labor corresponding to the economic and social categories that made women dominant within the village and its surrounding fields while men dealt with the outside world (43)."

39 Jennings, ed., *Iroquois Dipolomacy*, 124.
40 Trigger, *Natives and Newcomers*, 94–108. An example of the archeological work that allows one to historicize the Amerindian past is James F. Pendergast and Bruce G. Trigger, *Cartier's Hochelaga and the Dawson Site* (Montréal and London: McGill University Press, 1972), see especially 155–6, 158–61.
41 Sagard mentions women and girls kept by Hurons from war as wives or to be used as gifts, *Grand Voyage*, Part 1, ch. 17, 239. *JR*, 9: 254–5: Le Jeune, talking of some Iroquois prisoners seized by Algonquins, comments more generally: "Il est vray que les Barbares ne font point ordinairement de mal aux femmes, non plus qu'aux enfans, sinon dans leurs surprises, voire mesme quelque ieune homme ne fera point de difficulté d'épouser une prisonniere, si elle travaille bien, et par apres elle passe pour une femme du pays."
42 *JR*, 40: 180–1.
43 Elizabeth of France, sister of Louis XIII, was the wife of Philip IV of Spain; Anne of Austria, sister of Philip IV, was the wife of Louis XIII. John Elliott, *Richelieu and Olivares* (Cambridge: Cambridge University Press, 1984), 12, 113.
44 Pierre Esprit Radisson, *The Explorations of Pierre Esprit Radisson*, ed. Arthur T. Adams (Minneapolis: Ross & Haines, 1961), 26. *JR*, 41: 102–3.
45 I treat and give further bibliography on the issues in this paragraph in "Boundaries and the Sense of Self in Sixteenth-Century France," in Thomas Heller, Morton Sosna, and David Wellbery, eds, *Reconstructing Individualism*.

Autonomy, Individuality, and the Self in Western Thought (Stanford: Stanford University Press, 1986), 53–63, 332–5 and "Fame and Secrecy: Leon Modena's *Life* as an Early Modern Autobiography," in Mark Cohen, trans., *The Autobiography of a Seventeenth-Century Venetian Rabbi: Leon Modena's "Life of Judah"* (Princeton: Princeton University Press, 1988), 50–70.

46 *JR*, 16: 226–9; Trigger, *Children of Aataentsic*, 58–9, *Natives and Newcomers*, 104; Campeau, *Mission des Jésuites*, 22–6.

47 Fenton, "Structure, Continuity, and Change," in Jennings, ed., *Iroquois Diplomacy*, 16; Jennings, *Iroquois Empire*, 34–40; Trigger, *Children of Aataentsic*, 162–3, and Richter, *Ordeal of the Longhouse*, ch. 2. Grumet talks of "Coastal Algonkian confederacies" in the "early historic contact period" ("Sunksquaws," 47), but he may be referring to alliances rather than federations. White, *The Middle Ground* does not give evidence for Algonquin confederations in the Great Lakes region until the late eighteenth century. Of course, these alliances must also have stimulated diplomatic and oratorical skills.

48 Horatio Hale, ed., *The Iroquois Book of Rites* (Philadelphia: D.G. Brinton, 1883), ch. 2: a historical telling of the founding work of Deganiwidah and Hiawatha, collected during Hale's visits to the Reserve of the Iroquois nations in the 1870s; 180–3: the stories he collected about the death of Hiawatha's daughter. J. N. B. Hewitt, "Legend of the Founding of the Iroquois League," *American Anthropologist*, 5 (April 1892): 131–48 (the legend of Deganiwidah, Hiawatha, and Thadodaho, collected by Hewitt in 1888). Clark, *Indian Legends*, 138–45; Erdoes and Ortiz, *American Indian Myths and Legends*, 193–9. Fenton, "Structure, Continuity, and Change," 14–15; J. N. B. Hewitt, "The Status of Woman in Iroquois Polity before 1784," in *Iroquois Women*, 61–3.

49 Brébeuf in *JR*, 10: 256–7. "Ils haussent et flechissent la voix comme d'un ton de Predicateur à l'antique." "Raise and lower the voice" would seem a better translation than "raise and quiver the voice," the translation given on 257.

50 Champlain, *Works*, 1: 110; Sagard, *Grand Voyage*, Part 1, ch. 15, 220; and especially Brébeuf in *JR*, 10: 254–63. Le Jeune on the Montagnais, *JR*, 5: 24–5: "They do not all talk at once, but one after the other, listening patiently."

51 On mnemonic devices and wampum belts strung by women, see Fenton, "Structure, Continuity, and Change," 17–18, and Michael K. Foster, "Another Look at the Function of Wampum in Iroquois-White Councils," in Jennings, ed., *Iroquois Diplomacy*, 99–114. Captain's tone and walking back and forth: *JR*, 41: 112–13. Cartier, "Deuxième voyage," 132: "Et commença ledict agouhanna . . . à faire une prédication et preschement à leur modde, en démenant son corps et membres d'une merveilleuse sorte, qui est une sérymonye de joye et asseurance."

52 Barthélemy Vimont in *JR*, 27: 252–3. Vimont himself was depending on an interpreter for the words, and admitted that he was getting only "some disconnected fragments" (264–5).

53 Brébeuf in *JR*, 10: 256–9, 278–9. Fenton, "Structure, Continuity, and Change," 16 and "Glossary of Figures of Speech in Iroquois Political Rhetoric," in Jennings, ed., *Iroquois Diplomacy*, 115–24; Petrone, *Native Literature*, 27–8.

54 "Narrative of the Captivity of Mrs. Mary Rowlandson, 1682," in Charles H. Lincoln, ed., *Narratives of the Indian Wars, 1675–1699* (New York: Charles Scribner's Sons, 1913), 150. It would be interesting to know what speech strategies Weetamoo used when she negotiated her support for King Philip in his war against the English in the 1670s. When a Wyattanon woman spoke

to President Washington together with other delegates from Prairie Indian communities in 1793, she did so only because her uncle, Great Joseph, had died and she was representing him. In the transcription made by Thomas Jefferson, she said "He who was to have spoken to you is dead, Great Joseph. If he had lived you would have heard a good man, and good words flowing from his mouth. He was my uncle, and it has fallen to me to speak for him. But I am ignorant. Excuse, then, these words, it is but a woman who speaks." Thomas Jefferson, *The Writings of Thomas Jefferson*, ed. Andrew A. Lipscomb, 20 vols (Washington, DC: Thomas Jefferson Memorial Association, 1903), 16: 386–7.

55 Marie de l'Incarnation to Mother Ursule de Ste Catherine, September 13, 1640, *Correspondance*, no. 50, 117–18. This is the only account we have of the woman's speech; Marie must have heard about it from one of the Jesuits on the Huron mission, and with her characteristic sensitivity to women's words and actions, included it in her letter to the Mother Superior at her former convent at Tours. In the *Relation* of 1640, the Jesuit Superior Jerome Lallemant talks about the conflict about the Jesuits at this same "conseil general," but does not mention a woman speaker (*JR*, 19: 176–9).

56 "Hiawatha the Unifier," in Erdoes and Ortiz, *American Indian Myths*, 198; Marie de l'Incarnation, *Correspondance*, no. 168, p. 565. Jennings, ed., *Iroquois Diplomacy*, 13, 124, 249. "Speaking through my mouth" is the phrase used by envoys and ambassadors: "Escoute, Ondessonk, Cinq Nations entieres te parlent par ma bouche" (*JR*, 41: 116).

57 *JR*, 5: 180–1; 10: 258–9; 27: 262–3; Sagard, *Grand Voyage*, Part 1, ch. 15, 220. Le Jeune also comments on Montagnais reaction to the French talking all at the same time: "A Sagamore, or Captain, dining in our room one day, wished to say something; and not finding an opportunity, because [we] were all talking at the same time, at last prayed the company to give him a little time to talk in his turn, and all alone, as he did" (*JR*, 5: 24–5).

58 Leonardo Bruni, "Concerning the Study of Literature, A Letter to . . . Baptista Malatesta," in W. H. Woodward, *Vittorino da Feltre and other Humanist Educators* (Cambridge: Cambridge University Press, 1897; reprinted New York: Teachers College of Columbia University, 1963), 126. Margaret L. King, *Women of the Renaissance* (Chicago: University of Chicago Press, 1991), 194. For a few well-born Italian women with training in good letters who managed to give orations, see Margaret L. King and Albert Rabil, Jr, *Her Immaculate Hand. Selected Works by and about the Women Humanists of Quattrocento Italy* (Binghamton: Medieval & Renaissance Texts & Studies, 1983), nos. 2, 4, 6, 7. For an overview of queenly strategies, see N. Z. Davis, "Women in Politics," in Natalie Zemon Davis and Arlette Farge, eds, *A History of Women in the West*, 3: *Renaissance and Enlightenment Paradoxes*, (Cambridge, Mass.: Harvard University Press, 1993), ch. 6.

59 Phyllis Mack, *Visionary Women: Ecstatic Prophecy in Seventeenth-Century England* (Berkeley: University of California Press, 1992). [Margaret Fell Fox], *Womens Speaking Justified, Proved and Allowed of by the Scriptures* (London, 1666 and 1667). Natalie Zemon Davis, "City Women and Religious Change," *Society and Culture in Early Modern France* (Stanford: Stanford University Press, 1975), ch. 3. Elizabeth Rapley, *The Dévotes. Women and Church in Seventeenth-Century France* (Montréal and Kingston: McGill-Queen's University Press, 1990). Linda Lierheimer, "Female Eloquence and Maternal Ministry: The Apostolate of Ursuline Nuns in Seventeenth-Century France" (Ph.D. diss., Princeton University, 1994).

60 *JR*, 43: 288–91.

61 Ann Eastlack Shafer, "The Status of Iroquois Women," in Spittal, ed., *Iroquois Women*, 108; Tooker, *Ethnography*, 91, n. 75. It has been suggested that the False Face society was created among the Iroquois during the 1630s (Trigger, *Natives and Newcomers*, 117) and that the Midewiwin society of shamans developed in the central Great Lakes region in the course of the eighteenth century (Phillips, "Art in Woodlands Life," 64–5). Could one find archeological, visual, or other evidence that would allow one to historicize the relation of Amerindian women to religious action in the healing and other shamanic societies?

62 Marie de l'Incarnation, *Correspondance*, no. 65, 165–6.

63 Marie de l'Incarnation, *Correspondance*, no. 65, 165–9; no. 73, 201; no. 97, 281; Appendix, no. 9, 975; no. 11, 977 (letter from Thérèse); no. 18, 988, (letter from an Ursuline, almost certainly Marie, to Paul Le Jeune, 1653: "Nous avons appris que nostre Séminariste Huronne, qui fut prise il y a environ dix ans par les Iroquois, estoit mariée en leur pays; qu'elle estoit la maistresse dans sa cabane, composée de plusieurs familles; qu'elle priot Dieu tous les jours et qu'elle le faisoit prier par d'autres." Campeau provides the name Khionrea (*La Mission des Jésuites*, 86).

64 Juchereau and Duplessis, *Hôtel-Dieu de Québec*, 161–3.

65 Marie de l'Incarnation to Claude Martin, 12 October 1655 in *Correspondance*, no. 168, 565–6. François du Creux, *The History of Canada or New France*, trans. Percy J. Robinson, 2 vols (Toronto: The Champlain Society, 1951–2), 2: 698–700. Du Creux's report was based on the letters sent to him by Marie de l'Incarnation (referred to in her *Correspondance*, 642, 719), which he simply incorporated into his *Historia canadensis* (Paris: Sébastien Cramoisy, 1664).

66 See the fine discussion of Jacqueline Peterson in her essay "Women Dreaming: The Religiopsychology of Indian White Marriages and the Rise of Metis Culture," in Lillian Schlissel, Vicki Ruiz, and Janice Monk, eds, *Western Women. Their Land, Their Lives* (Albuquerque: University of New Mexico Press, 1988), 49–68. I am treating the relation of Amerindian women to Christianity from other points of view in my chapter on Marie de l'Incarnation in *Women on the Margins* (forthcoming Harvard University Press).

67 Cholenec, *Life of Katharine Tegakoüita* in *The Cause for Beatification and Canonization . . . of the Servant of God Katharine Tekakwitha*, 257, 299.

68 *JR*, 10: 286–7. Alexander von Gernet analyzes the evidence for Huron beliefs regarding souls after death and the various ways in which the qualities of the dead could be saved for the living in a remarkable essay, "Saving the Souls," in Mills and Slobodin, eds, *Amerindian Rebirth*.

69 "The first wampum (Iroquois and Huron-Wyandot)," in Clark, *Indian Legends*, 55–6 from a story collected by Erminnie A. Smith, in 1883 (170, 176). Another Iroquois version of the origin of wampum, which also connects it indirectly with feathers and directly with treaty use, in "Hiawatha and the Wizard (Onondaga)," ibid., 138–41, from a story collected by J. N. B. Hewitt in 1892 (172, 174). See Hewitt, "Legend of the Iroquois," 134–5.

70 The twin motif is widely discussed in regard to Indian stories (for example, Erdoes and Ortiz, eds, *American Indian Myths and Legends*, 73ff.) and is the central theme of Lévi-Strauss, *Histoire de lynx*.

71 Brébeuf, *JR*, 19: 126–9. Erdoes and Ortiz discuss the "fall through a hole" as a motif in *American Indian Myths and Legends*, 75, and there are several examples analyzed in Lévi-Strauss, *Histoire de lynx*.

72 Curtin, ed., *Seneca Indian Myths*, 70–5. Curtin collected myths in the Seneca reservation in Versailles, NY in 1883 as an agent of the Bureau of Ethnology of the Smithsonian Institute (v). Curtin's version given in Clark, ed., *Indian*

NOTES

Legends, 37–40, and in Susan Feldmann, ed., *The Story-Telling Stone. Traditional Native American Myths and Tales* (New York: Dell, 1991), 161–6.

15 ANDEAN WITCHES AND VIRGINS
Seventeenth-century nativism and subversive gender ideologies
Irene Silverblatt

1 Some of the formulations of the problem and analysis presented here are in Irene Silverblatt, *Moon, Sun, and Witches: Gender Ideologies and Class in Inca and Colonial Peru* (Princeton: Princeton University Press, 1987). I would like to thank the Department of Anthropology, Western Michigan University, for inviting me to participate in the "Origin of Gender Inequality" Conference, and encouraging the presentation of the paper on which this essay is based. A longer and somewhat different version of it is to be published in a volume of the conference's collected papers. Special thanks here go to Margo Hendricks and Patricia Parker for their helpful criticisms, editorial skills, adroit use of modern technologies, and intellectual commitment.
2 The literature on resistance is extensive and growing. This essay has been inspired by Eugene Genovese, *Roll Jordan Roll: The World the Slaves Made* (New York: Vintage, 1974). Among other intellectual contributions of Genovese's Gramsci-oriented analysis is the careful delineation of the now fashionable conceptual dynamic of "resistance and accommodation." This essay hopes to contribute to our awareness of the gendered nature of this process (also see Irene Silverblatt, "Women in States," *Annual Review of Anthropology* 17 [1988]: 427–60).
3 R. T. Zuidema, "Inca Kinship," in *Andean Kinship and Marriage*, ed. R. Bolton and E. Mayer (Washington, DC: American Anthropological Association, Special Publication no. 7, 1977), 240–55.
4 Silverblatt, *Moon, Sun, and Witches*, pp. 20–65.
5 R. T. Zuidema, *The Ceque System of Cuzco: The Social Organization of the Inca Empire* (Leiden: E. J. Brill, 1964), pp. 40–1, 168.
6 Silverblatt, *Moon, Sun, and Witches*, pp. 67–80.
7 Ibid., pp. 81–108.
8 Karen Spalding, "Indian Rural Society in Colonial Peru: The Example of Huarochirí" (Ph.D. dissertation, University of California, Berkeley, 1967), pp. 122, 126.
9 Felipe Guaman Poma de Ayala, *La nueva crónica y buen gobierno* [1613?], ed. L. Bustíos Gálvez, 3 vols (Lima: Editorial Cultura, 1956), vol. 2, p. 111; vol. 3, p. 130.
10 Guaman Poma, *La nueva crónica*, vol. 2: 34, 61, 117, 144, 175.
11 Virgilio Roel, *Historia social y económica de la colonia* (Lima: Editorial Grafica Labor, 1970), p. 109.
12 See Maria Rostworowski, *Curacas y sucesiones, Costa Norte* (Lima: Minerva, 1961), p. 29.
13 Archivo Arzobispal de Lima: Legajo 2, Expediente XIV, f.2v. (Hereafter cited as AAL: Leg., Exp.).
14 H. R. Trevor-Roper, "The European Witch-Craze," in *Witchcraft and Sorcery*, ed. M. Marwick (London: Penguin, 1972); Keith Thomas, *Religion and the Decline of Magic* (London: Weidenfeld & Nicolson, 1971). There is no evidence that "witches," as testified to in the European trials, existed in Europe. What is significant here is the way in which the stereotype of "witches," with its vitriol against women, was carried to Peru.
15 Pedro de Cieza de Leon, "El señorio de los Incas" [1553], in *Biblioteca*

peruana, ser. 1, vol. 3 (Lima: Editores Técnicos Asociados, 1968), pp. 84–8; Cristóbal de Mena, "La conquista del Perú, llamada la Nueva Castilla" [1534], in *Biblioteca peruana*, ser. 1, vol. 1, pp. 133–70.

16 José de Acosta, *Historia natural y moral de las Indias* [1590] (Madrid: Biblioteca de Autores Españoles, 1954), p. 172; Martín de Murúa, *Historia del origen y geneología real de los Incas* [1590], ed. Constantino Bayle (Madrid: Consejo superior de investigaciones científicas, Instituto Santo Toribio de Mogrovejo, 1946), p. 301.

17 Pablo José de Arriaga, *The Extirpation of Idolatry in Peru* [1621], trans. L. Clark Keating (Lexington: University of Kentucky Press, 1968), pp. 11, 23; Hernando de Avendaño, "Relación sobre la idolatría" [1630?], in *La imprenta en Lima*, ed. J. T. Medina (Santiago de Chile: Imprenta Elzeviriana, 1904), vol. 1, pp. 380–3.

18 For the classic European case, see the pioneering Carlo Ginzburg, *Night Battles* (New York: Viking, 1985).

19 See AAL, sección idolatrías. Note that while similar in practice to the Inquisition, the "capaigns to extirpate idolatry" were not under the institutional jurisdiction of the Holy Office of the Inquisition, but rather, were under the ecclesiastical authority of Bishops.

20 Pierre Duviols, *La Lutte contre les religions autochtones dans le Pérou colonial: L'Extirpation de l'idolâtrie entre 1532 et 1660* (Lima and Paris: Institut Français d'Etudes Andines, 1971).

21 Acosta, *Historia natural*, p. 181; Juan Pérez Bocanegra, *Ritual formulario e institución de curas para administrar a los naturales* . . . (Lima, 1631), pp. 389–90; also see Michael Taussig, *The Devil and Commodity Fetishism in South America* (Chapel Hill: University of North Carolina Press, 1980).

22 Pérez Bocanegra, *Ritual formulario*, p. 114; AAL: Leg. 1, Exp. VII; Leg. 1, Exp. XII.

23 AAL: Leg. 4, Exp. XIV.

24 AAL: Leg. 4, Exp. XIV, f.1v.

25 AAL: Leg. 4, Exp. XIV, f.9.

26 AAL: Leg. 4, Exp. XIV, f.9.

27 AAL: Leg. 4, Exp. XIV, f.12v.

28 AAL: Leg. 4, Exp. XIV, f.12v.

29 AAL: Leg. 4, Exp. XIV, f.24.

30 AAL: Leg. 4, Exp. XIV, f.23v.

31 Ibid., f.2v.

32 Ibid., f.3v.

33 Lima archives hold manuscripts describing how women challenged colonial authority. See AAL: Leg. 1, Exp. s.n.; AAL: Leg. 3, Exp. XVIII, f.7v.

34 Ibid., f.37, f.37v.

35 John Earls and Irene Silverblatt, "La realidad física y social en la cosmología andina," *Proceedings of the XLI International Congress of Americanists* 4: 399–425.

36 Arriaga, *The Extirpation of Idolatry*, pp. 32–5; Bernabé Cobo, *Historia del Nuevo Mundo* [1653], 2 vols (Madrid: Biblioteca de Autores Españoles, 1964), vol. 2, pp. 225–9.

37 AAL: Leg. 2, Exp. IV.

38 AAL: Leg. 4, Exp. sn.

39 AAL: Leg. 4, Exp. XVIIIA, f.3v.

40 Ibid., f.28.

41 Ibid., f.2.

42 Note that the four chosen women from Otuco were called María, as were the

women who composed the leading women's group in the Taki Onqoy nativist movement of the 1560s.

16 INVADED WOMEN
Gender, race, and class in the formation of colonial society
Verena Stolcke

1 "Yo soy un hombre, / aunque de villana casta, / limpio de sangre y jamás / de hebrea or mora manchado."
2 Christoph Hein, *Horns Ende* (Berlin: Aufbau Verlag, 1985), pp. 279–80.
3 Irene Silverblatt, *Moon, Sun, and Witches: Gender Ideologies and Class in Inca and Colonial Peru* (Princeton: Princeton University Press, 1987), pp. 109–24.
4 See Marcel Bataillon, "La herejía de Fray Francisco de la Cruz y la reacción antilascasiana," *Miscelánea de Estudios Dedicados a Fernando Ortiz* (La Habana, 1955–7), vol. 1, pp. 135–46.
5 See Silverblatt, *Moon, Sun*, p. 112.
6 Inga Clendinnen, "Yucatec Maya Women and the Spanish Conquest: Role and Ritual in Historical Reconstruction," *Journal of Social History* (1982), pp. 427–41.
7 See Siverblatt, *Moon, Sun*, p. 120.
8 See also Juan José Vega, "La poligamia española en el Perú" *Cantuta* (Peru: Ediciones Universidad Nacional de Educación, 1968), pp. 3–36.
9 See Mary Poovey, "Scenes of an Indelicate Character: The Medical Treatment of Victorian Women," in Catherine Gallagher and Thomas Laqueur, eds, *The Making of the Modern Body: Sexuality and Society in the Nineteenth Century* (Berkeley: University of California Press, 1987), p. 145.
10 Werner Conze, "Rasse," in Otto Brunner, Werner Conze, and Reinhart Koselleck, eds, *Geschichtliche Grundbegriffe: Historisches Lexikon zur politisch-sozialen Sprache in Deutschland*, vol. 5, pp. 135–78.
11 Joan Corominas, *Diccionario crítico etimológico Castellano e Hispánico* (Madrid: Editorial Gredos, 1982), pp. 800–1.
12 Henry Kamen, *La inquisición española* (Barcelona: Ed. Crítica, 1985), pp. 156–81.
13 Ibid., p. 158.
14 Diaz de Montalvo, quoted in ibid., p. 158.
15 Ibid., p. 158.
16 Henry Kamen, "Una crisis de conciencia en la Edad de Oro de España: Inquisición contra la 'limpieza de sangre'," *Bulletin Hispanique* 88 (3–4), (1986), pp. 321–56.
17 José Luis Martinez, *Pasajeros de Indias* (Madrid: Alianza Editorial, 1983), p. 32.
18 Henry Méchoulan, *El honor de Dios* (Barcelona: Editorial Argos Vegara, 1981), p. 58.
19 Richard Konetzke, "La emigración de mujeres españolas a América durante la época colonial," *Revista Internacional de Sociología* (1945), pp. 124–50.
20 Méchoulan, *El honor de Dios*, p. 57.
21 Richard Konetzke, *Colección de documentos para la historia de la formación social de Hispanoamérica, 1493–1810* (Madrid: Instituto Jaime Balmes, CSIC, 1958), vol. II (1), p. 148.
22 Nicolás Sánchez Albornoz, "The Population of Colonial Spanish America," in Leslie Bethell, ed., *The Cambridge History of Latin America* (Cambridge: Cambridge University Press, 1984), vol. 2, pp. 3–35, esp. p. 16.
23 Konetzke, *Colección*, vol. II, p. 128.

24 Ibid., p. 148.
25 Ibid., p. 148.
26 Quoted in ibid., p. 126.
27 Konetzke, *Colección*, vol. III (1), p. 217.
28 Aunción Lavrín, ed., *Sexuality and Marriage in Colonial Latin America* (Lincoln and London: University of Nebraska Press, 1989), pp. 47–95.
29 Konetzke, *Colección*, vol. III (2), pp. 473–4.
30 Verena Martinez-Alier, *Marriage, Class and Colour in Nineteenth-Century Cuba: A Study of Racial Attitudes and Sexual Values in a Slave Society* (Cambridge: Cambridge University Press, 1974; 2nd edn, East Lansing: Michigan University Press, 1989), p. 24.
31 For the case of Mexico, see Patricia Seed, *To Love, Honor and Obey in Colonial Mexico* (Stanford: Stanford University Press, 1988), pp. 75–91.
32 Ibid., pp. 161–76.
33 Konetzke, *Colección*, vol. III (1), pp. 401–5.
34 Seed, *To Love, Honor and Obey*, p. 201.
35 Konetzke, *Colección*, vol. III (1), pp. 438–42.
36 See Martinez-Alier, *Marriage, Class and Colour*, pp. 11–14.
37 Daisy Ripodas Ardanaz, *El matrimonio en Indias. Realidad social y regulación jurídica* (Buenos Aires: Fundación para la Educación, la Ciencia y la Cultura, 1977).

17 OTHELLO'S IDENTITY, POSTCOLONIAL THEORY, AND CONTEMPORARY AFRICAN REWRITINGS OF *OTHELLO*
Jyotsna Singh

My thanks to Don Wayne for his crtique and comments.

1 Quotes from Lamb and Coleridge are cited by Sylvan Barnet, "Othello on Stage and Screen," reprinted in *Othello*, ed. Alvin Kernan (New York: Signet Classic, 1986), 273.
2 Aimé Césaire, *Selected Poetry*, trans. Clayton Eshleman and Annette Smith (Berkeley: University of California Press, 1983), 77–9.
3 William Shakespeare, *Othello* (New York: Signet Classic, 1989), V.ii.338–9. All subsequent references will be from this edition of the text.
4 See Alvin Kernan, "Introduction" to *Othello*, Signet Classic xxiii–xxxv, for one such moral reading.
5 Ibid., xxxiii.
6 Karen Newman, "'And wash the Ethiop white': Femininity and the Monstrous in *Othello*," *Shakespeare Reproduced*, ed. Jean E. Howard and Marion O'Connor (London: Methuen, 1987), 150.
7 For a discussion of the play's critical history see Michael Neill, "Unproper Beds: Race, Adultery, and the Hideous in *Othello*," *Shakespeare Quarterly* (Winter 1989), vol. 41, no 4, 391–2. Also see Newman, "'And wash the Ethiop white',", 143–5.
8 Cited by Neill, "Unproper Beds," 392.
9 Kernan, "Introduction," xxvi–xxvii.
10 Essays by Newman, "'And wash the Ethiop white'," and Neill, "Unproper Beds," cited earlier, are representative of the recent interest in the reproduction of *Othello* within colonialist and racist ideologies. Also see Martin Orkin, "Othello and the 'Plain Face' of Racism," *Shakespeare Quarterly* 38 (1987), 166–88 and Eldred Jones, *Othello's Countrymen: The African in English Renaissance Drama* (London: Oxford University Press, 1965). For a feminist

analysis of Othello's self-divisions, see Dympna Callaghan's *Woman and Gender in Renaissance Drama* (Atlantic Highlands: Humanities Press, 1989).

11 Newman, 157.

12 Ibid., 145.

13 See Angela Davis, *Women, Race, and Class* (New York: Vintage Books, 1983), 172–201, for her discussion of the myth of the black rapist and how it led to mass lynchings of black men in America after the Civil War. This myth has had many earlier incarnations throughout colonial history, whereby black men were cast as sexual predators. I am also grateful to Dympna Callaghan for her astute analysis of this subject in our frequent discussions.

14 Newman, "'And wash the Ethiop white'," 157.

15 Kernan, "Introduction," xxvii.

16 For a perceptive discussion of the play's final scene, see Neill, "Unproper Beds," 411–12. I am also indebted to Michael Neill for his comments on my reading of *Othello*.

17 In *Black Skin, White Masks*, trans. Charles Markmann (New York: Grove Press, 1969), Frantz Fanon develops a detailed theory of the struggle for black identity within European colonialism – a struggle that is self-defeating because it is underpinned by a "wish to be white" (14). I use the term "black man" throughout the chapter, not generically to refer to people, but specifically, to identify black men of all ethnic groups in African history.

18 See Kernan's formulation of *Othello* as a "morality play, offering an allegorical journey" ("Introduction," xxxiv–xxxv).

19 Nancy Leys Stepan's essay, "Race and Gender: The Role of Analogy in Science," in *Anatomy of Racism*, ed. David Theo Goldberg (Minneapolis: University of Minnesota Press, 1990), 38–57, elucidates on the discursive strategies of nineteenth-century scientists in which "gender was found to be remarkably analogous to race, such that the scientist could use racial difference to explain gender difference and vice versa" (39). Even though today we recognize the dangerous elisions between racism and sexism in such "scientific" formulations, many political critics still seem to collapse the categories of race and gender, though often for progressive social goals.

20 A number of studies have noted that English literature played a role in ensuring the hegemony of the British empire. A representative work is Gauri Vishwanathan's essay, "The Beginnings of English Literary Study in India," *Oxford Literary Review* 9 (1987), 2–26. Also see my essay, "Different Shakespeare: The Bard in Colonial/Postcolonial India," *Theatre Journal*, (December 1989), vol. 41, no. 4, 445–58.

21 Quote from Thomas Babington Macaulay's 1835 *Minute on Colonial Education*, cited by Ania Loomba, *Gender, Race, Renaissance Drama* (Manchester: Manchester University Press, 1989), 31.

22 See Jean Paul Sartre's "Preface" to Frantz Fanon's *The Wretched of the Earth* (New York: Grove Press, 1963), 8–9, in which he discusses Fanon's resistance to "becoming European" and to the "nauseating mimicry" of the colonized races. Fanon's resistance and critique of the ways in which the empire produced subservient, though Europeanized, subjects is a theme in many postcolonial works. V. S. Naipaul's famous title, *The Mimic Men*, captures the postcolonial dilemma that others like Homi Bhabha have theorized more fully.

23 Fanon, *Black Skin, White Masks*, 18.

24 Homi Bhabha, "Of Mimicry and Man: The Ambivalence of Colonial Discourse," *October* 28 (1984), 132.

25 Robert Young's analysis of Bhabha's theory in *White Mythologies: Writing*

History and the West (London: Routledge, 1990), 146–8, specifically draws on the essay " Of Mimicry and Man: The Ambivalence of Colonial Discourse," *October* 28 (1984): 15–33, to point to the complexities of mimicry.

26 Césaire, *Selected Poetry*, 79.

27 Murray Carlin, *Not now, sweet Desdemona* (Nairobi and Lusaka: Oxford University Press, 1969), 2–5. All quotes will be taken from this edition of the text.

28 Ibid., 2.

29 Fanon, *Black Skin, White Masks*, 14.

30 Ibid., 69.

31 Western feminists have recently offered useful insights into the ways in which race, gender, and class oppressions interact. In many instances, however, they tend to collapse these categories as a convenient discursive strategy that often makes their critique somewhat apolitical. For instance, Elizabeth Foxe-Genovese, in *Feminism Without Illusions: A Critique of Individualism* (Chapel Hill: University of North Carolina Press, 1991), cites W. E. B. Du Bois's theory of the feeling of "twoness" among African-Americans and applies it to the experience of women. She preempts a critique of such a move by stating:

> It is no part of my intention to trivialize the particular meaning of Du Bois's words by equating female and African-American experience. But however different the problems and histories of women and African-Americans, the living of twoness applies to both.
>
> (139)

This emphasis on shared experience, while well-intentioned, is ultimately a move to elide very *distinct* histories, even while the critic acknowledges the differences among them.

32 Tayib Salih, *Season of Migration to the North*, trans. Denys Johnson-Davies (Washington DC: Three Continents Press, 1969), 38. All quotes will be taken from this edition of the text.

33 Barbara Harlow, "Othello's Season of Migration," *Edebiyat: Journal of Comparative and Middle Eastern Literature*, 4 (1979), 166. This essay reads Salih's novel in the context of Arab encounters with colonialism and reinforces parts of my argument. I am grateful to Ruquayya Khan for recently bringing this piece to my attention.

34 By the nineteenth century, one "idea" of the Orient (symbolically encompassing African and Arab cultures) that passed off as "knowledge" produced a sexual fantasy, reflected in works like *Madame Bovary* and Richard Burton's Introduction to his translation of *Thousand and One Nights*, and packed with "Oriental clichés: harems, princesses, princes, slaves, veils, dancing girls." See Edward Said, *Orientalism* (New York: Vintage Books, 1979), 190. Also see Harlow's account of such clichés in Burton and elsewhere, 166. The stereotypical images of non-Europeans from antiquity through Hakluyt's narratives of the early modern encounters with the "New World" natives to Richard Burton's sentimentalized prurience are all largely a conglomeration of facts, exaggeration, and pure fantasy. Therefore, similar images of "cannibals," "monsters," and "harems" or of naked "beasts" appear in haphazard combinations of "facts" in texts ranging from Columbus's *Journals* to Conrad's *Heart of Darkness*.

35 I am indebted to Harlow's discussion of this quote from the novel, in "Othello's Season of Migration," 166.

36 Ibid., 162.

37 See Malek Alloula, *Colonial Harem* (Minneapolis: University of Minnesota

Press, 1987).

38 I am indebted to Patrick Brantlinger's analysis of cultural studies as a counterdisciplinary practice, especially as it has been articulated by Raymond Williams. See P. Brantlinger's *Crusoe's Footprints: Cultural Studies in Britain and America* (London: Routledge, 1990), 42.

CONTRIBUTORS

Lynda E. Boose is Professor of English at Dartmouth College. She is co-editor of *Daughters and Fathers* (1989) and has written on Shakespeare's *Taming of the Shrew* and *Othello*, as well as issues of war and gender based on her experience in Viet Nam. She is currently working on the figure of the shrew in early modern English literature.

Laura Brown is Professor of English at Cornell University. She is the author of *English Dramatic Form, 1660–1760* (1981), *Ends of Empire: Women and Ideology in Early Eighteenth-Century English Literature* (1993), and, with Felicity Nussbaum, co-editor of *The New Eighteenth Century: Theory, Politics, English Literature* (1987).

Dympna Callaghan is Assistant Professor of English and Textual Studies at Syracuse University, where she teaches feminist theory and English Renaissance Drama. She is the author of *Woman and Gender in Renaissance Tragedy: A Study of Othello, King Lear, The Duchess of Malfi and The White Devil* (1989), feminist essays on theory, drama, and poetry, and *The Weyward Sisters: Feminist Politics and Shakespeare*, with Jyotsna Singh and Lorraine Helms (forthcoming).

Natalie Zemon Davis is Henry Charles Lea Professor of History and Director of the Shelby Cullom Davis Center for Historical Studies at Princeton University. She is the author of *Society and Culture in Early Modern France* (1975), *The Return of Martin Guerre* (1983), *Fiction in the Archives: Pardon Tales and their Tellers in Early Modern France* (1987), co-editor of volume 3 of *A History of Women* (1993), and author of *Women on the Margins* (forthcoming from Harvard University Press).

Margaret W. Ferguson, Professor of English and Comparative Literature at the University of Colorado, is the author of *Trials of Desire: Renaissance Defenses of Poetry* (1983) and co-editor of *Rewriting the Renaissance: The Discourses of Sexual Differences in Early Modern Europe*

(1986), *Re-memberingMilton: The Texts and the Tradition* (1987), and *Feminism and Postmodernism* (a special issue of *boundary 2*, 1992). She has recently co-edited Elizabeth Cary's *The Tragedy of Mariam* and *The Lady Falkland: A Life* by one of Cary's daughters (forthcoming from the University of California Press). She is completing a book entitled *Partial Access: Studies in Female Literacy and Literary Production in Early Modern Europe*.

Carla Freccero is Associate Professor of Literature at the University of California, Santa Cruz. She is author of *Father Figures: Genealogy and Narrative Structure in Rabelais* (Cornell University Press, 1991). She has written numerous articles on early modern European culture and on US popular culture. She is currently completing a book-length project entitled *Marguerite de Navarre and The Politics of Maternal Sovereignty*. This article is part of a project on early modern masculinities.

Kim F. Hall teaches English and Women's Studies at Georgetown University. Her essay is from her forthcoming book, *Acknowledging Things of Darkness: Race, Gender and Power in Early Modern England*, which explores the gendering tropes of blackness, and the transformation of such tropes during England's imperial expansion in the sixteenth and early seventeenth centuries.

Margo Hendricks is an Assistant Professor of Literature at the University of California, Santa Cruz. She is author of "A Painter's Eye: Gender in Middleton and Dekker's *The Roaring Girl*" (*Women's Studies*, 1990), "Feminism, the Roaring Girls and Me," in *Changing Subjects: The Making of Feminist Literary Criticism* (Routledge, 1993), "Managing the Barbarian: The Tragedie of Dido Queene of Carthage" (forthcoming in *Renaissance Drama*). Her current project is a book-length study of the dramatic works of Aphra Behn.

Jean E. Howard is Professor of English at Columbia University. She is co-editor of *Shakespeare Reproduced* (1987) and author of *Shakespeare's Art of Orchestration* (1984), and of numerous articles on early modern drama. Her new book, *The Stage and Social Struggle in Early Modern England* (1994), is published by Routledge.

Stephanie Jed teaches Italian and comparative literature at the University of California, San Diego. Her publications include *Chaste Thinking: The Rape of Lucretia and the Birth of Humanism* (1989). Her current research focuses on intercultural relations in the sixteenth-century "Old" and "New" Worlds and their role in the construction of gender, nationalities, and the European "world system."

Ania Loomba has taught at Delhi University and Jawaharlal Nehru University in New Delhi. She is currently Associate Professor of English at the University of Tulsa. She is the author of *Gender, Race, Renaissance Drama* (1989) and articles on colonial discourse, Shakespearean appropriations, pedagogy in India, and the women's movement.

Felicity Nussbaum, Professor of English at Syracuse University, was recently Marta Sutton Weeks Fellow at Stanford Humanities Center. Her most recent book, *The Autobiographical Subject: Gender and Ideology in Eighteenth-Century England* (Johns Hopkins University Press 1989) was awarded the Louis Gottschalk Prize. Her current project is a book on maternity, sexuality, and empire.

Patricia Parker, who has taught at the University of East Africa, the University of Toronto and as a visitor at Berkeley, is currently Professor of English and Comparative Literature at Stanford University. Author of *Inescapable Romance* (1979) and *Literary Fat Ladies: Rhetoric, Gender, Property* (Routledge) and co-editor of *Shakespeare and the Question of Theory* (Routledge) and of *Literary Theory / Renaissance Texts*, she is currently completing books on Shakespeare and on gender in the early modern period.

Juliana Schiesari, Associate Professor of French and Italian at the University of California, Davis, is author of *The Gendering of Melancholia: Feminism, Psychoanalysis and The Symbolics of Loss in Renaissance Literature* (1992) and co-editor of *Refiguring Woman: Perspectives on Gender and the Italian Renaissance* (1991), as well as author of articles on feminist theory, psychoanalysis and Italian Renaissance literature. She is currently writing a book on the culture of women and animals, in relation to the politics of domestication.

Irene Silverblatt teaches cultural anthropology at Duke University. The author of *Moon, Sun, and Witches: Gender Ideologies and Class in Inca and Colonial Peru* (Princeton University Press, 1987), she continues researching and writing on feminist theory in Anthropology and the cultural work of state-making and colony-building in the Peruvian Andes.

Jyotsna Singh is Assistant Professor of English and Cultural Studies at Southern Methodist University. She has published essays in *Theatre Journal* and *Renaissance Drama*, and co-authored *The Weyward Sisters: Shakespeare and Feminist Politics* (with Dympna Callaghan and Lorraine Helms). She is currently writing a book on colonial narratives and cultural dialogues in India (seventeenth to nineteenth centuries).

371

Verena Stolcke, a social anthropologist, teaches at the Universitat Autònoma de Barcelona. She is the author of *Marriage, Class and Colour in Nineteenth-Century Cuba* (1974), which recently appeared in a new edition from Michigan University Press; and of *Coffee Planters, Workers and Wives: Class Conflict and Gender Relations on São Paulo Plantations, 1850–1980* (1988). She is presently engaged in research on "the nature of nationality."

INDEX

Special thanks are due to Jude López for her assistance in preparing this index.

373

vernacular literacy?